LARGE
PRINT
EDITION

RANDOM
HOUSE

A Golfer's Life

ARNOLD PALMER

with

JAMES DODSON

Published by Random House Large Print
in association with Ballantine Books
New York   1999

Library of Congress Cataloging-in-Publication Data
Palmer, Arnold, 1929–
Arnold Palmer : a golfer's life /
Arnold Palmer with James Dodson.
p.   cm.
ISBN 0-375-70574-0
1. Palmer, Arnold, 1929–   .   2. Golfers—United States—
Biography.   3. Large type books.   I. Dodson, James.
II. Title.   III. Title: Golfer's life.
[GV964.P35A3   1999]
796.352'092—dc21
[B]   98-33139
CIP

Random House Web Address: http://www.randomhouse.com/
Printed in the United States of America
FIRST LARGE PRINT EDITION

This Large Print Book carries the
Seal of Approval of N.A.V.H.

To my wife, Winnie,
and my daughters, Peggy and Amy

CONTENTS

ACKNOWLEDGMENTS

Perhaps the best way to put together your autobiography would be to isolate yourself from all distractions for a few months and write away. In my case, that simply was not possible. I had too much going on . . . then, and now, ahead of me. Quite obviously, I needed some help in getting all of my words down on paper in proper, thorough, and interesting fashion and then in being certain that what I had roughed out in my dictation was complete and accurate.

Certainly, the most important assistance would have to come from the writer who would collaborate with me in creating the finished manuscript. Through the years I have known most of the finest golf writers in the world, but, at the urging of my wife, Winnie, we wound up entrusting this job to a talented man we had just met. Winnie had read his book *Final Rounds*, a wonderful account of a father and son's long-planned and final golfing trip to the British Isles. Winnie thought that the son, author Jim Dodson, would be the perfect person to work with me on this project. I agreed. Jim has been wonderful, and I think, or at least hope, that this book bears out the wisdom of this decision. Considering that Jim is a three-time winner of the Golf Writers Association of America Award, a longtime contributing editor to

Golf magazine, and the Golf Editor of *Departures* magazine, and that *Final Rounds* was picked as the top golf book of 1996, the choice was obvious.

Jim has shaped and organized my words and thoughts into a flowing account of the wonderful life I've had the good fortune to live. I am most grateful to him for his dedication, understanding, and reliance on others when appropriate, and his diligence in completing the manuscript in a timely fashion.

Both Jim and I relied heavily on my family and close friends and associates in getting everything right. You can never depend totally on your memory to come up with all the facts and stories of a lifetime of nearly seventy years and get them just right every time. That's where Winnie, Doc Giffin, and Bev Norwood, in particular, came in. Winnie and Doc, who both have been encouraging me to undertake this autobiographical effort for many years, but only under the right circumstances, made many suggestions as I began to present my thoughts to Jim Dodson and pored over the manuscript as it took shape in his hands. Nobody, of course, knows more about me and the last forty-five years than Winnie, so her input and total interest in achieving just the right story of this golfer's life was invaluable.

To a lesser extent and from a slightly shorter period of acquaintanceship, Doc Giffin, my personal assistant and confidant for the last thirty-three years, contributed significantly to bringing this story to life. I'm certain—and I think Jim Dodson will agree—that we could not have done as well without him. A journalist by profession, Doc might have been the "with" on the cover of this book himself. Realizing that he could not relinquish his other duties to give full attention to the project, Doc instead devoted himself to a careful, superb editing of the manuscript, suggesting additions, corrections, and deletions when appropriate. Most of the time they were.

We had the benefit of another journalist, too, in Bev Norwood, who was involved with this book as a literary executive at the International Management Group and is also a good friend, knowledgeable about golf and my career. He also read the first draft of the manuscript meticulously and made a number of valuable suggestions that prevented inadvertent mistakes and enhanced the finished product.

My siblings—brother Jerry and sisters Lois Jean and Sandy—were particularly helpful in reconstructing the early years in Latrobe and Youngstown. So were my daughters, Peggy and Amy, in bringing back family memories. When we turned to the significant business side of my life, we counted heavily on the input of Mark McCormack and Alastair Johnston as well as that of Ed Seay, my frequent traveling companion, when we got into the exciting (to me) subject of golf course architecture and design, which became more and more important to me as the years went by.

Since this is the last of my books, I have been able to draw from the work and words put down by previous writers I've collaborated with—Tom Hauser, William Barry Furlong, Ernie Havemann,

Norman Cousins, and Bob Drum—so their fine efforts have been renewed, in a way, in these pages.

Finally, I must offer sincere thanks to Judith Curr, Senior Vice President and Publisher at Ballantine Books, who originally approached me with the idea of finally writing my autobiography. Perhaps the timing was right, but so were Judith's guiding editorial insights. She was ably assisted in the production of the manuscript by Gary Brozek, Editor at Ballantine Books, and the ever-diligent Managing Editorial and Production departments there.

Thank you all, from the bottom of this golfer's heart.

Once Upon a Time

Clear September evenings are beautiful in the little town of Latrobe, Pennsylvania, in the foothills of the Allegheny Mountains, where I grew up and still live. A few days after my sixty-eighth birthday, on just such an evening, my wife Winnie and I left home and drove down the hill to the township road that hasn't changed much in the past half-century, crossed over, and started up the winding driveway of Latrobe Country Club.

The driveway crosses a small brook and two fairways, the steep downhill first and the long uphill 18th. We paused to allow a couple of late finishers—two boys carrying their own bags—to hit their final approach shots on 18. Winnie reached over and took my hand and commented that I seemed awfully quiet—and was driving awfully slowly—for a man who had a big speech to make in a few minutes.

Under normal circumstances I enjoy giving speeches, and I seldom use a prepared text, because years ago I discovered that speaking to people straight from the heart about a subject you love may be a bit more risky, but the rewards are almost always greater in the end. That's just my style, I guess—the way I prefer to play golf and the way I prefer to speak to people.

This crowd was different, however. The occasion was my fiftieth high school reunion, and at that moment almost two hundred people from Latrobe High's Class of 1947 were gathered in the upstairs dining room or sipping cocktails on the adjacent lawn, waiting for their unofficial host to arrive and get the festivities under way.

I hadn't seen many of these folks in over half a century—a thought that probably astounded them as much as it did me. How could that time have gone by so rapidly? Most of those in attendance, I knew, now lived other places and had come back to Latrobe from great distances. Others there were some of my closest friends on earth. But all of them had known me long before I became a famous public figure named Arnold Palmer. To them, I was simply "Arnie" Palmer, the skinny, golf-crazy son of Deke and Doris Palmer, the boy who would grow up and do well enough to buy the club where once upon a time he was permitted on the course only before the members arrived in the morning or after they had gone home in the evening.

I peered through the windshield and watched as one of the boys made a strong swing, and I remember commenting to Winnie, as his ball flew away in the twilight toward an unseen flag up the hill, "He may like that better than he knows." I knew what that boy was feeling, because I'd hit that final shot— perhaps from that very spot—thousands of times myself over the past fifty or sixty years. And every time, it filled me with a mixture of hope and wonder.

The boys picked up their bags and moved on.

Wrapped in the spell of the game, they probably didn't have a clue or a care in the world who was watching them, and that's exactly as it should be, a tribute to this marvelous game we play. There is something magical about finishing a golf round in the dusk.

Driving on, I admitted to Winnie that I was a bit worried about what I was going to say to the folks on the hill, and she knew why without my having to say anything more. It wasn't being sixty-eight that was chewing away at me or even the slight bitter-sweet feeling I often experience with September's arrival—brought on by the knowledge that another golf season is slowly winding down. The truth was, several things had happened to us in the preceding year that made this homecoming all the more poignant, and therefore somewhat difficult for me.

She simply squeezed my hand and assured me that when it came time to speak, she knew I would do just fine.

"Oh really?" I said, with mock annoyance. "And what makes you so sure about that?"

She smiled that simple, no-nonsense smile of hers I've always loved and found so comforting, whether I set the course record or shot 80 in the final round.

"Don't forget, lover," she said, "I've known you a few years, too."

In life as in golf, we all encounter turning points, moments of trial when everything accomplished up till then falls away and everything we stand for and

believe is summoned forth for thorough examination. On the golf course, I've been fortunate enough
to come out on the happy end of several such trials.
But a few days after the 1997 New Year's holiday, I
faced a more urgent moment of self-reflection. The
phone rang at La Costa Resort and Spa, in Carlsbad,
California, where I was preparing to give a speech
and present the Arnold Palmer Award to Tom
Lehman at the annual PGA Tour Awards dinner at
the kickoff event for the PGA Tour's new season.
Winnie was on the other end of the line, and her
voice immediately told me something was wrong. A
moment later I knew what it was. For several years
during my regular periodic physical examinations,
I'd scored elevated PSA tests, but several precau-
tionary biopsies had all come back negative. The
most recent one, however, had not. Winnie had
called to inform me I had prostate cancer.

The very word *cancer* can send a cold blade of
terror cutting through the strongest man or woman. I
remember feeling a great gutted hollowness inside,
followed by a wave of anger at the injustice of the
verdict. *Why me? Why now?* My physicians were
quick to point out that there was no particular hurry
to confront this frightening opponent—I could delay
surgery indefinitely, even decline it, if I so chose.
There were even other procedures and treatment
strategies available. The decision was up to me, they
said.

"Well," I remember replying almost without hesi-
tation, "if you're leaving it up to me, I think there's
only one thing to do. Let's get the damn thing out."

In retrospect, this was the only course of action I could honestly think to follow. Get it out, get it done with, so I could get on with my life—back to the golf course and back to my work and family. I had so much I still wanted to do, so many things I still wanted to accomplish; why, even my golf game was showing new signs of vitality after a few years of less-than-inspiring play. The cancer couldn't have come at a more inconvenient moment (if there ever is a convenient moment). I'm sure everyone who faces this terrifying news has felt this way at some point or another.

I promptly canceled all my business appointments and withdrew from the following week's Bob Hope Chrysler Classic, a tournament I had played in since it was started in 1960 and had won five times. Then I flew home to Orlando to be with Winnie and my daughter Amy and consulted with my doctors. The next day, we flew north to the famed Mayo Clinic in Rochester, Minnesota, and three days after that the job was done.

For the first time in my adult memory, I didn't play much golf that spring. I spent weeks recovering at our condo at the Bay Hill Club and Lodge in Orlando, watching the golf season unfold on television and reading an avalanche of get-well cards and letters I received from concerned people all over the world. I can't really express how grateful I was for these cards and letters. Cancer can make you feel so alone. Friends I hadn't spoken to in twenty years got in touch, strangers shared their own inspiring medical stories with me; some simply offered prayers, while others sent small gifts. It was powerful medicine to think I'd somehow touched so many lives—and now they were touching mine.

It's also probably just as well that I can't tell you how frustrated I was—what a pain in the rear end I must have been to Winnie, who had the unenviable task of trying to keep me in one place, off the golf course and out from underfoot at the office—to have to sit on the sidelines while one of the most memorable golf seasons in history was brilliantly unfolding. Within weeks of the new season's debut, it was clear young Eldrick "Tiger" Woods was going to fulfill his early promise of greatness and make maybe the most sensational rookie entrance to the professional ranks since a fellow named Jack Nicklaus came along in 1962 (an event I happen to remember very well), and I set my goal to be back on my feet and playing—perhaps even playing decently—by my own Tour event, the Bay Hill Invitational, in mid-March.

Thanks to Winnie and others who stayed after me to give my body proper time to heal, I was able to be back on my feet and functioning pretty normally by early March. My golf game even showed flashes of surprising sharpness, but I found I tired with almost frightening suddenness—a phenomenon that's not at all unusual, as it turns out, after cancer surgery. My stamina simply wasn't what it had always been, and I reluctantly had to accept that it would be months, instead of weeks, before I really began to feel like my old self again.

Even so, playing two rounds with Jack Nicklaus

at the Masters was a boost for my morale, a real tonic for what ailed me, certainly one of the year's highlights. Proving perhaps that time is no friend of champions, Jack was limping a little bit, too, from a nagging painful hip. But we had a lot of laughs and both agreed we wouldn't have missed it for the world. The Augusta crowds gave us a lavish welcome, and it seemed somehow fitting that Tiger Woods demolished the field to capture his first major, a breathtaking performance that will live in Masters history.

Unfortunately for me, by the time I began to get my old energy back and was charging to the golf course again, it was almost September—the American Ryder Cup team was headed to Spain and Valderrama and the golf season had come and gone almost without me. Well, I told myself, the important thing is to realize that I've licked a big opponent, or at least subdued him, and it's time to set my sights on next year.

That's when the second blow came.

Ken Bowman was one of my oldest and dearest friends. We'd palled around together since our school days in Latrobe, and his father, Lloyd, a vice president with Vanadium Alloy Steel, had belonged to the club where my father, Deacon Palmer, was head professional and course superintendent. Ken was your basic "Hill" boy, as we called kids who grew up on the more prosperous side of the spur of the Pennsylvania Railroad tracks that bisected the town of Latrobe from east to west. But early on, perhaps because of our mutual passion for sports, Ken and I developed a strong attachment to each other. We were best pals in high school, dated some of the same girls, and when I started playing in state golf tournaments, his father generously helped underwrite some of my traveling expenses. Ken himself often caddied for me in big tournaments, including the first state championship I ever played in. He went off to Amherst College; I went to Wake Forest. He joined the U.S. Navy; I enlisted in the U.S. Coast Guard. But we always stayed in touch. He eventually married Susie Cook, and I met and married Winnie; we built houses on the same wooded ridge across from Latrobe Country Club, raised our families together, played bridge and golf, and for well over thirty years developed as close a bond as two neighbors possibly can.

A few weeks before our high school reunion, I stopped over to see Ken. I was on my way over to the club to test some new equipment on the range and perhaps play an afternoon round with a couple of members. He had been having difficulty with his vision, some sweating and nausea, but eerily, he experienced no pain to speak of. I remember he described it as "kind of weird" and explained that the doctors were stumped. A few days later he went in for more tests, and it was determined that a series of blood vessels that fed the rear portion of his brain were rapidly deteriorating. Ken was effectively suffering a series of mini-strokes that would kill him unless the condition could be surgically halted. The operation was extremely risky—it had been successfully performed only a few times—but it was just like him to elect to try it. They opened him up and realized it was too late. The doctors sent him home to be with Susie, and I saw him for the last time on a Saturday on my way over to play at the club. He suggested that I come by afterward and we'd have a vodka on the rocks, as we always did after a round. I promised him I would, and told him I would love nothing better.

Two days later, Ken was dead. He was sixty-eight years old.

Whatever my own bout with cancer failed to drive though my thick skull about life's fleeting nature and fragile preciousness, Ken's death drove home with the force of a steelyard hammer. It wasn't just that Ken and I were the same age that shook me to the core. It was simply that I'd lost perhaps my oldest friend.

These things, which I can really only now begin to speak of, remind a man of his fragile mortality. But luckily, there are other things—many other things, in my case—that give him joy.

Everyone I shook hands with at the reunion seemed to have a delightful "Arnie Palmer" story to tell me. That's how the homefolks know me—"Arnie" rather than "Arnold." Many of these tales I'd heard before; others I'd somehow forgotten or—here's the amusing part—maybe never even knew.

We reminisced about the two-room schoolhouse in Youngstown where many of us went for eight grades before catching the trolley to high school in

Latrobe, and someone remembered how on snowy days a gang of neighborhood kids would always come to our little house off the sixth fairway, where my mother would give everybody hot chocolate. Someone else—an old teammate from my abbreviated days on the gridiron—reminded me of how passionate my father was about my *not* playing football, stopping just shy of dragging me off the football field at Latrobe High because he thought football was the quickest way on earth to get permanently injured. A woman I hadn't seen since the tenth grade remembered how I was so unspeakably shy in Miss Jones's public speaking class that she forced me to stand before the class and asked me to explain the importance of making solid eye contact with the people I was addressing—something, come to think of it, I always try to do to this day. Another man recalled watching Winnie and me roll out of town one afternoon in 1955, pulling a small trailer behind our two-door Ford, headed for my first year on the Tour. I decided not to tell this man his memory was off a bit, that we didn't actually buy the trailer he remembers in Latrobe. In fact, we bought the trailer outside Phoenix, Arizona, and returned home with it only at the end of the golf season, literally coasting down the last hill into Latrobe with a Ford whose engine was nearly shot from hauling that damned little house on wheels. "That's right," I told him, not wishing to disappoint him by correcting his memory. "That's the same trailer Winnie insisted we park and never use again."

The stories flowed on and on, and each one, I

must say, almost without my being aware of it, began to ease my worry. There was a lot of laughter and joking around, and a few tears shed, and all I could think as I made my way around the room to shake hands and share embraces and spin reminiscences was how my own parents would have thoroughly enjoyed being at this party. Pap, as we called my father, would have enjoyed the rough-and-tumble stories of life in old Latrobe, and my mother, given her deep compassion for people, would have known most if not all of the names of everybody in the building—and I daresay many of their most touching family stories, too.

That's small-town life for you. Perhaps not as true today as it once was in America, but still true in my hometown and perhaps yours, too.

When the room quieted and I finally stood up to speak, I must say, my emotions nearly got the better of me. I briefly hesitated. But then I quickly recovered and the thoughts just seemed to stream straight from my heart to my lips. I thanked everyone for coming and specifically thanked Dolores Pohland for allowing me to copy off her paper so many years ago, thereby permitting me to graduate from Latrobe High—the room rocked with laughter at this. Then I admitted to them that for a number of reasons, some public and some private, I'd been shy about hosting the reunion and a bit worried about what I would say to everybody. I told them this was one of the most special evenings of my life. "We've all gone a lot of places since our days growing up here in Latrobe," I said, looking at as many faces as I could. "And if there's one thing I've learned in all those years, it's this: Your hometown is not where you're from. It's who you are."

They seemed to really appreciate this remark, applauding vigorously. When they quieted down again, I explained to them that this was why I still made Latrobe my home and would always come back, as I put it, until they spread my ashes out there somewhere near my Pap's on one of the club's fairways.

Everybody laughed again. But they knew I couldn't have been more serious.

Then I thanked them for coming and gave them all umbrella pins, making everybody official members of Arnie's Army.

I should have known that Winnie would be right. The proper words had come to me in the nick of time, and I was deeply grateful for having been able to say them. A short while later, with the band going full tilt, we slipped out of the clubhouse and walked to our car in the darkness.

"You did pretty well," she said with that way she has of gently sticking the needle in me but also somehow meaning it.

"I did, *didn't* I?" I said, again with mock surprise. I was really pleased that what I had wanted to say had managed to come out all right.

Winnie patted my hand reassuringly.

*   *   *

Remembering one's life, someone said, is to live twice. If that's true, I realize I've been fortunate enough to live many lifetimes since I was a small boy following his dad around the fairways of Latrobe Country Club, that once-upon-a-time place where this tale really begins. Or maybe it really begins someplace before that.

In any case, on the drive back down the hill to home and bed, I was thinking fondly about all the wonderful stories that had been swapped that clear September night. I loved hearing every one of them. The funny thing is, I hear these stories all over the world now. A few of them are even true.

Of course, I have a few of my own to tell. If you have a little while, I'd like to tell you some of them.

CHAPTER ONE

Good Hands

I sometimes think it's odd, and in no small part revealing, what you manage not to forget. In almost fifty years of public life, the shape and strength of my hands have been written about hundreds, perhaps even thousands of times, by writers who saw them as metaphors for what I've accomplished and as clues to who I really am. True enough, they're distinctive in that they are large, gnarled, and unusually strong. A blacksmith's hands, they've been called. Good workingman's hands. I got these hands from my father, Deacon Palmer.

My two earliest memories involve my father and my hands. I was three years old and we were living in a small house across the street from my paternal grandparents, Alex and Agnes Palmer, on Kingston Street in Youngstown, a small working-class village just outside Latrobe. At that time my father was the head greenskeeper at Latrobe Country Club, which he'd helped build with his own hands in the years just prior to my birth in September 1929. As an economic measure to combat the effects of the Great Depression, he would soon also be made "temporary" head professional by the club's directors—a job he managed to keep, and perform tirelessly, for over forty years until his death in 1976. But at that moment in time, my world was only about one block long, the distance between my parents' house and my grandparents' front porch.

I loved to go over to my grandmother Agnes's house, because she was a superb baker and always had a special treat for me and my little sister Lois Jean, whom everybody called Cheech. Sometimes it was a fresh piece of pie and chocolate milk, sometimes it was her terrific homemade bread and the wonderful apple butter she made from scratch. I remember a large grapevine growing just outside her kitchen door, and the tart jellies that came from those grapes. On this particular morning, I was carrying a quart of fresh milk up her three front steps when I stumbled and fell on the milk bottle, shattering the glass and slicing open nearly the entire side of my left hand. I remember being frightened, but I don't remember the pain that surely must have come immediately afterward and as the doctor stitched me up.

I suspect I may have cried—though perhaps not. It certainly wouldn't surprise me if I didn't, because even then I knew my father and grandfather were tough and seemingly unsentimental men, and I instinctively knew I wanted to be like them. My grandfather, Alex Jerome Palmer, was a housepainter by trade who served on the Youngstown school board and constantly fought for education funding—a fact that, considering his own minimal education, reveals something impressive about his character or at least his good common sense.

Palmer men did things with their hands and were

justifiably proud of that fact. According to family records, Palmers had been scraping out a living on small farms and in the coal mines of the rough Allegheny Mountains since the late 1780s, when they probably arrived in the area as English immigrants. Alex Palmer's three sons were no different. They were strong willed and independent minded. My father, Milfred Jerome Palmer, was the oldest, followed by Uncle Francis, or "Spook," and their kid brother, Harry, or "Dude," Palmer. For years, at holiday or other family gatherings, whenever these three got together, an argument or debate of some kind was likely to erupt, fueled by blue-collar philosophy and beer. Uncle Francis later went to work for the management at Latrobe Steel, and Uncle Harry, a union man to the core, not only led a strike against the company that briefly turned into a rock-throwing melee, but took to calling his older brother a "scab" until my grandfather put an end to that. A little healthy disagreement was one thing, but Alex Palmer wasn't going to tolerate rudeness at the family's dinner table. He had firm ideas about how grown men should behave. Also present was their pair of sisters—my aunts Dorothy, or "Doll," Palmer and Hazel, the baby sister. I remember how fondly they treated my sister Cheech and me at Thanksgiving and Christmas—the uncles bouncing us around, the aunts constantly trying to feed us more desserts or simply making a fuss over us.

I don't know who came up with "Cheech" for Lois Jean, but everyone (except perhaps for me) in those days seemed to have a nickname. Exactly how my father got his nickname—"Deacon" or, more commonly, "Deke"—remains a bit of a family mystery. Sometime back when he was a young man, he apparently helped out a local black minister in some kind of trouble, and people took to calling him "Deacon." Perhaps the name was bestowed in derision or jest. No one knows for sure, and my father certainly wasn't going to discuss it. In his view, someone else's troubles were their own business, not a proper subject for public discussion.

While a deacon is an elder of the church who helps the minister caretake the flock, my father never felt comfortable going to the little Lutheran church in Youngstown where Cheech and I were sent every Sunday from the time we could walk until confirmation at around age thirteen. I eventually came to learn that, even though he wasn't a church-going man, our father really was a caretaker to many people around town. A man who took care of people regardless of their background or race. A deacon with strong hands. So the name stuck, and it suited him. As I say, most people simply called him Deke.

I called him Pap from the beginning.

Pap was the only Palmer son with a physical disability, a deformed foot from a bout of infantile paralysis that in those times was popularly referred to as a "game foot." I'm convinced this only made him tougher, doubled his determination to be independent and strong. As a boy, he lifted weights and practiced chin-ups with one arm in order to build his upper-body strength. He could chin himself with either arm at least ten times, and his hands and upper torso, as a result, were splendidly muscled while his hips remained slim, his legs fairly weak.

At about age fifteen, he quit school and went to work at American Locomotive in Latrobe (now Standard Steel) as a mail runner, but he didn't like being indoors and heard somebody planned to build a golf course a couple of miles from his parents' house in Youngstown. He knew nothing about golf, even less about growing grass or shaping fairways and greens, but he went out to the site of the new Latrobe Country Club and applied for a job as a laborer. He began his long career at Latrobe Country Club by literally digging ditches on a three-man construction crew.

When the nine-hole course was more or less finished, in 1921, my father, then just seventeen, was asked by Latrobe Steel—which owned most of the stock in the new club—to stay on and help maintain the course. But there was a catch: the job wasn't a year-round opportunity, and he would be laid off when the golf season ended. After tearing down, cleaning, and repainting every piece of the club's maintenance equipment, he remedied this shortfall by finding a second job running the poolroom at the Youngstown Hotel, a pretty rough-and-tumble place where local workingmen, including several Polish and Slovak men who would eventually come to work for him at the golf course and become like surrogate uncles to me, relaxed and drank shots of whiskey with their beers, wagered on pool, and sometimes got into fistfights. Thanks to his weight lifting, Pap was a young bull nobody dared give much lip to.

Pap's personality and character, I see now, from the vantage point of many years, undoubtedly was shaped by those years struggling to teach himself to walk again, long before there were doctors and re-habilitation programs to help people manage the various difficulties associated with types of polio. His father drilled into him the importance of doing a job to the best of your abilities, never complaining about your lot, and always conducting yourself with as much dignity as possible. Early in his married life to my mother, for example, Pap worked a second job at night in the steel mill to bring in extra family income. According to Mother and others, he worked so hard (at a job he hated, no less) he sometimes angered the other workers, and one night some fella tried to spill molten metal on him. I don't know what came of that incident, but if I'd been that man I sure wouldn't have wanted to have met Pap in the alleyway after work that night.

Because of his handicap, Pap learned he had to be tougher than the next fellow, regardless of his social position. As a result, I think, he developed even more rigid beliefs about what was right and what was wrong, what a good man did or didn't do. You didn't borrow money. You didn't take what wasn't yours; you didn't lie, cheat, or steal. If you did any of those things, you weren't anybody in Deacon Palmer's eyes.

Once, as a boy of about five, I lifted a packet of

glue from the drugstore in Youngstown, just slipped it into my pocket and sidled nonchalantly out the door. I was nuts about building model airplanes in those days. Anyway, I'd barely reached the pavement out front when I began to worry that someone had seen me or would somehow find out and tell my pap what I'd done. The truly amazing thing is, I worried about that theft for the next sixty-five years, and the truth is I *still* worry a little bit that my father, wherever he is, will somehow find out I took that glue and lower the boom on me.

Pap wasn't big on spanking either Cheech or me. He left that task to our mother, Doris Palmer—and she did it only once, as far as I can remember, when Cheech and I burst out laughing at her after she tried to discipline us for some rules infraction. But the sound of his voice—combined with the size of his hands and their potential menace—was almost enough to freeze me in my tracks and set my bony knees quaking when I was caught doing something I shouldn't have been doing.

I began this reflection by saying I had two earliest memories involving Pap and hands. Here is the other one: When I was three, perhaps just before or some time after the broken milk bottle incident, my father put my hands in his and placed them around the shaft of a cut-down women's golf club. He showed me the classic overlap, or Vardon, grip—the proper grip for a good golf swing, he said—and told me to hit the golf ball. Because the Vardon grip involves overlapping the small finger of one hand on the index finger of the other, it's not the easiest grip for a small-fry to master. But an easier, baseball, grip would never have done, so I worked hard to learn the grip Pap showed me. It probably helped that my hands were larger than the average kid's.

His initial thoughts on the golf swing weren't complicated, though. "Hit it *hard,* boy," he said simply. "Go find it and hit it hard again."

Pap took basic lessons from the Latrobe Country Club's first professional, a Scotsman named Davy Brand, and spent years refining his own swing enough to become a solid single-digit handicapper. Even though by this time he was regularly giving lessons to members, that was pretty much all the swing instruction he gave me for many years. *Get the right grip. Hit the ball hard. Go find the ball, boy, and hit it hard again . . .*

From the beginning I took his advice to heart and swung at the ball so hard I often toppled over. I remember how a prominent member once saw me take a cut at the ball and commented to him, "Deacon, you better do something about that kid's swing. He swings so hard, he can't even stay on his feet." Without missing a beat, my pap leveled his gaze at this member and told him in no uncertain terms, "Dammit, J.R., you let me worry about the kid and you take care of your own game, all right?" Years later, after I began to have some success in junior golf and even when I was first playing on the PGA Tour, well-meaning people would watch me slug a golf ball with my unique and essentially

homemade golf swing—a corkscrewing motion
that relied almost entirely on my great upper-body
strength, producing low-boring shots that seldom
rose above eye level and flew a long way in the form
of a bold draw and the occasional monstrous hook—
and offer me tips and insights about how I could
improve and refine it. Others marveled that it worked
as well as it did.

A case in point is an incident that took place on
the practice tee at Chick Harbert's club in Detroit
during my rookie year on the Tour in 1955. I was hitting balls with my driver when I realized George
Fazio and Tony Penna were standing there watching
me. I knew Fazio a bit—he once gave me a lift when
I was hitchhiking back to Wake Forest, a funny story
I'll get to in a while—but Penna was a ball-striking
legend. I really wanted to show off, so I teed up some
balls and let out the shaft, pounding drives to the rear
of the range.

I heard Penna ask Fazio if he knew who I was.

"Sure. That's this kid Arnold Palmer. He just won
the National Amateur."

"Well, better tell him to get a job," Penna said
with unmistakable disdain, almost mockery. "With
that swing of his, he'll *never* make it out here."

I really burned inside at that remark. Many years
later, after I'd won the Bob Hope Classic for the
third time, I saw Tony again. He came up to me and
winked and said, in that same slightly mocking
voice, "Palmer, you're beginning to swing that club
pretty good."

I guess I was. The point is, early on my views

about the golf swing—and, for that matter, life in general—were shaped by a man who believed in the virtues of hard work and following the rules but essentially doing things your own way in this world.

Almost from the moment he put that cut-down club in my hands, Pap would tell me in no uncertain terms to permit nobody to fool with or change my golf swing—and it's a tribute to him that anytime I ever got in trouble with my swing, lost the feel or touch in a shot, it was usually because I became enamored of some popular teacher's ideas about the "mechanics" of the golf swing and gave their advice a try, often really screwing myself up for a time.

Mine was, and remains, almost the antithesis of a "mechanical" golf swing. Everybody has their theories about what makes a good golf swing, but Pap's basic premise was that once you learned the proper grip and understood the fundamental motion behind the swing, the trick was to find the swing that worked best for you and your body type, maximized your power. The rest of it was a lifelong learning process of refinement by trial and error, seeing what worked by how the club felt in your hands. Even at the pinnacle of my success in the middle 1960s, I would be practicing at Latrobe for hours, beating balls like you wouldn't believe, and look up to discover him watching me. Typically, he might make some small comment about my swing, but overall he didn't have much to say on the subject. It was inconceivable to think of a Sam Snead or Byron Nelson consulting a swing doctor or even asking another Tour professional for advice on their golf swings. As

Ben Hogan later said, the answer was in the dirt, and pounding balls was the only way to find it. That was pretty much my father's attitude, too. And it inevitably became mine.

If that sounds simple, my father prided himself on simple, clear logic—a way of looking at life that I eventually accepted as "Deacon's gospel." Not surprisingly, he had the same simple reverence for the rules of the game. The rules were there to be followed, because that meant the game would be the same kind of challenge for everybody. Beating an opponent was meaningless unless it was done by the rule book. Unless winter rules were in effect or an area had been designated as under repair, for example, improving a lie would have been utterly unthinkable to him. Wherever you hit the ball and found it, *that* was the spot you played your next shot from. No casual rolling the ball in the rough or fairway. He was as rigid and unyielding on the rules of the game as any USGA official I ever knew, and that's one reason I learned the rules thoroughly at an early age, something that would benefit me enormously down the road in my career.

Because Pap was both head professional and course superintendent, he knew what it took to both build and maintain a golf course. He preached relentlessly on the importance of replacing divots and repairing pitchmarks, and woe be unto the player—regardless of whether it was his own son or the club president—who failed to treat the golf course with the kind of respect Pap deemed necessary and proper.

Pap's other big concern was manners—how you behaved in the presence of your superiors or while eating and certainly the way in which you conducted yourself on the golf course. At the dinner table or in the company of grown-ups, for example, a kid didn't speak until he was spoken to, and he or she had better eat *every* scrap of food they bothered to take on their plate. You also had to hold your knife and fork properly, or he'd go through the roof. And God forbid you dared to enter a dwelling or be in the presence of a woman and forget to remove your cap. Pap would snatch it off and take part of your scalp with it! Cheech and I both learned these cardinal rules early in life—and in my case sometimes the hard way.

Likewise, from the beginning it was also drilled into me that a golf course was a place where character fully reveals itself—both its strengths and its flaws. As a result, I learned early not only to fix my ball marks but also to congratulate an opponent on a good shot, avoid walking ahead of a player preparing to shoot, remain perfectly still when someone else was playing, and a score of other small courtesies that revealed, in my father's mind, one's abiding respect for the game. In a nutshell, Pap had no patience with people who chose to ignore the rules and traditions that made golf the most gentlemanly game on earth. Especially if the offender was *me*.

As I got older and began to work at the golf course myself, I also began to build my upper-body strength, just as he had done, from pushing heavy greens mowers and raking and cleaning out ditches, and eventually the same well-meaning members warned me that building shoulder and arm muscles like Pap's would eventually ruin my golf swing. As near as I can tell, it never did. In fact, I never lifted weights to build muscle until my senior career started in the early 1980s.

I simply wanted good hands like his, the hands that shaped Latrobe Country Club.

But all that came a bit later, of course. To begin with, as I say, my introduction to golf came when I started swinging myself out of my shoes with that old cut-down ladies' club at age three and was taken by my father to the golf course, where I was permitted to ride on his lap while he was mowing fairways with gangmowers pulled by the club's old Fordson steel-wheeled tractor.

Red Yazvec and Slim Balko worked for Pap, and sometimes I think they helped raise me, or at least taught me to curse in Slovak and to fight. They would tease me into such a froth of anger, I would run and jump on them and pound them with my fists. They were both big friendly men, and I remember how, when everyone broke to eat lunch and drink fresh cold milk under the trees, they would often get to horsing around and wrestling with Pap. Thanks to his massive upper-body strength, they simply couldn't overpower him, and he'd nail them every time. I loved that.

Another man, Charlie Arch, more or less kept an eye on me when my father was busy. Charlie worked in the club pro shop. He was born with malformed arms that were very short and with no elbow joint, and he had only four fingers on each hand. He was such a great and generous guy, we became friends almost instantly. For years when I needed money, Charlie would always come through and "advance" me ten or twenty without telling my father about it. Pap didn't believe in borrowing money you couldn't pay back, and he would have been livid if he found out I'd accepted Charlie's little loans. What nobody but me knew was that I was careful to keep track of how much Charlie advanced me over the years, hoping the day would soon come when I could pay him back. Eventually the sum came to around $600. The year I married Winnie and started playing the Tour and made a few bucks, I gave Charlie Arch a check for $1,000 and sincerely thanked him.

There were other men who benefited from Pap's caretaking. Slim Balko's brother, Paulie, worked at the club for a time, as did Jack Byerly, whose brother, R. A. Byerly, was an engineer at Latrobe Steel and a lifelong friend of Pap's—they were so close, in fact, that my parents chose to use his middle name, Arnold, when naming me. Then there was Pickles Vilk, a coal miner who got injured and came to the club, where he worked as a caddie for the rest of his life.

Pap was protective of his employees. By the time my sister Lois Jean and I came along, he had clearly earned the respect and friendship of the club's most prominent members, like Harry Saxman and Dr. H. R. Mather, and he often spent his Friday nights playing poker with men who were the movers and shakers in Latrobe and the surrounding area, businessmen, steel executives, and so forth. These well-attended poker games became legendary, but I think it was his friendships with Slim and Red and Jack Byerly and the rest of them, who were such a major part of our day-to-day lives, that meant the most to him.

He loved drinking "shots and beer" and shooting pool with his buddies at the firehall or Amer's Hotel in Youngstown, and in the winter, when the club closed its doors, thanks to his connections in town, Pap was able to find most of these fellows good-paying jobs in the steel mills or, after the repeal of prohibition, the Latrobe Brewing Company. Some of the jobs he found them were so good, they never came back to the golf course. One of the Balko boys, for example, went to a management job at the steel mill and never came back. Red Yazvec started a tire business in Youngstown that's going to this day. But they obviously never forgot what Deke Palmer had done for them, because I heard it straight from their mouths for decades.

The year I turned six, we moved to a small frame house adjacent to Nine Mile Run and the old sixth hole at the golf course, and I began walking the mile or so up the hill and through the village to the two-room Baldridge School. I had to pass my grand-mother Palmer's house on the way, and every time I got into a fistfight with a playmate like Bert Lam-bert, Karl Burkhart, or Berkey Shirey, it seemed to happen directly in front of Grandma Palmer's house.

Even then I had a strong temper, and though I

usually wound up on top, there was a curious aspect
to my fighting: I never could really bring myself to
try to hurt an opponent. Instead, I would just kind of
sit on them and warn them, "Now, look. Give up or
I'm going to have to hit you," and that usually did
the trick. By then, of course, it was usually too late
for me to avoid my father's wrath, because my
grandmother had called home or the club to report,
"Arnie's fightin' in the street again," and my father
would stop what he was doing and come get me.

Curiously enough, I can think of only a couple
times my father actually laid a hand on me. The first
time was when I was about nine or ten, and it
involved another scrap in the village with a kid
named Jimmy McCracken. Pap was in the Amer's
bar having a drink with his friends, and I was outside
arguing with Jimmy McCracken when fists began to
fly. Pretty quick I had Jimmy on the ground, warning
him to give up or else, when a hand suddenly pulled
me off him. It was Fat Rushnoc, an older man who
knew my father. Fat told me to quit picking on
Jimmy because I was bigger than my opponent, and
I told him to let me go. He refused to do it. We happened to be standing in front of the village grocery
store, and a display of fresh fruit was out front. Desperate to get free and back to my business, I im-
pulsively grabbed a peach—a *very* ripe peach, as
my poor luck would have it—and smashed it on the
front of Fat's shirt, smearing it all over, really ruining the shirt.

Fat let me go and disappeared into the Amer's
bar, and a few moments later my father appeared

and just from the look on his face I knew I was in big trouble. Because it was raining, Pap had an umbrella with him, and he used that big umbrella to whack my butt all the way down the hill to our house, probably half a mile at least. I can still feel the sting of that umbrella, and I never quite forgave Fat Rushnoc for turning me in to Pap. A dozen years or so ago, Fat dropped by Latrobe Country Club just to say hello, and I told him, "What are you doing here! Thanks to you I got my rear end smacked all the way down the hill, and I want you to know I haven't forgotten it!"

We had a laugh about that—but the truth is, I wasn't really kidding.

One other time I remember wasn't the least bit amusing. In fact, it was pretty terrifying. But it says something about the place and time I was from—as well as the direction I was headed in life.

The incident happened on my sixteenth birthday. Pap came home to dinner after having a few drinks with his friends and began picking at my mother. He sometimes did this, nitpicked at her about this or that after a few drinks and a hard day at the club. I hated when he was drunk, because alcohol often brought out a side of him none of us liked to see. It troubled me that the man who rode me so hard about knowing the difference between right and wrong often did something—after too many shots at the firehall—*he* knew was wrong.

Well, on this particular evening I decided I'd had enough of it. I didn't like it one bit, and I stood up and told him flat out that I didn't like the way he was talking to my mother. I insisted that he leave her alone. I remember how he looked at me with surprise and then rage. Cheech and I, as I said, were raised to be seen and not heard, and it was unthinkable that I would challenge him in his house. Almost before I knew what hit me, Pap grabbed me by the shirt and lifted me off the floor with those massive hands of his and slammed me against a galvanized stovepipe, flattening it against the wall, scaring the living daylights out of me.

Perhaps it scared him too. These days some people might regard such violence as an act of child abuse, and I think even then my father realized he'd gone too far. Some part of him may have even admired the way I'd stood up to him—Pap admired toughness based on principle. In any case, the evening was in shambles, and a little later that night I ran away from home.

I grabbed a few things and slipped out of the house, trying to cool down and figure out which direction to go. I don't even remember if I took my golf clubs, to tell the truth. I was sixteen and regularly winning my high school golf matches, but I had no clue where to go to find a more interesting life, so I followed Nine Mile Run for a while and then wandered around the golf course for several more hours until I realized I simply had no place else I really wanted to go.

For better or worse, my father's house was my home. It was where I belonged. A little while later, I let myself back into the house and climbed quietly into bed. In the morning, my father didn't say a word about the incident. He never mentioned it again.

And he never laid a hand on me in anger again, either.

CHAPTER TWO

Mother

Not too long after we moved to the golf course and I started first grade at the Baldridge School, Mother went to work as the club's bookkeeper and took up golf. She usually played in the early evenings after dinner with the Bouches, Matt and May. Pap would go back to the club to give an evening lesson, and I was free to tag along after her.

My mother wasn't a good player, but she was as patient as the day is long and I owe my first playing experiences on a golf course entirely to her. One of five daughters, Doris Palmer was a classic "people" person, interested in just about everyone and every-thing, always enthusiastic in her approach to life, and she never met a stranger she didn't like. I'm deeply flattered when people who knew us both say I inherited her personality, for she was magnetic and charming and nobody ever had a bad word to say about her.

I don't remember a lot about those early outings with the Bouches, to be honest, except how much fun they were and how great it was to be with my mother, because I was anxious to show off for her. I was clearly the apple of her eye, and almost anything I did seemed to thrill her. Many years later, when reporters commented on a mannerism that became a kind of personal signature, hitching up my pants while stalking up a fairway in the heat of competition, I often explained that it was simply a means of handling nervous tension, something to do with my hands between shots. In fact, it was a reflex that dates from those first outings onto the golf course at Latrobe with my mother and the Bouches, when she would look over at me chugging to keep up and affectionately chide: "Hey, fella. Pull up those britches before they fall off you."

She always called me "fella." No aspiring golfer ever had a greater, more nurturing golf mom.

Maybe more important, though, given the restrictions inherent in my father's position as the club's head professional, she instinctively knew how important it was for me to actually *play* the golf course. I was paid a nickel to shag balls on the practice range, and when I wasn't with Pap or one of his work crews I sometimes was permitted to hack a ball around in the rough. Occasionally, when nobody was looking, I'd sneak onto a putting green for a few stolen moments of practice. But actually playing on the golf course when any of the members were present was another matter, strictly forbidden, simply out of the question.

The same policy applied to the club swimming pool. Cheech and I were employee children and therefore were never afforded the privilege of swimming there. Our swimming place was Nine Mile Run, the rock-edged stream that skirted the golf course and our house near the old sixth hole. Ironically, that creek was the source of the pool's water, and our favorite running joke for years was that we at least got to pee in the club's swimming pool water before the country club kids did.

Though I probably would have killed to swim in that pool, I don't think we resented the kids who got to swim there, some of whom I would later compete against on the golf course and others who would soon become some of my best friends. Many of them, like my friend Ken Bowman, hailed from the prosperous "Hill" section of town.

Any resentment we may have felt at being excluded, I'm convinced, like so many things in our lives, was softened considerably by the presence of our mother. People were drawn to her, and because of her almost consistently upbeat temperament, she had a way of placing the proper perspective on any situation, good or bad.

In some ways she was a complete and welcome contrast to Pap. Where he was pure discipline, she was complete generosity; where he was hard work and almost no play, she was playful and life nurturing. She encouraged, by her actions, the development of the gentle side of our personalities. She was good for Pap that way, too.

Pap had what might be termed classic "Scottish" ideas about a club professional's place in the world. When he wasn't overseeing maintenance on the course or giving a lesson, he stayed put in the shop. He would take meals either in the clubhouse kitchen or at home, and he would enter the clubhouse locker room, dining room, or bar only upon the explicit invitation of a member. The members wouldn't have lifted an eyebrow if Deacon Palmer ventured into these places on his own, but to him that breach of personal protocol was unthinkable. This policy naturally extended to his family.

Thanks to my mother, though, I had the opportunity to play on the golf course at Latrobe Country Club, learning to wield my women's brassie (a 2-wood) and a set of cut-down irons well enough to break 100 for eighteen holes before I turned eight. The course in those days was just nine holes, no par 5s, two par 3s, and the rest a bunch of surprisingly tough par-4 holes, a par-34 layout few players were good enough to get around twice and break 70. The fact that I could hit the ball over 150 yards pretty quick gave me the opportunity to make some unexpected movie money.

On summer days, I'd hang around the ladies' tee near the sixth hole waiting for Mrs. Fritz to come along. An irrigation ditch crossed the fairway about a hundred yards out, and Mrs. Fritz could never quite carry it. "Arnie," she'd call over to me sweetly, "come here and I'll give you a nickel to hit my ball over that ditch."

I did, too. I can't recall ever failing to get her ball safely across the ditch. The nickels mounted up. I made my first money playing golf that way.

Going to the movies in Latrobe was our big Friday-night event. Pap drove us in his '39 Chevrolet to see Roy Rogers movies or other western cowboys at the Manos and Olympic Theaters, and we often stopped for ice cream at Strickler's Drug Store (which claims to have invented the banana split in the 1920s) or visited my other set of grandparents in Latrobe, Charlie and Inez Morrison, who lived on Fairmont Street. My mom's father worked as an engineer for the Pennsylvania Railroad most of his life, and if I wasn't as close to him as I was to my father's father, I nevertheless enjoyed Grandpap Morrison's company a great deal. He wasn't a "physical" man the way the Palmer men were, but he did take me hunting once in a while and he spent a fair amount of time with both me and Cheech.

I remember this period, roughly between ages five and twelve, as a surprisingly social time for my family. My father was working hard at the club—even then there were discussions about expanding the course to eighteen holes, and he was forever tinkering with the existing nine he'd helped build—and my small world felt safe and secure. On Friday nights after he took us to the movies, my father hosted a big poker game at the house. In the beginning, his old friends from the pool room or firehall in town came to these late-night card games, but, increasingly, so did many of the club members—a measure of how welcome and comfortable they felt in our house, thanks to my mother.

Saturday-night get-togethers at Deke and Doris Palmer's place also became fairly commonplace, except on that night it was mostly couples. My mother would cook a big dinner, and couples from the club would come to play cards. Someone would always bring a bottle of good whiskey, and there would be a great deal of discussion about politics and a lot of laughter.

For a man who held such rigid ideas about right and wrong—and seemed almost puritanical at times—my father was remarkably liberal minded about the consumption of alcohol. As I explained with the stovepipe incident, that confrontation led to its own set of problems and complicated feelings I eventually had to work out for myself, about his—and later my own—drinking habits. When we were young, he would allow Cheech and me a sip of beer or wine if curiosity got the better part of us. I suppose some would say that was encouraging a bad habit.

I think, in fact, it was just the contrary. He had an extremely practical sensibility about it. He often commented that if he and my mother attempted to hide their own social drinking from us, that would all but guarantee we'd grow up to abuse alcohol. Though he was as human and real in his failings as any man, as the stovepipe incident revealed, Pap basically believed honesty and moderation were the best policies. There was no question he sometimes drank more than he should have, but over the years I've come to realize that drinking alcohol in a social setting served a very useful function for my father. His belief systems were so tightly formed and his attitudes about proper behavior so rigid, I think the drinking genuinely relaxed him and allowed him to lower his guard just a bit. For all of his exterior toughness, I would eventually learn, my father's emotions ran deep, and he had a sentimental side that rarely revealed itself—perhaps because he thought people would think he was weak. In any case, drinking allowed him to display that side of his personality, good or bad, but I think that release was beneficial for him.

Not surprisingly, my attitude about drinking has always been pretty much the same. When our girls came along, Winnie and I followed a similar pattern of allowing them to taste an adult beverage if curiosity got the better of them. By not hiding our belief in moderate drinking, we hoped to demystify the attraction of consuming alcohol and send a proper message. It must have worked, because Peg, our oldest, will only have the occasional beer, and Amy never touches alcohol in any form.

These family social rituals, I see now, were critical to the formation of my attitudes about life and meeting people, for all sorts of people were forever coming to our house. My father kept chickens and pigs in a side yard, and every autumn we made a kind of ritual of slaughtering pigs and making sausage. I loved the sausage but hated seeing the pigs killed. I loved hunting rabbits and pheasant with my father up on the forested ridges above our house. As with golf, there was a right way and a wrong way to hunt, and my father was fanatical about safety and proper behavior in the woods. And yet, at these moments, I was sometimes given the opportunity to see the deep-feeling man inside him. One afternoon while we were hunting, for example, we came across a big oak that had fallen over. The air was swarming with honeybees, and inside that oak was the most stunning honeycomb you've ever laid eyes on. Before we took the honey, Pap sent me to the store for two twenty-five-pound sacks of sugar, which we placed in the tree for the bees. That was the Pap few people got to see—a man who insisted on giving something to the bees in exchange for their fabulous honey.

In winter, when the snows came, my parents' house was also a gathering spot for folks out sledding and skiing down the hill from the seventh hole. My father turned a small maintenance shed at the club into a place to wax the skis of club members with paraffin, using an old laundry iron to melt it. Mother always made hot chocolate for the piles of kids who showed up, and there was warmed whiskey for the adults.

These gatherings were very festive, but one snowy night a near tragedy occurred that took the shine off the sledding outings forever. My mother and aunt Hazel were riding a toboggan down the hill in the darkness, racing my father, who was on skis. They ran straight into a guy wire holding up some of the new trees my father was always planting on the course. The guy wire caught my mother just below the nose and nearly tore off her upper lip. She was lucky—it could easily have snapped her neck and killed her instantly. Fortunately, a doctors' meeting was going on at the club at the same time, and the fact that Pap was able to fetch one of them fast probably saved her life. That night Cheech and I were both at home in bed at the time of the accident, completely unaware of what had happened. In the morning, Mother attempted to downplay the potential tragedy. But Pap's furrowed brow and alert eyes told us how serious the consequences could have been for us all. Maybe it was that sledding accident, or perhaps less dramatic things that happened shortly afterward, that slowly made Cheech and me aware of the harsher realities of what until then had seemed an almost perfect childhood.

Unquestionably the glue that held us together as a family, Mother somehow made the fact that Cheech and I were excluded from the pool and other places at the club seem . . . well, not such a big deal. But I do remember listening to the easy banter of the club's golfers as they came and went, watching members and their families coming and going to dances and dinners and such, and secretly wishing that we could be part of that larger world, too.

I was forever peeking in windows at the club, and one winter evening just before Christmas, I witnessed a very strange sight: all of the guests at a holiday dinner were dressed up in flowing white gowns of some sort, participating in some kind of formal ceremony. The scene was startling and a little bit upsetting to me. After all, I knew most of the people in the room—the club's top members and a lot of Latrobe's leading citizens. The club had nothing like the social diversity it enjoys today, no Jewish or Catholic members, no black members, and few or no other ethnic minorities to speak of. Today, it's highly tempting to make more of the gathering than it was—a holiday party built around the theme of celebrating the dominant Anglo-Saxon heritage of the membership. I remember shooting straight home to report to my mother that something kind of spooky was going on up at the club, and I remember how she smiled and assured me it only meant those people were simply proud of who they were and where they were from. No more, no less.

As usual, she was right, of course. My mother had a gift for being able to look at any situation and see the essential truth. In time I would come to know many of the older people in that room, and some of them would provide great support to my budding golf career. I wouldn't discover people who harbored secret racist views, though I suspect there were some who had them. On the contrary, for the most part I would find people who were, as my mother said they were, decent and proud of who they were and where they came from.

Several other remarkable things happened about that time that would have a lasting influence on me. One thing was my first ride in an airplane. Tony Arch, Charlie's older brother, hoping to go to the war brewing in Europe, had come home after washing out as a fighter pilot. He had his pilot's license and had volunteered instead to fly glider planes. That should have been some kind of tip-off to me about Tony's recklessness in the air. After all, the mortality rate among glider pilots was frighteningly high. But I was young and cocky and planning to live forever and, please pardon the pun, almost *dying* to fly. So Tony took me up in his Piper Super Cub and flew so low over the golf course, the rudder

tail actually dragged on the ground. In a nutshell, he
scared the blazes out of me.

After an experience like that, some people would
vow to never fly again. On the contrary, that hair-
raising stunt made me realize how much I really
wanted to learn to fly an airplane. Building model
airplanes and flying them with Rudy Melichar, the
club manager's son, had been one of the great pleasures of my childhood. Flying with Tony simply
made me vow to learn to fly a real plane the *proper*
way.

The arrival of war in 1941 brought great changes
to America in general and Latrobe in particular, with
acute shortages of manpower and material. The
supply of local labor, in fact, was so diminished that
there seemed to be no shortage of jobs around the
golf course my father wanted me to do.

In the summers, I worked at the golf course full
time, days that started before dawn and ended after
dark, cutting fairways with the gangmowers and
greens with a push mower in the mornings, then
working in the pro shop in the afternoons. I also
served as the club's caddie master and often caddied
for members myself. When I started winning golf
tournaments many years later, some members would
comment to the press that I was so full of myself I
couldn't resist telling them which club to hit, and
actually got a little sulky if they rejected my advice.
Perhaps I did. If so, it was because I was beginning
to learn more and more about the game and know
that golf course my father built like the back of my

own hand. I'm happy to add that many of those same members were careful to note to reporters that I was usually right about my advice on a particular shot or choice of an iron.

Many years later, Pap told a reporter that the worst "hire" he ever made was placing me in charge of the pro shop, because I was always running off to hit practice balls from the ladies' first tee when nobody was looking. Also, in those days a pair of slot machines sat in the clubhouse entryway, and when things got slow I'd sometimes sneak over there as well to plug dimes—dimes, I must confess, I took from the pro shop—into those one-armed bandits. Once, to my complete astonishment and sudden horror, I hit the jackpot and twenty dollars' worth of dimes flooded out. I frantically scooped up the money and took it to Johnny Shirey, Berkey's older brother, the locker room attendant, and begged him to keep it for me. I was scared to death that my father was going to find out about it, but Johnny agreed to keep my windfall—and keep mum. I waited nearly forty years to tell my father this story, and he was not too pleased to hear it even then.

I'll never forget the December afternoon we learned that Pearl Harbor had been bombed by the Japanese. It was a cold day and I'd just caddied nine holes for Pap and Dr. Mather. They'd gone into the pro shop to warm up, and I was dearly hoping that was all they planned to play that day. Latrobe winters were difficult and extra-lonely times for me; I hated the cold because it kept me from being out on the golf course, playing.

The radio in the pro shop was on, and I remember how still everybody became as the announcer described the devastation at Pearl Harbor. I remember my father shaking his head and swearing softly, and I thought that meant there would be no more golf that day. Unfortunately, my father told me to go get the bags because they were going to play another nine. In retrospect, it wasn't an unpatriotic gesture on his part to go out and play golf after hearing such awful news. He was helpless to do anything about the sneak attack and the arrival of war, and knowing him as I did, I can say that he was probably spitting nails about it and wishing he could personally have a crack at the Japanese. In any event, I made fifty cents for my trouble that afternoon, double my usual rate for carrying a bag.

Being a caddie had other perks. Among them, I was allowed to play the golf course on Mondays with the other caddies, when the course was officially closed. My game, as a result, progressed rapidly. The course had small but moist (or heavy) greens that received a low, hard shot best, so I grew up hitting low-liners that would land and roll rather than high lofted shots that would settle where they landed. Because the course had several demanding tee shots that required almost pinpoint accuracy, I became pretty adept at swinging a 1-iron, a club few if any players carry today and manufacturers never even bother to include in "matched" sets of clubs anymore. Because of its extremely low loft, I found I could get anywhere from 210 to 230 yards from a 1-iron shot. It was often easier to maneuver than a comparable fairway wood, and it helped me bend or shape a shot as needed. As a result, the 1-iron became very useful in my "training" at Latrobe Country Club, a tool I didn't hesitate to reach for when a shot required deadly accuracy.

Some things never changed, though, like my father's attitude about proper boundaries. I won the club's caddie tournament five times, beginning at about age eleven. But I never got to take the trophy home with me, a fact that deeply disappointed me at the time. Trophies were for other kids, even for other kids who were employees of the club. But they were never for me, and I secretly stewed about that for years.

Even so, with Latrobe's fairways as my laboratory, my old Walter Hagen driver and Patty Berg brassie, and either a set of Tommy Armour irons or Wilson Top Notch flat-backed blades I got just before high school, I began to experiment with all types of shots, learning how to move the ball by putting a certain spin on it. One area remained a problem for me, though: the short game, chipping and sand shots. For reasons of economy, Latrobe didn't have many bunkers in those days (sand traps require a lot of attention and are expensive to properly maintain). Also, Pap was a tyrant about people chipping around his greens, and he sure wasn't going to tolerate my endlessly practicing chip shots. As a result, my chipping and sand shots were the weakest parts of my game for years.

I became obsessed with the idea of practicing, and there's a little anecdote about this evolving passion that also helps to show the respect my father commanded from the members at Latrobe Country Club. On another hot afternoon when no one was around, I locked up the shop and went to practice hitting balls. Unfortunately, just about then, J. R. Larson, the chairman of the grounds committee— the same man who worried that I swung the club too hard—showed up at the shop, anxious to get his clubs and play a little. He found the place locked up and went to find my father, and soon all hell broke loose.

As Larson looked on, my father chewed me out good, describing my stubborn unreliability and warning me about the dire consequences of future mistakes, and so on. When he paused for a breath, Larson said to my father, "Tell you what, Deacon. Send him down to the steel mill to work. We'll straighten him out fast."

I was surprised by my father's quick response— and so, I'm sure, was J. R. Larson.

"Don't tell me what to do with my kid," Pap snarled at him, perhaps recalling his own time in the steel mills. "You take care of your business, Mr. Larson, and I'll take care of mine."

That was Pap's philosophy to a T, and he didn't back down from anybody, including powerful club members. For some head professionals that might have been the kiss of death, but on more than one occasion I overheard him say to Harry Saxman, his boss and the club's longtime president, "Harry, if you don't like the way I'm doing the job, feel free to go hire somebody else."

They never did, of course. They knew they would never find a man who worked harder and understood Latrobe Country Club the way Deacon Palmer did.

It was also about this time that I started reading books about golf, instruction books and biographies about the game's greatest players, picking up ideas here or there, even beginning to seriously fantasize about a professional career of my own. I was naturally drawn to the exploits of Bob Jones, and I remember thinking if I could fashion a golf career along the lines of his, that would be a dream come true. Byron Nelson's writing, his ideas about the golf swing and the way he'd come up through the game from the caddie yard to stardom and treated the game with such personal grace, also had a tremendous influence on me. That still wouldn't stop me from beating him or Ben Hogan or Sam Snead or anybody else on the course at Latrobe, though, and sometimes whipping them pretty soundly, on the perfect fairways of my vivid daydreams. I sometimes played two balls, for instance, one for Ben Hogan, say, and one for me: Palmer versus Hogan for the PGA Championship; or one for Byron and one for this brash young upstart named Arnie Palmer with the National Open Championship hanging in the balance. I was such a big dreamer in those days, perhaps because I was alone so much of the time on the course. Sometimes I think that kids these days could really use less planned activities and fewer structured choices and more time alone—time to

develop their imaginations, play games, and find out
who they really are. Years later, musing about those
slow boyhood days, I joked to a reporter that I lost a
lot of Opens on the fairways of my imagination. But
I won more than my share, too.

My first junior tournament took place the summer
I was twelve, at Shannopin Country Club in Pittsburgh. A slightly older golf buddy named Tommy
Smith drove us in his parents' car to the tournament,
but when we got there we encountered an unexpected problem. Just before I was scheduled to tee
off, I was informed that I was ineligible to play
because the tournament was sponsored by the Western Pennsylvania Golf Association, and Latrobe
Country Club didn't belong to the association.

I was stunned, crushed, and angry. I rushed to a
phone and called Pap and told him what had happened. He told me to calm down and stay close to
the phone. A few minutes later he called back to say
he'd spoken with Harry Saxman, who also belonged
to nearby Greensburg Country Club. Greensburg,
where Tommy Smith's family belonged, happened
to belong to the West Penn Golf Association, and
Harry's novel solution was that I would be declared
an "instant" member of Greensburg Country Club
by head professional Perry Delvecchio—and hence
be eligible to play.

I shot 82 in the qualifying round, good enough for
third or fourth qualifier. I thought that made me
pretty hot stuff, to tell the truth, and in the first
match the next day I drew a guy named Jack Kunkle
from St. Clair Country Club in Pittsburgh. Jack

was two years older than me, one of two golfing brothers—the other was named Bob—I would play with for years at junior tournaments around Pittsburgh. I watched Jack hit his first drive off the tee, a blast that sliced straight into the trees, and smiled. I was so cocky that I was sure I already had him beaten, especially since my drive found the heart of the fairway.

Off we went, with Jack in trouble and me already feeling the match was mine. A few hours later, Jack waltzed me in 4 and 3, and I'd learned one of the most valuable lessons of my career: Never take any opponent for granted on a golf course. It was a dose of humility I needed and carry to this day. Play your own game, as my father would have counseled, and mind your own business and you'll do much better. You control what you do, not what the other guy does. The only good news was that I didn't need to worry about how I would get to Pittsburgh the rest of the week because I was out of the tournament.

When I was thirteen, my year was full of a lot of junior golf tournament experiences like that around Pittsburgh, Greensburg, and Ligonier, where I met strong junior players I would compete against for years and forged many lasting friendships. My mother used to drive me to these events in the family Chevrolet, and whether I won or lost, played brilliantly or just survived, it didn't matter to her. Her enthusiasm was unwavering. Pap, on the other hand, seldom saw these early matches because he couldn't get away from the course, though he never missed any of the action if the match was played at Latrobe.

And if I came home and boasted of thrashing another kid, he would typically nod and remind me with a sobering note of skepticism not to get too cocky and to keep practicing if I knew what was good for me. The implication was, there was always going to be somebody tougher waiting out there to clean my clock and I'd better be prepared. I must admit, I really burned inside to earn a simple compliment from my father. After all, by that age I could routinely get around Latrobe in even par and was already regularly beating the boys on the high school golf team. But that compliment never came, which probably explains why I tried all the harder to please him.

I'm not entirely certain, but I believe that was the summer Babe Didrikson Zaharias came to Latrobe and put on an exhibition match, playing with Pap, me, and a promising young golfer named Pat Harrison, whose daughter is LPGA star Muffin Spencer-Devlin. The Babe was one of the great women of American golf, with sparkling wit and a swing as strong as garlic. I remember how she stepped to the first tee, pegged up her ball, and turned to the gallery and joked, "Okay, ladies and gentlemen. Hold on for a second while I loosen my girdle . . ." She proceeded to nail the ball a mile down the fairway with one of the sweetest and most compact swings you've ever seen. She made it look so easy.

The crowd ate up her showmanship, and I think I became aware of my own budding desire to show off and please people in that manner. Babe had a flair for the spectacular and the talent and personality to pull it off. Though no one but me realized it then, so did I. Prior to that, the only people I aimed to please with my golf shots were my father and mother. I was always pestering Pap to come watch what I could do in hopes he would praise me, which of course he never really did. That simply wasn't his style.

But, watching Babe do her thing, it occurred to me how great it would be to make *lots* of people— complete strangers at that—ooh and aah over a golf shot. It's impossible to say that's when I realized I loved performing in front of galleries, because the truth is, only a handful of people had ever seen me play in competition up to that point. But something in me was clearly drawn to the kind of public admiration I witnessed that day Babe Didrikson Zaharias came to Latrobe.

I already knew all the names of the game's greatest stars. But probably the first Tour professional I met about that time was Lew Worsham, older brother of a young man who would soon change my life. At that time Lew was the head professional at Oakmont Country Club in Pittsburgh. The Tour's season was so short in those days, players invariably kept head professional jobs at clubs. Worsham would capture the U.S. Open in 1947 over Sam Snead in a playoff that was as exciting as any in Open history.

A professional I knew even better and someone who had an even greater influence on me in those days, however, was a guy named Steve Kovach, an unpolished Pittsburgh steelworker who could simply do magical things with a golf club in his hands.

When Byron Nelson saw Steve play at the Canterbury Open in 1946, he commented that Kovach was
as good as anybody he'd ever seen. That was no
small compliment, and Kovach did have incredible shotmaking skills. I knew this because as a
schoolboy golfer I got to play with Steve a great deal
around Pittsburgh. He could produce high floating
shots that would settle as sweetly as anything you'd
ever seen, and I recall how at Ligonier, where the
greens were small and the mounds so fierce, he
could bounce balls off those slopes like nobody else.

I learned a lot from watching Steve play golf. But
I also learned a lot from watching what *happened*
to Steve Kovach as the result of his success. Kovach, as I say, was an unpolished gem, a blue-collar
worker whose grasp of proper English was marginal
at best. People would snicker when Steve spoke, and
reporters made fun of the way he butchered the language while attempting to explain his magical shots.
Some well-meaning people got together and paid for
Steve to attend language school in Cincinnati. The
strategy, however, backfired and only compounded
the problem. Steve emerged from these tutorials
using—and misusing—big words he scarcely knew
the meaning of. The laughter only intensified, and
Steve eventually suffered a mental breakdown and
wound up in an institution, out of golf. It was a genuinely sad story, and one that I took to heart. My
father had drilled into me the importance of knowing who you are and being true to that, not putting
up appearances or trying to be something you
simply aren't and can never be.

But I also drew another lesson from Steve's ordeal—the importance of learning to speak well. I came to understand how the words you say can make or break any situation.

Admittedly, I wasn't the best student in high school. I made decent marks in math because it had a useful purpose on the golf course (keeping score and tallying up bets), and pretty ordinary ones in English and history. Socially, as difficult as it may be for some people to believe, I was almost painfully shy, at least early on where girls were concerned. Thanks to Cheech, I went out with a number of pretty girls from the Latrobe area, but the idea of having a "serious" girlfriend didn't enter my mind.

I guess at that time I was much more comfortable beating my buddies on the golf course or playing football and baseball with them. Those two sports were the reigning kings around Latrobe, and, despite my relatively small size, I earned letters playing halfback and defensive tackle in junior high school. I went out for the football team my freshman year at Latrobe High only to be told by the coach, Bill Yates, that the team didn't have a uniform for me. This really stung. I was so upset I went home and told Pap, who, instead of being sympathetic, really chewed me out. "Boy," he said, "you shouldn't be playing football anyway. If you really want to play golf, stick to that!"

Ironically, I grew a lot physically over the next year, and by the time my sophomore year rolled around, Yates, who was also the school golf coach, almost begged me to come out for football. By then it was too late, though. Ken Bowman played on both teams, but I had no interest in playing anything but golf.

My first high school match was against a kid named Bill Danko, now a retired radiologist in Los Angeles whom I still see from time to time. Bill was from Jeanette High School, a powerful lefty, really a very good player and a heck of a nice guy. I was nervous as hell the first time we played, but I shot 71 and somehow beat him. We played two matches a year for the next four years, and Bill got close many times but never managed to beat me. He remains a good sport about it.

I was progressing fairly rapidly now. My first West Penn Amateur came at fifteen—I finished second and was bitterly disappointed that I didn't win. Lew Worsham wasn't the only golfer to have a great year in 1946. That was my junior year at Latrobe, when things really began to take off for me. First I won the West Penn Junior title and, later that fall, with Ken Bowman as a caddie, the PIAA, or state high school championship, on one of the fine old courses at Penn State. We hitched a ride to State College, I remember, with the tennis team because my usual ride to tournaments, my mother, was home with a new baby, my brother, Jerry.

Something important happened in the final match at Penn State that, in retrospect, would become another so-called signature of my game—though it was hardly a conscious thing at the time. Somewhere near the end of the match, holding a slight lead, I found my ball in the heavy rough with only a narrow gap through the trees to the green. An errant shot like that was fairly typical—I had them all the time at Latrobe—the result of my aggressively strong swing. The smart play was to pitch the ball back to the fairway. The truth is, though, that thought never really entered my head. There was no way I was *not* going for broke at that green, because I knew I could pull off that shot. I selected a 5-iron and fired my ball through the trees, right up onto the green. For the first time, there was a little gallery following me, and I remember how enthusiastically they cheered over that shot. Their response genuinely surprised me. They loved it . . . and so did I. For years I'd been motivated to hit spectacular shots principally in order to please my father; now, like Babe Zaharias, I had it within my grasp to please people I didn't even know with my golfing skills! What a thrill!

Something else happened that summer that would have a lasting impact on how I approached and played the game. Both my parents were on hand to watch my match in the West Penn Junior finals. Frustrated at having missed a short putt, I turned and threw my putter in disgust over the gallery and some small trees. My elation at winning quickly vanished when I was greeted with dead stone silence in the family car. "If you ever throw a club like that again," my father told me, barely restraining his fury, "you'll never play in another golf tournament."

I remember what a long ride back to Latrobe it was. Thank God my mother was there, slipping me affectionate quiet glances to let me know how proud she was of me. I know my father was brimming with pride as well, but I'd violated one of his cardinal rules about life and golf—that learning to be a gracious loser is at least as important as being a gracious winner. Being an *ungracious* winner was perhaps the worst thing he could imagine.

I was enough like my mother, I guess, that I was incapable of hiding my emotions at either winning or losing. But thanks to Pap, I learned the value of never publicly displaying my frustration—frustration every golfer experiences—and keeping my emotions in the bottle when I lost, regardless of the depth of the disappointment, of which there would be plenty. More to the point, I never threw a club like that in anger again. At least not when my father was anywhere around to see it.

I also played for the first time that summer in the Hearst juniors at Oakland Hills in Detroit. Al Watrous, whom Bob Jones once beat to capture the British Open at Lytham, was the head professional there, and I was pretty excited about meeting him. Unfortunately, it turned out that Watrous was coaching a player named Mac Hunter, my opponent in the finals, whose father, Willie, was head professional at Riviera Country Club in Los Angeles. I suppose you could call it healthy home-field advantage. In any event, it wasn't my time to win and Hunter beat me by a significant margin. I vowed I would go back the next year an improved player and take the Hearst title from him.

Something else happened at Detroit, though, that would have far greater impact on my career and life than winning the tournament, which, by the way, I

never managed to do. It was there I met Buddy Worsham, the younger brother of Lew, soon to be the
new National Open champion. His family called him
"Bubby," a nickname that didn't suit him, in my
mind. I called him "Bud" from day one—it simply
seemed to suit him better. Bud and I were the same
age and loved to horse around. We liked the same
kinds of foods and the same kinds of girls (we were
both painfully shy, but he was even shyer than me, if
that was possible), and our rambunctious boyish personalities meshed wonderfully even if our golf
games were distinctly different. For one thing, Bud
had severed a tendon in his leg as a child and walked
with a noticeable limp. Amazingly, he taught himself to stand on one leg and hit a golf ball, a feat that
always astounded me because he could hit it a mile
that way. Both of us hailed from golf families and
wanted to be professionals ourselves.

I did make it back to the Hearst National Junior
Championship the next year, the summer of 1947.
It was conducted at the now-defunct California
Country Club in Los Angeles. Bud Worsham and I
rode the train west together, and perhaps the long
two-day train ride exhausted me, or maybe I simply
wanted—or expected—to capture that Hearst title
too much. In any case, I was eliminated in the first
round.

This hurt, because my golf game seemed to be at
the top of its form. That year I would win both the
West Penn Junior and West Penn Amateur titles (the
first of my five WPA titles), capture my second
straight Pennsylvania schoolboy championship held

at Penn State, win a host of smaller invitational tournaments, and even make the semifinals of the Pennsylvania Amateur Championship.

But the whole way west to California on the train, Bud Worsham talked up a storm about where he was going to college. Some place down south called Wake Forest. Down there, Bud said, you could play golf *all winter long* and never have to interrupt your game for cold weather. That sounded great to me, almost too good to be true. The winters in Latrobe, as I've admitted, sometimes really got me down. Maybe at least as impressive to me, Bud had been offered a full athletic scholarship to play golf at Wake Forest—full tuition, room and board, the whole nine yards.

The truth was, I hadn't really given a whole lot of thought to going to college. Part of me, I suppose, thought I might join the U.S. Army to get my military service out of the way—World War II was over, but the draft was still in business—then come out and turn professional and try my luck at tournament golf. Thanks to my handsome schoolboy press clippings in Pennsylvania, Penn State and the University of Pittsburgh had expressed some interest in me, both of which offered full-tuition scholarships but not one penny of room and board.

My family wasn't in the kind of financial position to pay for my feeding and housing elsewhere. Pap and I had talked about college and pretty much decided that if I couldn't find a full ride like the one Bud had received from Wake Forest College, wherever it was, then I'd stay put at home, work at the club to make money, and maybe attend classes at St. Vincent College in Latrobe to try to earn a business degree.

As we headed over the rails to the Hearst tournament, though, Bud's bright idea was that maybe he could convince the powers at Wake Forest, specifically Jim Weaver, the school's athletic director, to give me a similar deal. It was almost too late—the start of the fall term was literally days away at that point—but Bud called Jim Weaver from California and I called my mother and asked her to hurriedly send my high school transcripts to Wake Forest, a place I knew nothing about except it was *somewhere* in North Carolina and sounded like heaven.

My disappointment at being knocked out early at the Hearst tournament was quickly tempered by a letter I received a few days after I got home. My mother, fittingly enough, gave me the letter from Wake Forest offering me the same full scholarship deal as Bud Worsham got.

I'd never been south of the Pennsylvania state line, but there was no question which direction I was headed.

CHAPTER THREE

Wake Forest

In the spring of 1997, a special gathering took place at the Bay Hill Club and Lodge in Orlando, Florida. Twenty-six of the world's finest collegiate golfers assembled to contest the first-ever Palmer Cup, a three-day team match-play tournament modeled after the popular biennial Ryder Cup matches, pitting the best young players of America against their British and Irish counterparts. The event was the brainchild of several prominent college golf coaches, and I was proud to have my name on the cup and be a title sponsor and host of the fledgling event, because, as the Ryder Cup's success proves, playing for pride and country invariably makes for thrilling drama. This tournament was no exception. The Americans won going away, but everyone who was involved with the event, I think, went away smiling, and believing that a valuable contribution to the game had been made and perhaps a new tradition born.

On a more personal level, though, the Palmer Cup symbolizes the deep and somewhat complicated feelings I have about the amateur golf of my own collegiate days playing for Wake Forest College. In many ways, they were among the happiest years of my life, where, out from under my father's stern sphere of influence for the very first time, I spread my wings and had a hell of a lot of fun, forged a host of lifelong friendships, and got my first taste of winning golf tournaments on a national level. With freedom comes joy and pain, though, and in other ways the education I got at Wake was far more than I bargained for. Amid the winning and friendships I learned what real emotional pain felt like, because of some of the saddest days of my life.

When I periodically go back to visit the sprawling modern Wake Forest University campus that now occupies a particularly lovely corner of Winston-Salem, North Carolina, I'm struck by how powerfully life can change in half a century. To begin with, obviously, Wake is no longer the sleepy Baptist college I discovered tucked off in the pine woods east of Durham—it's now a major, thriving university with over 6,000 undergrads and graduate students, home to a world-class medical teaching hospital and a respected law school. Its academic programs are distinguished, and its sports programs, as they say, are big time. Eventually, if plans go as hoped, and my lobbying efforts on the board of trustees yield dividends, Wake may eventually become home to a world-class collegiate golf course facility created by Palmer Course Design.

That eventuality would have more than symbolic meaning to me, because fifty years ago, using wheelbarrows and shovels, during a lull in studies during our sophomore year, Bud Worsham and I and a few other members of the Wake golf team built the college's first grass greens, replacing the modest nine-hole course's original sand greens with something that at least resembled a competitive putting surface. As I recall, the athletic department paid us fifty cents an hour for our efforts, and we were very proud of our handiwork, though I doubt very much that the administration—or, for that matter, anybody but us really—expected the improved practice grounds to increase Wake's chances of achieving golf prominence.

The truth is, in those days Wake's golf team was something of a doormat in the old Southern Conference. The University of North Carolina at Chapel Hill was the dominant conference power, underscored by the presence of Harvie Ward, the best amateur player in the country at the time. Duke University was a close second, thanks to Art Wall and Mike Souchak. Sixteen miles to the south, North Carolina State was also considered a comer, with Jim McNair and a host of young and promising southern-bred golfers on board.

Nationally, it was a fertile time in collegiate golf. Dow Finsterwald, who would win the 1958 PGA Championship and become one of my closest friends on the PGA Tour, was at Ohio University, and Ken Venturi—the man I would battle down to the wire in the 1960 Masters and then again in the 1964 U.S. Open—was already making a name for himself at San Jose State. Gene Littler, the Open's 1961 champion, was at San Diego State. And North Texas State, meanwhile, was something close to a collegiate golf dynasty with the likes of Don January, Billy Maxwell, and Joe Conrad.

Wake had a long history of producing great

teachers and ministers, not athletic stars—certainly not golf stars. In a sense, my unheralded arrival at the campus in the fall of 1947 pretty well summarizes that complacent atmosphere. After a long overnight bus ride from Pennsylvania, during which I slept only in fits and starts, I literally got off the bus in the hot and sleepy village of Wake Forest with only my golf bag and suitcase in hand. The bus drove off, and there I stood on a loop of U.S. Highway 1, the town circle, wondering where the blazes to go next.

I saw a group of handsome brick buildings and decided that must be the college and started walking that way, ending up a little while later by an open office door in the school gymnasium. Two men were sitting in a small office talking. When they saw me, timidly loitering just outside the doorway, the larger one asked with a deep southern voice what I wanted. I told him I was looking for Jim Weaver. I saw the men exchange glances. The other man, I soon learned, was Peahead Walker, the school's football coach.

"Who the hell are you?" the first man asked.

"Arnold Palmer," I told him, swallowing dryly.

He gave me a small smile. "Well, Mr. Palmer," said Jim Weaver, getting up to offer me his hand, "welcome to Wake Forest College."

I was told to report to a rooming house on the circle that was owned by Johnny Johnston's mother. Johnny, the school's golf coach, was finishing his military service, and except for weekend leaves wouldn't return to campus until the spring of my freshman year, so in the meantime we had Jim Weaver as a coach. What I failed to realize then was that Weaver, who really didn't know all that much about golf, was itching to show the rest of the conference that Wake would be a pushover no more. Weaver was a born competitor and terrific motivator, a large man with a big heart and bear-like enthusiasm, qualities that made him a great choice to become the Atlantic Coast Conference's first commissioner. Jim was still smarting, I think, from a remark made to him not long before by Carolina's golf coach, Chuck Erickson, who confidently assured him Carolina's crop of golf prodigies would wipe Wake's collective derriere on the golf course, though in language slightly less suitable for use on a Baptist college campus. These were fighting words to Big Jim Weaver.

Besides, Wake Forest wasn't without promising young guns of its own. Mickey Gallagher and Ray Harris were solid veteran players and constituted the team's nucleus, while Bud Worsham and I were the highly touted newcomers. Jim Flick was also there on a combined golf and basketball scholarship. And a year behind us would come a couple of fellas named Dick Tiddy and Sandy Burton.

The highlight of my freshman year, just about the time Johnny Johnston returned from the U.S. Air Force, was beating Harvie Ward and Art Wall at Pinehurst Number 2 to win the Southern Conference championship. I'm sure many of the reporters on hand considered this a major upset—Harvie, after all, was considered by many to be the best collegiate player in the country—but I never had any doubt in my mind that I could beat them or anybody else. The tournament was medal play, and I remember watching Harvie play the final hole, needing to make two to tie me. He made it very interesting to the last shot—nearly holing out his approach. When my heart started beating again, I realized I'd won my first Southern Conference championship and Jim Weaver was nearly out of his mind with happiness.

I came home that summer bubbling with confidence and with a college-boy spring in my step and won the Sunnehanna Amateur and reached the semifinals of the North and South Amateur. My routine was now a little more varied and fun. I still worked most mornings for my father at the club—mowing grass or tending the shop, whatever he told me to do—but thanks to Harry Saxman and other prominent members at Latrobe, I was more or less accorded membership status and was free to play the golf course as much as I wanted to in the afternoons. I suppose it's fair to say I was thoroughly obsessed with golf, thinking of little else and practicing long hours every day before hanging out with my old gang at night. That summer I flew to Memphis, Tennessee, and met a man named William Barrett, Jr., in the first round of the United States Amateur championship at Colonial Country Club. I felt pretty confident about my chances, but as one of the youngest players in the field I also remember feeling a little awed by the fact that this was the most coveted amateur event in the world.

As strange as it sounds, perhaps I was both a little

bit too awed *and* cocky—both being major sins in my father's eyes. I failed to play as well as I should have and was beaten fairly handily, 6 and 5, by the much older Barrett in the first round. I took losing hard, mentally kicking myself for a number of missed opportunities. But once I'd resolved to fight my way back to the Amateur the next year and go deeper into the rounds of competition, the pain of disappointment was muted by a friend of my father's named Bob Thompson. He invited me over to a big invitational tournament in Indiana, where we really cleaned up in the Calcutta portion of the tournament and I almost won the regular tournament. I did win several smaller pro-am and regional invitational tournaments that summer, and I had more pocket change than I'd dreamed of.

By summer's end, though, I couldn't wait to get back to Wake and see Bud and resume my college life. Wake Forest was a Baptist-affiliated institution, which, in those days, allowed no drinking or dancing on campus. Students were required to take their partying and social life elsewhere, usually to taverns and hotels in Durham or Raleigh, a drive of about twenty miles over twisting backcountry roads. I understood the scriptural basis for such a policy, but, quite frankly, even now I question the wisdom of segregating a young person's academic life from his social one. The fact is, there were a lot of unsupervised parties off campus in those days. Like Pap used to, I now think the school's rigidity on this issue probably contributed to underage drinking problems and made consuming alcohol seem much more glamorous than need be, by extension increasing the possibility of irresponsible driving.

Socially and academically, Bud and I had a system of sorts worked out where we more or less looked after each other. Our strengths and weaknesses beautifully complemented each other's. I had a stronger physical constitution that allowed me to handle alcohol, sometimes showing little or no effects, so I was always the one who drove Bud's Buick when we went out on dates or in a group to party in Durham or Raleigh. As I've said, Bud was shyer than me, so it was left to me to speak to girls and arrange our "dates," if you want to call them that.

On the academic front, Bud had a strong work ethic and was forever on my case about keeping up my grade point average to avoid losing my scholarship and being put on academic probation, or worse, getting kicked out of school and probably drafted. Quite honestly, I really wasn't much of a student. For a while I thought fleetingly about a career in law but then switched to a business major, figuring that I could at least graduate to a nice businessman's job somewhere that would allow me the freedom to make a decent living *and* play the kind of top amateur golf I envisioned myself playing.

The idea of turning touring professional was also always somewhere in the back of my mind, I must confess, but not if it involved having to do the kind of demeaning jobs I'd always seen Pap do in order to support my family. Several years after my college days, I commented to a reporter that above all else I was determined to avoid the second-class life of my father's profession. I meant no disrespect to Pap and the life of a club professional. Back then a club professional's status was so different from that of today's professional, and I knew in my gut there was no way I could put up with the things I'd seen Pap put up with over the years.

Golf would be my ticket *somewhere*, I told myself, I just couldn't say where it would lead me. But life at Wake for the time being, even with the social restrictions, couldn't have been better. After constructing the new grass greens on the school golf course, I was free to play as much as I wanted and sometimes even invited my dates to be human targets on the greens. God only knows why they agreed to do it; perhaps I had more charm than I realized in those days, except with a certain academic dean who took to summoning me to his office for friendly chats about my casual academic performance.

During my sophomore year, I captured a second straight Southern Conference championship and became the medalist (or low qualifier) at the National Intercollegiate finals at Ames, Iowa, where I lost to Tom Veech of Notre Dame in the semifinals. Harvie Ward beat Veech in the final match to take the NCAA championship. I remember being furious with myself because I'd never lost a match to Harvie Ward, and it would have been great to have the two of us, both representing the Southern Conference, vying for the national collegiate championship. It wasn't to be, though.

What was to be, however, in the summer break

between my sophomore and junior years, was another West Penn Amateur title—I beat Jack Benson over a difficult Oakmont Country Club course, my first real glimpse of the famous course set up to tournament specs—and once again I was a semifinalist at the North and South Amateur. In midsummer, I managed to make it to the third round of the U.S. Amateur at Oak Hill Country Club in Rochester before being eliminated with surgical precision, 4 and 3, by Crawford Rainwater of Pensacola, Florida. Two steps closer to the big prize, but ultimately another disappointment and a new resolution.

My junior year at Wake was, in retrospect, maybe the most fun of all my college years. There were plenty of parties and plenty of pretty girls and lots of laughs and more competitive golf than I suppose I'd ever played in my life. Bud and I grew socially more confident but were still basically inseparable, always ready to drop everything at the chance to beat each other on the golf course. This had been our standard operating procedure since our very first week at Wake Forest, when we managed to cajole a couple of coaches into taking us over to the Carolina Country Club in Raleigh for a four-ball match. Bud shot 67 that day, and I beat him by a stroke—on a course neither one of us had seen before. That set the tone for our matches, which always had something riding on them—at least the drinks afterward. My grades still weren't great, but, once again, thanks to Bud Worsham, I was holding my own, and with

Johnny Johnston's return as the golf coach, I found a true friend and confidant for life.

On weekends, I sometimes went to Bud's home in Maryland, or he went to Latrobe with me. My younger brother, Jerry, and little sister Sandy (my parents had another set of children almost twenty years after Cheech and me) fell in love with Bud, and we both grew close to each other's families. It was while we were hitchhiking back to school one weekend with our golf bags in tow that we met George Fazio. We had our thumbs out on U.S. 1 south of Washington when a big Cadillac pulled over. I recognized Fazio instantly, but he didn't know us from Adam's house cat until Bud told him who his older brother was. We told him we were headed back to college at Wake Forest, and he told us to hop in, asking if either of us was old enough to drive a car. I said yes. He promptly told me to drive, climbed in the back, issued firm orders to shake him awake when we got to North Carolina, then fell into a deep, noisy sleep. That was the first Cadillac I ever drove. I remember being impressed by that car, its big purring engine and nice interior, a true symbol of American success.

We failed to win the Southern Conference team title, but my game had never been sharper and I captured the Southern Intercollegiate championship and once again was low qualifier at the NCAA finals, firing a record pair of 68s at Albuquerque, New Mexico, in a tournament that featured Billy Maxwell, Don January, and Jack and Jimmy Vickers, gunning for All-American fame. Unfortunately, as often happens after a record-setting performance, I let down my guard and played poorly in the semi-final round, and was beaten by a dark horse named Ely Barristow of San Jose State. Being sent home early really hurt, but it only made me buckle down and practice that much harder. Later that summer the intense work paid dividends; I won my third West Penn Amateur and the Greensburg Invitational, tune-ups for what I hoped would be my big break-through at the U.S. Amateur at Minneapolis Country Club in Minnesota.

Frank Stranahan of Toledo, Ohio, was my oppo-nent in that first round. To be honest, this sort of pleased and worried me. Stranny, as I called him, was a pretty good friend against whom I'd competed several times in our amateur playing careers, most notably at the North and South Amateur in both '48 and '49. Curiously, in 1948, Harvie Ward beat me in the semifinals and Stranny in the championship match; the next year, I played Stranny in the semis and he really cleaned my clock, something like 11 and 9 over a thirty-six-hole match, before going on to whip Harvie. The way I figured it, I was a good-luck charm for both of them.

Maybe this time Lady Luck would be in my corner for a change and my third trip to the Amateur would prove the charm.

My other nickname for Stranny was Muss. He was not only a tenacious competitor but also some-thing of a weight-lifting addict and health nut to boot, a classy fellow whose father was chairman of

Champion Spark Plugs in Toledo. Early on I learned never to take our matches lightly, because Muss was a steady player who was capable of going on a sudden birdie binge like nobody you've ever seen— as he did at Minneapolis, beating me once more, 4 and 3, to knock me out of the National Amateur yet again. If I had to lose in the first round, I suppose it helped slightly that it had been a friend who beat me.

On the other hand, I was somewhat bitter that I'd missed another golden opportunity. But as Pap had trained me to do, I put on a good face and was a perfect gentleman about the loss, smiling and graciously congratulating Stranny and wishing him the best of luck. I really meant it—he deserved to win and dearly wanted the National Amateur title for himself and his family. Inside, however, I was seething mad at myself for having blown my chance to capture the prize I wanted more than anything else at that time in golf.

A great deal of emotion and high expectation surrounded Wake's homecoming football game of 1950. We were playing Carolina on our turf, and Carolina was the dominant pigskin power in the conference at that time. Wake, as I recall, had merely a so-so year. But with all those Baptists at home in the stands praying for an upset, it stood to reason that something big just might happen. Incidentally, the story that Peahead Walker had attempted to recruit me for the football team is true. Like Frank

Stranahan, I was physically stronger than most golfers and pretty agile. I loved watching and playing football, but by that point had accepted Pap's belief that it was foolish to play a game in which I could easily be injured and jeopardize my golf career.

As usual, a group of us planned to attend the game together and maybe go out to dinner afterward or to the homecoming dance that night at a hotel in Durham. Bud threw us a little curve by announcing he planned to sell programs that afternoon to make some extra spending money but agreed to join us at halftime. True to his word, he showed up and we had our usual laughs, plus a few discreet bourbon and Cokes.

I honestly can't remember who won the game that day, because in my mind the game and the events afterward take on the quality of an eerie and troubling dream. We all went back to the Community Club, as the athletic dormitory was called in those days, and some of our friends either went on to dinner or slept to rest up for the evening festivities. I decided to take a nap and quickly dozed off on my bed, only to be shaken awake by Bud a short time later. He told me that he and Gene Scheer, Jim Flick's roommate from next door, were going to get some dinner and go to the dance in Durham and he wanted me to join them. He was really keen on that idea and lobbied hard, I suppose mostly because I was always the one who was able to talk to pretty girls.

I shook my head and sleepily told him I wasn't

interested in the dance, explaining that Jim and I had discussed going to a movie later.

"Come on, Bud," I said to him. "Stay with me. Go with us to the movie."

"No," he said. "Gene and I are going to the dance."

So I fell back to sleep.

Later, I did get up and Jim Flick and I went out to the movie and were back at the dorm before midnight. In the morning, I looked over and saw Bud's bed hadn't been slept in, and this surprised me. It wasn't like Bud Worsham to stay out all night—at least not without me along to take care of him.

Surprise gave way to worry and worry turned to panic when I went next door to see if Gene had come home. Gene hadn't reached his bed either. I remember several of the guys were in Jim and Gene's room, shooting the breeze about the game and the dance, and I remember telling them to let me know if anybody heard from Bud or Gene. Then I went back to my room to wait.

About an hour later, Jim Flick appeared at my door and said Coach Johnston wanted to talk to me. The instant I saw Jim's face I knew something terrible had happened. "Arn," Johnny told me somberly, "we've got a problem. We think maybe Bud's had an accident."

Within minutes, we were all in Johnny's car headed toward Durham, and it was while we were riding in the car that Johnny broke the news to me that he thought Bud and Gene were dead. I remember how incomprehensible that sounded, but a little while later, crossing a narrow bridge over a rocky creek, we passed the site where their Buick had run off the road, skidded briefly along a support rail, then landed upside down in the rocky streambed, crushing both boys to death.

We drove to Durham in silence, searching for a funeral home where the authorities might have taken the bodies. We had a devil of a time finding the right one. Johnny's brother was a highway patrolman, and it was through him, as I recall, that we finally learned Bud and Gene had been taken to Raleigh.

"Who are you, family?" the funeral director asked me.

I told him I was Bud's best friend.

"Would you be prepared to identify the body?" he added.

I didn't know what to say. I was numb with disbelief. I suppose part of me did wish to view the body—if only to prove that the nightmare was real.

"I guess so," I said.

He led me into a room and there they were, both of them, lying together on a table. It was the worst thing I'd ever seen.

For some reason, Johnny and I then went searching for the car, Bud's car, the car in which we'd had so many good times. Perhaps the shock was so great we needed to see the physical evidence of this unimaginable nightmare. Or perhaps I wanted some other mental image to replace the one I'd just seen— twisted metal in place of those broken bodies. We found the car a little while later at an auto junkyard just outside of town, crushed almost beyond recognition. But it was unmistakably the Buick. Essentially, the vehicle had been torn in half.

Johnny took me back to the dorm at Wake. That was the last place I wanted to go, to tell the truth, but I couldn't imagine where else to go except home—and home was over four hundred miles away. I called my parents, and their shock and grief almost matched mine.

Jim Flick moved his things into my room that night, and I remember that we sat up late talking about what had happened, what we would do, and I don't know what else. Perhaps this was good for us both, a necessary venting of grief and anger. Grief is one of the most powerful forces on earth, and almost always unpredictable. I'd never felt anything like the emotions and conflicting feelings suddenly turning over inside me. I wanted to play golf, but staying at Wake Forest suddenly felt empty and pointless without Bud there. I didn't want to go to war, but I suddenly no longer wanted to be in college. I wanted to run away, but I wanted to be comforted. I wanted to sleep, but I wanted to wake up from this nightmare. Jim must have felt the same confusion and loss of direction.

It's strange. Over the years Jim and I have remained friends, but more distantly than you might expect. I wouldn't say we are terribly close even today. He's gone on to have a distinguished career as one of the game's premier teachers, including his long association with Jack Nicklaus, and I sometimes wonder if the shared intimate horror of Bud's and Gene's deaths and the subsequent soul-wrenching conversations we had in those long days and nights after the tragedy sealed our friendship in place, froze it in time—maybe prevented anything deeper from forming.

Some things go beyond words, and I simply can't say for sure. And, I'll wager, Jim can't either.

Bob Jones, my first golf hero, once commented that he never learned anything from a golf tournament he won. It may sound absurd to compare the death of my best friend to losing a golf tournament, but I've learned life really does resemble a golf round in its crazy ups and downs. For better or worse, those moments of unaccountable loss or failure teach us the most about who we are, where we've come from, and where we may be headed.

After Bud's wrenching funeral in Maryland, I went home to Latrobe and told my parents I needed a break, some time away from college. I thought I might enlist in the U.S. Coast Guard, because the guard required only a three-year service commitment, unlike the U.S. Navy or Air Force. My father, I could tell, wasn't pleased to hear this news. He was unshakable in his belief that I should finish my studies and earn a degree, perhaps rightly fearing that if I got out of the service and started earning a buck I would probably never go back and finish what I'd started. On the other hand, perhaps either out of respect for Bud or simply because of the ordeal I'd just been through, he made no comment one way or the other. But he did say the final call was mine to make because I'd have to live with it. Both my parents, I believe, were still in a state of shock. They'd loved Bud like a son, and I think they were also deeply relieved I was still alive.

My mother had an almost infallible instinct for knowing how I felt about almost anything, whether it was for golf or for people. And I think that, unlike my father, she understood the depth of the grief I was reeling from. Pap was a great believer in the curative powers of working hard and doing your job, toughing out any misfortune, but Mother was a natural sympathizer and I think she fully understood that my whole world had been turned upside down. Some kinds of grief require additional airing, perhaps a new landscape for better perspective, in order for the healing to begin.

She told me to follow my heart on this one, in effect to live my life the same way I played the game, my own way.

The simple truth is, I was haunted by a feeling I couldn't escape, that if I'd only gone that night to Durham with Bud and Gene things might have turned out very differently. I'd probably have been driving the Buick, and we would have all returned safely from Durham and gone to bed and gotten up that Sunday morning and maybe gone out and played golf and the world would have been exactly as it had always been for us, spinning happily on its axis.

But that was now all gone. Wake without Bud

was unthinkable. He was the reason I'd gone there in the first place, the reason I'd stayed, the reason I'd become one of the best college golfers in America.

I did return, briefly, after Christmas, to finish out the term and be alone with my thoughts. Though I never broke down publicly, I shed plenty of tears in private. My last days there were a quiet torture for me.

One day in mid-January I picked up the phone and called the United States Coast Guard recruiting office in Washington, D.C. A couple of days later, I was on a bus headed north, hoping to outrun a grief I still feel like a cool evening shadow almost fifty years later.

CHAPTER FOUR

Turning Point

By the time I arrived at the U.S. Coast Guard's basic-training facility the third week of January 1951, the coldest, bleakest part of the winter had set in at Cape May, New Jersey, at the southern tip of the state where the Atlantic Ocean joins Delaware Bay.

I've seen it written that during at least the first two of my three years of Coast Guard service, due to Bud's death, I lost interest in playing golf, but that's simply not true. My passion for playing the game was probably as intense as it ever was. In fact, golf was the foundation of my life. Because everything else in my life had been shaken up in the aftermath of Bud's accident, golf was a refuge for me. Out on the course, things still made sense. It was the one place where I felt in control of what was happening to me. The reason I didn't play much in the Coast Guard is simply that I had little or no access to golf courses—a situation that dramatically improved by my third year in the service.

A true little-known irony, however, is that this same passion for golf nearly prevented me from being accepted by the Coast Guard. The reason was flatfeet. After signing up in Washington and being sent for routine physical exams, I was informed that—a big surprise to me—I'd ruined my arches by running barefoot on the golf course so much many years before. I was put through a battery of additional physical tests to see if I could meet the physical requirements, made to run sprints, walk on my toes, all sorts of things I never imagined having to do to qualify for service.

That was tough, but I passed their tests and life soon got tougher. I was shipped to boot camp at Cape May, where my company commander was rumored to have been kicked out of the U.S. Marines because he was too rough on the men in his command. That may have been something they told every green recruit—especially college boys who played golf—but after I got to know him I had every reason to believe the rumor was correct. He was one tough SOB, and I tried my best to do what was expected of me and stay on his good side.

The Coast Guard receives less publicity than the other three major branches of military service, but the fact is that during the years of the Korean War—which was raging full blast at that point in time—the guard lost a higher percentage of its people in the conflict than any of the other branches of service. Its skill in escorting ships and troops as well as its legendary search-and-rescue expertise were about to be depicted, as it turned out, in a new movie, aptly called *Fighting Coast Guard,* starring Brian Donlevy. Just as I was finishing up my boot camp training, word came down from on high that an honor guard detail of twenty Coast Guard cadets would be selected to attend the movie's world premiere in Washington. Being the enterprising fellow I was, I decided that making the detail would give me an opportunity to go see my sister Cheech and her new husband, Ron, who lived just across the Potomac in Alexandria. I also hoped to get some welcome R and R and maybe play a little bit of golf while I was at it.

Clever me—almost too clever, as it turned out. I wasn't the only guy scheming for a break. Over four hundred men volunteered for the detail, and weeks of hard drilling and ruthless marching ensued. Every few days, names would be dropped from the list for the slightest infraction or breach of discipline. One mistake and you were out. The list quickly dropped to 300 names and then 200 names, and my name was still on it. It went from 200 to 100 prospects, and I was still there, getting more confident every day. In retrospect, it was a little bit like trying to make the cut of a major golf tournament, and I was really pleased with myself when I made the top fifty. Finally, after two months of exhaustive training and nerve-racking worry, the names of the twenty lucky cadets who would be going to the movie premiere in Washington were posted . . . and Arnold Daniel Palmer's name was on the list! I could have jumped over the moon.

They put us in our best dress whites and sent us south to Washington on a bus. That evening, when President Truman and Brian Donlevy and all the other celebrities arrived at the theater, the honor guard was in place and the flashbulbs were popping. After a few words from dignitaries and so forth, everyone trooped inside to see the movie, and the honor guard was left standing out front. We stood there for another hour before being ordered back onto the bus and taken to a cheap hotel. The next morning before sunrise, we were informed there was no leave and we were being sent straight back to Cape May.

So much for a family reunion and my brief golf vacation plans.

A few days later, though, I was called into my commander's office and asked if I would accept "permanent party" status. That meant the brass wanted me to stick around Cape May and train recruits. Someone else got the bright idea that since I was a hotshot college golfer, perhaps I might agree to build a nine-hole golf course on the base. I enthusiastically agreed to do the job and was summarily handed a rake and a shovel, placed in charge of an elderly hand-push mower, and directed to a weed-choked grassy patch of ground located between the base's air runways.

Of the 250 or so golf courses I've designed and built over the past fifty years, that first one was probably not the most challenging layout but certainly was the most physically exhausting to create. In addition to the fact that it was suddenly summer and surprisingly hot on the Jersey shore, I essentially had to do most of the shaping and grooming and mowing myself. When I was done, it was a pretty rudimentary layout—a nine-hole chip and putt, really—but I was pleased with my efforts, and the officers who played it were delighted to have a place to hit balls. For a while, a small eternity it seemed to me, that was about as close as I got to a golf course. Then I finally got a coveted weekend leave and was able to play a private course in Wildwood, New Jersey, discovering to my dismay that my game had more than a few barnacles on it.

In the Coast Guard there is seldom rest for the weary. On top of my course-building duty, I often had lifeguard duty at the base beach, sinking barrels for buoys or watching recruits swim in our restricted area next to the public beach. One afternoon I saw a couple of young recruits in trouble, maybe 150 yards offshore, and was off the lifeguard stand like a shot. I was a good swimmer, but realized as I swam out that I was clearly no match for a couple of guys drowning. Luckily, two girls from the public beach saw what was happening and swam out to lend a hand, and we somehow managed to haul them to shore. Safe on land, I realized my heart was pounding wildly, as much out of fear as fatigue. We could have all been in big trouble, they for idiotically straying where they shouldn't have been, I for letting them do it.

As I think back on it, it seems to me that I was always on the verge of being in trouble with my superiors. For one thing, it was obvious to anybody who knew me that I was simply fulfilling my military obligation and itching to get back to the world of playing golf. For another, the workload and constant discipline didn't appear to faze me as much as it did some of the other young guys. Thanks to Pap, hard work and being chewed out for something were fairly routine for me, and I think the ease with which

I went about my days irritated a particular lieutenant who used almost any excuse to pick on me. I think he knew I was a college-boy golfer, and that didn't sit well with him. At any rate, he was always looking for an excuse to try to bust my chops.

One day in the base gymnasium I nearly gave him that excuse. Because of the strength in my hands and upper body, I taught preliminary jujitsu to the recruits. It was nothing fancy, just some basic simple escape maneuvers. Typically, a hundred or so men would line up and run at me one at a time, and I would show them a simple break-and-fall technique. Well, proof that a little knowledge is a dangerous thing, one guy came at me and decided to throw in an extra move—I tossed him on his back and broke his arm.

I got a captain's call for that and was sure I was in big trouble.

"Mr. Palmer," the captain began, looking somberly at me, "we've made a decision to transfer you . . ."

Now I was really scared.

". . . and I'm going to give you an opportunity to go anywhere you wish to go."

I couldn't believe my ears. After a moment, I told the captain I'd like to go either to Washington, D.C., or Cleveland, Ohio, if it was okay with him. Both were fairly close to home, I reasoned, and both places had plenty of golf courses nearby.

A few days later, I was sent to the 9th Coast Guard District Headquarters in Cleveland, Ohio.

*   *   *

During those long and tough nine months at Cape May, I had played golf only a handful of times—at a private course in Wildwood, New Jersey, and once or twice back home in Latrobe during three- or five-day leaves.

Though I managed to successfully defend my West Penn Amateur title and won a memorial invitational held that summer in Bud Worsham's honor, the lack of practice took a large toll on the quality of my game, and my father was none too pleased when I signed up to play in the Greensburg Invitational. The tournament was held a few miles down the road from Latrobe, and I'd won it three times in its first four years. The trip home sort of set the tone for the dismal weekend. I was wearing my uniform and hitch-hiking with my gear and my golf bag when a guy pulled over in a Cadillac. He asked me to drive. With pleasant memories of George Fazio and our amusing ride south in mind, I happily got behind the wheel. We hadn't gotten two miles down the road when this character suddenly reached over and placed his hand on my leg. "Pal," I said to him, "you see this uniform? We've almost killed a couple guys who did what you're doing." I told him to get his hand the hell off me and if he didn't I was going to ram his Cadillac into an embankment. At the next exit, I pulled over and got out, disgusted and spitting mad. When I got to Latrobe that night, still shaken, things didn't get any better. Pap told me he thought I was pushing myself and had no business trying to play in the tournament the next day.

I played anyway—if you want to call it playing. I got beaten badly, and Pap really let loose, chewing me out good for attempting to play when I was so unprepared. As usual, he was right. My game was so rusty, I should have skipped the tournament and just practiced at Latrobe. But I was hungry for tournament play and foolish enough to think I could actually win.

On the plus side, reassignment to Cleveland held the prospect of more time to play golf because, as I was pleased to learn, Admiral Rainey, the district commanding officer, was a golf enthusiast. By another stroke of luck, I was assigned to the Coast Guard Auxiliary, a civilian outfit that would allow me more contact with the public and, ostensibly, a little more operating room where my free time was concerned. Thanks to amateur golf I had a number of friendly contacts in the metropolitan Cleveland area, and within a short time following my arrival a couple of gentlemen named Art Brooks and Laurie Purola would even offer me a membership in their club, Pine Ridge Country Club.

I'd barely settled into my new job in Cleveland when I was summoned to the admiral's office. I wondered what I'd done *this* time and was surprised when the admiral informed me he was interested in recommending me for Officers' Candidate School. He thought he was doing me a big favor. In fact, it would mean two more years of service would be tacked onto my tour of duty, which was about the last thing I wanted.

I did some pretty smooth talking. I thanked him for considering me to be officer material but explained that all I really wanted to do was get out of the service and play tournament golf in some form or another—as an amateur or maybe eventually as a touring professional. Under NCAA rules I still had some college eligibility left, and the idea of returning to Wake Forest to finish my degree and play golf also had some new appeal. All in all, he was very decent about it. He said he would instead send me off to Yeoman Storekeeping School in Groton, Connecticut, and then bring me back to my job in Cleveland. He also mentioned the idea of building a base driving range and maybe giving him a few swing pointers. I was relieved about not being headed to OCS and was pleased to do both chores for the admiral.

My game may have been on hiatus in late 1952, but the golf world at large was hardly mourning my absence. My old Tar Heel opponent Harvie Ward would win the British Amateur that summer and the next year nearly take possession of a Masters green jacket as an amateur—proving conclusively that he was the best college golfer at that moment. Billy Maxwell and Don January were leading North Texas State to a third NCAA championship, and Gene Littler was about to leave San Diego State, but not before capturing the National Amateur and the San

Diego Open the next year. Similarly, Ken Venturi, a junior at San Jose State, would soon make his presence known to the golfing world.

On the professional scene, Ben Hogan was now almost more legend than man, but he still ruled golf like an icy monarch determined not to give up the throne. Two years after his miraculous recovery from a car crash, Hogan brought mighty Oakland Hills to its knees to win his third Open championship. In 1952 he was anxious to give his weary legs a rest, and as a consequence played mostly exhibition rounds and entered only three tournaments: the Masters, where he finished seventh, the Colonial, which he won, and the Open, a third-place finish. Curiously, that Open was won by a burly, placid, thirty-two-year-old ex-accountant from Bridgeport, Connecticut, who'd been a professional only two years. Julius Boros had great tempo and a beautiful, languid swing, but Hogan, the most methodical attacker of golf courses of his era, would come back the very next year to have the greatest year of his competitive life—playing six seventy-two-hole tournaments and winning five, including wins at the Colonial, the Masters, the U.S. Open, and the British Open, a feat some compared to those of Jones in his prime. If Ben Hogan's career had a peak, that was it.

Other greats were fading, though. Byron Nelson, another of my boyhood heroes, had effectively been in retirement at his ranch since 1946, and even the ageless Sam Snead's game was losing some of its youthful zest. Tommy Bolt and Porky Oliver were still hanging around, factors in almost every tournament they played, but a new generation of players was coming along, symbolized by the emergence of a tall, lean southerner named Cary Middlecoff, who won the 1949 U.S. Open and, like Nelson, was a long and extraordinary driver of the ball. Mike Souchak, my old Duke nemesis, would also turn pro in 1952 and eventually win sixteen Tour events, and there was a host of other promising young players waiting in the wings to challenge the game's old guard, including Gardner Dickinson, Peter Thomson, Paul Harney, Bob Rosburg, Dow Finsterwald, and soon, Littler and Venturi.

As I say, at that moment I was still on the sidelines, so to speak, champing at the bit to get back into the game. Thanks to an understanding admiral and the friendship of Brooks and Purola, who arranged a place for me to play regularly, I was able to start playing golf and practicing a lot—almost every weekend, as it evolved, starting early Friday afternoon and ending late Sunday afternoon. They introduced me to a host of the city's golfers, some skilled players as well as your typical weekend golf addicts, and before too long I was supplementing my modest Coast Guard salary by as much as $100 off two-dollar nassaus, having more fun playing the game than I'd had in years. I even started going out with a young woman who was modeling around Cleveland, though admittedly my attention to her was a distant second to that in my revived golf life.

One of the businessmen I was introduced to was Bill Wehnes, a paint manufacturer's rep who sold industrial paints and tapping compound, a substance used to cool metal when holes are being drilled through it. Bill was a member of Canterbury Country Club and a pretty cool customer himself. He and his wife, April, more or less adopted me as their surrogate son. Bill knew I worried a great deal about money and the dilemma I would soon face—how to support myself *and* make the kind of commitment I yearned to make to playing tournament golf—and he proposed a nifty solution. Upon completion of my obligation to the Coast Guard, now just slightly over six months away, he would pay me to go back to Wake Forest and finish up my business degree, then hire me to work as a paint rep for him in the Cleveland area, allowing me as much time as I needed to polish my game and compete in tournaments. It was an offer that was too good to turn down, so I accepted it.

The summer of 1953 was a good one for me on and off the golf course. I won the Ohio Amateur at Pine Ridge and another Greensburg Invitational. I won the Cleveland Amateur, sponsored by the *Plain Dealer,* and an open tournament where a number of the top touring professionals like Porky Oliver and Jimmy Demaret competed. After a two-year absence from the event, I went to Oklahoma City and made it all the way to the fourth round of the U.S. Amateur before being nipped at the wire, beaten one-up by a pleasant Ohioan named Don Albert. A short while later, my first effort to make the cut at the U.S. Open came up a couple of strokes shy.

I was disappointed but not discouraged. The confidence I felt in my game was almost frightening, and the rekindled desire to play was practically all-consuming. When winter came and the private clubs around Cleveland closed down, several of us routinely went down to Lake Shore golf course and beat balls at frozen cups. Golf nuts in woolies.

Suddenly, it was late January and I was out of the service. My time with the Coast Guard was finished. I made a beeline to Wake Forest, where my scholarship had been reactivated, and arrived a few days after the spring semester had begun. People there couldn't have been nicer, and because Johnny Johnston was now occupying Jim Weaver's job—Weaver had gone on to become commissioner of the new Atlantic Coast Conference—I was named interim golf coach. The team played pretty well that spring and I played exceptionally, winning the ACC championship and a number of other smaller invitationals and pro-ams, setting the stage for bigger wins.

In retrospect I was probably playing too much golf, because, once again, I ran afoul of the academic dean. One afternoon he summoned me to his office and pointed out that the scholarship that had been generously reactivated was in serious jeopardy because, just like old times, I was missing classes in the afternoons. It was true—I couldn't deny any of his charges. Most afternoons, and many of the mornings, I played thirty-six holes and practiced my chipping and putting. The bookkeeping course I was supposed to be taking met for two hours two afternoons a week, but I reasoned that rather than sit there and fall asleep it was better for everybody if I did something useful with my time, like work on my short game. Unfortunately, the dean didn't see it like that. After chewing me out, he warned me in no uncertain terms that I'd better start attending classes or I'd be in big trouble—and back on the bricks.

I think I did make it to a few afternoon sessions of bookkeeping after that, but it turned out to be almost immaterial, because by the end of the semester I found I was still a few hours short of having earned my degree. That was too bad; I really did want that business degree in my pocket, and part of me regrets to this day not finishing my task at Wake.

But summer had come and tournament golf beckoned, and better yet, thanks to Bill Wehnes, I suddenly had a job that complemented my ambitions to compete on a higher level of the game. I knew nothing about selling paint, but I liked people and could talk to almost anybody, and very quickly a kind of wonderful routine established itself: Every weekday morning I'd get up and shower and go out and make calls on prospective clients, then meet Bill for lunch at Canterbury. In the afternoon, we'd play golf. Weekends were taken up entirely with the game, almost sunrise to sunset.

It was through these expanding golf connections that I met John Roberts, a successful manufacturing executive from Columbus, Ohio, who loved golf, served for a time on a USGA committee, and befriended me at a critical moment in a way that nearly altered the direction of my career and life. Here's what happened:

John had a friend at another Cleveland manufacturing firm who had invented a golf course maintenance vehicle they believed would have immediate appeal to course superintendents everywhere. The vehicle was a nimble trailer-like device equipped with a special hydraulic lift that would permit a superintendent to move mowing equipment from one point to another point on the golf course much more quickly than the conventional manner of driving it, thereby saving time and money. It was a clever idea, the kind of machinery you see at every course these days, and it was the clincher.

John and his partner offered to pay me a flat salary of $50,000 a year plus expenses to play the PGA Tour as an amateur while representing them. The idea was that I'd go, say, to the Tour site in Phoenix (we talked about that being my first stop) and try to qualify for a spot in the field, then make a pitch to the course superintendent. As enticing schemes go, this one appeared to have no downside whatsoever. I'd get to play tournament golf without worrying about my income, while selling this practical piece of machinery to a sympathetic buyer.

I told Bill Wehnes about the deal, and he was nearly heartbroken. He urged me to stick with him and even offered to double my salary, which still wouldn't have come close to the fifty grand. We both knew it was a deal too good to refuse, and he reluctantly gave me his blessing. I called Pap to tell him about the deal, and he admitted it sounded pretty good. Pap still wasn't convinced golf was much of a paying proposition, but the fifty grand got his respect.

I'll never forget the morning I went to see John's business partner at Warner Swazey, the manufacturing firm where he was plant manager, to finalize the deal. I got there early, only to be told I'd have to wait because my future employer wasn't back yet from Florida. It seems he flew south every weekend to be with his wife and children.

I sat for a small eternity in that office waiting room, trying to keep my anxiousness to *get going* at bay. Finally, the man's secretary came out and apologized, saying her boss wouldn't be in that day. Something had come up in Florida and someone, she said, would contact me later. I remember leaving that waiting room really disappointed and a bit worried that the deal might somehow fall through.

The deal did fall through, because my prospective boss had been killed that weekend in a car crash. I felt deeply sorry for his family, but I also felt sorry for me. I'd been *that* close to having a financial angel and the kind of dough that would have allowed me to keep my amateur status but ease my way onto the Tour without having to scrape by and live out of the trunk of a car as so many pros did. When I called my father to break the news, he said, "Well, Arn. It's probably for the best. You've got a good job with Wehnes. You stick to that and do a good job and keep playing golf." It was so typical of him. Nothing in life came easy, in Pap's view, and not everything that glittered was gold.

Bill Wehnes was a perfect gentleman about the whole thing, sympathetic even, and more than happy to let me continue in my repping job for him. But that wasn't the end of the prospective deals. A few days later, another acquaintance from the course called me to his office and said he and a group of fellows would stake me to $10,000 to play the Tour for a year, but the catch was a big one: they wanted the first ten grand I won back and fifty percent of everything else I won after that. The deal was absurd. I was sorely tempted to tell the guy to shove it. Instead, I got up, politely shook his hand and thanked him, then stormed quietly out of his office, wondering what I was going to do next.

There are moments in life when you feel the deck is stacked against you. I felt that way when Buddy Worsham died, and I felt that way when my golden sponsorship deal fell through. I was twenty-five years old and owned nothing more valuable than my golf clubs. Money, or lack of money, was always what kept good players from taking a stab at the vagabond life of a touring professional. Sponsorships weren't nearly as commonplace or as lucrative as today, and the byways were littered with scores of topflight amateurs who, burdened by families or other financial responsibilities, either took a halfhearted leap and failed or never quite worked up the means or the nerve to try to become the next Snead, Hogan, or Nelson. I knew I had the nerve, possibly the ability, and for one giddy moment I'd even had the means to be the next Hogan. But now my guy was gone and, it seemed, so was my one best shot at a professional golf career.

I knew what my father would have told me. He would have said to pick up my head and quit complaining and get back to work. So I did that—in more ways than one.

A great deal has been written about my sixty-one tour victories, seven major championships, and various comebacks and charges. But none of it could have happened without things falling into place the way they did, the sequence of events that took place over the next few weeks at the end of the summer of 1954. In many respects, this was the turning point of my life.

First I drove to Chicago's Tam O'Shanter Country Club for George S. May's extravagant two-week golf shindig, which consisted of two back-to-back tournaments—the All American Open and the World Championship of Golf. I was low amateur in the All American, tying for fourteenth in the field, nine strokes ahead of Frank Stranahan. May upped the purse for the World Championship, his crown jewel, to the unheard-of amount of $100,000. The winner that year, Bob Toski, took home $50,000 in cold, hard cash, and was guaranteed an additional $50,000 in the form of fifty confirmed $1,000 exhibition matches. In comparison, an average Tour purse that year was less than $20,000.

In many respects, George S. May was the P. T. Barnum of American golf, a short, stocky, flamboyant former Bible salesman with a well-fed stomach who favored outlandish costumes and was whispered to have had as many pals in the mob as he did in Chicago politics. Someone once commented that May took a game that evolved from humble Scottish peasants and gave it back to them. There was no question he considered golf more of a popular entertainment than a serious game, because between 1941 and 1957 the controversial promoter established the richest purses on the Tour (more than $2 million in prize money), brought television coverage to the course for the first time, and was believed to be the first to identify players for the convenience of the spectators, many of whom had never been anywhere near a golf course.

I remember hearing what a character George May was long before I ever set eyes on him. Say what you will about him, the man had a flair for promoting golf. Among his innovations, he publicized his events in full-page newspaper ads, was the first to pay hefty appearance fees to top professionals, and was the first to erect spectator bleacher seats beside greens. Among his less dignified antics, he employed clowns and a "masked marvel" golfer to roam the premises and entertain the paying customers, and he gave away hefty door prizes that had nothing to do with golf. His galleries were massive, unschooled in the gentler courtesies of the game, and invariably rowdy. Some players, Ben Hogan for one, were offended by May's antics, feeling with some justification that his commercial ploys demeaned the game. For example, at one point, to help fans identify the players better, he proposed

having them wear numbers on their backs, as athletes do in team sporting events. You should have
heard the intense outcry of protest from many
players who thought such a stunt was far below their
dignity. It was eventually decided that caddies would
wear identifying numbers instead, and some time
after that, the players' names wound up on the caddies' backs.

May's tournaments were one part sporting event,
one part Roman spectacle, and, whatever else was
true about him, his timing couldn't have been better,
because the advent of television was suddenly
changing the social landscape of American life. This
was, fittingly, the setting where Lew Worsham
played one of the most exciting shots ever struck,
holing a wedge approach for an eagle two on the
final hole of the World Championship to beat Chan-
dler Harper by one stroke. Worsham didn't see the
ball go in the hole, but millions of people who had
never set foot on a golf course did, thanks to the fact
that the moment was broadcast live on television.
Some have speculated that the event did almost as
much to popularize golf and the Tour as my own
televised charges in the decade that followed. While
I prefer to think my athleticism and personality were
helpful in attracting a new generation of Americans to the game, there's undoubtedly truth in that
assertion.

The same year that I played in the All American
and the World Championship, Sam Snead had edged
out Ben Hogan in an eighteen-hole playoff at the
Masters, and the debate simmered over who was

really the best player in the game at the moment. May grandiosely offered to settle the issue once and for all by tacking an extra $25,000 on the purse for his World Championship; if either man won the championship he would collect no less than $75,000. But Hogan, disgusted as much by May's antics as by his belief that the PGA Tour should be run by an executive committee instead of the players themselves, stayed home in Texas.

The really interesting news that year was made on the amateur side. Stranahan won low-amateur honors at the World Championship by neatly reversing the outcome from a week before, edging me by a hole. I remember that as we were standing together at the presentation ceremony, Stranny turned to me and said, "You know, Arn, if I don't win the Amateur next week, I've made up my mind to turn pro." He'd won the British Amateur in 1948, but the U.S. Amateur had always somehow eluded him.

"Muss, why would you want to do that?" I asked him. I was genuinely surprised. After all, even though purses like May's gaudy windfalls were awful tempting to a working stiff like me, Frank had enough family money to play the game purely for the love of it for an eternity. I certainly would have, in his position.

"Well," he said, "we'll see what happens in Detroit."

The 54th United States Amateur Championship was to be held at the Country Club of Detroit, on a

great old golf course recently refurbished by the re-
nowned architect Robert Trent Jones. It was a layout
I had never seen. To win the Amateur, it was necessary to play six straight eighteen-hole matches in
just four days, then endure the thirty-six-hole semifinals and finals. It was match play all the way, and
though 1953 champion Gene Littler wouldn't be
defending (he opted to turn pro instead), the field
included the likes of Harvie Ward; Billy Joe Patton,
the golf sensation of the year who almost won the
Masters and was low amateur at the Open; Don
Cherry, the reigning Canadian Amateur champ; public links champion Gene Andrews; the great Willie
Turnesa (Amateur champion in 1938 and 1948, and
1947 British Amateur champion); Bill Campbell
(Amateur champ in 1964, future president of the
USGA, and captain of the Royal and Ancient Golf
Club of St. Andrews); and finally the man who'd
won every major amateur event in the world save
this one—Frank Stranahan.

My first match, beginning at 8:06 on Monday, the
twenty-third of August, was against Frank Strafaci, a
seven-time winner of the New York Metropolitan
title, and it was one of the closest matches I'd played
all year. The highlight for me came at the difficult
460-yard par-4 17th, played as a par 5 by the club's
membership, when I decided to hit a 4-wood from a
fairway trap. The sand shot failed to reach the
putting surface, but my pitch was within five feet of
the hole. I holed the putt to win after Strafaci took
three to get down from the fringe. Frank's total score

for the round was 71, one more than my even-par total.

An amusing footnote: I don't remember if it was that evening or the evening before the start of the tournament, but in an effort to keep myself loose and in a relaxed frame of mind, I invited the model I'd been going out with in Cleveland to come over to Detroit for the week. Unfortunately, Bill Wehnes arrived almost simultaneously and lit into me as my own outraged father would have. "Get her out of here," he snarled at me paternally. "You're here to win the Amateur, and you're not going to do it with her here."

He knew I would need every ounce of my concentration to make it through the ordeal dead ahead, and he was right. The model went packing.

For my second match I drew a Florida State golfer named John Veghte, and thanks to a lot of bold long putts, I survived another close match to beat him one-up. My third match—against Richard Whiting, a former captain of the Notre Dame golf team—was also unexpectedly tough and required the full eighteen to determine the outcome in my favor, 2 and 1. Again, I attacked pins and putted boldly, though my teenage caddy cheekily informed the press afterward that I was fairly "erratic inside six feet."

Finally, on Wednesday, for my fourth-round match, I got a break from the USGA, or at least from the golf gods. Walter Andzel fell pretty quickly, 5 and 3, which allowed me to get off the course just as a savage thunderstorm broke, suspending play for almost an hour. The headline for the day, however, was written in the morning rounds when Stranny defeated Harvie Ward one-up in an eighteen-hole thriller that still had the gallery buzzing.

Of course, he was my next opponent.

Despite our friendship, I had plenty of reasons to fear Stranny. In previous match-play challenges his age and experience had dominated, most notably at the North and South, where he whipped me 11 and 10 in a thirty-six-hole semifinal, and at the 1950 Amateur, where he smoked me 4 and 3. This was Frank's eleventh run at the National Amateur title, and I knew he would be tougher than a two-dollar steak.

Fortunately, I played nearly perfectly from tee to green and was one under par for the front side, including a couple of deuces, leaving me two up at the turn. Stranny uncharacteristically sprayed his drives into the menacing rough on six of the first twelve holes. I, on the other hand, committed only a couple of costly mistakes—at the 14th, where I drove into the rough, and at 16, where I hit into a bunker. The wind had come up by then, I remember, blowing harder than it had all week, and I was fortunate enough to hit a fine wedge shot to within four feet on 15 to salvage par. Another good approach left me six feet from the cup on 17. I rolled in the birdie and won the match, 3 and 1.

Stranny's father was the first person on the green to congratulate me after Frank and I shook hands. What class and generosity of spirit that took, to come forward so enthusiastically and shake the hand of the kid who broke his own son's heart. You could see the emotion in his eyes as he pumped my hand and wished me well. As Frank and I walked off the green together, he said to me, "That's it. I'm turning pro tomorrow."

The next day, true to his word, Muss did just that, signing a sponsorship contract with Wilson Sporting Goods.

I had something more immediate to worry about—an afternoon quarter-final match against Don Cherry, the reigning Canadian Amateur champ. I didn't know much about Cherry's game, but I found myself two down to him at the turn and had to battle back to square the match by 16. At the long 17th, both of us missed the green, but I pitched close enough to make four. Cherry bogeyed and we halved 18, meaning I moved on to the semifinal round.

I don't remember how I slept the night before the thirty-six-hole semifinal match. I do remember that after beating Cherry, I went straight into the club-house and called my parents in Latrobe. They hopped in the car and drove eight hours to Detroit so they could be on hand the next morning. That meant more to me than anyone could ever have known.

Now it was Friday, and my opponent was Ed Meister, a former Yale golf captain and thirty-six-year-old veteran of thirteen U.S. Amateur campaigns. I'd beaten Meister once in the Ohio Amateur, but neither of us had any inkling we were about to make history at the National Amateur.

The match was a seesaw battle. I patched together

a shaky 76 and was lucky to be one up after the morning round. Neither of us seemed to be on our games, and one sportswriter later reported, "The contestants hit shots that cheered the hearts of duffers in the gallery." The low point came when we halved the 425-yard 18th with double-bogey sixes. Nerves were killing both of us, I think.

Meister was one up after twenty-seven holes, but I squared the match on 28 with a fine pitch and run that stopped four feet from the pin. We traded leads twice more and reached the 36th hole all square. This was the darkest moment of the tournament for me. Ed's drive found the heart of the fairway, and a beautifully struck 5-iron left him eight feet from the pin. My drive was in the rough, and my 5-iron shot flew into a grassy area behind the green. The grass was deep and the green sloped dangerously away from me; I knew I was in big trouble. Meister was looking down the barrel at birdie, and I would have my hands full just to get up and down for par. I lofted a high wedge shot that came to rest five feet above the hole. Meister missed his birdie attempt but tapped in for four.

Now I faced the ultimate nightmare: the slick downhiller to halve the hole and keep the match alive. I took a long time studying the putt, trying to calm my nerves and remind myself to hit it firmly enough to hold the line. I finally stepped up and stroked the putt and felt massive relief when it dropped into the cup. Later, a reporter asked me how I could take so long over a pressure putt. Perhaps he thought I was joking when I replied that I waited until I was sure I would make it. Fact is, I was dying over that putt, and I needed the time to calm myself down.

Meister missed another short putt and a chance to win at the first playoff hole; we halved with bogey fives. For the third hole in a row—putts of ten, eight, and five feet, respectively—he'd had the chance to slam the door on me but failed to convert. The same thing happened at the 38th hole. He was sixteen feet from a birdie and the championship—and failed to capitalize. On the par-5 third, I smashed a drive 300 yards to the center of the fairway, then used a 3-iron to reach the green on my second shot. Meister had trouble in the trees, and having left his fourth shot short of the green, conceded the match. He looked physically whipped, and I'm sure I did, too. We didn't realize it then, but we'd just finished the longest semifinal match in the fifty-four-year history of the U.S. Amateur.

Bob Sweeny, my opponent for the thirty-six-hole final, was a debonair, forty-three-year-old investment banker from Sands Point, New York. He was movie-star handsome, wealthy, Oxford educated, with a golf swing as smooth as a Rolls-Royce engine. Sweeny was no casual socialite golfer who somehow woke up to find himself contending for the biggest prize in amateur golf. On the contrary, as his 1937 British Amateur title proved, Sweeny was a player's player—a guy who gave strokes to Ben Hogan, I later learned, when they played together at Seminole in the winter months. He was also one heck of a nice man.

To look at us side by side, though, you might well have thought we hailed from different galaxies. Sweeny was a middle-aged millionaire, a member of London's swanky parkland club called Sunningdale, and an international playboy elegantly dressed in crisp pressed linen pants, with the most beautiful young woman I'd ever seen following him like an adoring puppy from hole to hole. I was a twenty-four-year-old ex–coast guardsman and paint sales-man with his nervous parents in the gallery.

I don't have any memory of Pap giving me advice before the match, though it wouldn't have been his nature at all to do that. And I can't even seem to recall what we all did the night before the final. I suppose we went out to an early dinner somewhere and I must have turned in fairly early, as is my habit. I was probably a bit quieter than normal, but I was often quiet before a big match, and I don't think in this instance I was particularly nervous about meeting Sweeny. I had a lot of confidence in my abilities, and I think I slept pretty well, all things considered.

The first three holes seemed to indicate, however, that I wasn't just outclassed but also outmatched. Sweeny calmly rolled three birdie putts into the cup, and I was left standing on the fourth tee won-dering what train had hit me. Others among the 3,500 or so spectators watching must have thought the same thing, perhaps sensing a real slaughter in the making. To make matters worse, as we started down the fourth fairway after hitting our tee shots, the beautiful girl following my opponent suddenly

came through the ropes and out onto the fairway and
waltzed right into his arms, giving him a real double-
feature kiss. I remember watching them in disbelief—
and maybe a little envy—thinking what a cruel game
golf could be. Here I was getting pasted in the tournament I'd always dreamed of winning, and my opponent was not only rich and handsome and hitting
perfect golf shots but getting the girl as well! With
slumping spirits, I glanced over at my parents,
walking quietly along in the gallery. Mother looked
worried but smiled her usual reassuring smile. Pap
wore his usual stoic face on the evolving drama.

Sweeny, it seems to me, never let up, never hit
what you would call a bad shot. He made me have to
come get him, which I did finally on holes eight,
nine, and ten, winning them to halve the match. By
lunchtime, Sweeny's twenty-nine putts gave him a
70 on the card versus my 72. He was two up going
into the afternoon round.

At the break, I reminded myself that I wasn't
trying to beat the man on each hole; rather, I figured,
if I could play consistently and manage to beat the
course, I'd have an excellent chance of beating
Sweeny as well.

This proved to be a wise strategy, one I would
attempt to adopt in match-play competition thereafter, because it forces you to keep your concentration where it should be—on the golf course instead
of your opponent and the interesting things happening to him. We were nip and tuck all over the
final eighteen, and every time I would make a move,
he responded with a clutch birdie or a salvaged par

to win. On the 22nd hole, for example, I dropped a twenty-five-footer for birdie, but Sweeny came back to win 23 when I carelessly three-putted. I tied the match at the 465-yard 27th with my best 2-iron shot of the week, but Sweeny took the lead at the next hole by nailing a thirty-five-footer for birdie. I caught him again at the 30th hole, and thanks to a burst of fine iron play I finally moved a hole ahead of him at the 32nd.

A birdie on the 33rd put me two up, but I lost the 35th with a three-putt. My drive at the 36th found the fairway and my second shot safely reached the putting surface. Sweeny's drive was errant and he couldn't find his ball. After several minutes of fruitless searching, he looked at me and graciously lifted his arm and called, "Congratulations, Arnie. You win."

I confess I felt a bit woozy—the heat, stress, and fatigue of the week's ordeal all sort of came rushing over me. The sudden elation I felt was almost overwhelming. I gratefully shook Sweeny's hand, and as I started up the fairway to the green, still a bit dazed, Joe Dey, the wonderful, longtime USGA official who was overseeing the match, came over to me and said, "Mr. Palmer, if you don't mind, we'll call this a one-up victory." I nodded, unable to speak.

To this day, I don't know why Joe insisted on that, but that's how it reads in the record books, a one-up victory over Robert Sweeny. For his part, Sweeny couldn't have been more gracious.

As the media swarmed around us, my mother was the first one to hug me when I walked off the final green. As we embraced, she was crying tears of joy. "Where's my father?" I called out. "Let's get Pap in here. He's the man who really won the U.S. National Amateur." For several moments I couldn't find him in the crowd, but suddenly he was there, quietly smiling for the first time that week. I could tell he was happy. As a flurry of cameras clicked around us, he put his hand on my shoulder and squeezed it.

"You did pretty good, boy," he said simply, and my heart swelled nearly to the breaking point.

This meant the world to me, and I felt my own tears coming. I'd finally shown my father that I was the best amateur golfer in America. It was the turning point of my life, and I don't know if I've ever felt as much happiness on a golf course.

CHAPTER FIVE

Winnie

My extraordinary week in Detroit proved how quickly lightning can strike in the game of golf. Arriving there, I'd simply been one of a thousand dreamers who'd made it close to the pinnacle of amateur golf, a working-class guy with more grit than polish, more strength than style. But as the rounds of parties commenced and the flood of telegrams from well-wishers seemed to pour in from every direction, the press was suddenly writing head-turning things about me that I suppose I'd never noticed or perhaps simply always took for granted. They wrote about the intense excitement my "come-from-behind" victory and "go-for-broke" style of play seemed to stimulate in galleries; they wrote about the affectionate way I often spoke to spectators and paused to joke around with little kids in the crowd, my changing facial expressions, the lucky red baseball cap I wore all week, my composure under fire, the way I hitched my pants as I walked up a fairway, the openness of my emotions.

The truth is, I loved these stories. Not only were they the first to identify a host of personal characteristics and eccentricities people would come to associate with the name Arnie Palmer and apparently admire in coming years, but they also confirmed what I dearly hoped was true—namely, that for all my rough edges and boyish lack of refinement, I belonged among golf's elite. When Jack Clowser of the *Cleveland Press* wrote that "Arnold Palmer was born to be a great golf champion," I daresay my pride and confidence grew immeasurably, as they did a few days later when John Dietrich of the competing *Plain Dealer* informed his readers that the Amateur had witnessed the birth of a "new super champion." My crusty old friend Bob Drum of the *Pittsburgh Press*, who'd been writing about me since my schoolboy days in Pennsylvania golf, wrote slightly less breathless dispatches from the front lines about my alleged heroics at Detroit, while the major wire services sent these stories flying to all corners of the globe. I *still* get chills thinking about those first stories.

Lightning had struck, and my life would never be the same. In hindsight, though, it's amusing how I misjudged the effect of the Amateur. Suddenly the press wanted to know about my future plans and any aspirations to turn professional. I remember hearing Pap reassure a reporter that I wouldn't turn pro. Well, he was my Pap, and I dutifully echoed, "I like selling paint. I have no intention of turning professional. I am very happy, and my new title automatically puts me on the Walker Cup team." At the moment I said this, I really meant it. With a six-month apprenticeship required by the PGA Tour, a period during which you could take no official prize money, I simply couldn't imagine how I could make a living out on tour. So I pointed out that the Walker

Cup would be contested in England the next spring
and I couldn't wait to go there. I also noted that my
next golfing goal was the British Amateur crown.

They say lightning never strikes the same spot
twice, but my tale is proof that it sometimes can
strike you again when you least expect it to. In this
case, lightning of a very different nature struck me
within days of hoisting the Amateur trophy. My
words—to say nothing of the direction of my life—
abruptly changed.

Mother hadn't been back home in Latrobe for
more than a few days when she got a phone call
from Fred Waring, the celebrated bandleader of the
Pennsylvanians, inviting me to play in his annual
golf tournament, the Waite Memorial, at Shawnee-
on-the-Delaware. Fred had invited me to his annual
golf shindig before, but I could never afford to go.
Now that I was the new National Amateur champion
I was even more anxious to go, but I'd been away
from my job so much of the summer I felt bad
asking Bill Wehnes for yet another week off.

Bill solved the problem nicely by telling me,
"Tell you what, Arn. If you can get Mr. Waring to
invite April [Bill's wife] and me to the tournament,
we'll all three drive down there."

I placed a call to Fred, who happily extended the
invitation, and almost before I knew it the three of us
were rolling down the highway to Shawnee-on-the-
Delaware in Bill's big Cadillac.

The tournament festivities began over Labor Day
weekend. We arrived on Monday and checked into
the Shawnee Inn, a beautiful rustic lodge abuzz with

tournament activities. I immediately went out on the golf course to play a practice round, and as I was coming back into the inn I saw a couple of pretty girls coming down the stairway that led to the main lobby. One of them was Dixie Waring, Fred's daughter. But it was the quieter, prettier, dark-haired one that really caught my eye. She had smoky good looks, and her demeanor had a clear sheen of class. Fred's longtime secretary, Cora Ballard, a whiskey-voiced redhead, paused and introduced me to the two girls she was chaperoning for the week, the tournament's official "hostesses," and I shook hands with Winifred Walzer.

"If you don't have anything to do," I said jauntily to her, "why don't you come out and watch the golf."

"Perhaps I will," she replied demurely, and smiled at me.

I think I learned she and Dixie Waring were old chums from Shawnee, and I must have been thinking Winnie must be a rich girl from Philadelphia's Main Line. She was so refined and polished. Little did I know she was really from the village of Coopersburg, just outside Bethlehem, and though her father, Shube, was successful enough in the canned foods business to afford a summer cottage at Shawnee, the Walzers were by no means wealthy in the sense of Philadelphia wealth. She only hobnobbed with girls from the Main Line. Winnie was nineteen, studying interior design at Brown University's affiliated design school at Pembroke College, aiming to be an interior decorator. Unbeknownst to me she was a veteran of Shawnee's social swirl and had even dated some of the most eligible bachelor golfers, including my old adversary Harvie Ward.

I don't think I saw her at the dinner that was held that evening, but I was pleased when I glanced over the next afternoon and saw her watching from the edge of the 11th fairway. Years later I learned that was purely an accident—she was really en route to watch her "Uncle Fred" Waring play golf. Fred, who was in the foursome directly behind mine, was deeply fond of Winnie and almost jealously protective of her. Anyway, I sauntered over and asked if she "planned to tag along" and made small talk with her and wondered if she would be interested in sitting with me at the dinner dance scheduled for later that evening. She said she would, and I went on about my business with a new spring in my step.

Winnie, I began to learn that night, was unlike any girl I'd ever met, not just pretty and comfortable in almost any social situation, but also smart, well traveled (she'd just come home from a big European trip), engagingly independent minded, even something of a would-be social rebel. The only girl in a close-knit Moravian family that included two brothers and a host of boy cousins, she had a grandfather who was a minister and uncles who were college professors. She had grown up absorbing blows from baseball games and kick-the-can with her male cousins, but also kept her father's books from an early age. She had pluck and ambition, and she didn't suffer vain or pretentious fools easily. Her mother, Mary, was something of a sweet social butterfly who may have entertained hopes that Winifred would become a proper debutante in due course, but feisty Winnie Walzer wanted none of that.

We became inseparable for the rest of the week, but that first evening at the dinner dance she got a taste of the unexpected impact sudden "fame" can have on a young man's life. I happened to be dancing with an older golf professional's wife when she suddenly seized my shoulder and whispered damply into my ear, "Take me *away* from all of this. Let's me and you run away together!"

The poor woman sounded desperate—and frighteningly serious. She had four children and a swell husband, and she scared the daylights out of me. So I slunk back to the table. After a while, I told Winnie what had happened, and she laughed. That was another thing I loved about Winnie Walzer, her robust and infectious laugh. She had a no-nonsense, down-to-earth way of placing everything in perspective, I was discovering, including alcohol-fueled dance-floor confessions from older married women. What I didn't know then was that, despite our wonderful week of intimate conversation about family and golf and life in general, typically held after my rounds in the club bar where underage Winnie could sip her favorite Fitzgerald Old Fashioneds, come Friday night my beautiful escort was watching me go through the buffet line with more than casual interest. One subject we hadn't touched upon was religion, and I later learned she was watching to see if I ate meat on Friday. Apparently one of her suitors at

Brown had been a passionate Catholic boy. For reasons I can't begin to understand or explain, Shube Walzer took pains to chase him away from his only daughter, and she wasn't anxious to repeat the experience. She later admitted that she was deeply relieved when I took a healthy helping of roast beef.

What I guess I failed to notice, smitten as I was with her, was that almost *everybody* around us save Shube Walzer (who was back home in Coopersburg, by the way) was shamelessly promoting a match— and all these years later it amuses me how many people claim *they* had the critical hand in bringing us together.

Nobody had to bring us together or promote the match. By Friday night my amateur partner, Tommy Sheehan, and I were leading the tournament, but more important, I was completely taken with Winnie Walzer and a plan was forming in my brain. At the dinner, I reached under the table and took her hand and said, "What would you think if I asked you to get married?"

The question appeared to startle her—though only for a second or two. "Well, I don't know. This is so sudden. Can I have a day to think about it?" she replied.

"Not too long," I said to her. "I've got places to go."

I told her my grand plan: we would get married in the spring and use the Walker Cup tournament as our honeymoon. She assured me that her mother and aunts would love that romantic plan—as they did. She told me her father would probably grumble a lot but would eventually come around because he wanted his only daughter to be happy. For such a crack judge of character, she either overestimated her father's capacity to appreciate romance or underestimated his contempt for unconventional suitors for his daughter. As it turned out, the last thing Shube Walzer wanted was his daughter marrying a golf bum, which is pretty much what he thought of all tournament golfers in those days.

But, of course, my "grand plan" was to be a highly successful businessman who could not only support a wife in the manner to which she was accustomed but also have the time and financial wherewithal to play top amateur golf. If paint selling wouldn't do it, maybe I'd switch to selling insurance; insurance men always had time to play golf.

I suppose it was no surprise that word quickly leaked out about the proposal. Winnie quickly informed her mother, who was happy as expected, and her mother broke the news to her father—who wasn't remotely happy to hear about it. Shube had heard such declared attentions from his headstrong daughter before and, I think, felt love would run its course in due time. At the final presentation dinner, Fred Waring startled everybody by announcing that I wasn't taking only the tournament trophy home from Shawnee-on-the-Delaware, but a fiancée as well.

My mother and Pap took an instant shine to Winnie when they met her the following week in Latrobe. Back in Coopersburg, the female family think tank already had big wedding plans well under way, but there was still no movement on the Shube Walzer front. Shube was a tough customer, a successful businessman who loathed Roosevelt and the socially liberal policies of just about any other Democrat. Pap, on the other hand, was a strong Democrat and devoted Roosevelt man who thought the late president hung the moon. In some ways, the families hailed not just from different ends of Pennsylvania but different ends of the planet.

Winnie assured me all would be well in time.

What was really missing, I quickly realized, was some material sign of my intentions—namely, an engagement ring.

Back in Cleveland, my old golf gang from Pine Ridge helped solve that problem. Art Brooks, Bill Wehnes, and Ed Preisler all chipped in a couple grand each to help me purchase a decent ring, and Bill even managed to get a good deal from a local jeweler. My salary didn't pay me enough to afford even the payments on the ring, and I now had an $8,000 debt on top of everything else.

It was about this time that one of them proposed a weekend golf trip to Pine Valley. It would be a way, I realized, to maybe pay off my borrowings—or go even deeper into debt. Pine Valley, the famous George Crump layout that meandered through the scrub and sandy hills in the New Jersey pine barrens, was a place I'd always heard about and dearly wanted to play but had never had an opportunity to. Before I knew it, two foursomes were headed that way. On the drive down, the guys started telling me how ruthless Pine Valley was and how even I probably wouldn't break 90 on it.

"Ninety?" I looked at Bill Wehnes incredulously.

"That's right."

Well, one thing led to another and I soon had half a dozen wagers going, $20 nassaus with automatic presses and an intriguing side bet with Bill: for every stroke I was 70 or under, he'd pay me $100, and for every stroke I was 80 or over I'd pay him the same.

In retrospect it was pretty foolish. I could have *really* lost my shirt and been so indebted to the gang I would never get out of Cleveland. But you're only young and cocky and in love once, I suppose, and I had no doubt I could bring celebrated Pine Valley to heel.

Foolish thought number two, or so it appeared from the outset.

Day one, hole number one: I pull-hooked a 5-iron approach over the green into the brush, chipped *over* the green, and was forced to make a thirty-footer for bogey five.

Pine Valley certainly had my respect and full attention. I think Bill and the guys must have been mentally spending all of my money, and for a while I thought I was in big trouble.

Frankly, I'd never seen anything like the place, the way holes were integrated so beautifully into the rolling scrubby sand landscape. It looked wild *and* manicured. The greens were immaculate, with slopes so subtle or murderous I could see why many famous pros had come there only to be reduced to screaming fits of despair. At nine, I made a bogey and shot 36 out, thanks to a flurry of much-needed birdies. Not bad—but still a long way to go.

The back nine treated me a little better. I holed a fifteen-footer for birdie on the tough finishing hole to card 67. That was four hundred Ben Franklins in my pocket. I cleaned up on all the nassaus and that night even cleaned up at gin rummy. The next two rounds I went 69 and 68, and by the time the weekend was through I had pocketed nearly five grand, almost enough to pay off the ring.

It was while we were there in that ultimate golf terrarium that I had time to think about what Winnie and I were really up against. My salesman salary scarcely covered my own expenses, much less those of a married couple in need of a first house and possibly children in the near future. Winnie was still scheduled to begin classes at NYU in a few weeks—practical girl that she was, she'd transferred there from Brown to begin studying business—and as much as I liked the proposed scenario of a big church wedding in the spring and steaming off to England for the Walker Cup, in my heart I saw only one way for us to make it as man and wife.

I would need to turn pro.

Instead of heading straight back to Cleveland, Bill and April suggested we go to New York City for a few days of dinners and shows, their treat; I called Winnie, and she enthusiastically agreed to meet us there. Shube wasn't budging any on her momentous decision, but she could get away because she needed to register for fall classes anyway. We met in the afternoon at the New Yorker Hotel and—talk about a potentially bad omen—checked in just as some poor chap committed suicide by leaping from an upstairs window. A little later in the bar, still shaken, Winnie probably thought our plans were crashing, too, when I informed her of my change of strategy—namely, that I'd decided to turn pro and that we should probably get married as soon as possible, certainly before the start of the new Tour season out west. England and the Walker Cup were out; the uncertain life of a Tour rookie's bride was in.

Her face fell, but she didn't seem as upset as I thought she might be at this idea, though she needlessly pointed out that her father wasn't going to like this news any better than the last. Through shows and dinner, we talked about this all weekend long, and I convinced her that she shouldn't enroll at NYU after all, but maybe should return to Coopersburg and take courses in the local business school, a plan Shube Walzer would have eagerly endorsed under other circumstances. She agreed, and we parted with a whole new game plan established.

On November 18, I drove by myself to Chicago and met with the marketing people at Wilson Sporting Goods Company. Preceded by a long line of golf champions, amateur and professional (Sam Snead and Byron Nelson had represented Wilson on tour), I was pleased to represent them, too, though the endorsement contract I signed was hardly the stuff of princes. It was Wilson's standard contract and amounted to $5,000 per year as a base, plus a $2,000 signing bonus. Under the terms of the Tour's established apprentice program, I wouldn't be able to earn a nickel of official money until sometime the next summer. By my rough calculations, though, with luck and good bookkeeping, if we watched our coins carefully, Wilson's money and whatever else I might pick up at pro-ams and unofficial events just might get us to the heart of the next summer, when I could begin earning official prize winnings.

I remember feeling pleased and deeply relieved when, prior to meeting with Wilson, I broke the news to Pap and he nodded his head and said he thought it was the right thing to do. I couldn't do any worse selling paint, to be honest. And who knew? Maybe I'd break in the way guys like Doug Ford and Ken Venturi and Gene Littler and my buddy Dow Finsterwald were already doing, making names for themselves as up-and-coming Tour professionals and banking a few bucks to boot.

I asked Pap to accompany me to my first event, the Miami Open. We drove down in my two-door Ford and checked into a motel, and I went out to the course a bundle of nerves but also pumped up with a lot of confidence. After all, I'd recently beaten guys like Ted Kroll and Bob Toski and Tommy Bolt at the Azalea Open in Wilmington, so I knew in my heart I could compete.

Perhaps I was too pumped, though. I missed fairways right and left and couldn't sink a putt to save my life. A funny thing happened that afternoon, though, something that quickly helped me get my priorities straight.

I missed the cut and was boiling mad at myself. I returned to the motel only to find a message from my old girlfriend, the Cleveland model; she was in town working and wanted to get together for a few drinks. That seemed like just the remedy I needed, so I went out and returned sometime after midnight only to find Pap waiting up for me—and as mad at me as I'd ever seen him. Through clenched teeth he asked me where the hell I'd been and I told him truthfully—out for some drinks and a few laughs with an old friend, nothing too serious, all pretty innocent.

"You're engaged and you've got an obligation to that girl back in Pennsylvania," he snarled at me.

"But, Pap—" I began.

"Do you love her?" he snapped, cutting me off.

"Well, *sure* I love her. I asked her to marry me, didn't I?"

Pap gave me a look I'll never forget. It was withering. I think he and my mother were so fond of Winnie they couldn't stand the idea of losing her. I think they were fonder of her than of me, their own son. Pap chose his words very carefully.

"Then you better go get her and get married and get on with your business and quit screwing around like a college boy. Do you understand me?"

I did indeed.

"Okay," I said. "Then how are you going to get

home?" I offered at least to drive him. He would have none of it.

"Just do what you have to do. Let me worry about myself."

Early the next morning, I dropped him off at the Miami airport and turned onto U.S. Highway 1, headed north. Fifteen or sixteen hours later—pretty late, as I recall—I arrived at Winnie's parents' house in Coopersburg and found her waiting up for me. The next morning, after a good sleep, we went into Bethlehem to Christmas shop and I suggested to Winnie that I wait in a local bar while she shopped. She agreed, and I was soon sitting alone over a beer smoking L&Ms and wondering if she would agree or tell me to hit the bricks when I laid my latest idea at her feet.

"Are you ready?' I asked when she joined me.

"Ready for what?" she asked innocently.

"To hear me out."

"I guess so."

So I laid it out. I told her I thought we ought to go get married right away, elope if we had to, just get the job done and get on with it. I explained to her about being out with the model and what Pap had said to me—and admitted that I knew, as usual, he'd been right.

Winnie sighed. I think she would have ordered a double Old Fashioned if she'd been old enough to legally drink. Unfortunately, she wasn't even old enough to legally marry, and Pennsylvania law required that we have her parents' consent. I knew we could count on her mother, but Shube still acted as if he thought I was asking his precious daughter to marry a convict.

"Boy, this won't be easy," she admitted.

I told her I already had a plan in mind. We would call my sister Cheech and her husband, Ron, in Alexandria, Virginia. Cheech would arrange the church and party afterward. We would invite both sets of parents and maybe a few other people. We could drive down and be married before Thanksgiving Day.

"My father will *never* let that happen," Winnie promised me.

"Then we won't tell him," I said.

We did inform her mother that night, though. I think Mary was alternately thrilled by the romantic haste of the plan and worried sick what her husband, Shube, would do when he found out what we were up to.

In any case, the next morning when Shube was already safely out of the house, Winnie and I quietly hustled our bags out to my Ford, bid goodbye to her mother—who promised to try and intercede with her husband on our behalf—and hit the road for Alexandria.

Cheech arranged everything—the church, the minister, and the reception, everything except the actual wedding license. We called my parents, and they enthusiastically agreed to drive down. We called Winnie's parents and found Shube had no interest whatsoever in being party to our elopement. The next day, the whole plan nearly came unraveled when Winnie and I went to get a marriage license.

The clerk, an older man who probably had a daughter at home about Winnie's age, behaved as if he, too, thought the idea was completely ridiculous. "How old are you?" he demanded, looking at me.

"Twenty-five," I said, truthfully. My birthday was a few days after Winnie and I met.

He glared at Winnie for a moment and then glared at me. I was terrified he knew the truth, that she was underage by two years.

"Is she old enough?"

"Yes, sir," I answered solemnly, sweating bullets.

The next afternoon, license in hand and blood tests complete, we had a brief little ceremony at Falls Church Presbyterian Church, and a nice little party at Cheech and Ron's house afterward, and then we climbed into my car and started up the highway as man and wife. We spent our honeymoon night at a trucker's motel off the Breezewood exit of the Pennsylvania Turnpike. It wasn't terribly romantic, and in retrospect it makes me realize what a true gem I had found in Winifred Walzer. Here was this classy, educated, beautiful girl who risked her father's eternal wrath and gave up her girlhood wedding dreams and goodness knows what else to follow a guy who'd never made a plugged nickel as a professional golfer. It was the beginning of a host of disappointments both large and small that she and any other Tour wife in those days would have to endure. Winnie never complained, though, and I've spent years trying to make it up to her in various ways. She would tell you it was no big deal, honeymooning that first night in a trucker motel off a lonely turnpike. But I know it was, and I also know we've done all right ever since.

There was one problem with her, though.

Winnie couldn't cook a lick. Actually, that's not entirely correct. She could make great icebox cake, a recipe she'd been taught as a girl. But when it came, say, to boiling water—she was out of her depth. Our first tiff developed over the subject of cooked sausage, and I still feel a little bit bad about it. After spending a quiet Christmas holiday and calling Shube to see if he was adjusting any better to the news (he wasn't), Winnie and I went to the club for a New Year's Eve party. Afterward, as I prepared to drive the baby-sitter home—my brother, Jerry, and sister Sandy were still young enough to require one—I suggested to Winnie that she fry up some country sausage and make us a great midnight breakfast. She probably aired her insecurity about cooking, and I must have laughed and told her not to be ridiculous—how hard could cooking sausage be? Anyway, a short time later I returned and found the sausage cold in the pan and her tears flowing. Boy, did I feel like a real heel. I apologized and cooked the sausage myself and told her not to worry because my mother was a great cook and would teach her all she really needed to know.

Mother did, too. Like Pap, she adored Winnie, and she knew that Palmer men could be somewhat insensitive to certain needs of a young woman. For instance, several weeks before, Winnie had taken the train to Latrobe to spend Thanksgiving with us. I'd grumbled how blasted cold it was in Latrobe and how I dearly wished I could hit some balls in the warmth because the start of the new Tour season was only a few weeks away.

"Well," Pap had proposed, "why don't we just get in the car and drive down to Pinehurst and play."

He meant just the two of us, not the women in our lives. I regret to say that it never occurred to either of us to invite them along. The next day, Friday of Thanksgiving weekend, mind you, we tossed our clubs into the car and drove to Pinehurst, leaving Winnie and my mother to face the long holiday weekend without us. I failed to realize how much the holiday meant to Winnie, who was devastated by this impulsive act. In her family's tradition, Thanksgiving meant a lot, and she normally would have been surrounded by family and childhood chums at the big Walzer celebration back home. When we left she burst into tears and no doubt wondered what kind of life she was getting herself into. I later learned that Jerry and Sandy were very comforting to her, agreeing that their older brother was being a jerk, and once again my mother came to the rescue by proposing that the girls simply put the kids in her car and drive to see Cheech in Virginia. They did just that—and had a swell time without us, we later learned.

On the second day of the New Year, 1955, I left for the McNaughton Pro-Am at Normandy Isle in Miami. Winnie and I had been married for ten days, but I went alone. As it wasn't an official Tour event,

I stood the chance of picking up a few much-needed bucks. I didn't play particularly well, but I picked up $750, enough to afford a plane ticket to the next event, another unofficial tournament, the Panama Open, which preceded the official start of the Tour season out west.

I flew down to Panama with Porky Oliver, Lew Worsham, Chick Harbert, Ted Kroll, and Bob Toski. The tournament was a seventy-two-hole event, and Panama City was a pretty wide-open place for a good time, if you know what I mean. I was down there to try to make some serious money and prove to Winnie that she hadn't married the golf-world equivalent of a carnival-ride operator. On the first night there, a number of the guys invited me to go out drinking and looking for homegrown female companionship. I don't think they took me seriously when I protested that I was now a married man and, tempting as it was, I didn't go in for that sort of thing anymore.

They left, and I pulled my mattress out onto the hotel room's veranda because the night was extremely hot and sticky. I stretched out on the mattress and went to sleep, only to awaken a while later from what I thought was a provocative dream about my bride. I was startled to find a naked Panamanian girl cavorting around the porch and the guys laughing their backsides off. They'd brought a local lady of the night back to the room to try to test my newlywed resolve. I bolted up off that mattress ready to flatten somebody, and after I came to my senses I threw them all out of the room in a rage,

locked the door, and went back to sleep on the bal-
cony, worrying about how in the world I would tell
Winnie about this.

If this was a glimpse of the rollicking Tour life to
come, it would be good to have Winnie and her
common sense by my side. Perhaps still annoyed at
the guys for their drunken stunt, I fired a blistering
65 in the tournament's opening round, followed by
rounds of 68, 70, and 71. I lost by a stroke to Argen-
tine Tony Cerda, but my second-place finish was
good enough to earn me a thousand dollars. Really
pleased with myself, I phoned home to break the
good news to Winnie and suggested she meet me in
Miami so we could drive west and start the PGA
Tour together.

I still wrestled with the question of whether or not
I should tell her about the incident on the hotel bal-
cony, and finally I decided to risk it. Winnie and I
had such an honest relationship, she simply had to
know *everything*. So I told her the story and waited
in a bit of suspense to hear her response.

I should have known she would laugh. I'd married
a woman who knew how to roll with the punches
and keep things in perspective. She knew what was
important and she knew I loved only her. That was
the beginning of a forty-five-year journey of learning, through the usual marital ups and downs,
through Tour triumphs and personal disappointments she'll never speak of, all magnified by my
evolving success, how extraordinary my wife truly
is. No wonder Shube Walzer was such an unyielding
papa bear on the subject. He knew he was losing

more than a strong-headed daughter who could keep his books and decorate his summer cottage on a frugal dime.

I was just beginning to discover what I'd really found.

CHAPTER SIX

The Tour

Winnie and I had a great time driving across America in my old coral pink Ford. In many ways, the trip west to join the Tour in California amounted to a perfect honeymoon. It's worth remembering that Winnie and I had known each other less than four months, and if you ever want to learn a lot about somebody fast, good and bad, driving across the country with them is one way to do it. I drove, and Winnie navigated. We also decided her experience keeping accounts for Shube Walzer made her an invaluable asset, the logical choice for the traveling Palmer team secretary and bookkeeper. We had an offer of a place to stay in California but really didn't know a soul along the way, so we drove leisurely through the days and slept in inexpensive motels and motor courts, stopped wherever and whenever the spirit moved us, ate in cozy roadside diners and cafés, saw a few tourist sights, talked about children and plans for a house, and held hands like the runaway newlywed lovers we were, falling more deeply in love.

Most of the regulars on the Tour were starting play at the Thunderbird Invitational in Palm Springs, but I hadn't been invited to play there; I was signed up to try to qualify for the Brawley Open in

Brawley, California, scheduled to begin the same day as the Thunderbird. I remember that we drove to Palm Springs anyway to see what it was like. I guess that because we knew of it only by reputation and all the glamorous associations we made with million-aires and movie stars, we were surprised at how small it was—why, it was hardly bigger than Youngstown! On the other hand, it was also incre-dibly beautiful, with its swaying palms and pretty sun-splashed streets tucked in a majestic bowl of desert mountains under an always-blue winter sky. We found a nice inexpensive place to have lunch, then cruised over to the tournament site to take a peek at the proceedings—literally looking in from outside the gate, dreaming of the day we would be invited in.

Then we drove on to Brawley and met Grace and John Stadler, a farmer and his wife who were friends of someone we knew, two of the most gracious and welcoming people Winnie and I ever met in our years of travels. They put us up in a pretty room in their little farmhouse and fed us handsomely, and I went out that Monday and qualified and shot a total of 277 in the tournament against a strong field, good enough for seventeenth place. Not a bad start, except for the fact that it would be six months before I'd have an official Tour payday.

So on we motored to Phoenix. Somewhere en route it occurred to us that we were spending far too much for motel rooms. By the time we hit the city limits of Phoenix we'd more or less made up our minds to go shopping for an inexpensive trailer.

Given the nomadic nature of the PGA Tour in those days, it's not surprising that there was a thriving culture of trailer-haulers on tour. Several of the young professionals and their wives even traveled in caravans from one Tour site to the next, including Bill Casper and his wife, Shirley, the Doug Fords, the Littlers, the Dick Mayers, and several others. (Impressively, they hauled everything from their china to family heirlooms and were able to set themselves up with all the comforts of home in no time flat.)

The trailer we found was a neat little rig shaped like a loaf of bread, nineteen feet long, with a small kitchen, small bedroom, and a *very* small bath. The key word here is *small*. The only thing that wasn't particularly small about it was the price. To afford it, we had to phone my father and—even more difficult—Shube Walzer and ask to borrow $500 from each. Pap readily agreed, and I was surprised by Shube's willingness to chip in on the trailer. Perhaps the ice was beginning to thaw after all.

Speaking of ice, our first morning in that little love nest on wheels turned out to be an adventure neither Winnie nor I will ever forget. After hooking up the trailer and provisioning it with homemaking supplies, we drove to a trailer park near the tournament site and set up housekeeping, both so proud of our little place-on-wheels we were about to pop. Later, at the tournament site, I invited a fellow professional and his wife over for breakfast. (By then my mother had given Winnie her crash cooking course, and Winnie could do a pretty fair breakfast.)

Anyway, perhaps forgetting that we were parked in the desert in winter, I got up early and went to shower, only to find there was no water. It was so cold outside, I quickly discovered, the trailer's hose line to the spigot was frozen solid. Well, I thought, no problem. I went back inside and heated some water in a pot and poured it on the frozen line. I must have done this half a dozen times, but the line remained frozen as a Popsicle. Finally, I lost my patience altogether and kicked the spigot in frustration. The head snapped off clean as a whistle and water spouted up like a baby geyser. "C'mon, Winnie. We're going over to the club for breakfast!" I shouted to my bride. And that's exactly what we did—leaving that gusher for the management to handle.

I finished tenth at Phoenix, and we moved on to Tucson and then San Antonio, followed by Houston and Baton Rouge. My best finish in those initial tournaments was sixth place at San Antonio. What I remember most about that period of time, aside from wrestling with and cursing at that trailer, was practicing my rear end off before and after each round.

I seemed to live on the practice tee and putting greens, beating balls off the rock-hard ground from dawn till dusk. In those days, it was kind of a running joke that the trajectory of my tee shots was so low you could always tell when Arnold Palmer had been on the tee—the grass in front of it was scorched by the ball. It's true a lot of my tee shots rarely got higher than twenty feet off the ground and did indeed occasionally ricochet off the turf. I could still outdrive almost anybody out there, but I knew I would need a broader range of shotmaking skills if I wanted to win the two tournaments that most interested me—the Masters and the U.S. Open.

Earlier in this account I talked about my father's stern admonition that the quickest way to wind up back in Latrobe was to accept swing advice from other players or fall under the spell of teachers. I pretty much accepted his words as gospel, but I did receive help of a sort from a larger-than-life character named George Low.

George was the son of a famous Carnoustie golf teacher and a widely acknowledged putting genius whose professional career was marginal at best on these shores but who epitomized the kinds of characters who were still around the professional tour in those days. Like a figure out of a Damon Runyon tale, George was a charming rogue who lived off a small inheritance from his father and whatever he could make at the horse track, at cards, or from the big-money private matches he always seemed to be in the middle of somewhere. He was proud of his Scottish heritage and not opposed to making an easy buck and supposedly once dressed up in a kilt to play the "part" of the "Scottish" professional in George S. May's elaborate Tam O'Shanter productions. As I fondly recall, old George always had some kind of action going somewhere—a putting match he never lost, if nothing else. Anyway, though Tony Penna questioned whether my swing would keep me out on tour long, George had no doubt about my abilities whatsoever. He took a shine to me very early—perhaps because I was a professional's son like him—and gave me the one putting lesson I ever had. It was short and sweet, as I'll explain.

From the beginning, my putting stroke was also the subject of some conjecture on the parts of commentators and other professionals and observers. The way I hunched over the ball, knock-kneed and leaning, and gave the ball a firm, wristy rap that often sent it speeding ten feet past the hole seemed to trouble some people, who thought I should stand straighter, use less body English, and make a smoother stroke rather than the stab that sometimes crept into my putting technique. I rarely left a ball shy of the cup, figuring it was easier to make the comebacker than a putt that never reached the target to begin with.

I also learned early on from my own experimentation that there's absolutely nothing wrong with having "wristy action" in a putt if you're able to keep the putter head square and the face on target, which I was able to do by standing very close to the ball, allowing my wrists to "hinge" back and forth. George was from the old school—the school where players taught themselves to play and used whatever worked for them—and gave me the most useful putting lesson I ever had. After watching me putt for a while, he took me aside and growled: "Listen to me, Arnie. There's not a damn thing wrong with the way you putt. You putt great. Don't ever let anybody fool with your putting stroke or you'll be damned sorry." George Low believed in the Gospel of Deke Palmer, and I was deeply grateful to have his support. It may or may not have been George who gave me an interesting tip—namely, to dig the ends of my thumbs into the putter grip whenever I felt undue pressure or my stroke wasn't up to snuff. I used that technique a few times in big tournaments when I really needed to get the ball in the hole or felt my stroke wasn't working quite right.

Early on, George sort of adopted Winnie and me out on tour, and a few years later when Peg and Amy came along he served as a kind of Dutch uncle to the girls. Once, in Phoenix, when the girls were maybe four and six, "Uncle George" showed up at the hotel and insisted on baby-sitting while Winnie and I went out to dinner with some other folks. I remember how reluctant we were to leave the three of them, but George was nuts about the girls and vice versa, so we eventually gave in and went out to dinner. Much later we returned to find the girls still up and having the time of their lives. Uncle George had taught them how to play poker and, for all I know, roll dice. Peg and Amy adored him even before the time, some years later, when Uncle George showed up in Latrobe with bicycles for them, a gift from his "winnings."

With George, a good rule was to not ask too many questions. I remember the time in Palm Springs he came to the house for dinner with a paper sack—what we used to call a "poke" back in Latrobe—in hand and asked Winnie and me to keep it for him "for a while." But there was a catch: he also asked us not to look in it under any circumstances. We reluctantly agreed, but not long after he was gone curiosity got the better of us and we opened the bag to find it was full of money. We knew it had to be George's winnings from the track. Winnie and I looked at each other and shook our heads. Later, when I handed the bag back to George, I told him there was no way Winnie and I could keep money for him and he ought to put it in a bank. George screwed up his face and told me he didn't trust banks. Especially not with $27,000. Winnie and I nearly fainted.

Anyway, I practiced hard, a slave to the range before and after each round, and by the time of our arrival at St. Petersburg, Florida, the seventh week of the season, all that heavy-duty practicing had taken an unexpected toll on my body. One morning I woke to discover an excruciating pain in my upper torso; I could barely lift my arms above my shoulders without severe pain. I'll admit to being a bit panicked—I had no idea what was wrong with me.

Some players were superstitious about how they practiced and played golf, and others—like Frank Stranahan, who passed along his weight-lifting and fanatical conditioning regimes to some extent to his protégé, a young man named Gary Player—performed elaborate pregame routines, always eating certain kinds of meals, abstaining from sex and alcohol, wearing certain types of clothes. You name it and they did it, all in an attempt to find the mental comfort zone where good golf is played. Still others carried four-leaf clovers or rabbit's feet or lucky charms from their travels. Some openly prayed to God to let them win.

I've never been very superstitious, and my religious faith is more like my father's, a strictly private matter between my maker and me. I did say prayers but never asked the Almighty to let me win a golf match or a tournament. My prayer was basically pretty simple and direct: Please let me stay healthy enough to compete. That was my biggest fear—that an injury or illness would keep me from being able to use my God-given physical abilities to win a golf tournament.

Now, in St. Petersburg, I faced the first test of my faith—this horrifying pain in my arms and shoulders. It had me shaken up because I couldn't imagine what the hell was wrong. I somehow got through my practice round, and that evening Winnie and I went out to dinner with professional Skip Alexander and his wife and their friends, a Dr. Needles and his wife. Dr. Needles was a heart specialist, and when I mentioned my problem to him he explained that I'd nearly beaten my shoulder and arm muscles to death, or at least to the point of extreme exhaustion, and that I would have to give them a rest or at least be very careful not to do serious or permanent injury.

He suggested I come to his office, adding that he had a brand-new "wonder drug" that might ease the inflammation. The next day, the aptly named Dr.

Needles administered several injections of cortisone directly into my shoulder muscles. For several long minutes, I wondered if I'd made the biggest mistake of my life. Those injections hurt more than the sore muscles they were supposed to be helping. For a while it seemed as if the medicine might kill the patient, rather than cure him. The inflammation grew worse overnight, but somehow I gutted out the tournament, managing a 68 in the third round for a total of 284, good enough for seventeenth place. I joke about the episode now, whenever I feel a twitch of pain in those muscles after a round. But this experience gave me the first taste of what it's like to play with serious pain, and I wouldn't wish that fate on anybody.

As sore as I was, I suppose I must have been tempted to withdraw from the tournament. I did that five times that first year, pulled out of tournaments when things for one reason or another weren't going to my liking. Today, when a professional pulls out of a tournament it's considered big news—I suppose because the financial commitments are so large and the press corps so hungry for any whiff of controversy. In those days it wasn't such a big deal. That's not an excuse for quitting. Life sometimes gets in the way of golf, and life invariably comes first. I'm not proud of the fact that I pulled out of those five tournaments, but on the other hand, if I hadn't done it I wouldn't have eventually learned the larger value of sticking with the game to the very end, regardless of the outcome. In time, as my name became better known to the galleries, I became aware of my obligation to stay in a tournament that wasn't going particularly well, out of respect to the sponsors, to the galleries, and even to myself, who I was and where I'd come from—the son of a man who never abided the word "quit."

Anyway, that week in St. Petersburg wasn't exactly our best—on top of the acute pain in my shoulders we had trouble with our elderly Ford two-door. I remember taking the car to a service station to have the oil changed and the alignment checked out—there was a funny shimmy at sixty or seventy miles per hour—and the service attendant put her up on the lift and had barely begun examining the front tires when the left front wheel simply fell off. It startled us both, and the attendant remarked on the obvious—we were lucky that that wheel hadn't snapped off while we were hauling a trailer at seventy miles an hour.

Speaking of the trailer, our little Phoenix love nest, its diminutive size was now too much—or, rather, too *little*—to bear. Winnie and I decided it had to go in favor of something larger and more accommodating. More phone calls to Latrobe and Coopersburg ensued, followed by two more loans of $500 from each of our families. A day or so later, we rolled into a trailer park in Florida pulling a new trailer that was twenty-six feet long.

This was living, but my shoulders were still killing me. I went to Seminole Golf Club to play in a pro-am where I could pocket money and shot a dismal 87 and 86 on successive days. Luckily, by the start of the Miami Open a day or so later, the pain had backed off enough to permit me to find my stroke again, and I recorded three rounds in the 60s, a respectable warm-up for my first appearance at the Masters.

I remember like it was yesterday the feeling as I drove up Magnolia Lane into Augusta National Golf Club for the first time. I'd never seen a place that looked so beautiful, so well manicured, and so purely devoted to golf, as beautiful as an antebellum estate, as quiet as a church. I remember turning to Winnie, who was as excited as I was by the sight of the place, and saying quietly, probably as much in awe as I've ever been: "This has got to be it, Babe ..." I felt a powerful thrill and unexpected kinship with the place. Perhaps that's partially because Augusta was built by Bob Jones, who was one of my childhood heroes, but also because the Masters, though still a relatively modest event in terms of money, was like a family gathering of the game's greatest players, ruled with a firm, unbending hand by Clifford Roberts. They were all there— Jones, Sarazen, Snead, Nelson, Hogan. Though I'd met them all before, just seeing their names together on pairing sheets or chatting with each other on those perfect putting surfaces was an almost religious experience for me. Privately, I admitted to Winnie that it was like dying and going to heaven. I was there, of course, courtesy of my National Amateur title, and though I was rendered a bit agog by the lush surroundings and famous players, I was also surging with confidence. After weeks of playing courses on tour that were rock hard and in some cases in pretty woeful shape, coming to Augusta's exquisitely manicured fairways and pristine greens was a royal treat I was anxious to experience. As it was not an official Tour event, I also stood to pocket some much-needed moola.

I played pretty well, all things considered, in that first Masters outing. I opened with a pair of discouraging 76s, but then settled down a bit and shot 72 in the third round, followed by a final round of 69. Ironically, standing on the tenth tee on Sunday, I calculated that if I got home in 32 on Augusta's famous back nine I might be a serious factor in the tournament's outcome. That realization got me so worked up, I regret to say, I made a double-bogey six on ten and wound up finishing in tenth place. I made a paycheck for $696 that week—money that came just when we needed it most—but more importantly, I had made the acquaintance of a special place and numerous people who would soon mean more to Winnie and me than I could ever have imagined.

At first glance, the course, designed by Alister Mackenzie with helpful insights from Bob Jones, didn't particularly suit my style of game. There were numerous places where a high, soft fade worked best, and the undulating and fast putting surfaces favored approach shots that stuck like darts rather than ricocheted like bullets, as mine sometimes did. I quickly saw there were things I would need to learn to do if I intended to conquer the golf course and win the Masters—notably, hit the ball a bit higher and know when to back off intelligently at a hole where finesse and not power would bear more fruit.

As Pap would have pointed out, though, you're invariably stuck with the golf swing you're born with, and I wasn't going to alter that much of my game to try to tailor it to Augusta's swirling winds and daunting putting surfaces. I learned, instead, *where* to hit my drives in order to have approaches to greens I was comfortable with—in other words, put the ball where I could hit into the green on a straight, low line. In time I became pretty adept at knowing Augusta's "angles," as I thought of it, knowing where I could roll a ball through an opening or use a mound or hillside to pull off a shot and snug the ball close.

I remember meeting Clifford Roberts, the club's legendary chairman, then at the height of his power, and being almost instantly scared to death of him. Though a New York investment banker by profession, he reminded me of an old schoolteacher, reserved, tough, a headmaster brooking no opposition or even debate on any subject. He was clearly a one-man show, and the small membership of Augusta National obviously liked it that way. I was determined to stay out of his way, recalling that a few years before he'd tossed Frank Stranahan off the premises for allegedly hitting extra practice balls during a round—something that was against the club's policy. Being friends with Clifford Roberts, I would discover, was like learning Augusta National's proper angles—it took time, but the friendship, when it evolved, would be a lasting and genuine one.

I met Bob Jones there, too—by then far past his playing prime and only a year or so away from being stricken by the illness (syringomelia) that would rack his body and eventually force him to use a customized golf cart to get around the grounds to see players and meet people. Mr. Jones, as I called him from the outset, was as unfailingly polite and kind-spirited as anybody I ever met at Augusta. Perhaps because amateur golf had meant so much to him—he won the Grand Slam as an amateur in 1930 and then retired from the game, as he described it, before he "needed" to make money in order to play—Jones harbored a special affection for amateur champions who found their way to Augusta, treating each and every one like the special young men he thought they were, myself included.

I'd seen Ben Hogan at various tournaments and even played in a group close to him at Wilmington, but I met him for the first time in Augusta. To be honest, I was so in awe of the man, and so naturally shy, I felt he was utterly unapproachable. At the Masters someone introduced us, and we shook hands. He was polite enough, but I felt the cool distance others sensed while in his presence. Hogan was still limping from his 1950 car crash but remained the most dangerous player of his age, maybe the best ball-striker who ever lived. I was at first surprised by—and later angered about—the fact that he never, in the years I knew him, called me by my first name. Ten million golf fans have felt completely comfortable calling me "Arnie," but Mr. Hogan never spoke my real name. He only called me "fella." To give him the benefit of the doubt, he called lots of young, ambitious players "fella." Perhaps he couldn't remember their names (after all, a lot of talent was streaming out of the college ranks into the professional ranks), or maybe he sensed the others and I were gunning for his records, which of course we were. But he was a living legend and inspiration. Golf is, at its core, life's most good-hearted and socially complex game—one of the "most humbling things on earth," as my good friend George Low once quipped—and I wouldn't have minded being called "Arnie" by a man I only admired from afar and played for on a Ryder Cup team. But it never happened. You draw your own conclusions from that.

I learned a valuable lesson at that first Masters— that *wanting* something so much I could almost taste it wasn't the best approach to winning golf tournaments, especially major ones. I learned that, at a place like Augusta National, where every shot is potentially so decisive, I couldn't afford to get ahead of myself as I did that Sunday afternoon on the final nine, blowing myself right out of contention. I had to play my own game, shot by shot, and not permit myself the luxury of thinking what it could mean—a lesson I was destined to learn and a mistake I was destined to repeat. But that's a tale to come.

Sam Snead and I had met before, but we got to be pretty good friends at that first Masters. I always enjoyed my time with Sam, the rounds we played together, the rustic pearls of wisdom he dropped

about the game and life, even the colorful and sometimes downright raunchy jokes he told and tall tales
he spun. Sam had a dark side that emerged when his
game faltered, but he was at heart a big old country
boy who loved golf and had a zest for life, swallowing it in gulps (especially if someone else was
buying the beer—he was also one of the tightest
guys with a buck I ever met), and surely one of the
most natural talents who ever swung a golf club. He
and I took an instant liking to each other, and it was
Sam who personally invited Winnie and me to his
own little shindig, the Sam Snead Festival, which
was scheduled, as I recall, to take place the week
after the Tour stop at Greensboro, North Carolina, a
tournament with lots of Wake Forest alums in the
gallery. For that reason alone, I always dearly
wanted to win there. Unfortunately, I never did.
Once again, perhaps I could taste my desire to win a
little too much. I shot four rounds in the 70s and
wound up thirty-third. Not a great showing, and
proof we needed some rest. We headed on north for
home.

Our old Ford needed rest, too—perhaps a permanent rest. That much became clear when we got off
the Pennsylvania Turnpike at the Donegal exit to
take a familiar shortcut to Latrobe out of the mountains. Big mistake. The road was narrow and steep,
and we'd not even reached the summit when the
radiator began to spew. We had to pull off and wait
for the engine to cool down before we could add

more water. Then we resumed our crawl to the top. The trailer we were pulling was so loaded down with all our stuff, Winnie and I actually had to get out and push the car at times. So much for shortcuts.

What should have taken a few minutes required several hours' worth of work and worry until, mercifully, we reached the top. It didn't dawn on us until we had started down the mountain into Latrobe that the final five miles (down the same road where Cheech and I used to ride a toboggan) could be an even bigger problem. Within minutes of starting our descent, the Ford's brakes were smoking, and it was all I could do to keep the car from running away and the trailer from running over us. We finally got stopped on the shoulder and basically had to inch our way that last mile down to Latrobe. Wheezing and exhausted, car and owners, we crept into my parents' driveway by the 15th hole at the club and switched off the engine. As long as I live, I'll never forget Winnie's reaction.

She got out of the car, shut the door, turned and looked at me with her jaw set, and calmly declared, "That's it. I'm never going anywhere in that trailer again."

I knew she was dead serious about that, and I didn't disagree. The novelty and charm of traveling America in a trailer had run its course. The next day, we put the rig up for sale in the Latrobe newspaper. A newlywed couple bought the thing and, I gather, lived quite happily in it for years somewhere just outside of town. The only people who were really disappointed to see that trailer vanish for good over the hill were my little brother, Jerry, and even younger sister Sandy. For several days they got to use it as a playhouse, their very own palace on wheels.

The message was pretty clear that life on tour wasn't going to be easy on either of us and might possibly be very tough on a prospective family. Though we didn't know it, Winnie was already pregnant, or shortly would be, and there had to be a better way to travel than a small trailer and a worn-out Ford.

After all those weeks beating across America, Sam Snead's invitational tournament at The Greenbrier in West Virginia was just the tonic we needed, in more ways than one. First of all, it was an unofficial event with a large Calcutta (where teams are purchased in a wagering pool), meaning I stood a decent chance of picking up some needed money. A little like Fred Waring's shindig at Shawnee, there were a lot of parties and socializing in addition to the golf tournament. The event took place at the luxurious old Greenbrier resort in White Sulphur Springs. Speaking of luxury, a friend in Latrobe who was a pilot offered to fly us to the site, so we chartered a small plane and spared ourselves the long drive through the Blue Ridge Mountains.

By some stroke of fortune, I got paired with an amateur partner named Spencer Olin, the chairman of a large chemical firm, who not only had a splendid private plane of his own but turned out to be a pretty fair player as well. Spencer bought our team in the Calcutta and followed up that confidence by playing just great, shooting several strokes beneath his handicap. The first day I shot 69, and we were leading the field.

On an amusing note, after that nice opening round, I remember Dutch Harrison sidling over to me and telling me *he* had arranged for me to have Spencer Olin as a partner. "Don't you forget ole Dutch, Arn," he growled at me, and winked. Quite frankly, I didn't know whether to believe him or laugh in his face. Dutch was a character in the same way George Low was—you never quite knew what sort of action he had going. All I knew was, hard pressed as Winnie and I were for funds at that moment, regardless of whether or not Dutch had somehow arranged the pairings, the last thing I wanted to do was give him a percentage of my winnings as some kind of personal gratuity!

The pressure seemed to get to Spencer a bit; he blew to a 94 on the second day, but I shot 67—good enough for third in the professional division and enough for us to tie for first in the pro-am team division. I collected $1,500.

The PGA Tour stop the next week was the Colonial in Fort Worth. But before that I had arranged to play an exhibition, and Spencer graciously offered to fly us there in his private DC-3. I remember thinking, as we got airborne, that this was the *only* way to go to golf tournaments; perhaps it was then and there that I made up my mind to get that pilot's license I'd always dreamed about and maybe to buy a plane. In any case, especially in light of Dutch's less than subtle request, Spencer Olin made the trip even more memorable by coming to me and saying, "Arnie, it's traditional for the winner of the Calcutta to give his pro partner a percentage of the winnings. Here's yours." He presented me with $5,000, bringing my total earnings to a princely $6,500. What a great weekend it had been!

I played poorly that week at the Colonial and then missed the cut at Kansas City, before flying on, after a stopover in Latrobe, to Fort Wayne. This was the the first event where I could take official money. My six-month apprenticeship was finally up. Perhaps I tried too hard, or maybe I was just a little road weary. I wound up twenty-fifth and took home $145 as my first official tournament paycheck.

No matter how much I'd made, it was good to go home to Latrobe for a couple weeks of rest and relaxation before playing in my first National Open as a professional. Winnie went to visit with her folks in Coopersburg for a few days, and I hung out at the club with Pap. He was busy planting trees on the golf course and talking about making other changes. (As long as he lived Pap was always making changes to the golf course at Latrobe, a trait I inherited.) When Winnie came back, we took our Sam Snead Festival money down to Forsha Motors in Latrobe and purchased a brand-new, beige-and-tan Chrysler New Yorker, a real sweetheart of a car, and a few days after that, loaded up with golf clubs and clothing, we hit the turnpike headed west.

That trip—our second across America inside a year—was memorable and fun for a number of reasons. First of all, we saw more sights and our trip was still a little bit like a honeymoon; the big difference was that this time the car was a sheer joy to drive. Winnie wasn't crazy about the fact that I got the New Yorker up to 120 miles per hour while crossing the Great Salt Lake, but that evening in Elko, Nevada, we put up in an inexpensive casino motel. We had decided we didn't have enough money to risk any gambling, but returning from a hamburger and a beer, just for fun, I dropped our dinner change on the roulette table—double ought—and hit the jackpot, collecting thirty-five silver dollars! Talk about a couple of naive kids; we hustled straight back to our motel room, showered and got in bed, clutching our winnings. I was so worried about being robbed of our bounty, I propped a chair against the doorknob just like I'd seen in the movies!

The next day, Winnie took over the driving, and she was no slouch in the speed department either. In fact, at one point we roared over a hill, and I suddenly saw cops on motorcycles scattering wildly in several directions, looking like Keystone Kops. Without knowing it, she'd nearly wiped out several young state patrolmen who were on a routine motorcycle training mission! Sirens wailed, and the police gave brief chase. Winnie, bless her, was scared out of her mind, and the captain who asked for her license must have known that. To tell the truth, I wondered what he was going to do to her myself.

"Young lady," he said sternly. "I see you're from Pennsylvania."

"Yes, sir," she answered meekly.

"Well, you're in California now and I really want you to obey the speed laws. I want you to drive very safely from here on out. Is that understood?"

A solemn nod.

The officer smiled. "I'm going to let you go this time. But you remember what I said, all right?"

Winnie smiled sweetly up at him. Luck is a lady, and this seemed to be our lucky week. First we win $35 out of the blue, then we don't have to part with the cash for speeding!

Perhaps Lady Luck would be with us at San Francisco's famed Olympic Golf Club, too. That was my hope, anyway, because I'd never played the famous narrow, eucalyptus-lined Lakeside Course, which sits mere yards from the Pacific Ocean. The world's greatest golfers were gathering, and Ben Hogan was gunning for the record books and a fifth U.S. Open championship.

We drove straight into San Francisco and found the Olympic Club, met official hosts Ed and Rita Douglas (who would become cherished longtime friends), and they directed us to a reasonably priced motel not far away where, as coincidence would

have it, we found Tommy and Shirley Bolt checking in.

I was quite fond of Tommy Bolt. He was ten
years my senior and was generous enough to take
me under his wing and explain to me how things
worked on Tour. It's a shame that Tommy is best
known for breaking clubs over his knees or throwing
them around (like at the U.S. Open I won at Cherry
Hills where he hit a poor drive and hurled his
favorite driver into a lake, then chased the kid who
retrieved it). In fact, Tommy was one of the most
able ball-strikers I've ever seen, with a skill that
made him dangerous anytime he was around a leader
board. Tommy's temper, his inability to control his
impatience and rage at the game's small injustices or
bad luck, really proved his undoing far too many
times. Off the course, Bolt was justly known for his
quick-witted one-liners, and you've never met a
more charming and interesting fellow. To this day,
I'm convinced his temper is the only thing that stood
between Tommy and the Hall of Fame status he's
always greatly desired and probably deserves. As I
say, I was lucky to have Tommy as a friend early on,
because I learned an awful lot from him—not least
of which was the importance of harnessing my own
temper on the golf course, a lesson I would soon
need.

Anyway, sometime that week at Olympic,
Tommy and Shirley and Winnie and I agreed it
might be fun to travel together from one Tour stop to
the next, and that was the plan we made. The

Western Open was the next scheduled stop, but before that Tommy and I both had our sights set on Olympic.

From the outset, it appeared to be Tommy's week. Of the 162 starters, eighty-two—more than half the field—failed to break 80 that first round, and only Tommy Bolt managed to break par, cruising around the course in a smooth 67 thanks to eleven one-putt greens and some superb chipping. I carded a miserable 77, hacking balls out of calf-deep rough and getting to know some of Olympic's 43,000 eucalyptus and pine trees far more intimately than I had planned or wanted.

Bolt slipped to 77 in the second round, still good enough to give him a share of the lead with Harvie Ward at 144; I failed to improve my chances by firing a discouraging 76. The dangerous Ben Hogan and the then-unknown Jack Fleck were a mere stroke behind Bolt and Ward, and by the end of the third round it appeared Ben Hogan was en route to a record fifth Open. The best I could accomplish were closing rounds of 74 and 76, good enough for twenty-first place. But no one noticed what I was doing, because the real drama belonged, of course, to Hogan and Fleck, an outcome that many think of as the biggest upset in all of golf history. Early in the afternoon of Open Saturday (in those days the tournament concluded with two rounds on Saturday), Hogan finished with a surgical round of 70 and, amid 6,000 wildly cheering fans gathered on the amphitheater hillside by the 18th hole, was all but presented the Open trophy by a beaming Gene

Sarazen, who was doing television commentary of the great moment.

The rest of the story proves what a wonderfully mysterious game golf really is, but it proved a sad tale to Ben Hogan. Out on the course, Fleck's putter got hotter than it had ever been before, and a couple of hours later he holed an eight-foot putt to force a playoff. By then Hogan was showered, dressed, and had packed up his clubs to head home to Texas. Fifty-four years old, still hurting from his terrible car accident injuries, the last thing he wanted or expected was to have to play some unknown guy from Iowa for the National Open title. Now he would have to wait one more day to collect his record fifth Open, but his legs—and possibly his heart—really weren't in it.

All the betting was in Hogan's corner the next day, but it was Ben who faltered. He needed a birdie at the 18th to tie, but drove into the ferocious rough and made six; Fleck parred for 69 and became maybe the greatest human curiosity in the history of golf—the "Giant Killer," as the papers hailed him, who never managed to win anything significant again.

Was it a fluke? Some called it that. But nobody I know who's played this game on the level we played it that week at Olympic would dare call it that. It took courage, great intelligence, and superb shot-making for Jack Fleck to win that U.S. Open, knowing that virtually everybody watching was rooting against him. Contributing to that anti-Fleck sentiment was Jack's appearance. He was not a glamorous figure. Though he'll go into the history books as a giant killer, he looked more like a beanstalk—tall and gangly and undernourished. He also seemed uncomfortable at times—at war with himself—so reserved he seemed almost dour. Aptly enough, his hero was Ben Hogan himself.

In any event, people wanted to see history made, and he made it in a most unexpected way. You've got to give Jack his due. It was a great performance, and if you get only one great performance in your life, may yours be on as grand a scale as Jack's.

The next week at Portland Golf Club, site of the Western Open, I learned something about my own composure under fire on the golf course. I was playing with Doug Ford and Marty Furgol in the first round when we came to the par-5 tenth hole, a hole I planned to try to reach in two. Both Furgol and Ford had played their second shots and the group ahead of us was still putting, so I had to wait before shooting. Doug Ford was a pleasure to play with—he'd come out on tour a few years ahead of me and enjoyed early success, giving me a boost of confidence—but Furgol's host of eccentricities made Jack Fleck's personality quirks look tame. As I was preparing to hit, I saw Furgol standing down the fairway between me and the green. I yelled at Doug to ask him to move and Doug did, but Marty moved only a few feet. I yelled again, and he moved a couple more feet. With each passing moment I grew hotter and hotter. I swung too hard and the ball flew over the green right, and I should have chipped up for an easy bird, but I missed the putt, too.

Coming off the green I was as mad as I'd ever been on a golf course. I seized Furgol's collar and said to him, "Let me tell you something, Mr. Furgol. If you ever pull a stunt like that again I'll take my fists and beat the hell out of you, and if I can't do it with my fists I'll use a golf club."

I think it really shook him up, and probably a few of the spectators watching, as well. Marty knew what he'd done, but he feigned complete innocence. The truth is, I really wanted to flatten him on the spot, and that really shook me up, too, because I'd never lost my composure like that during a golf tournament. One consequence of the blowup was my score, an opening 76. That night at dinner I observed to Winnie that Pap would have been furious with me for losing my cool like that, and I vowed to myself, and to her, that I wouldn't let my temper get the best of me again. I shot 66 the next day and finished the tournament with a respectable 284. I also reported Furgol to Ray O'Brien, the Tour's head man. He admonished Furgol, telling him to avoid such stunts in the future. For years Marty and I kept our distance from each other, which was probably a good thing for both of us.

The next four weeks were an adventure, traveling with the Bolts up to Vancouver for the British Columbia Open, then on to St. Paul, where Tommy won and I scored my first top-five finish, a third— worth $1,300 to the family till. Then it was on to Milwaukee, Toledo, and George S. May's All American and World Championship at Tam O'Shanter in Chicago.

I failed to play well there, but I felt my game was getting closer to really clicking—a hunch that proved correct the very next week in Toronto at the Canadian Open. I opened with a blistering 64, followed that with rounds of 67 and 64, and enjoyed a six-stroke lead at the start of the final round. One of my playing partners was none other than Tommy Bolt, and at one point a funny and revealing incident occurred. I duck-hooked my drive into the woods on the sixth hole and found my ball lying near an old fallen tree. There was no penalty for moving a loose obstruction, but as I was pushing the tree aside, Tommy suddenly appeared and growled at me, "For God's sake, Arnie. Chip it out into the fairway. You've got a six-stroke lead!"

"Tommy," I said evenly to him. "You mind your own business and I'll mind mine." There is, after all, a penalty for accepting advice from and giving advice to other players. More than anything, I wanted him to shut up and go away.

I'd seen a small gap through the trees and was determined to fire my ball through there and up onto the green. Tommy left me, shaking his head as if I were the kid who would never learn. I took my 6-iron and hit the ball cleanly. It flew through the gap and landed on the green. The gallery let loose a tremendous cheer. I think that made Tommy even madder at me!

I held on to shoot 70 and win my first professional golf tournament by four strokes over Jackie

Burke. Talk about timing. I was so elated with my first win that I failed to realize it was one year to the day since I had captured the National Amateur Championship. I believe it was Winnie who finally pointed this sweet irony out to me. My oh my, how my life had changed in just one year!

All was forgiven by the time Tommy and Shirley and Winnie and I got to the fish camp east of Toronto where we had planned, some weeks before, to stop and relax for a couple days before the start of the Labatt tournament in Montreal. I was the new Canadian Open champion, I'd won my first PGA tournament, and, sitting on the end of a small dock fishing and drinking cold beers in the beautiful summer dusk, I couldn't have felt happier or more at peace.

Too bad the goodwill didn't extend to the Bolt cabin, where post-tournament cocktails fueled one of the Bolts' legendary arguments. Shirley and Tommy were pretty well matched in the temper category, and as Winnie and I watched in horror through the screen door from several yards away, the yelling escalated to pan throwing, and soon steak knives were flying through the air.

"Winnie," I said with quiet conviction, "I think our time traveling with Tommy and Shirley just came to an end. We probably ought to get out of here. Don't you agree?"

She agreed, but we wondered how to do it without hurting either Tommy's or Shirley's feelings, assuming one or both survived the night. Shirley's teenage son, Richard, had just shown up, and we had planned to go to Montreal together. Winnie was looking forward to trying out her finishing-school French on Montreal's waiters but was already suffering from morning sickness.

We departed before dawn the next morning, leaving the Bolts a friendly goodbye note. Not a mile down the road, we found Richard by the side of the road with his thumb out. Apparently the fireworks had been too much for him, too. He was hitchhiking, and we offered to give him a ride to Montreal, but he said he was headed back to the United States.

A week or so later, we made the same trip south toward home, and a few weeks after that, I completed my first season as a professional golfer with a record of one win and $7,958 in official prize money. By Christmas, Winnie was well along with our first child and we were talking about buying the piece of land near Latrobe Country Club. Living out of a suitcase, we agreed, was no way to raise a baby, and we really needed a home of our own.

A few weeks after that, we bought the land from Ed Anderson, a wealthy member of Latrobe Country Club who owned perhaps a hundred acres on a hillside across from the club. Mr. Anderson didn't take me seriously when I explained to him I wanted to buy as much of that parcel as he would sell me. I'm afraid he didn't think I would be able to come up with the money. He thought about it a bit and finally agreed to sell me a three-acre lot on the property where so many years before Pap and I used to hunt pheasant and once upon a time came across that extraordinary honeycomb.

What a year, what a beginning it had been.

That's me at age two standing outside my maternal grandparents' (Charles and Inez Morrison) home.

Baldridge School, Latrobe, Pennsylvania, 1938. Have you ever seen a more serious bunch? I'm at the end of the first row at the far right.

The 1945 Latrobe High School varsity golf team. We were known as the Wildcats, and we all had our sights set high—especially that fellow on the far left.

Here I am preparing to take a shot in the Ellwood City tournament when I was in high school. I had some pretty fair success coming up through the junior ranks.

What a wonderful friend I had in Buddy Worsham. That's him standing next to me at the 1946 Hearst National Junior Championship held in California. Stan Weil of Pittsburgh is the other fellow.

This was taken shortly before Buddy died tragically in a car wreck while we were both attending Wake Forest.

The love of my life—the beautiful and irrepressibly charming Winifred Walzer Palmer.

Though Winnie's father was none too keen on the two of us getting married, my family was thrilled. I guess they knew who was getting the better of the deal. From left to right are Charles and Inez Morrison, my maternal grandparents, Winnie, me, my mother, Doris, my brother, Jerry, my father, Deacon, and Alex and Agnes Palmer, my paternal grandparents.

Winnie and me posing for a publicity photo for Wilson Sporting Goods, shortly after I turned pro in 1954.

Sharing a Lone Star (milk, that is) and a laugh at the 1955 Houston Open. Even though the life of a touring pro can be grueling, Winnie is my rock and my foundation.

Winnie has always been a great help and support with my many business and golf ventures. Here we review some correspondence in the first office we had in our house in Latrobe.

As tough as it is out on the course, it's no easier on the sidelines—as this photo of Winnie attests.

Unfortunately, playing golf meant that I was away from home a lot of the time. Here, in 1960, Winnie feeds Amy, while Peggy concentrates on her placemat. The girls are age two and four, respectively.

Posing with my mother, Doris. I've always said that she was the glue that held our family together.

Pap doing two of the things that he loved most—being out on a golf course and spending time with two of his granddaughters.

*Left:*One of my proudest moments on a golf course.
I defeated Bob Sweeny in the final match to win the
1954 U.S. Amateur.
Right: I took seriously my role as a member of the
U.S. Coast Guard and was grateful for all those
experiences taught me.

In 1989 this plaque was dedicated at the Country
Club of Detroit to commemorate my shot to the
eighteenth green as I defeated Bob Sweeny for the
1954 U.S. Amateur.

As the reigning U.S. Amateur champion, I got to play my first competitive rounds in 1955 at Augusta National. It started a love affair that continues to this day.

The great Bob Jones was one of my golfing idols, and it was a thrill to receive his congratulations after winning the Masters in 1960.

Jack Nicklaus helps me on with the traditional green jacket following my win in 1964. As the previous year's champion, he took part in the presentation ceremony.

Just moments before, I'd holed a putt on 18 to wrap up the victory in 1964. What a sweet feeling, and one that I was privileged enough to experience four times in Augusta.

Jack Stephens presided over a 1995 ceremony dedicating this plaque commemorating my four wins at the Masters. It now rests on a drinking fountain behind the 16th tee.

CHAPTER SEVEN

Augusta

Good players win golf tournaments, but great players win major championships. If you hang around golf long enough, you'll hear this chestnut of wisdom stated repeatedly in the media tent and the locker room, especially when a phenom like Tiger Woods or David Duval bursts on the scene and starts winning everything in sight. I'd had winning major golf tournaments in my mind almost from the beginning, at least since those days when I used to beat Sam Snead or Byron Nelson for the National Open in the fairways of my imagination. It was a perception reinforced at every turn by my father, who used to tell me, boy and man, whenever he thought I was in danger of getting too big for my britches, "Listen here, boy. Anytime you think you are the best you can be, just remember there is always some guy out there just waiting to beat you. Don't brag about what you've accomplished and don't tell people what you're gonna do—keep your mouth shut, keep your mind on your own business, and *show* them!"

Pap, in almost every respect, was a modest man, but he burned with a wisdom and intensity about what it took to accomplish great things that was far beyond his own experience. His way of looking at things would prove invaluable to me.

During the next two years on tour, 1956 and 1957, I won six PGA tournaments and nearly $50,000 in prize money, money that enabled me to pay back my father and Shube Walzer (who slowly came around to the realization that I would, indeed, be able to support his only daughter after all) and pay for the modest six-room house that Lou Pevarnik built for us on that sloping tract of land that overlooks Latrobe Country Club. I wanted a house with a "modern" look and feel, whereas Winnie had her heart set on something colonial in style. We compromised on a style Lou called a "colonial ranch," with three bedrooms and two baths and a small carport and an extra room for Peggy, our one-year-old, who arrived about the time I was putting out on the 72nd hole at Houston, in late February of '56. I remember flying home all night a nervous wreck, aware only that Winnie had gone into labor, uncertain of the outcome or any complications, imagining all sorts of frightening first-time-father scenarios. By the time I reached Newark and trans-ferred to another flight to Allentown (in eastern Pennsylvania), the sun was coming up. It was a stunning winter's morning and Winnie's aunt Peg (the baby's namesake) was there to pick me up, in-forming me that I was the proud papa of a little girl and that everyone, except perhaps for me, was doing just fine.

Winnie and the baby both looked radiant that morning. When I got to the hospital and finally held my new daughter, I was smiling from ear to ear. But frankly, I was exhausted after my all-night race home from Texas. After a couple hours of sleep and a hot shower, I returned to the hospital even happier about our new prosperity but eventually found myself wondering what to do next. It was Winnie, as usual, who solved the dilemma. "Arnie, you're driving yourself crazy. Even worse, you're driving *me* crazy. Go get your golf bag and go to Baton Rouge," she told me sternly from her hospital bed.

So I did just that, and I recall thinking, as I made the lengthy trip, how useful it would be if I had my own airplane that I could fly home at the drop of a hat. It's no coincidence that at the conclusion of that season, I went out to our small airport at Latrobe to see Babe Krinock about taking flying lessons, the beginning of another of my lifelong passions.

Through the early part of the Tour in '57, while waiting for our house to be finished on the ridge, Winnie and I carted baby Peggy and an unbelievable assortment of parenting paraphernalia from one tournament stop to another. Fortunately, we weren't alone in this nomadic attempt to have a "normal" family life. A number of younger Tour players and their wives dragged an assortment of household goods, baby-sitters, and playpens along with them; we sometimes filled up motels with these extended Tour families.

Pleasant as that often was, it was a major relief to finally move into our new house that autumn. Thanks to my four wins that year—including a win at Houston where, fittingly, one-year-old Peggy aped adorably for press photographers while sitting in a crystal trophy filled with prize money—we paid Lou

Pevarnik in cash, $17,000 for our house, including all the amenities, like the $600 bay window Winnie simply *had* to have. That Christmas, we planted the first of a succession of evergreen trees around the house, and every holiday season for many years after that we made a little family ritual of adding another one.

Finally having a home was a major relief to us all.

Maybe even more important to our family fortunes, that same year, 1957, I edged a little bit closer to the tournament I perhaps wanted to win as much as any at that time—the Masters.

As I've said countless times over the years, from the first moment I walked onto the property and the golf course of the Augusta National Golf Club in 1955, I knew—because I could feel and even smell it—that there was no place and no other golf tournament quite like Augusta, Georgia, and the Masters. It was where the best players in the game annually convened at the behest of Bob Jones, the club's cofounder and the tournament's patron saint. It was a tournament run with such autocratic perfection by New York banker Clifford Roberts, you simply felt *privileged* to have been invited to play there.

Which reminds me of a darkly amusing little incident that preceded my first Masters win in 1958. After a win at St. Petersburg a few weeks before, and a loss in a Monday playoff to Howie Johnson at Wilmington's Azalea Open, I arrived at Augusta in the wee hours of the morning.

My pal Dow Finsterwald had arranged for us to team up and play with Ben Hogan and Jackie Burke

in a practice round. After my bone-wearying midnight drive across South Carolina (to say nothing of
the deflation I felt at losing the playoff) I went out
on the course that morning and played abysmally. I
felt doubly bad that Dow had to carry us both—he
played brilliantly and we collected $35 apiece off
the wager. A little while afterward, as we were
changing in the club locker room, I heard Ben
Hogan remark to Jackie, "Tell me something,
Jackie. How the hell did Palmer get an invitation to
the Masters?"

That really stung me. I'll never know if Hogan
knew I overheard the comment. But he certainly
was aware that I was nearby and *could* have heard
it. I knew he was probably the most precise shotmaker who ever played the game and no particular
fan of my style of play, having once said of my
game, "Palmer's swing might work for him, but no
one else should try it." In any event, the question
burned me up and set my mind on showing him
why the hell I'd been invited to the Masters. So perhaps I owe Ben a tip of the cap for helping me focus
my mind on my business the way Pap always
insisted I would have to in order to win a major golf
tournament.

I went out and shot opening rounds of 70, 73, and
68, and arrived Sunday afternoon at the infamous
12th hole, arguably the toughest par 3 in tournament
golf, with a one-stroke lead over the field. My concentration was great and my adrenaline really
pumping—a bit too much, perhaps. My tee shot carried over the green and embedded in the soft turf

between the putting surface and the rear bunker. Walking toward the green, I had no idea the ball was embedded and fully expected to be putting from the fringe. When I saw the situation, I called the rules official over and explained to him that I intended to take relief without a penalty. Because of the heavy rains earlier that week, the tournament was being played under wet-weather rules. This meant that a plugged ball could be lifted, cleaned, and dropped without a penalty.

The official, Arthur Lacey, shook his head and said, "You don't do that at Augusta."

"I beg your pardon?" I replied. "We're playing wet-weather rules."

"No, sir," he said. "You can't do that. You've got to play it as it lies."

For a moment I thought about my dilemma, trying to keep my growing anger at this injustice at bay. Finally, I told him I would play *two* balls and appeal his verdict to the tournament rules committee.

"Nossir," he said crisply. "You cannot do that either."

Now I was really steaming inside, but I tried not to let him know that.

"Well," I said, "that's exactly what I'm going to do."

I dug the ball out with my wedge, moving it only about eighteen inches, then chipped onto the green and two-putted for a double-bogey five that apparently dropped me from the lead. Then I walked back to the original spot of the dispute and reached for another ball from my caddie, Nathaniel "Ironman" Avery, and placed it at the same spot on the fringe where my tee shot had come to rest. I chipped the second ball a few feet from the hole and coaxed the putt into the cup for a par 3. I'm sure there were plenty of people in the gallery who were certain they'd just watched Arnie Palmer disqualify himself from the Masters. Ken Venturi, who was contending that afternoon, was among those who felt he'd been cheated by my actions at the hole. But I knew the rule, and I believed I was well within my rights to do what I had done.

At the par-5 13th, after hitting a good drive to the middle of the fairway, I saw Mr. Jones coming down the fairway in the familiar green riding cart he used in those days to get around the course. That made me nervous as hell, but I also wanted to show him what I was made of, so I took out a 3-wood and smoked my second shot to the rear of the green. I made the twenty-foot putt for eagle and parred 14. Then, in the fairway at 15, I was summoned over to meet with members of the tournament's rules committee, all of whom had gathered around Mr. Jones's cart. Jonathon Winters, the committee chairman, said to me: "Mr. Palmer, the committee has ruled in your favor. You will have a three at the twelfth hole."

That was music to my ears, and I finished 18 with a birdie, for a final-round 73 and a four-round total of 284. To be honest, I was so tense and focused, I don't even remember the walk up 18—and hardly remember the birdie putt that gave me the one-stroke victory. I left the green and went into the clubhouse to be with Winnie and have a Coke and a calming cigarette, while a dozen players still on the course had a run at my posted total. I remember telling Winnie that I'd done all I could and she gave me her usual kiss and hug, win or lose. Doug Ford and Fred Hawkins both finished strongly, but they missed tying putts on 18, and my 284 held up. I'd captured my first major golf tournament.

Curiously, there wasn't a lot of hoopla and cere-mony surrounding the presentation of the coveted green jacket at Augusta in those days. As the spring darkness gathered around us, the club's members assembled on the practice putting green, and Mr. Roberts made the official presentation of the trophy, the green jacket, and the first-place check of $14,000. My parents weren't there to enjoy this breakthrough moment, and even the galleries had pretty well dispersed by the time I went off to fetch the Chrysler. Winnie, our traveling secretary and accountant, paid Ironman his wages plus an extra percentage for the win. A group of us, including sev-eral people from Wilson Sporting Goods, drove downtown to the Town Tavern for an impromptu victory dinner. The festivities were interrupted a short while later, though, when someone from the club tracked us down and informed me that there was a bit of a "problem" with the check Winnie had written Ironman.

In all her excitement, instead of writing out a

check for $1,400, she had written him a check for $14,000!

We still laugh about that slipup.

Another amusing sidelight from that first major victory: That was the year Winnie, who didn't have much in the way of nice jewelry, got to be friendly with the owner of a fine jewelry store on Broad Street, not far from the old Richmond Hotel where we were staying in Augusta. Earlier in the week, she had picked out a single-link golf bracelet that cost $75—far above our budget—but didn't tell me about her "extravagant" purchase until that night at the Town Tavern.

An amusing kind of superstition set in then and there, I guess. Every year we returned to the Masters Winnie joked that she really had to purchase something we couldn't afford or else I wouldn't have a chance of winning the tournament! She devotedly did her part, and for more years than I care to remember we left town on Masters Sunday with expensive new shoes and outfits. I'm happy to say we still have a laugh about that, too.

Winning that first Masters was a real shot in the arm in several important ways. First, it meant that I was now playing in a whole new league of golfers— winners of major golf championships—and the opportunities that newly forged status would suddenly bring my way would inevitably lead me to Cleveland attorney Mark McCormack. Mark became my lifelong business manager, friend, and agent shortly afterward. That mercifully relieved Winnie of many of the accounting and management tasks that threatened to overwhelm both her and the small guest room in our house where she kept the books and arranged my schedule.

But perhaps more important, on a deeper psychological level, winning that first of my seven majors as a professional told me something I needed to know about myself—that with the right kind of focus and hard work and maybe a little bit of luck, I could be the best player in the game. What a dizzying thought! Before slipping on that first green jacket, I must admit, I used to privately quip to friends that winning golf tournaments was really the most important thing to me—that winning major golf tournaments, for goodness' sake, wasn't *everything*.

In some respects, I still believe this. The game of golf, after all, is far bigger than one individual's achievements or even the prestige of winning major tournament championships. Even then, I suppose I sensed that nothing I might ever accomplish in professional golf would match the excitement and provide the kind of satisfaction winning the National Amateur had done for me. That was a tournament I never expected to win—and it changed my life in ways I couldn't have even imagined.

In contrast, as strange as it may sound, I always had a gut feeling that the Masters title would eventually be mine—that is to say, it was simply a matter of time before I won the tournament. Part of that came from the way, year after year, I studied the course and learned how to play it, and part of it came from the almost childlike excitement I always felt going up Magnolia Lane each spring at Augusta National. Perhaps there are moments in life when we can feel destiny's invisible hand brushing our shoulder.

I always felt *something* powerful in Augusta, and I knew my time would come.

It's funny how stories, once they enter the public domain, get changed around and sometimes transformed into myth. One such tale concerns my first meeting with President Dwight D. Eisenhower. A persistent myth tells how we met and played golf after that first Masters win, but that wasn't the case at all. In fact, I met President Eisenhower later that year at Laurel Valley Golf Club (the golf club in Ligonier I helped found in 1958 and have represented on tour all these years), and we didn't actually play our first round together until after my 1960 Masters win. I'll get to that in a bit.

At Augusta in 1959, it's fair to say, I suffered the first of my *major* stumbles, resulting from the same aggressive style of play that seemed to endear me to the press and so many golf fans. I once quipped to a reporter who asked about my "patented" final-round charges that perhaps the reason people enjoyed watching me play so much was that they could relate to my predicament: I was often where they were as I came down the stretch, in the rough, the trees, or up the creek. The same go-for-broke kind of play that won me seven majors perhaps cost me at least that many more. But that's life and that's golf.

Fittingly, it was a creek—infamous Rae's Creek in front of good old number 12—that sank my hopes at the 1959 Masters. Leading the tournament with seven holes to play, I plunked my tee shot in the water and staggered off the hole with a triple bogey. I recovered with a birdie at 15, briefly retaking the lead, but then missed an easy three-footer for par on 17, and failed to make a four-foot birdie at 18, missing at the worst possible moment. Art Wall, on the other hand, executed one of the most brilliant finishes ever at Augusta, with birdies at five of the final six holes, and rightly donned the green jacket, nipping Cary Middlecoff by a stroke. My disappointment was immense. I'd had the tournament in my grasp but had been unable to close.

On the positive side, though, if I fondly recall anything about that Masters, it is my growing awareness of how the galleries enjoyed watching me perform in the clutch, their hopes sometimes living and dying on every shot. In those days, the Masters was still a wide-open golf tournament for spectators and a pretty low-key affair. As unimaginable as it may sound now—especially if you've tried to get tickets to the event recently—you could stroll up to the gate off Washington Road and pay five bucks for a day ticket and walk just about anywhere behind the greatest names in the game. There was a relaxed but almost reverential calmness about the place. Women often wore dresses and men sometimes wore neckties, out of respect for the tournament created by Bob Jones and Clifford Roberts, but the genteel atmosphere only made the final acts that much more dramatic. A brilliant management stroke on Mr. Roberts's part was using volunteer soldiers from nearby Fort Gordon (in those days it was called "Camp" Gordon) to man the scoreboards. It may have been in 1959, the second year that the tournament was televised, that I first looked up and saw one of the scoreboard GIs holding a small sign announcing the presence of "Arnie's Army." That gave me an electric thrill, I can tell you, as I acknowledged the tribute, to think that in just five years' time my fans had grown from a few hometown folks following me around the Country Club of Detroit to a whole *army* politely rooting for me at Augusta.

Nineteen sixty was a watershed year for America. With the election of the youngest president in history and talk of space exploration literally pushing our collective vision to new heights, Americans in general were reaching for new personal horizons, trying new things and forging new paths. As I've said before, it was a moment when many Americans, infused with the optimism of youth and prosperity, secure in their national identity, felt they could achieve almost anything—if they were only bold enough to try.

Count Arnold Palmer in those ranks. At the outset of the 1960 season, with my home life settled and, thanks to my new partnership with Mark McCormack, the first significant money from endorsement deals beginning to ease my natural worries about supporting my family, I was determined to achieve more than I ever had before on the golf course. That effort started very well, in the weeks leading up to the Masters, with wins at Texas, Baton Rouge, and Pensacola. Not insignificantly to me, this was also the year of the first Desert Classic, which I won. They added Bob Hope's name to the marquee the next year, and it became one of my favorite stops in the game, as my four subsequent wins perhaps suggest.

In any case, my game had never felt sharper, and my attitude almost verged on cocky in the weeks preceding the Masters. I suppose it's a measure of that confidence that, at Pensacola, after I complained bitterly to George Low about shooting 73 in the final round, having to birdie six of the last ten holes and barely pulling out the win, he snapped at me with perfect Scottish indignation: "For God's sake, Arnold. You made 78 into 73—and won the tournament. Count your blessings."

He was right, of course. The truth was, though, I was far too busy concentrating on my game to stop and count any blessings. As a measure of how my thinking had changed, I'd set my sights on winning majors and knew that the first big test came at Augusta, where larger-than-ever galleries and a national television audience would be waiting to see if I could make up for the previous year's collapse.

I birdied the first two holes of the tournament and took the first-round lead with a 67. Despite a blister on my foot (which I eased by padding my shoe with a torn scorecard halfway through the round) and my lackluster second-round 73, I maintained that one-stroke lead over Hogan and Finsterwald at the halfway post. That good fortune continued in round three, when no thanks to my shaky putter I was able to get around in 72 and still keep a one-stroke lead over Finsterwald, Boros, Hogan, and Venturi. Just behind them was a twenty-four-year-old South African who'd won the 1959 British Open and struck me as one of the most dedicated young golfers I'd ever seen, Gary Player.

With record crowds expected that Sunday, it promised to be a dramatic finish. Winnie and I were renting a small house with Ken and Susie Bowman, our friends and neighbors, not far off Washington Road (the first of a succession of private homes we would occupy during Masters week), and, as Winnie likes to joke, she had a hunch it might be a good week for Team Palmer. I basically never heard a word she said to me all week. She could have asked for a divorce, and I would have only grunted and nodded, so strong was my concentration as I practiced my putting on the house's short green carpet.

Augusta's glassy greens were capable of giving me living nightmares. Admittedly, I was never a strong fast-green putter, and my reputation for ramming putts into the cup from all over the place stems, in large part, I think, from my ability to make comeback putts that had rolled precarious distances past the hole. At that time, standing over a ball, I never had any doubt whatsoever that the ball was going to roll into the cup. And when it missed, as more than a few did, I honestly was surprised and not a little angry about it.

Casper, Boros, and Player all faded fast on that Sunday, shooting numbers in the mid-70s, and Ben

Hogan, who attracted perhaps the largest gallery, surgically hit greens but putted woefully to a disappointing 76. That left three of us to decide the outcome—Finsty, Venturi, and me. Paired together, the two of them played what appeared to be a match-play final, each of them winning holes but neither gaining much ground on the other. Finally, they arrived at 18, all even. Dow missed a difficult eight-footer to save par, and Kenny parred to finish with a two-under 70, and a total of 283 for the tournament.

Out on the course, I was chain-smoking L&M cigarettes and swigging Cokes to try and keep my nerves at bay. Starting on the back nine, a stroke behind the leaders, I got a lift when I saw one of those scoreboard signs saying, "Go Arnie. Arnie's Army." I had two excellent birdie chances coming up at 13 and 15, but poor chipping cost me both opportunities. After a dreadful chip at 15, I flipped my wedge disgustedly toward Ironman. He fixed me with a stare I'll never forget. "Mr. Palmer," he said in a low rumble, "are we chokin'?" His scowl was eerily reminiscent of the disapproving glare Pap used to give me as a kid whenever I threw a club or failed to keep my mind on my job.

Ironman wasn't the greatest caddie. I'd be less than honest if I said he was. His distances were often inaccurate, and I relied, instead, on my own calculations and knowledge of the course to get around Augusta. But his understanding of what made me tick was perhaps instinctive and definitely profound. I stared back at him and realized he was right—I was foolishly beating on myself instead of taking care of the business of playing the golf course.

The closing three holes at Augusta are tough birdie prospects. At 16, the demanding par 3 over water, I put my 3-iron shot safely on the green but twenty-five feet below the hole. Because of the severe contour of the green, I was unable to see the cup from where my ball lay. I chose to leave the flag in the cup, an option not available to players today, and struck the ball firmly. Had the pin been out, it might have dropped, but it struck the pin and stopped a couple of feet away instead. I made the par and went to 17, commenting to an official that I would have to make two birdies to beat Ken Venturi, who was already in the clubhouse and, I was later told, already being measured for his green jacket.

A good drive at 17 was followed by something less than a perfect 8-iron shot that left me thirty feet from the cup. Twice I took my stance and twice I backed away. The uphill line was much the same as the three-footer I'd missed there in the clutch the year before. I decided I wasn't going to be short this time and took my stance for a third time, gathered my concentration, then hit the ball hard. It rolled up the slight incline and seemed to stop on the very edge of the cup—then dropped in.

I jumped excitedly into the air, punching skyward with my fist. I don't think I ever heard the roar of the gallery, though everyone later talked about what a sustained excitement that putt created. People sprinted from the green to find a spot along the 18th fairway. I made one of my best drives of the week and struck a 6-iron approach that dropped the ball about five feet from the cup.

Walking up that final fairway, having just hit maybe the finest clutch shot of my career to that point, I knew I now faced the biggest putt of my career. Even though I was probably as nervous as I'd ever been on a golf course, I knew I could make the putt. My father and mother were there, along with Winnie and Cheech and Ron, and I calmed myself by thinking of my father's familiar advice to keep myself still over the putt and make a smooth stroke.

This time I didn't hesitate, but just as I was about to putt, I heard an announcer chattering excitedly in the television booth above the green. Distracted, I looked up and saw a sheepish Jim McKay. I smiled at Jim, then refocused on the task of somehow getting that ball across five dangerous feet and into the cup. I took my stance, and stroked the ball, and watched it curl lazily into the hole for a birdie. I stayed in my familiar hunched-over stance for a beat or two longer, as the crowd roared and Jim McKay shouted over and over that I'd won the 1960 Masters.

After that I looked up, grinned, walked a couple steps, and once again jumped ecstatically into the air.

There's no feeling quite as satisfying as entering the media room to face the press after winning a big golf tournament—or, at the other end of the spectrum, as potentially painful when you've blown it. During my game's peak years, which I consider to have been roughly between 1958 and 1972, I had more than my share of both experiences.

Nineteen sixty has been called the "Golden Year" in American golf, for several reasons. To begin with, thanks to television, millions more people than ever were suddenly watching golf and taking up the game in record numbers. Fueling the grassroots explosion, every major tournament that summer seemed to come down to last-second heroics like my birdie-birdie finish at Augusta.

Others have correctly noted that the summer was golden because representatives from three distinct eras of the game were contending for the same recognition of being the top golfer in the world. Ben Hogan was a living legend and symbol of the game's postwar resurgence. As he would prove at Cherry Hills later that summer, though slowed a bit by age and the effects of his near-fatal car crash, he was still the man to beat in major golf tournaments. To the growing number of recruits who followed me and counted themselves part of "Arnie's Army," I represented the optimism and excitement of the game at the moment.

Finally, whispering of things to come, there was also a stout young amateur phenom from Ohio State with a butch haircut and a high fade, who announced his presence that summer by simply posting the lowest amateur score in Open history. His name was Jack Nicklaus.

It was undoubtedly also a golden time to write

about the game of golf, and luckily for us there were
some simply marvelous reporters and writers doing
it. I vividly remember walking into the interview
room minutes after winning the 1960 Masters and
receiving the hearty congratulations from a sea of
faces I'd come to trust and admire. My curmud-
geonly old friend Bob Drum was there, along with
Tom Birks from the Pittsburgh *Sun-Telegraph* and
Phil Gundelfinger from the third Pittsburgh news-
paper, the *Post-Gazette.* I remember seeing Jack
Clowser from Cleveland and Irwin Smallwood from
Greensboro, Dana Mozley from New York's *Daily
News* and Link Werden from the *Times,* Ron Green
from Charlotte, Charlie Bartlett from the *Chicago
Tribune,* Nelson Cullenward from San Francisco,
Herb Graffis, the late great Jim Murray from Los
Angeles. Joe Looney was there from Boston and
Bob Sommers from the *Washington Post,* Larry
Robinson from the *World Telegram,* Dave Eisenberg
from the *Journal American,* Al Laney from the
Herald Tribune, Dan Jenkins from the *Ft. Worth
Star-Telegram,* Fred Byrod from Philadelphia, Al
Wright from *Sports Illustrated,* the eloquent Herb
Wind from *The New Yorker,* and the ambassadorial
Alistair Cooke from Britain. Watching from off in
the corner, down from the broadcast booth, were
Chris Schenkel and Jim McKay and the ever-dapper
Jack Whitaker.

I'm sure I've missed some other important
writers. But that's still a pretty small fraternity compared to the monstrous packs of journalists that
cover a major golf tournament these days. On that

note, permit me to say that it surprises and dismays me a bit to realize how aggressive, impersonal, and controversy-driven much of today's sports reporting has become, even in golf—the last refuge, as someone once described it, of the true sporting man. I'm sure some will brand me an old fogey for saying this, but considering the way gossip-column and tabloid-style reporting have crept into golf writing in the past decade or so, I miss the days when reporters judged a player largely by his public actions and the way he conducted his affairs on or around the field of competition, and left his private affairs out of their columns. I daresay few of us could stand up to the scrutiny and sometimes mean-spirited reporting that certain charismatic modern players—John Daly and Tiger Woods come immediately to mind, in this respect—are subjected to. Both of these gifted young men have had to grow up in full public view, as it were, barraged by constant psycho-analysis or criticism from sideline "experts," who won't grant them the benefit of being able to make mistakes, and learn from them, as all young men must do.

I counted many of these scribes of my time as good friends, and respected the rest as men who wrote about golf with the best interests of the game at heart. There is no question that their writings about Jack and Gary and me stoked the public excitement about the blossoming PGA Tour and transformed all of us into larger-than-life figures. It made us stars and wealthy men, and we owe them a deep debt of gratitude.

Some of these reporters came to my home in Latrobe, and we'd traveled thousands of miles together on the PGA Tour, and in doing so a definite environment of mutual trust had developed among us. I didn't have to say something was "off the record" because, typically, they knew when to stop writing. They appreciated that, win or lose, I spoke straight from the heart, and I appreciated that they worked hard to get the story right—neither hesitating to praise my exploits when they deserved it, nor failing to hold my feet to the fire when I'd blown a tournament I should have won. After hours, we loved nothing better than to share a beer, play cards, and shoot the breeze.

Given this intimacy, which I'm certain some today might criticize as being "too cozy," I can only recall a couple of incidents where reporters took what I regarded as unfair shots at me in print. Early on I learned the value of cultivating friendships with these opinion makers by taking a genuine interest in their work and lives. Not to beat a dead horse about it, I sometimes think both players and reporters of today are guilty of having forgotten—or simply abandoned—this old-fashioned ethic of mutual respect and cooperation. It would be good for golf were it to return.

Many of those same fine wordsmiths chronicled my collapse at the 1961 Masters in minute detail. It still makes me wince to think about it.

Here's what happened:

My opening-round 68 was good enough for the lead, and I kept it going with a 69 on Friday. That meant I'd been in first place after each of six consecutive rounds over two years at Augusta. But on Saturday, the streak came to a halt when I skidded to a sloppy 73 and Gary Player, capitalizing on everyone else's mistakes, vaulted four strokes into the lead. Sunday dawned dark and stormy and the round was washed out. Such a wait can be murder on a leader's psyche, and the delay seemed to take a toll on Gary, who was otherwise one of the best front-runners who ever played the game, a real mongoose who never let up.

His game slipped and he finished with a two-over 74. Meanwhile, I recovered my putting touch and "charged." I came to the final tee three under for the day, holding a one-stroke lead, needing just par to become the first man in history to win consecutive Masters championships.

Then I simply blew it.

My tee shot was fine, slightly down the left side of the fairway. I walked to my ball feeling really good about the situation. All I had left was a 7-iron approach shot I'd executed dozens of times. As I neared my ball, however, I saw someone at the gallery rope motioning me over. It was none other than my good old friend George Low, looking dapper as ever in his jacket and necktie. "Nice going, boy," he said to me, patting my arm affectionately. "You won it."

I made the biggest mistake you can make in such a situation—I accepted his congratulations prematurely and, in doing so, completely destroyed my concentration.

As I stood over the ball, my brain seemed to completely shut down. I was suddenly unsure what I should be thinking about. Instead of seeing nothing around me except the business at hand—which is what any player needing birdie or par to finish and win at Augusta must do—I suddenly seemed to notice everything around me, the color of the sky, the expectant faces of the people in the gallery, you name it. The pin was in its customary Sunday placement, front left, behind the bunker. I remember telling myself to focus only on getting the ball on the green and two-putting. That was where I made my big mistake. As Pap had always sternly advised me in such situations, I should have been thinking only about swinging the club properly and keeping my head still through the impact. Instead, I lifted my head a little and came out of the shot too soon. The ball went right into the bunker.

I compounded that mistake with a worse one. Instead of taking a moment to compose my thoughts and regain my cool, I hurried to the ball and struck an explosive shot that sent it flying out of the sand, across the green, and down a slope toward the television tower. Now, dying inside, I needed to get down in two simply to get into a playoff with Gary. My fourth shot ran fifteen feet past the hole, and my attempt for bogey failed. I'd double bogeyed the final hole to lose the Masters by a stroke.

The friendly fraternity of reporters I faced in the pressroom now felt more like a hanging tribunal. They appeared almost as shell-shocked as I, and their questions were tough, as I recall, but fair. After all, I'd blown it and the whole world had been watching and what was there to say? I had no excuses to make.

I remember walking briskly to our car afterward, in quiet fury and agony, feeling as awful as I ever had coming off a golf course. In self-disgust, I slammed my golf shoes onto the front seat, denting the lovely engraved silver cigarette case Clifford Roberts had presented as a gift to the players' wives that year. I really knocked the hell out of that little box—and later felt pretty bad about that.

What really tore me up inside was the knowledge that I'd lost because I'd failed to do what Pap had always told me to do—stay focused until the job is finished. This wasn't the first tournament I'd blown in such a manner. It was simply the biggest to that point. Unfortunately, there would soon be others.

Today, that same dented silver box sits on my office desk in Latrobe. I use it to hold business and membership cards. It also holds a lot of memories and a painful reminder.

One of the first Augusta members to privately express his sympathies to me was Clifford Roberts.

That might seem a bit odd to those who knew Mr. Roberts only from his public persona as the austere, dogmatic, seemingly unsympathetic chairman of Augusta National Golf Club.

But both Winnie and I had gotten to know Clifford Roberts pretty well since I won the tournament in 1958, and we found him to be a deep and surprisingly warm man who cared immensely about Augusta National and the Masters and what they symbolized not only in the world of golf but in all of sport. As Frank Stranahan had discovered the hard way, Mr. Roberts could be a ruthlessly unforgiving presence if you dared cross him, challenged a club policy, or behaved in a manner he deemed unsuitable. He believed to his marrow that if you made a rule, you lived by it.

There's no question that the tournament rose to the prominence it enjoys today because of the personal drive, conviction, and vision of Clifford Roberts. Among other things, he warned that if and when the prize money offered at the Masters—or any golf tournament, for that matter—became the primary attraction to the game's best players, the tournament would be in danger of losing its purpose, integrity, and uniqueness. A highly astute New York banker whose private client list read like a Who's Who of business and political leaders (including President Eisenhower), Mr. Roberts was convinced beyond a shadow of a doubt that the major threat to the golf tournament he and Bob Jones created to celebrate the game's finest traditions, the only factor that could really undermine the Masters, was *too much* money.

I think about his concerns these days, as purses continue to spiral to unimaginable heights and an increasing number of top young players seem almost blissfully ignorant of the game's history and traditions, the people who made the game what it is today, and above all the fact that it is at heart still a *game*—not a business. It's true that my dramatic success in the 1960s and 1970s—particularly my domination of the Masters between 1958 and 1964—helped fuel the popularity of tournament golf and provided the basis for my success in the business world. But I never confused the two, the love of competitively playing the game, and the good fortune of enjoying the financial rewards that come from playing it well. It greatly distresses me to hear modern players base their decisions to play in this tournament or that one simply on the prize-money values. It angers me to think there have been name players who snubbed a Masters invitation simply because they didn't think the money was good enough or didn't care for the way Mr. Roberts or his successors as chairman operated the tournament.

Speaking from personal experience, I can tell you Mr. Roberts took a while to size you up, and I, for one, was almost scared to death of the man for years. But as our friendship grew, I found him a surprisingly warm, generous, and even compassionate man who quietly did things for a broad range of people that the public had obviously never heard boo about.

His close relationship with President Eisenhower, in my book, spoke volumes about the man's character and integrity. As our own friendship deepened with the years, we enjoyed many hours of pleasant, frank conversation, either at Augusta or out at Eldorado in Palm Desert, where he went for a month or so every winter, on a host of subjects near and dear to both our hearts, everything from politics to putting surfaces, Wall Street to world war.

The man was as tough as nails. But he was also as decent as the day is long, and brilliant. Far less known, beneath that stern headmaster exterior he possessed a schoolboy's wry sense of humor. One year, just prior to what Augusta's members know as "Jamboree," a club tournament that takes place two weeks before the Masters, Mr. Roberts ordered the water level in the pond by the 16th tee drawn down by about eight inches. He then had workmen construct a small boardwalk across the pond before raising the water level back to normal. At a critical moment during the members' tournament, Cliff strolled expressionlessly off the tee and straight out onto the pond—proving, to anyone who doubted it, that the godlike chairman of Augusta National Golf Club really could walk on water!

I was pleased when, around 1965, Cliff invited me to make suggestions about how the golf course could be improved. My actual belief was that there wasn't a whole lot to do—that Alister Mackenzie's wonderful design ought not to be tampered with very much. For such a sturdy guardian of tradition, some of the changes Mr. Roberts said he wanted to make surprised me. For example, he wanted to create a new lake that would stretch almost the entire length between tee and green of the par-3 fourth. But I argued that a lake in that spot simply wouldn't fit the tradition of the course. He accepted that argument and the lake was never built (and I hope it never is). He also wanted to switch the greens from Bermuda to bent-grass surfaces, and I wasn't a bit keen about that idea, either, because it would drastically alter their character, in my view. Bermuda is a tougher, coarser grass that causes a ball to bounce slightly when it lands. Part of the challenge of hitting a ball onto a green at Augusta National was allowing for the tricky undulations of the putting surfaces.

When they put in the smoother, finer bent grass, some of those undulations had to be flattened out or else the greens would have become unplayably fast. Today, the course's putting surfaces are extremely fast, as you may know from the ritual spring chorus of gently complaining Tour players, owing to the firm bent-grass surfaces, but I'm not sure they are any better than the old Bermuda greens, which required a lot of imagination and courage to get your ball close.

My major contribution to Augusta's endless process of re-creation, I suppose, was to suggest that the tees on holes one, two, seven, eight, nine, 15, and 18 be moved back to accommodate the longer modern game. Mr. Roberts also championed the creation of the club's adjacent par-3 course, and I fully agreed with him that it was an excellent idea— adding a bit of useful mirth and even comic relief to the air of tension that normally precedes the high drama of Masters weekend.

Sometimes, as the saying in golf goes, it's better to be lucky than good, and at the Masters of 1962, I think I was a little bit of both. As someone in the press tent wrote, that particular Masters showcased the best and the worst of Arnold Palmer's style of golf. Doggedly determined to make up for my embarrassing collapse at 18 the year prior, I played superb golf for three rounds, shooting 70, 66, and 69 to take a two-stroke lead heading into Sunday's action.

A record crowd estimated at 40,000 was on hand, and I began the fourth round miserably by missing a short, easy putt for par on the first hole. My problems were compounded after that by a mind that seemed to drift in and out of focus. I hit balls into the woods and missed putts I normally could have made in my sleep. As a consequence, I finished the outward nine in a dreadful 39 and after fifteen holes found myself two behind Gary Player and Dow Finsterwald. In retrospect, I was lucky to be just two back—it could have been much worse.

Golf is a game composed of human failings, and I don't suppose, given the way the first fifteen holes had gone, that anybody in the gallery gave me much hope of catching Gary and Dow—especially after I missed yet another green on 16 and faced a difficult forty-five-foot chip to try to get up and down for par. As the gallery was being moved and I stood looking

over my dismal situation with disgust no doubt
showing on my face, I happened to overhear on-
course commentator Jimmy Demaret remarking to
his audience that I faced a nearly impossible shot,
that I'd be extremely lucky just to get down in two.
The much-needed birdie was unthinkable. "This
shot will perhaps put Arnold Palmer out of contention for the Masters championship."

I think I turned and looked at Jimmy wearing a
little smirk of exasperation. I can tell you his comments really revved me up inside, and when I
chipped the ball into the hole and the crowd went
crazy, I felt a rush of adrenaline that seemed to have
been missing all day long. The charge was now on,
in my mind. At 17 I made a twenty-footer for a
birdie and at 18 missed my birdie attempt and had to
settle for par. The Masters championship had its
first-ever three-way tie.

Al Wright of *Sports Illustrated* described the
drama as "characters by Saki, plot by Hitchcock"
and also cheekily noted, though fairly enough, that I
blew my two-stroke lead that Sunday "by hitting
golf shots that would have sent a duffer scurrying
over to his pro for help."

It was true. I was damned lucky to have made the
playoff. But, once again, I'd also pulled off the
miraculous shot when I had to.

The playoff threesome provided an interesting mix
of styles. Dow epitomized regal conservatism—
always taking the intelligent and safe path to greens,
seldom risking his gains with a chancy, low-percentage
shot. Gary, as I've noted, was the complete grinder,

the hardworking little opportunist who never seemed to back up and always remained upbeat. I suppose I was by far the most unpredictable factor in the group, prone to either charge for the green jacket or blow myself out of contention with a risky shot. After the first nine holes on Monday, it appeared to be the latter option. I started poorly and trailed by three at the turn. Dow's putter utterly abandoned him, too—perhaps mental exhaustion had set in. For his part, reliable as a Swiss watch, Gary valiantly battled Augusta's lethal greens to finish with a solid one-under 71.

I suppose I was the really "lucky" one of the threesome that afternoon. My form of the first three rounds returned on the back nine, and I ripped off birdies on four of the first five holes down the backstretch to take the lead and held it to earn my third green jacket in five years. My 68 beat Gary by three strokes and Dow by nine.

I admitted in the pressroom afterward that I felt very fortunate to have won the tournament and really looked forward to the day when I might walk up the 18th hole with the tournament safely in hand, actually able to enjoy the experience of knowing I didn't have to pull off another miracle shot to win my favorite golf tournament.

They laughed at this remark, already punching out wire stories and newspaper dispatches about how my "heroic" putting had once again saved the day at Augusta National. I suppose some of them thought I was kidding.

*   *   *

The Masters of 1962 was significant and perhaps even lucky for me in a couple far less visible but meaningful ways. If you had been a part of the frenzied crowds following the playoff on Monday, you might have noticed a trim young fellow with a portable phone in hand, battling the galleries as they rushed from one vantage point to the next. His name was Donald Webster ("As in dictionary") Giffin, but he was Doc to just about everybody on or around the Tour. Doc had just left his job that year as a sportswriter at the *Pittsburgh Press* to join the PGA Tour as its press secretary. His job that Monday was to phone in the hole-by-hole action on the course to the crowded pressroom, where wire-service reporters and writers sat poised on deadline.

Four years later, after admiring Doc's hustle and organizational skills from afar, I spotted him crossing the empty grillroom of Rio Pinar at the old Florida Citrus Open (which eventually became the Bay Hill Invitational, by the way), where I was grabbing a bite alone and doing some hard thinking. I called him over and told him that the rapidly expanding demands of my work and family life were driving me a bit crazy. I explained that even with the capable business management of Mark McCormack and his various people, my personal affairs on the road and back home in Latrobe had become almost too much for both Winnie and me to manage ourselves. What I really needed was, in effect, a traveling secretary and somebody to run my home office, and Doc Giffin was the man I wanted to do it. He agreed to take the job, and after a couple of months spent breaking in Bob Gorham, his successor as press secretary, just after the PGA Championship at Firestone, he came on board with Arnold Palmer Enterprises.

I count that as one of the wisest choices I ever made. Ironically, on a sadder note, Doc's arrival coincided with the death of one of the Tour's newest stars, Tony Lema. Tony was killed in a plane crash while flying from Firestone to an exhibition in Chicago. Doc's first duty as my assistant was to phone me in Latrobe, where I'd just arrived by my own plane, to inform me of the tragedy.

The second change in my life that began to quietly manifest itself before the 1963 season was the realization that I probably should give up smoking on the golf course.

Much to Pap's dismay, I'd smoked pretty heavily since about age fifteen, first secretly with my teenage school friends, and later, by the time I reached Wake Forest, on the golf course itself. Coming down the stretch of a tournament, I found there was nothing like an L&M cigarette to steady the nerves and help me concentrate on the business at hand. One of my first business contracts negotiated by Mark McCormack, fittingly, was a deal to represent Liggett & Myers cigarettes, which I happily did for several years, puffing furiously whenever I needed the crutch of nicotine. My cardinal rule for representing any commercial product on tour was that I had to genuinely believe in the value of the product I was endorsing. My two-pack-a-day addiction spoke powerfully to that belief.

But increasingly troubling to both Winnie and me were stories beginning to appear in the popular press about the terrible long-term health effects of cigarette smoking, particularly among people who took up the habit as teenagers. During the 1963 season, I tried off and on to kick the habit, but it wasn't until the Surgeon General's Office released its report in late 1963 or early 1964 officially linking cigarette smoking to various ailments, including heart disease and lung cancer, that I knew the writing was on the wall for my own two-pack habit.

Simultaneously, the letters I received from concerned parents and teachers and physicians urging me to abandon my own "glamorous" addiction cinched the deal. I hated to think I could somehow be responsible for thousands of kids picking up golf clubs *and* cigarettes. Even my friend President Eisenhower advised me in no uncertain terms to kick the habit, and both he and Pap expressed their strong relief when I finally promised to try.

When my contract with L&M expired, I decided to go "cold turkey"—at least on the golf course. That proved easier said than done, and though I only slipped up and smoked publicly during a golf tournament on American shores once or twice more, my battle against addiction to coffin nails went on behind the scenes, painfully at times, for many years yet. In fact, it wasn't until a Christmas party at Bay Hill in 1970 that I kicked the awful habit for good.

Then, on a wager with eleven other friends—
including Dow Finsterwald, a nonsmoker who suddenly took to wildly puffing cigarettes just to get
into the wagering pool—we agreed that all of us
would kick the habit for good or else pay the others
in the pool $100 each for falling off the wagon.

I've never touched a cigarette since, and friends
still debate the effect quitting had on my career.

Even so, by the end of 1962, the year I quietly
began to quit smoking on tour, I was the Tour's
leading money winner, with $81,448 in official prize
money and nine wins, which included consecutive
victories at Texas, the Tournament of Champions,
and Colonial. The year's major highlights were my
second British Open championship title, at Royal
Troon, and a devastating playoff loss—before what
amounted to a hometown crowd at Oakmont Country Club in Pittsburgh in the United States Open
Championship—to a sensational Tour rookie who
possessed a game for the ages and no visible fear in
him. But I'll get to him in just a bit.

Approaching the Masters of 1963, I suppose I
really was a bit mentally and physically weary, and
maybe just dying for a cigarette or two when I
played. My tournament and business life was booming and the media focus on my family was at its all-
time high. We never had an unlisted phone number
in Latrobe, and as a result, the telephone would ring
at all hours of the night, with people calling and
asking to speak to me, convey their best wishes, ask
for favors, borrow money, sell something, you name
it. I always tried my best to be courteous to people,

to treat them the way I wanted to be treated, but honestly at times it made me wonder if the privacy you sacrifice for fame and fortune is really worth it.

As I think of those hectic days, looking at old cover stories on my career in *Time* and *Sports Illustrated* and a host of others, it seems to me that someone from the national press was always camped out at our house or staying at the nearby Mountain View Inn, dining with us, probing our family life, asking us to pose for pictures planting a family Christmas tree or taking a ride with my daughters on Pap's old tractor (the same one you see in Pennzoil commercials). Winnie, for her part, was good-natured about the constant intrusions on our family life but clearly had her limits and, thankfully, knew how to say no whenever I couldn't or simply promised too much. Watching all the reporters around me, Amy, who was born in Augusta in 1958 and was almost five, wondered to her mother, "Why does Daddy always have all those detectives asking him questions?"

From the mouths of babes . . .

At moments, as a result of these intense distractions, both on and off the course, when I felt my concentration beginning to waver and the tournament slipping away from me, I'll freely admit there would have been nothing better to soothe my jangled nerves than a long drag on a cigarette, but there was no way to go back on my pledge. As a result, I eventually put on weight—as much as fifteen pounds at one point—but on the positive side of the ledger I started fast in 1963 by taking the L.A. Open, a tournament I always dearly hungered to win but in which I had never done particularly well. I followed that good fortune up with victory laps at Phoenix and Pensacola and top ten finishes at Palm Springs and Doral.

I was thirty-four years old, the traditional peak of a Tour player's performance years, with forty-two professional wins in my column, and it stood to reason that I was the logical favorite to win my fourth green jacket at Augusta. But it simply wasn't in the cards for me that year. From the start, I felt uncomfortable—a rare circumstance for me at Augusta—and nothing I tried short of lighting up could fix the problem. I opened with a shaky 74, failed to summon the kind of concentration I always needed in order to contend, and finished a distant ninth with 291.

That Masters belonged to a history maker named Jack. In a very real sense, though I perhaps didn't fully appreciate it at that moment, I was suddenly staring at the future and my greatest rival in the game. Nicklaus, then twenty-two, the Tour rookie who beat me in a playoff in front of the rowdy home crowd at Oakmont nine months before, fired 286 to beat a hard-charging Tony Lema by a stroke in his first Masters, to become the youngest man in history to win the Masters. I remember slipping the green jacket onto Jack and smiling as he presented Bob Jones with his winning ball. It was an emotional moment, admittedly bittersweet for me, and I know neither Jack nor I have ever forgotten it.

Jack Nicklaus had come of age, and professional golf would never be the same. You could almost feel that in the air. I'd known Jack since we first met at an exhibition match in Athens, Ohio, in 1956. The event was "Dow Finsterwald Day," and Jack was a muscular, somewhat pudgy sixteen-year-old who even then could slug the ball farther than most professional Tour players. I remember that just for fun we had a driving contest and I beat him by a hair; I made a mental note on the spot to always keep an eye on this upstart kid, because with his skills and eerie composure under fire it was probably only a matter of time before he was giving us all a run for the prize money and tournament hardware.

And now that fate had come to pass. As if taking a U.S. Open trophy out from under me and my Army at Oakmont wasn't enough, Jack Nicklaus now had the temerity to stroll onto the hallowed grounds of Augusta National as a Tour sophomore and simply lay waste to the course in a devastating display of shotmaking not seen in that part of Dixie since a fellow named Sherman made his way from Atlanta to Savannah.

In all seriousness, if there was ever a course that was built to suit Jack's power-fade game, it was Augusta National. The way that he made his mark on the place, not to mention the game itself, so convincingly in 1963 stands as one of the great stories in golf this century. But, as I keep saying, more on him—and us—in a bit.

Curiously, a few of the same observers who only a year or so before had predicted that I would win seven or eight Masters titles now openly wondered if I had reached my peak of performance and would probably begin a slow decline. I suppose thanks to Jack it may have looked as if I was contemplating early retirement, but nothing could have been further from the truth. In the first five months of 1963, Jack won a couple of tournaments I'd won the previous year, prompting some wag in *Time* to reflect, "Whatever Arnie wants, Jack gets." Doug Sanders, the flamboyant one, commented to the press that "Baby Beef" (his name for Jack) was doing to me what I'd been doing to the rest of the PGA Tour for several years.

The truth is, for the first time in my career, I was nagged by an inability to mentally focus the way I had been able to do. As a result, my putting stats declined and even my drives lost some of their customary zip. Because of these problems, combined with an unexpected bursitis pain in my shoulder, I decided to do something I would previously never have considered doing at the height of the tournament season. I decided to take a month off. I went home to Latrobe and hung around the office, went swimming with the girls, and just basically tried to rest up for the U.S. Open at Brookline. The rest clearly did me good. A week before the Open, I beat Paul Harney in a sudden-death playoff to win the Thunderbird and went on to Brookline feeling like my old self, fashioning good enough golf to make a playoff with Julius Boros and Jacky Cupit. The popular story is that a stomach bug cost me a second Open championship title (I fired a miserable 76 in the playoff, and it's true I did feel woozy at times), but the real culprit was a foolish attempt to hit my ball from a tree stump. That's what cost me a chance to win in regulation.

Despite my roller-coaster ups and downs that year, counting a victory at the Australian Wills Masters and my team victory with Nicklaus in the Canada Cup, I collected nine wins on tour, six top tens, and enough prize money—$128,230—to make me, once again, the Tour's leading money winner. Not to put too fine a point on it—for a man some feared was in decline—becoming the first player to break the $100,000 earnings barrier that year was the kind of "decline" most players would hope for. Still, what weighed most heavily on my mind, and everyone else's, was that I hadn't won a major golf tournament in 1963.

Against that backdrop, Winnie and I arrived at our rental house off Berckmans Road in Augusta in 1964 with more than a little resolve churning in my gut to make up for my poor performance at the previous Masters. During a week of nearly perfect spring weather, the press wrote glowing accounts about the "Big Three of Golf"—Gary, Jack, and me—seeming to imply that the winner of the $20,000 first-place check and accompanying jacket was a foregone conclusion. One of us was bound to win it, and the serious betting was on Jack, the defending champion, as it probably should have been. That was fine with me, because one thing I'd finally begun to realize was that I almost always played sharper and more consistent golf when cast in the underdog role.

I was as determined as I'd ever been that Jack wasn't going to get the 1964 Masters, and I suppose some of my Army was, too. That year, and the year preceding it, our rivalry was plagued by a few unfortunate incidents where overzealous Palmer fans, in a foolish attempt to somehow boost their hero's

chances, expressed themselves in a most unsportsman-
like manner. The worst instances came from among
the hometown partisans at Oakmont in '62—as I'll
talk about later. Needless to say, Clifford Roberts
wanted no part of such shenanigans at *his* golf tournament and rightly responded in 1964 by printing an
expected code of spectator conduct on the back of
every Masters pairing sheet, as is done to this day.

Attempting to ignore a number of distractions, including a small airplane droning over Augusta National pulling a "Go, Arnie, Go!" banner, I
opened with a 69 and a 68 to take the 36-hole lead,
and a third-round 69 moved me five shots ahead of
the field—one of the best fields, I might add, in the
history of the Masters.

I can't emphasize enough that one private thought
was propelling me: I wanted to walk up 18 *knowing* there was no way I could lose the Masters
championship. Thanks to a strong front nine on
Sunday, I sensed that not only was that long-held
ambition within my grasp, but so was Ben Hogan's
tournament record of 274. In retrospect, it was
probably a mistake to be thinking about Hogan's
record, even for an instant. With that kind of lead,
most players would have been attempting to get to the
clubhouse—and a green jacket—as quietly and safely
as possible. But that wasn't my style, and this didn't
seem like the place to try to alter my personality.

Consequently, at 15, with the sun beginning to sink
low in the Georgia pines, my playing partner and

good friend Dave Marr looked at me as if I'd lost my mind when I pulled a 3-wood from the bag and decided to go for the green in two. I bore down and really crushed the ball but lost it flying into the glare of the sun. For an instant, I felt a true surge of panic. I glanced anxiously at Dave, and asked if my ball had safely cleared the dangerous pond in front of the green. Dave looked at me with that wonderful laid-back Texas smile of his and said dryly, "Hell, Arnold, your *divot* got over."

This is not an unimportant point to address. My reputation had been made pulling off gutsy shots like that, and it's reasonable to think somebody watching me go for the 15th green in two, while enjoying a five- or six-shot lead, would wonder why in hell I would risk everything on a gamble of that nature.

The simple answer, if there is one, is that that's the way I'd always played the game—or at least the way I played the game when I played it best. There's no question that my refusal to play safe or lay up cost me the opportunity to win scores of tournaments, including, by my calculation, three or four U.S. Opens, perhaps a Masters or two, and the PGA Championship on at least two occasions. Critics who have said that a safer shot here or there would undoubtedly have won me a few more tournaments are probably correct.

But the other side of that proposition—seldom mentioned by some of those critics—is equally true: if I hadn't had the instinctive desire to attempt those shots, regardless of the outcome, almost without thinking, I wouldn't have won half the tournaments I did win. Going for the green in two was who I was as a boy—and it's who I remain as a man. Asking me to lay up was like asking Jack to play a low hook or Gary to go a week without doing his morning workouts—it just wasn't in our constitutional makeups.

On the 18th tee, Dave Marr remarked to me that he really wanted to make a birdie and tie Jack Nicklaus, and I asked him kiddingly what I could do to help.

He gave me that sly flatland smile again.

"How about making a twelve?" he said.

Dave's joke came at just the right moment. It relaxed me and helped me keep my focus and hit a good drive and finally walk up Augusta's famous 18th fairway, basking in the pleasure of knowing I didn't have to make a putt to win or tie. I cannot emphasize enough how important this feeling of accomplishment was to me.

Dave, as it turned out, didn't require any assistance from me. He drained a bending thirty-five-foot downhiller to tie Jack, and at 5:26 in the afternoon on Easter Sunday, April 20, I sank a twenty-five-footer to miss Hogan's record by a stroke but become the first four-time winner in the history of the Masters.

In the hushed and crowded media room afterward, depleted by the power of my own gathering emotions, I told the assembled reporters that I felt this was my greatest achievement in professional golf.

Someone once said you should never speak too openly of your dreams—especially when they come true.

Perhaps that was the case that afternoon in the lengthening shadows at Augusta. I couldn't have known it then, but this was my last Masters win and the final time I would face the media to explain how I'd won a major tournament championship. The next year, in 1965, Jack shattered Hogan's old mark by three and won the second of his record six green jackets. I finished second, but nine shots behind. The next two years, I could do no better than fourth place. And as the decade drew to a close, so too, apparently, did my opportunities to win another Masters.

Perhaps it was because my "major" dreams had begun and ended at Augusta National, in golf's pine cathedral, that I've never stopped faithfully going back to Augusta and the Masters golf tournament each spring with a renewed feeling of gratitude in my heart.

In some respects, no gesture touched me as deeply as a ceremony on the Tuesday afternoon of Masters week in 1995. A big crowd was on hand as Jack Stephens unveiled a bronze plaque commemorating my four wins at the Masters. I became only the fourth player in history to be so honored. Sarazen, Nelson, and Hogan all got their own bridges. My plaque was mounted on a drinking fountain behind the 16th tee.

I'm really pleased by that. Take it from me, a walk up and down Augusta National's gorgeous rolling hills can be a draining experience. The fountain at 16 is a perfect spot to pause and have a refreshing drink of water.

CHAPTER EIGHT

D.D.E.

October 2, 1958

Dear Mr. Palmer,

Because of the general confusion the other day, I failed to realize when Ben Fairless introduced us that you were Arnold Palmer of 1958 Masters fame. I hope you will forgive my lack of reaction and accept, even this belatedly, my warm congratulations on your splendid victory.

Ben suggests that sometime we might have an opportunity to play at Augusta. This I should like very much though, judging from the brand of golf I have recently been displaying, I would be more than embarrassed.

Sincerely,
Dwight D. Eisenhower

Winning my first Masters gave me the thrill of a lifetime, but receiving this letter six months later out of the blue, from the president of the United States, typed and signed on his own personal stationery, just about put me over the moon. The framed letter still hangs in a place of honor in my Latrobe offices.

A casual student of military history and a slightly more than curious spectator of the brawl of American politics, I'd long been fascinated with President Dwight Eisenhower's long and distinguished career, initially as a military leader of the first rank, and later as president and leader of the free world through some of its most challenging days. I was deeply pleased when I learned that President Eisenhower was exceptionally keen about playing golf, so much so that he had the first putting green installed at the White House. He was also a member of Augusta National and had made over a hundred trips to Georgia during his two terms as president, to play golf and socialize with his close friend and adviser Clifford Roberts and other members of the club.

Though my father was a devoted Roosevelt man and lifelong Democrat, and I hailed from working-class stock in the heart of what might rightly then have been considered a Democratic stronghold, I suppose in my heart I always knew I was a middle-of-the-road Republican. What I mean by that is that the ideals President Eisenhower, Lincoln, and other leaders of the Republican Party seemed to represent—a passionate belief in the limitless benefits of personal freedom, governed by an equally strong sense of personal responsibility—were part of a belief system with which I was more comfortable.

Pap and I had more than one vigorous debate on the subject. After my first Masters win, President Eisenhower and I shook hands at Laurel Valley Golf

Club in nearby Ligonier. (This meeting took place a few months before that club opened, and I began representing it on tour.) Subsequently, my father grew to wholeheartedly agree with me on one thing: there were few men walking the planet who could match the character, charisma, and unpretentious charm of Dwight David Eisenhower.

From the beginning, I noticed that many of his intimates affectionately called him Ike, an indication of how comfortable President Eisenhower made people feel in his presence. He was a soldier's general and the president of the United States, though, and I never felt comfortable addressing him that way. To me, regardless of how close we grew over time, he was always either Mr. President or President Eisenhower. He once suggested that I feel free to call him Ike, but he didn't raise the subject again when, out of respect, I declined to do so. Instead, he always signed his frequent and warm notes of thanks and congratulations to Winnie and me exactly the same way—with his initials, D.D.E. I suppose that's about as casually as I could think of the man.

The day after I won my second Masters in 1960, we shook hands again, and he congratulated me on my big win, giving me that broad, easy, gentle and genuine Kansas smile of his, a smile that a decade or so before had bolstered the hearts of young men headed to the beaches at Normandy. "I hear you're a pretty good putter," he said with classic understatement.

I blushed and told him I was eager to see his

game. "Well," he said with a laugh, "you won't be
for long."

In fact, I was so in awe of the man I was almost
shaking with nervousness, but he was so gracious
and attentive he quickly put me at ease. President
Eisenhower, as it turned out, swung a golf club with
great conviction, if not tremendous dexterity, and it
quickly was apparent that even as he was retiring
from public life his interest in playing the game was
growing.

President Eisenhower loved golf for the social
and recreational aspects of the game, but he clearly
also took it very seriously. He dearly wanted to be a
good player, so he carefully watched, didn't hesitate
to ask intelligent questions about the mechanics of
the swing, and doggedly attempted to apply any tips
I invariably gave him about improving his own golf
swing—sometimes with alarming results.

A couple of weeks after I won my last Masters in
1964, President Eisenhower, Ray Bolger, Jimmy
Demaret, and I played an exhibition at Merion Golf
Club outside Philadelphia for the Heart Association
of Southeastern Pennsylvania. As it turned out, this
was President Eisenhower's only *public* golf performance on record. But it remains memorable to me
for the sudden horror I felt when I looked over and
saw blood all over the retired president's golf shirt.
Prior to the match, I'd noticed how his right elbow
"flew" away from his body on his swing, a common
habit of high handicappers attempting to generate
club-head speed, so I counseled him to always try to

keep his right elbow tucked "as close to your body as possible" to generate more power and hit the ball straighter.

Even playing golf, the president preferred to wear a rough military-style belt with metal buckles and adjustments. Bless him, like the good soldier he was, in his determination to keep that right wing tucked as ordered, he'd actually rubbed the skin off his arm and was bleeding! When I pointed it out to him, he acted as if it were nothing but a scratch and completely dismissed my concern.

After that first encounter at Augusta in 1960, our meetings on the golf course became more frequent and our playing companionship deepened into a genuine friendship that, for me at least, eclipsed any relationship I'd ever had with an older man besides my father. He loved to hear me talk about tour life, and I loved to hear him reminisce about his wartime experiences and reflect on current events. He was so down-to-earth and unassuming about his many accomplishments, I sometimes almost forgot who he was. I had to pinch myself sometimes as a reminder that I was interacting with not only a beloved figure in American history, a man who had been leader of the free world and a critical part of so much human drama, but someone virtually every American admired.

Being close to a president in this intimate manner is a thrill and an experience you don't take lightly, believe me, but in this instance I'm happy to report that the deep pleasure of our friendship seemed to work both ways. For years we would meet at

Augusta or I'd drop by his cottage at Eldorado in Palm Desert, and we would either sit and talk for hours after his round of golf, or play cards and have dinner, conversing well after evening turned to night. I liked the way President Eisenhower looked at the world, his endless reservoir of stories, his boundless optimism, which was firmly grounded in humility and an abiding sense of personal honor. Among other things, Winnie and I both came to deeply admire the highly ethical and almost humble manner in which the president and Mrs. Eisenhower applied their own sensible Midwest values to their public lives. Perhaps because they both hailed from farming stock and working-class families, the idea of wasting *anything* or abusing the privileges of their positions weighed constantly on their lifestyle choices.

It's perhaps a small thing, but, for instance, they declined to serve liquor at public functions and were even meticulously careful to use stamps they'd purchased themselves for personal correspondences. It never would have occurred to either of them to ask a favor of someone, and their gratitude for the smallest kindness rendered was instantaneous and the gesture graciously returned. President Dwight Eisenhower and his wife, Mamie, were, in my book, the epitome of American graciousness and civility.

Mostly, though, they were just so doggone comfortable to be with that Winnie and I almost couldn't get enough of their company—a welcome counterpoint to the public fervor that was surrounding our young family's attempt to have a normal private life in my peak years between '58 and '66. The girls, Peg and Amy, though mere toddlers when they first met him, were particularly fond of the president, as well.

One special day in September of 1966 stands out among many cherished memories. It was my thirty-seventh birthday and a pretty Saturday morning. I had planned to spend a relatively low-key day playing golf at the club, maybe practicing and building a new set of golf clubs in my workshop, followed by dinner with Winnie and friends later at Latrobe.

That was my plan. Others had something else in mind.

A friend of ours from Palm Springs named Molly Cullum just "happened" to stop by for a visit, and I greeted her on my way out the door to the workshop, but every time I attempted to leave, Winnie dragged me back into the kitchen. Frankly, this routine was getting pretty irritating. Finally, I walked Molly outside to say goodbye and was telling her how excited I was about my new aircraft, a Jet Commander, my first jet, when I heard a familiar roar, glanced up, and saw a jet making a wide approach for a landing at the Latrobe airport. "As a matter of fact," I said, pointing to it with surprise, "my plane is exactly like that one."

As a matter of fact, it *was* mine—transporting a very special passenger.

A few minutes later, I was once again ready to head to my workshop when Winnie insisted that she needed me in the house for "one more thing." I'm pretty sure I complained loudly that she was ruining my perfectly nice birthday morning, but I finally gave up and followed her inside one last time. A short time later came a gentle knock at the screen door, and I went to see who was coming by *this* time. I was startled to discover President Eisenhower standing on our porch clutching a small overnight bag.

"Say," he said, with that quiet photogenic smile of his, "you wouldn't have room to put up an old man for the night, would you?"

A host of folks had been in on the scheme: Winnie and Mamie, who planned the surprise get-together (Mamie, who was almost deathly afraid of flying, was being driven up from their farm in Gettysburg by the Secret Service); my pilot, Darrell Brown, who flew the plane to York Airport to fetch the president (the only time one of my planes went anywhere without my knowledge); Doc Giffin, who had somehow helped the Secret Service secure our place for the president's visit without being detected, and even set up a field base of operations in my club workshed on the property.

One of the nicest weekends of my life followed, characterized at least as much by what we didn't do as what we did. We sat for hours talking until Mamie arrived, and we then drove to Rolling Rock, another fine club at Ligonier, for that dinner with Ben Fairless and George Love. Then we came back to the house and the women watched the Miss America pageant on TV while the president and I disappeared into the master bedroom to catch the end of a college football game on the other set. For my birthday, he presented me with something I treasure: a small oil painting he'd done of a barn on his farm in Gettysburg. We hung it on the wall of our dining room, and it's there, one of my most cherished items, to this day. The next morning, a sunny Sunday, we got up early and ate a big country breakfast at the kitchen table, refilled our coffee cups, and sat idly talking for several more hours.

I can't tell you exactly what we talked about, but in my memory it was a little bit of everything— presidents and history, the new space program and old military campaigns, lots of family tales and laughter. The conversation went on a long time, and we never even moved from the table. I recall that we managed to even talk a little bit about golf, though we somehow never got around to swinging a golf club that weekend.

Quite frankly, I don't know when I've had a better time.

I wish I could say I played golf with President Eisenhower's successor, John F. Kennedy. I heard from a number of different sources of different political persuasions that he could really hit a golf ball and could have been an excellent player if his time—and his injured back—had permitted.

Kennedy's opponent in the famous televised presidential debates of 1960 was another example of a president who had a strong natural interest in golf, but for reasons mostly political in nature refused to indulge his passion. Richard Nixon was a member of

Baltusrol Golf Club during President Eisenhower's presidency and, despite his professed interest in the game, gave up his membership in the club because he feared the consequences at the polls if the public saw him on a golf course.

I liked Richard Nixon, despite his quirks and apparent lack of warmth. He was smart and engaging, and though, as I recall, we actually played golf together only once—nine holes somewhere—I think his decision to abandon golf for political purposes revealed something fundamental about the dark side of his character, or maybe his deep social insecurities, that Mr. Nixon never permitted himself to examine. Maybe, on the other hand, I'm just indulging in a bit of armchair psychoanalysis of the man— whom I never really knew very well. I do think golf fascinated Richard Nixon, though, and in his heart he wished he could have attacked it with the relish and joy his old boss President Eisenhower had. But, for one reason or another, that wasn't his style.

President Eisenhower hadn't cared a bit who saw him or who knew he was chasing the golf ball around Augusta or Eldorado (he just didn't want anybody to know his handicap, which was far worse than he would have liked—hence the bloody elbow). I think that attitude represented the fundamental honesty of President Dwight David Eisenhower. He wasn't going to put on airs for anybody or pretend to be something or somebody he wasn't. He took the heat and looked you in the eye, and even with a bad looping slice off the tee, he was the ultimate presidential straight shooter.

In Nixon's defense, it may have been the seriousness of the times that helped color his decision to
abandon golf. After all, with thousands of young
American men and women dying in Vietnam and the
college campuses of this country exploding with
antiwar demonstrations, it probably wouldn't have
sat well with the parents of those young people to
know the commander in chief had taken the afternoon off to beat the ball around Congressional or
Burning Tree.

At the end of the day, I have no way of knowing
what was in the man's complex mind, but I do know
that on at least one occasion, surprisingly, Nixon
wanted to know what was on *mine*. And I told him.
It happened one year while I was playing in the
Desert Classic. President Nixon summoned Bob
Hope and me to fly to his San Clemente home for
what somebody later called a "mini-summit"
meeting. I wasn't exactly sure what the subject of
discussion was going to be, but you can bet I was
highly interested in going to find out. It's not every
day that the son of a small-town golf professional
gets invited to sit in on a presidential meeting, with
cabinet officers and other senior advisers present. So
I was raring to go even before the U.S. Marine helicopter picked us up in the desert and flew us over the
mountains to San Clemente. There we found the
president, his friend and adviser Henry Kissinger,
Vice President Gerald Ford, and several other
national security people huddled in Nixon's living
room, with cold beverages, waiting for us to arrive.

It seemed that the president wanted to pick our

brains, of all things, about how to end the war in Vietnam. You could see the burden of it was seriously weighing on him, and I suppose he reasoned that because I'd been close to President Eisenhower and was even occasionally mentioned in the press as a possible political candidate myself I might have something useful to say on the subject.

No matter why I was included, I do remember the lengthy discussions about various strategic approaches, potential national security consequences, impact with allies and adversaries, and so forth, including the idea of bombing Hanoi back to the Stone Age to try to finally end the miserable, protracted war in Southeast Asia. When it finally came my turn to express an opinion, everyone looked at me.

"Well," I started, a touch reluctantly, "if the decision were mine to make, I guess I wouldn't pussyfoot around. Let's get this thing over as quickly as possible, for everyone's sake. Why not go for the green?"

They all had a good laugh at that. My remark seemed to provide some much-needed levity. But as I later said to Bob Hope, I really wasn't trying to be funny.

It wasn't that I'm such a political hawk. On the contrary, I'm a confirmed moderate thinker and as I've aged, I've learned the great value of diplomacy and seeking an honorable peace. But part of that wisdom is knowing when to fight, and another part is knowing when to fight even harder—a lesson I learned as far back as the streets of Youngstown. It seemed to me that the only smart and moral thing to do was to get the war over and bring our boys home as swiftly as possible. Whatever it took to do it, that's what I'd do.

I suppose that kind of decisiveness had a certain appeal to some people. A couple of years later, about the time Nixon's presidency was embroiled in the Watergate scandal, I was pulled aside at an outing for Chase Manhattan Bank in Houston by a wealthy oil man and invited to come meet a group of "interested friends" in a private meeting room. Waiting there was a group of true heavy-hitters from the business and financial worlds, and it was quickly explained to me that if I was willing to toss my golf visor into the public arena of high public office, these men would be "very interested" in providing the kind of political clout and financial wherewithal I would surely need.

I thought about it a moment and thanked them, explaining that I was genuinely flattered. I suppose in their minds my popularity as a sports figure and commercial spokesman, combined with the integrity inherent in the game of golf, made me irresistible candidate material at a time when the public opinion ratings of almost all politicians, owing to the war or the evolving Watergate scandal, were at an all-time low.

I would be less than honest if I didn't admit that the thought of running for office had crossed my mind before, probably on several occasions. As far back as my first Masters win I could remember fans holding up signs saying "Arnie for President," and on more than one occasion back home in Pennsylvania I was the object of grassroots campaigns to convince me to run for governor.

I liked politics, or more accurately the idea of performing the kind of public service that men like President Eisenhower performed so well. But as Pap had drilled into me from day one, I also knew myself well enough to know that in more ways than I cared to think about, I was really unsuited for a life in the political arena. For one thing, I'm prone to say what's on my mind without worrying about the consequences, and I really have no taste for the intense partisanship you see poisoning the political process these days. Besides, I probably have too many close friendships on *both* sides of the political aisle to ever throw my own hat into the ring. Golf is political enough without adding professional Democrats and Republicans into the mix!

At any rate, I smiled and thanked those men in the Houston meeting room, and admitted I was flattered but basically not interested in their offer. I may have even told them what my Pap used to say—that a smart man learned early what he did best and kept on doing it. Golf had made me what I was, and I intended to keep on playing it.

Gerald Ford, who succeeded Nixon, had no hangups about being seen on a golf course. He adored golf and didn't care a bit who knew it. I liked that about him. For such a strong man with an athletic background, Ford's game was frankly a bit of a puzzlement to me. In a nutshell, he should have been better than he was, and no president ever tried harder at the game than Gerald Ford. His reputation for beaning spectators at golf tournaments like the Hope was perhaps overstated a bit, but you clearly had to give the man points for daring to be so public with his golf game. His passion for the game was a joy to watch. One indication of his passion is that if you tried to give him a putt, he would never take it but insist on trying to make it. That's a true gamer, in my book.

I'm proud of the fact that during his term of office, President Ford and I together inaugurated the USGA's highly successful Associates (now Members) Program, aimed at getting the average golfer to support the amateur game. The day President Ford left office, he flew to California to play in the old Crosby tournament at Pebble Beach, arriving late and joining me on the third hole. I remember how hard he tried that day, and how errant some of his shots were. But that's Gerald Ford, as golfer and president. He may not have been a natural at either game, but he threw himself honorably into the fray at crucial points in history, did very good things for this country and his favorite game, and is still out there trying.

In his spare time Ronald Reagan preferred riding horses and chopping wood to playing golf, but Winnie and I were fortunate to get to know the Reagans pretty well during their years in office. Nancy and Winnie particularly hit it off, and some of my fondest memories of those years came out of the many state dinners we got invited to and attended.

There's nothing like a state dinner at the White House to grab your attention. I was a nervous wreck at the first one Winnie and I attended one cool spring night in 1968, shortly after Richard Nixon took office. I don't even remember in whose honor the dinner was given, though Frank Sinatra and a few other glamorous stars of his magnitude were there, causing the press photographers to go crazy and making me feel a little bit shy and wide-eyed, like a big kid. Winnie and I had flown up for the evening from Greensboro, North Carolina (where, as usual, I was in contention before I self-destructed in front of a lot of my old Wake Forest chums—I never managed to win that tournament, by golly, and always dearly wanted to). All I could think about during the actual dinner was my table manners, wondering whether or not Pap would have my head for the way I handled the presidential silverware. He was such a tyrant about "proper table manners," I felt deep relief when Winnie, sensing my high anxiety, reached over, patted my arm, and assured me that my table manners, thus far at least, were impeccable.

Speaking of wrecks, maybe my favorite story about attending a presidential state dinner concerns one that took place during the Nixon years and involved a car that only *looked* as if it had been wrecked. One night President Suharto of Indonesia was in town and had specifically requested that Mr. and Mrs. Palmer attend the dinner. (By the way, that's how you get your name on a state dinner invitation list—the guest of honor asks to have you present.) We were staying with my sister Cheech and her husband, Ron, at their place in Alexandria, and they graciously met us at the airport and offered to drive us across the Potomac to the dinner.

I used to joke that Ron and Cheech really ran the United States government, because for many years, Ron, a slow-talking Carolinian with a deadpan wit, was in charge of the navy's computer operations at the Pentagon while Cheech served as an assistant inspector general for the U.S. Army. That didn't cut much mustard with the Secret Service, I'm afraid, when we joined the queue of sleek black limousines and rolled up to the entrance portico of the White House in Ron's beloved 1964 Buick Wildcat, a bit of a rambling wreck that had seen better days. The stares we got from the Secret Service and the press photographers were pretty amusing—as if they were watching Ma and Pa Kettle arrive for the big night out on the town.

If Ron was bothered by their reaction to his heap, he didn't let it show. "Nixon invited us tonight, too, you know," Ron drawled at us as we prepared to step out into the glamorous setting and all those popping flashbulbs. "But I told him to go to hell."

If I'm smiling in any photos of that night, it's probably due to Ron's disarming remark. I still laugh when I recall that the Secret Service made sure that Ron and Cheech safely left the White House property.

State dinners are fun, but not half as much fun as

playing golf with a man who loves the amateur game almost as much as I do.

Such a man is George Herbert Walker Bush, whose grandfather founded the Walker Cup matches in 1922. During the Bush years in office, Winnie and I were fortunate to be invited to the White House several times (the experience, by the way, never became any less nerve-racking for me) for state dinners. President Bush and I played many times at a host of places, including his club in Houston or at Kennebunkport in Maine, Burning Tree, Pebble Beach, and once at the Tournament Players Club at Avenel—the place where I had back-to-back holes in one on the same hole on consecutive days in 1986. What you've heard about George Bush the golfer is true: he plays fast and takes no prisoners.

But like President Eisenhower, he *will* take a putt if you give it to him. Whether his ball was two inches or four feet from the cup, if you said, "That's good, Mr. President" to President Eisenhower, he wouldn't hesitate to slap the ball and pick it up, ready to move on. I never saw any president who hated to part with a buck more than Dwight D. Eisenhower did.

Unless, maybe, it's George Bush.

I feel comfortable calling him by his first name, I suppose, because we are close in age and he and his wife Barbara are so comfortable to be with and so warmly down-to-earth they make you feel as though you've known them forever.

Anyway, he will also take a gimme, and the flattering similarities between him and President

Eisenhower, in my view, go far deeper than their golf games. In terms of personal values and the way he looks at the world and treats other people, George Bush reminds me more and more of President Eisenhower. He has the same easy grace, keen mind, and unpretentious charm. He is also driven by a deep sense of honor, a strong New England sense of frugality, and has in his wife Barbara, in the shared view of Winnie and me, the greatest former first lady in the history of the presidency for a spouse.

If he worked on it, he could be a far better than average player in golf. He has a once limber athletic baseball swing and can knock down putts like you wouldn't believe when he's playing at a pace slightly less than warp speed. But with President Bush, I've come to realize after many enjoyable rounds, it isn't the scores he's after—it's the pleasure of the round's companionship that matters most to him.

For the grandson of the founder of the world's most important amateur team golf event, the Walker Cup, I think that's probably entirely fitting, and as it ought to be. I couldn't agree with him more.

As I write this, the current White House occupant, Bill Clinton, might like nothing better than to simply slip off and play a round of golf somewhere. It would probably do him a world of good, too.

Clinton is a nice man and fine golf partner. Without question, he's the best ball-striker of any president I've known. The first time we played together was several years ago in the summer of 1993 when I was invited to the White House to receive a National Sports Award as one of the so-called Great Ones along with Wilma Rudolph, Muhammad Ali, Kareem Abdul-Jabbar, Ted Williams, and representing Arthur Ashe, his widow, Jeanne.

President Clinton nearly brought tears to my eyes when he remarked at the presentation that one reason he wanted to be president was for the "perks"—and that presenting the award to Arnold Palmer was one of the biggest perks of his career.

When we played that time—and later again at the Hope tournament with Gerald Ford and George Bush—I was pleased to discover in Clinton a golfer who really loves the game and will get after the ball with great concentration and heart. He's got a big swing that can send the ball a long way, and a surprisingly gentle touch around the greens.

I'm happy to report that he also has a deft sense of humor, which is definitely what you need if you plan to stay sane while playing golf or, I suspect, serving as president.

Once, we found ourselves alone together back on a tee in a chute of trees. I watched as President Clinton teed it up, addressed his ball, and then took a mighty swing that sent a screaming fade hopelessly into the woods. I suggested he reload and try another shot. He smiled at me sheepishly.

"Hell, Arnie, I'm glad those reporters aren't back here to see that," he quipped good-naturedly, already re-teeing his ball. "They'd have me drifting to the right!"

*   *   *

Playing golf with presidents is merely one of many job perks the game of golf has presented me over the past four decades, and I'm proud to say that each of these men made me feel as if the contributions I've made to the game, whatever they may be, begin and end with inspiring young people—or at least the young at heart—to take up the game.

If that's true, it's perhaps because, almost from the beginning of our relationship at Augusta and later elsewhere, President Eisenhower constantly conveyed to me his deep concern about the welfare and lives of America's young people. It was a theme he returned to at every turn.

The old general who had sent men who were scarcely more than boys onto Normandy's beaches in defense of liberty was determined to make me aware of the valuable service I could perform as a role model to thousands of young people. In a tumultuous period of time that would soon begin to devalue such traditional notions, President Eisenhower believed fervently in the power of heroes to transform lives—and he spared no opportunity to remind me that I had the rare opportunity to be such a hero. If that's true, as we used to say on the streets back in Youngstown, it took one to know one.

Now approaching the age he was when we first met, I find myself thinking a lot these days about what a tremendous influence Dwight David Eisenhower had on my life. Like millions of Americans, I really liked Ike, though I would never have dared

call him that. You wouldn't be off the mark to say I
even loved him like a second father.

So it's no surprise that I was deeply thrilled and
moved almost beyond words to be invited to address
a joint session of Congress on the 100th anniversary
of his birth, March 27, 1990.

Winnie and Doc fretted for days about what I
should say in my speech, and Doc even thoughtfully
worked up a beautiful tribute speech for me to read.
They knew far too well how I hated reading from
prepared texts, though, and in the end I simply took
Doc's prepared notes, added some of my own,
and jotted down a few highlights I wanted to touch
upon. Amusingly, shortly before I was called to the
podium on the floor of the House, I was asked by
congressional aides for a copy of my speech—so
Congress could read along and copies could be
given to the press.

I blushed a bit and explained that I really didn't
have much to give them and, in fact, didn't really
know what I was going to say—until I said it. I don't
know if that rattled them or not, but it probably
proves why I would ultimately have been a terrible
politician. At any rate, I gave the speech, spoke from
the heart about a man I loved like a second father,
and I guess it was pretty good after all. Congress
gave me—or should I say President Eisenhower—a
standing ovation, and I had to wipe away a few
tears.

The last time Winnie and I saw the president was
Valentine's Day, 1969. We arrived at Walter Reed
Hospital about ten-thirty that morning and were

taken to the VIP floor, where we were offered coffee and heart-shaped cookies.

Mamie wasn't there—she was attending a scheduled Heart Association luncheon, ever the good foot soldier—but we had spoken to her earlier. She explained to us that Valentine's Day was the anniversary of their engagement, the day President Eisenhower presented her his West Point ring. She reminded us, unnecessarily, with emotion tinging her voice, that she was still his valentine.

We found President Eisenhower sitting up in bed, thinner but pink-faced and smiling, glasses on and a history book in hand. The second he saw us coming, he put aside the book. He seized Winnie and gave her a hearty smooch on the cheek, while reaching out to grab my hand and squeeze it vigorously. The man still had a field general's grip.

"Gosh, it's *great* to see you kids," he said to us, clearly excited that we'd come. "Sit down and talk to me."

So we did. We sat and talked as we always did, about this and that, politics and golf, Nixon and war, history and family, and invariably young people— particularly the campus unrest and drug culture that were beginning to spread like a cancer over American society. This really worried him. On a happier note, though, he talked fondly about his grandchildren and wanted to hear about my latest adventures on the Tour. He inquired about Peggy and Amy and wanted to know if I'd quit smoking *off* the golf course yet.

Far too soon, a nurse appeared and politely

informed us it was time to leave. The president had pills to take and needed time to rest.

We stood. He kissed Winnie again and we once more clasped hands. Beaming at us as always, he assured us that the next time we saw him, which would be soon, it would be back home at his farm in Gettysburg.

With tears welling in my own eyes, I told Winnie on the way out that I hoped he was right. But it was the last time we saw D.D.E.

CHAPTER NINE

Cherry Hills

A week after winning the 1960 Masters and playing my first round of golf with President Eisenhower, *Sports Illustrated* declared that an "authentic and unforgettable hero" had emerged in the pines at Augusta National, and *Life* weighed in with the verdict that I had replaced Hogan and Snead as the brightest star of the golf world.

What a wonderful moment it was for me, in some ways the fulfillment of my wildest childhood dreams. To have the press writing such breathtaking things about my exploits, to have people suddenly treating me as if I really was the best player of my generation—all I can say is, thank God I had Winnie and Pap and the folks back home to keep me humble. Even my Pap, though, was uncharacteristically moved to admit I'd done "pretty well" down in Augusta.

He knew better than anyone, though, that in my eyes the job was only partially done. My sights were set on the next big prize in golf, the United States Open Championship. The preeminent golf championship in the world was being contested that year at Cherry Hills in Denver, a course I knew a little bit about thanks to President Eisenhower, who happened to be a member there. President Eisenhower loved the course and predicted that I would do pretty well there. After nearly winning the Houston Classic, I didn't even worry too much about the mini-"slump" my game fell into during the month-long run-up to the Open. With reporters and photographers constantly underfoot both at Latrobe and on the road, I suppose the distractions of success took their toll on my ability to remain properly focused— a pattern that would increasingly become a problem for me in the coming years.

I played in my first Open championship at Oakmont in 1953, while still an amateur, firing 162 to miss the cut. I missed again in 1954 but finally finished the complete seventy-two holes at Olympic in 1955, the year Jack Fleck pulled off his miracle finish to beat Ben Hogan out of a record fifth Open trophy. I tied that year for twenty-first, so at least I was heading in the right direction. The next year, at Oak Hill, I was actually a threat for a while to Cary Middlecoff, before tapering off to seventh. After failing to make the cut at Inverness, I was never a factor at Southern Hills. The next year at Winged Foot, I finally made a decent run at the championship, but a weak finish, a 74, left me in fifth place.

But almost from the beginning, 1960 had a different feel about it. My confidence level had never been so high, my desire to go out and *play* the golf course so intense. Cherry Hills stretched 7,004 yards, but because of the added distance a ball would carry on a course that is located 5,280 feet above sea level, some believed Hogan's twelve-year-old tournament record of 276 might be in jeopardy. If the plus side of the equation was that a ball flew anywhere from ten to fifteen yards farther in that thinner atmosphere, the downside was that the decreased oxygen supply could sap your strength in no time flat. As a result, Hogan himself developed headaches and carried his own canister of oxygen with a breathing apparatus, and the sponsoring USGA arranged for similar supplies of oxygen to be made available to players at special facilities set up around the course. Something like forty players took advantage of these unusual arrangements.

Despite my surging confidence, I was in trouble from the opening swing, but breathing wasn't my problem. During two practice rounds, I'd driven the first green, a downhill par 4 measuring just 318 yards on the card, and I made up my mind to go for the putting surface in every round. Unfortunately, I pushed my first tee shot and the ball bounced into a small stream, Little Dry Creek, as it was fittingly called. The USGA had arranged to have water pumped energetically through the ditch, however, and by the time I arrived on the scene, frowning at my poor fortune, the stream had swept my ball farther down the hill toward the green. I remember commenting in jest to Joe Dey, the USGA's meticulous executive director and the rules official on the scene, that I would just "wait and follow my ball down the creek until it stops and take a drop there."

Joe clearly didn't think that was proper—or par-

ticularly amusing. After a bit of confusion determining where my ball had crossed the margin of the
hazard, a spot was determined and I took a drop with
a one-stroke penalty. My next shot glanced off a
tree, and my fourth attempt flew over the green. I
chipped five feet short of the hole for my fifth, then
sank the putt for a nice fat opening double-bogey
six.

You could have fried an egg on my forehead at
that moment. I was so furious with myself for blowing a hole I clearly should have birdied. As we
walked to the next tee, I remember hitching up my
trousers and having a sharp exchange with my caddie. Bob Blair, who often carried for me, had somehow engineered the assignment to my bag (in those
days, the USGA assigned caddies, who were mostly
from the host club or local area, at random to players
beforehand)—and I still don't think I want to know
what kind of maneuver Bob pulled off to get on my
bag. I don't remember what Bob had said that got my
dander up, but whatever it was it even caught the
attention of my playing partners, Jack Fleck and Cary
Middlecoff. I was obviously steamed, and I stayed
that way. Several factors contributed to that.

Perhaps due to the thinner air, play was much
slower than the normal slow pace of an Open, and it
didn't help matters that Fleck and Middlecoff, Open
champions both, were two of the most deliberate
players on tour. They could sometimes seemingly
anguish over the ball for a small eternity before
pulling the trigger on a shot. That habit was

anathema to my style of play—once I'd made up my mind what I needed or wanted to do, which was usually pretty quickly, the last thing I wanted to do was stand around and *think* about it some more. It was better, in my view, to make the shot believing it would work and deal with the consequences if it didn't.

In any case, the three of us wound our way tediously around the golf course over the next five hours. I had several moments when my putting stroke failed and my frustration deepened. I was fortunate to finish the opening round with a one-over 72, a respectable score that placed me four strokes behind leader Mike Souchak. Afterward, my friendly nemesis Bob Drum growled at me to summarize the round, and I reflected that I felt "wobbly and scrambling" all day long and never found my pace. Cary Middlecoff used those same words to describe my round when he wrote about our trio's frustrating escapades for his hometown newspaper. What I didn't come right out and say was that by my calculations the poky play of my partners had cost me four strokes on the round, because anytime I wasn't moving forward on a golf course my nervousness and anxiety level increased twofold and my scoring usually paid the price. That day, the agonizing pace of play seemed even too much for Cary. He could manage only a painful 77 for his afternoon's labors.

Of course, the real trophy for loss of composure under pressure that day went to Tommy Bolt, who in a rage of frustration flung his driver into the pond in front of the 18th tee after knocking two balls into the water, clearing the head of an astonished Claude Harmon by either inches or yards, depending on which account of the famous incident you choose to accept.

In the press tent, I was asked if I thought I was still in contention, and I wearily replied that I only hoped I would still be within four shots come Saturday afternoon. As tradition had held since 1895, the Open finished with two rounds on Open Saturday, a practice that would continue until 1965. Noting my poor start on the day, someone else wondered if, given the opportunity, I would use my driver again on the first hole, and I politely assured him I certainly would because you never could tell what could happen when you hit the green off the tee—you just might make a hole in one.

I know some observers thought that, under the circumstances, that was a foolish strategy. The course was playing a lot tougher than most had expected, and scarcely anybody was now thinking that Hogan's record was in danger of tumbling. But I meant every word of it, and I couldn't wait to get back to the first tee and take my revenge on the hole.

Winnie wasn't with me in Denver. She and the girls were visiting her parents at the family's cottage at Shawnee-on-the-Delaware, taking a breather from the rigors of tour life. I suppose it's a little ironic that, after being on hand for virtually every important tournament I'd played in since the day we met, she would miss one some would later describe as the greatest ever—where three eras of the game collided in the persons of Ben Hogan, Arnold Palmer, and a young amateur named Jack Nicklaus, and I would pull off the most dramatic charge of my career.

But, of course, we had no way of knowing ahead of time how things would play out and had already decided to leave the girls (then four and two) with Winnie's parents while we went on to the Canada Cup and the British Open at St. Andrews. The decision, from a family standpoint, made good sense.

My second circuit of the Cherry Hills course was hardly more encouraging than the first; I shot 71 and fell even further back of the hard-charging Mike Souchak, who tore around Cherry Hills in 67, setting a thirty-six-hole record of 137 in the process. I made several bold escapes from the rough and five birdies, but I failed to convert several pars at critical moments (including the par-3 12th, which I felt jinxed me all week) and was fortunate, I suppose, that my day's total wasn't any worse. I honestly felt I'd deserved better than the course gave me, but other observers, like the ever-downbeat Drum, said I was very lucky to finish at even par. The only good thing about losing ground to the leader was that I wouldn't be paired with slowpokes Fleck and Middlecoff again. I must admit, the two of them nearly drove me crazy at times.

Saturday, the day of the double finishing rounds, dawned sunny and warm, a perfect Rocky Mountain morning, and Mike showed the first signs of cracking, finishing his morning round with a two-over 73.

His score was still good enough, though, for a two-stroke lead over Julius Boros, Jerry Barber, and Dow Finsterwald. Ben Hogan, who was still the man to beat in my mind, hit all eighteen greens in that third round, as I recall, but his unpredictable putter was betraying him.

That morning, I woke up telling myself that if I was going to lose the Open, I'd do it kicking and screaming, so it didn't surprise anybody when I pulled out my driver on the first hole and went for the green. My ball landed in the short grass just in front but then rolled into the deep collar grass around the green. I made a poor chip and needed three more shots to get down in bogey.

Not the way to start Open Saturday.

I finally got birdies at three and five, bogeyed six, birdied seven, and parred the difficult and long eighth. I had yet to par the tough uphill ninth, made another poor chip from the rough by the green, ripped off my golf glove in disgust, and holed out for a careless double-bogey six. Despite three birdies going out, I'd managed only a mediocre 36. The struggle continued on ten, where I barely got out of the bunker and had to make a dangerous twenty-foot downhiller to save par. I pulled back to even par with a birdie on 11 and—finally—managed to par the watery 12th, the par 3 that had been trouble all week long. My fifth birdie of the round came at 13, but I knew I would need at least two, possibly three, more birdies to have a reasonable chance of catching Souchak and the eight or nine others ahead of me.

Of the remaining five holes, only the 17th offered a realistic birdie opportunity. I parred 14 and 15 and went for broke on 16—making bogey instead. To compound my woes, I settled for par on the "easy" 17th and followed that up by making a bogey on the finishing hole.

A disappointing one-over 72. At that moment, with eighteen holes to play, I was exactly where I had been at the start of the third round. I was still eight back of Souchak, and on top of that, four players in the two pairings that finished just ahead of me—Boros, Hogan, Player, and the kid Nicklaus— had all gained ground on the nervous leader. A few minutes later, thanks to a spectator taking an unau- thorized photograph—only the credentialed mem- bers of the press are allowed to use cameras on the premises—Souchak hooked his drive out-of-bounds on 18 and finished the hole with a double bogey for 73 and a three-round total of 208. That nudged all of us a bit closer to the lead, but thirteen players stood between me at 215 and Mike at 208.

Needless to say, I was angry with myself for my weak finish in the third round. I stalked into the club- house to get a hamburger and a Coke to try to cool down and compose myself for the final eighteen. I was brooding on the fact that I'd made twelve birdies in fifty-four holes yet was two over par.

I can't say I knew this at that very moment, but history was hardly on my side: In the fifty-six Opens that had been contested over seventy-two holes since 1895, no player trailing by more than five strokes after fifty-four holes had ever come back to win the championship. Still, Mike was clearly vulnerable—in the locker room he admitted to several reporters that he felt he'd just blown his chances with the double bogey at 18, a terrible thing to do to his confidence, in my view, what with Hogan, Nicklaus, Finsterwald, and Boros hot on his heels. After playing as brilliantly as Mike had, this was the moment to keep all negative thoughts out of his head.

I suppose I was looking for some consolation for my own self-inflicted troubles, or at least some reassurance that all wasn't entirely lost yet, so I took my burger to where Drum sat talking to Dan Jenkins and Ken Venturi and a couple of other players in the locker room.

I remember someone, possibly Ken, wondering if Souchak would fold. Somebody shrugged and reflected that anything could happen in golf—especially in a U.S. Open. That was true enough, we all agreed.

"What if I shot sixty-five?" I spoke up, chewing my burger. "Two-eighty always wins the Open. What would that do?"

I meant exactly what I said. But they all looked at me as if I'd grown a second head, and Drum gave his usual cynical snort of derision.

Drum and I had already locked horns on the course, when he barked at me to quit fooling around by trying to eagle the first hole; I knew he'd also thought it was a big mistake going for any of the par 5s in two, as I routinely did. Maybe he'd been right, but as I pointed out to him in the locker room, I still had a shot at 280, and 280 traditionally won the Open.

Drum looked at me with more amusement than sympathy.

"Two-eighty won't do you one damn bit of good," he pronounced bluntly.

I'd only taken a couple bites of my burger, but I stopped chewing, ready to explode with anger at his remark. I'd come looking for support and encouragement from a man I considered a friend—a man who was planning to accompany me and my wife to Britain in a matter of days, no less—and essentially he'd dumped a bucket of cold water over my head.

"Oh, yeah?" I said. "Watch and see."

I put down my sandwich, turned and left, yanked my driver out of the bag as I marched to the practice tee, teed up a ball, and slammed it to the back of the range. Still seething mad, I hit maybe one or two more such monster drives before I heard my name being paged, the official summons to the first tee.

I walked straight onto the tee, pegged up my ball, and drove it onto the front of the first green.

There was an explosive cheer from the gallery on the tee and around the green, producing one of the strongest thrills of my career. Marching off the tee, I felt a powerful surge of adrenaline, maybe the greatest I had ever experienced. By the time I reached the green, I knew something big was happening to me. The eagle opportunity was long and not the easiest to read from that position on the green, but I coaxed it close enough to make people gasp and then made a lengthy comebacker for a birdie—a vastly better start than the previous three visits to the green. Around me, the gallery was running to find places on the second tee and fairway. There, I missed my approach shot to the green, but I chipped in for a birdie from the fringe, producing another pulse-quickening roar. A good wedge approach at three left me only a one-footer to convert for my third consecutive birdie, and I followed that up at the fourth with an eighteen-footer that dropped for my fourth birdie in a row.

I was back in the Open now, two under for the tournament and only three back of Souchak. I'm told that some of the large galleries waiting for the tournament leaders to tee off heard the commotion of what has been described as the wildest cheering ever heard at an Open and broke away to go see what was happening.

On the par-5 fifth, 538 yards long, I blocked my tee shot a bit and drove into the right rough, hit a 3-wood into the greenside bunker, blasted out to twenty feet, and took two putts to get down—my first par of the round. I remember feeling let down a bit—mentally kicking myself for not making five in a row.

I went back to work at the sixth, nailing a curling twenty-five-footer for birdie, then followed that up with a strong chip up and tap-in birdie at the seventh. The gallery went wild, I'm told, but all I could think about was the difficult eighth, a long uphill par-3 of 233 yards. The pin had been moved from the morning round to a spot that was down front and left, and I chose to gamble and go at it; I went with a 2-iron and pulled the shot slightly, landing my ball just on the front of the green, and watched the slope send it back into the bunker. I blasted out and two-putted for bogey.

As I stood in that eighth-hole bunker, Jack Nicklaus was walking off the ninth green, also in the process of tearing up the course. He'd gone out in 32 and was five under for sixty-three holes. I was four under, but so were Souchak, Hogan, Boros, Fleck, Finsterwald, Jerry Barber, and Don Cherry.

For the next hour or so, the entire leader board was in utter chaos. Behind me, Ted Kroll and Jack Fleck were also blistering the course. Up ahead, leading the tournament by a stroke after twelve holes, Nicklaus was sizing up a dangerous downhill putt for par on 13 when his inexperience caught up with him. Aware of Hogan's gruff response to what he considered stupid questions, Jack, barely twenty years old at the time, was uncertain whether under the rules he was entitled to repair a pitch mark directly in his putting line. He was—but was too timid to ask either Ben or an official. He tapped the putt, and the indentation threw the ball off line and caused it to just miss the hole. The error shook Jack's confidence, and, still rattled, he three-putted the 14th as well.

It was around 4:45 in the afternoon when I finally got a share of the lead, tied with Hogan and Fleck at four under par after a birdie at 11. I cooled off a bit at that point and made five consecutive pars, arriving at 17 at four under after seventy holes of golf.

At one point before the turn, I looked over and saw wordsmiths Drum and Jenkins following along in the Army. Smiling at them, I couldn't resist a well-aimed barb: "Well, well. What are you guys doing here?" I don't recall if or what they may have answered, but the staggering tension was visible on their faces as well.

The 17th was a 550-yard par 5 with an island green sitting in the middle of a still lake. The hole's design forced even long players like me to go with an intelligent drive, careful lay-up, and safe pitch to the putting surface. The pin in the afternoon final round was positioned dangerously close to the front of the green—and the slope that led to a watery doom in front. A typical fourth-round Open pin placement, set up to make someone either a hero or a goat. Ben Hogan's putter had been shaky all week. Perhaps that explains why he, the premier precision shotmaker of all time, decided he needed to get his third shot as close as possible to the hole for a reasonable chance at birdie or even a two-putt. In a daring attempt that had some people scratching their heads for years, he went directly for the flag, his ball barely clearing the band of water in front of the green. It was almost a phenomenal shot, but he and the gallery watched in horror as it spun backward and trickled down the slope into the water.

You have to credit Ben. He did what a champion

does at such a crucial moment: play the shot he thinks will work best and the devil take the consequences. Facing disaster, he didn't hesitate to remove his shoes and socks and wade into the water to slash the ball out and onto the green—exactly what I would have done under the same circumstances. He somehow got the ball onto the putting surface but missed his par putt, and I think that finally took the steam out of him. At 18, his drive found the water a foot or so short of land and sank his hope of a fifth Open championship.

Behind him in the fairway, I saw much of what was unfolding and tried to keep Pap's stern injunction to "take care of my own business" in my mind, meaning I needed to keep my focus where it ought to be—on the next shot and nothing else. Even after I'd been informed that I alone was leading the tournament, and even after I successfully negotiated the moat and putted out for par at 17, I quietly sweated bullets.

One more par.

That's exactly what I was thinking. *Concentrate on the next shot,* I told myself. *Don't get ahead of yourself. Try to stay calm and keep your head still.*

I wanted to win a United States Open so badly. I'd dreamed of winning the Open as a small boy, and now all I had to do was make *one* par to achieve that dream. I don't recall whether I knew it or not, but two holes behind me, Jack Fleck was the only guy with a realistic chance of catching me. As he'd proven by stunning Ben Hogan at the Olympic Club, the man was capable of producing miracle finishes.

I hit a 1-iron across the pond and safely into the fairway at 18, feeling a massive surge of relief. I'd avoided the hazard that had undone Bolt and Hogan and God knows how many other world-class players that week. A few moments later, I felt my emotions seesaw when I pulled my 4-iron approach shot and wound up to the left of the green. The ball was eighty long feet from the cup and in the rough. United States Open rough, no less. I walked up and stared at the lie for several moments. I took a couple of deep breaths, trying to gain as much composure as possible.

If I got up and down, I'd have my 280. If not, Fleck or someone else would probably at least tie or might pass me.

You can wait your entire life for a moment like this. I took out my wedge, set up over the ball, and made a crisp little chip that sent the ball rolling slowly toward the pin. It stopped a couple of feet from the hole. On my way to the ball, I paused to repair a pitch mark and then straightened up and studied the line. When I finally stood over the ball, my hands were moist from the heat and the tension, and those couple of feet looked more like two miles. But I kept my head dead still, took the putter back slowly, and rolled the ball into the heart of the cup.

I suppose I didn't believe, for an instant, what I'd just done. After half a beat of silence, the air around the green exploded, fractured by wild cheers and whistles. I glanced around, took a step or two to the hole, and lifted my ball from the cup, then turned and flung my white visor toward the gallery at the back of the green.

I later learned that, in the excitement, an NBC announcer had prematurely announced to his audience that Arnold Palmer was the new National Open champion. But that certainly wasn't the case, with Souchak, Cherry, and Jack the Giant Killer still out on the course.

With my heart beating wildly, I signed my card and went into the press tent to get a Coke. I took a seat at the interview table and the place erupted into a noisy den of questions and activity. A few minutes later, word reached us that Don Cherry had gone for the green at 17 in two and topped his ball into the water, while Fleck, two back then thanks to a missed one-footer at 16, could do no better than par. He would need an eagle at 18 to force a playoff. Instead, after what felt like an hour, he tapped in for bogey and the U.S. Open championship was mine.

Somehow I got a call through to Winnie from the noisy pressroom to her parents' house in Coopersburg. They'd been on the road, as it turned out, when they heard on the radio that Arnold Palmer was about to pull off one of the biggest comebacks in Open history. By then, of course, the verdict was in amid the long shadows of that Denver afternoon. My final-round 65, in fact, had overtaken fourteen players and at that time was the best finish ever by an Open champion, beating Gene Sarazen's 1932 finish by one stroke.

When I finally got Winnie on the phone amid the

hubbub of excited voices, my heart was still thumping wildly. I decided to skip most of the details, though.

"Hiya, lover," I said to her. "Guess what? We won!"

Some would say the arrival of Jack Nicklaus in my "backyard" at Oakmont in Pittsburgh, two years later, was almost the match of Cherry Hills for sheer quality of drama. Though I didn't care for the outcome, I can't disagree. The Open that year had all of the classic elements: a hometown favorite son at the peak of his form, a brilliant tour rookie everyone feared, highly partisan crowds, and the intensity of a National Open on the line.

I'd had a great year, my best start ever, leading up to Oakmont—including back-to-back wins at Palm Springs and Phoenix (where I enjoyed a 12-shot margin of victory, the largest of my career), followed by my third win at the Masters in April, then those three consecutive wins at the Texas Open, the Tournament of Champions, and the Colonial.

The pre-tournament consensus had me as the man to beat, and the home-field advantage of Oakmont, a course I knew intimately, seemed like a storybook setting for a second Open championship. Frankly, after playing poorly and finishing twelfth at Oakland Hills in Detroit the previous year, I was determined to do well in front of the homefolks in Pittsburgh. But as I was careful to warn the writers and anybody else who would listen to me prior to that week, "Everybody says I'm the favorite, but you'd better watch the fat boy."

I wasn't trying to insult Jack. In fact, as I think back on that comment, I realize I was mimicking much of what was being written about Jack's weight and appearance, and his apparent threat to my dominance of the Tour. Since joining the Tour at Los Angeles the first week of the year and winning $33.33, Jack had steadily climbed the leader board, and it was clear to anybody who'd witnessed his power and finesse and almost unearthly ability to focus on his game that Jack Nicklaus's moment had arrived. Whatever image problems he had early on regarding his weight or appearance or personality were, in my mind, completely irrelevant. I knew he was perfectly capable of taking the Open at Oakmont, because golf courses play no favorites and young Mr. Nicklaus simply had the look of a champion about him. I could see it, and so could anybody else who cared to look beyond the image baloney. As I privately expressed to Winnie and a few others from Latrobe, I really did view him as the one man I feared could snatch away the second Open title, one I dearly wanted to win in front of my hometown fans—a prophetic hunch, as it turned out.

I suppose if I had an ace in the hole where Jack was concerned, it was simply that Oakmont was a dangerously narrow golf course, with punishing rough that could turn errant tee shots into major disasters. Jack had something of a "flying elbow" in those days, a tendency to get wild off the tee with those huge, high-power fades of his. U.S. Open rough, of course, is the great equalizer of the championship. Anybody who misses fairways probably has no chance to contend in a National Open.

I was pretty sure the heavy partisan fan factor wouldn't bother Jack; in fact, it might even be a motivating factor in his favor. With that year's Masters title already in my pocket, and the goal of a modern Grand Slam intensely set in my mind, the pressure was really on me to prove to the world that I deserved a second Open title. On top of that, the tournament was being held on ground that held great meaning for me. It's ironic that it was this same rugged Open rough, specifically the rough around the greens, that gave me fits and ultimately proved to be my downfall. Oakmont's glassy putting surfaces also played a part in my undoing. At best, I was a mediocre putter on very fast greens, and I probably should have practiced on a similar putting surface prior to the Open. But I didn't, and that oversight took its toll.

Almost from the opening bell, my fears began to materialize. Jack and I were paired together for the first round, and an estimated gallery of 12,000 spectators lined the first fairway, anxious to watch us do our things. Jack started with three consecutive threes, all birdies, but I gave my fans precious little to cheer about. After just three holes, I trailed Jack by five strokes and it looked as if the day would be a long one. Fortunately, I righted the ship and ripped off my own string of birdies while Jack faltered just a touch. I shot an opening-round 71, and by the end of the day I stood one better than Jack for the championship. Both of us trailed reigning Open champion Gene Littler, who shot 69 in a round that included an eagle on the par-5 ninth. But Gene had trouble figuring Oakmont's mighty lethal greens, too, and the next afternoon Bob Rosburg and I surged to the front of the pack, I with a 68 and Rossie with a 69.

After sixteen holes of the morning round on Saturday, Rossie took the lead, but I regained it a hole later by driving the green at the short 17th and making the putt for an eagle two. Unfortunately, I gave a stroke back with a birdie attempt that was too bold on 18, missing the comebacker for par and suffering yet another three-putt bogey. The 73 dropped me into a tie at 212 with Bobby Nichols.

I went to fetch a ham sandwich and Coke, feeling let down. Though I still had a piece of the fifty-four-hole lead, all those careless three-putts were killing my psyche. Jack, on the other hand, two strokes back, hadn't had even one of them. He'd putted brilliantly over some of the most treacherous greens in championship golf. The sandwich and Coke refreshed me. I even downed a pint of chocolate milk for an energy boost and walked back to the first tee, where my final round was set to begin.

"Go get 'em, Arnie!"

The whooping and cheerleading had intensified.

I remember being aware of how large the crowds had grown. By early afternoon, some 22,000 fans were on the grounds at Oakmont, and by the end of the tournament something like a total of 25,000 more spectators than had ever attended an Open before would come to Oakmont.

Some of them could have used crash seminars in proper sportsmanship—or basic civility. I didn't witness much firsthand, aside from the crowd's unusual boisterousness, but I later heard of several instances when zealous Palmer partisans called out unflatteringly to Jack and even cheered when he— and other contenders, for that matter—missed a shot. This was deeply distressing both to Jack's father and to mine, both of whom were in the gallery that week, and when I heard about some of the incidents they made me angry. There is no room for such shenanigans in the game of golf. But it also played right into Jack's hands, as far as I was concerned.

At the ninth hole of the final round, I faced an opportunity to put the Open out of reach. I was two under for the round at that point, three under for the championship. If I could reach the par-5 ninth in two and make birdie—better yet, eagle—that might cinch the deal. I don't suppose it surprised anyone that I went for the green, pounding a 3-wood right on the screws. The ball drifted a little too much, though, and settled in the heavy rough just off the green, about pin high. All I still needed to do was make a solid little flip chip and a putt for birdie; that just might be enough.

I don't recall being particularly concerned about the chip shot. I mean, U.S. Open rough is like no other, but, frankly, I was used to playing out of the longer grasses where careful players seldom ventured. Even so, this week the rough was giving me nightmares. I took my stance and aimed at the pin and drew back my wedge. The unimaginable happened. I stubbed the shot. The ball popped up and settled in the rough mere inches from where it had been. The gallery around the green groaned and then grew so eerily quiet I swear you could hear the blood pumping angrily through my veins. I glared at the ball and tried again, producing another poor effort that left the ball eight feet from the cup. Instead of an excellent shot at birdie I now had to scramble like crazy for par. I missed the putt, grazing the right edge of the hole. I'd turned a surefire birdie into bogey, which under the circumstances felt like a double bogey. Even worse, it gave Nicklaus just the opening he needed.

He birdied nine and 11, and when I bogied the par-3 13th, we were tied for the championship. Jack made a great recovery from the bunker on 17 and nearly holed a birdie at 18 to finish with 69 and a seventy-two-hole total of 283.

I knew what I needed to do and was in position to do just that. From tee to green, I'd played almost as well as I ever have, missing only four greens that day, twice reaching critical par 5s in two. All I needed was a birdie at 18 and I would have my second U.S. Open title in storybook fashion. But the hole is hardly a cream puff. It measures 465 yards and is studded with menacing bunkers. I hit maybe my best drive of the day to the heart of the fairway, then slashed a superb 4-iron shot to ten feet of the cup. I was certain I would make the putt, but once again I didn't.

After the regulation seventy-two holes of play, the United States Open Championship was tied, with a playoff scheduled for Sunday.

Winnie, Pap, and I drove home afterward to Latrobe, an hour away, and I remember feeling a little drained by my experience, replaying in my head blown opportunities and my failure to make a birdie when I needed it. On the other hand, despite all those depressing three-putts, I was relieved to still be in the hunt. By the finish, I would collect thirteen three-putts to Jack's one—and therein lies the tale, as far as I'm concerned.

The point is, as we all understand, that you never know what will happen in golf. The conventional view is that Oakmont was an Open I should have won because I was the better player at the time. Well, "should have" and "did" may be neighbors, but they don't always get along. Still, I was going to do my level best at Oakmont to make sure they did. Winnie, Pap, and I had a quiet dinner, and I slept well and got up early, ready to charge to the golf course in Pittsburgh and take care of business.

But I fell behind right from the start, and after Jack rolled a birdie into the cup at the sixth hole, I was already four strokes down. The crowds were eerily silent at that point, as though they were spectators at a state funeral. When I rallied, though, they rallied and cheered me on. I briefly got a charge going with birdies at nine, 11, and 12. That drew me to within a stroke of Jack. As my playing history showed, that was my preferred position, having to mount a charge and close hard upon the front-runner.

But, suddenly, that equation was different—or should I say the front-runner was different. In the past, whenever I mounted a charge I could almost *feel* that the player I was chasing was going to collapse and give ground. It sounds a bit odd, but it was almost as if I could will the leader to move over and permit me to pass. As I've said on numerous occasions, I was a far better closer than a front-runner. So it can be argued that after a trio of birdies got me back in the hunt, I was exactly where I needed to be.

But Jack Nicklaus was a different animal altogether, completely unlike anybody I'd ever chased. For one thing, he didn't seem the slightest bit bothered by the electricity of my charge and the lusty cries of my supporters. If anything, they seemed to drive him further into that hard cocoon of concentration he showed the world. But it would take the world years to fully appreciate how difficult a chore that was and how well he executed it. I had never seen anyone who could stay focused the way he did—and I've never seen anyone with the same ability since. In my view, that's why Jack Nicklaus became the most accomplished player in the history of the game.

You just couldn't crack that concentration. He had his own game plan and he stuck to it, come hell or high water—or even noisy hometown fans.

Once again, though, it was my own traitorous flatstick that did me in. I three-putted the 13th green, fell two strokes, and never recovered. Despite a drive into the rough at 18, Jack won his first U.S. Open, and a little bit later I reflected to a reporter, "I'll tell you something. Now that the big guy is out of the cage, everybody better run for cover."

Then I went and found Winnie, who gave me the same big kiss she always gave me, win or lose, and we drove home to Latrobe.

The popular historical view is that I was a dominant force in the next four Open championships and a major factor in Opens for at least the next decade. I would agree with that assessment, and note that by my own calculations, poor chipping and putting on Open greens cost me at least three Open titles, maybe even a shot at the fourth.

Not long ago, Doc Giffin asked me an intriguing question. "Arnold," he said (because he always calls me "Arnold"), "if you could have one mulligan anywhere in your career, where would you use it?"

I thought about it a moment and cheekily replied, "I'd divide it several ways."

Certainly the eight-footer to win at Oakmont would be the first part.

The second part I'd spend at Brookline, the very next summer, in 1963.

I arrived at the Country Club, on the fiftieth anniversary of Francis Ouimet's miraculous 1913 win over Harry Vardon and Ted Ray, in a virtual dead heat with Jack Nicklaus for the Tour money title, and, thanks to a rare month off, my game was rested but pretty well tuned. In thirteen tournaments I'd already registered four wins and five other top-ten finishes, one of my strongest starts ever, but Jack was also winning tournaments at an impressive clip, causing some in the press to openly wonder if I was beginning to slip a notch or two. The truth is, I was distracted by a seemingly endless array of new business deals brought my way by Mark McCormack, my business manager, by a new airplane, and by other factors that come with the kind of success I was suddenly enjoying. But my game, as my record that year indicated, was essentially fine. I simply needed that four-week rest from the public eye, and I got it, and I came back raring to go.

The week before Brookline, after defeating Paul Harney in a playoff to take the Thunderbird Classic, I traveled to Massachusetts and immediately liked what I saw of the Country Club's old-style meandering course, which placed a premium on accurate driving and intelligent shots to small greens. I hoped the more northern grasses would also mean the putting surfaces were a touch slower, and therefore more to my liking, though that didn't turn out to be the case.

The weather was a major factor in producing unusually high scores, cold blustery winds that constantly shifted direction, tossing balls hither and yon. Meanwhile, the USGA was up to its old tricks with the greens and rough, difficult to read, harder to play. I didn't play particularly well, in the first three rounds going 73-69-77. Most unexpectedly, Jack failed to make the cut, and I remember feeling slightly out of synch, never quite able to find my stride and get my rhythm going. I was lucky enough to hang on with a final-round 74 and find myself in a three-way tie with Jacky Cupit and Julius Boros at the end of regulation play. Our 293s were the highest scores to lead after seventy-two holes since 1935, when Sam Parks won at Oakmont with 299. Perhaps five other men had an opportunity to win it outright, including Tony Lema, Paul Harney, and even young Bruce Crampton. But none of them could convert when they needed to, and the Open did an odd reprise of its celebrated 1913 three-man playoff.

For me, the critical moment in the playoff came in the 11th-hole fairway. Boros, typically chipping and putting like Old Man River, was four strokes ahead, and if there was a moment for me to make my charge, it ought to have been then. After a bogey at the tenth, I tried to put some extra mustard on my drive, but it strayed, and I found my ball sitting in a rotten stump off the left side of the fairway.

I had three choices: accept the penalty, which amounted to two strokes, drop out of the stump or hit another drive, or else play the ball as it lay. There was doubt in my mind what I needed to do. But I had no margin to squander strokes, so I took out a 4-iron, figuring to simply advance the ball back onto the fairway and make a good recovery from there.

I hacked three times at the ball before I freed it from that damned stump. Once again my bold style of play had mortally wounded me. I made seven on the hole and finished six strokes back of Julius with a dismal 76. If I had it to do over—or if I had one of Doc's magic mulligans—I might have gone back to the tee and hit my drive over, because you never know what might happen. I might also spend my "do-over" on the short putt I missed at 17 in the final round, a devastating miss that might have given me the championship outright.

But golf is not a game of what might have been. It's a game of who did what when it counted.

What happened, of course, was that Julius Boros glided home with that magnificent flowing swing of his to become, at age forty-three, the second-oldest man since Ted Ray to capture an Open championship. It seemed oddly fitting, given all the history surrounding that hallowed ground.

But for the second year in a row, I'd lost the Open in a playoff, and frankly it hurt like hell.

The next year, at Congressional Country Club in Washington, I was the only man to break par 70 in the opening round of the U.S. Open, on a lush, green, newly irrigated course that had been stretched to 7,053 yards, making it the longest Open test ever. Washington was in the midst of a terrible heat wave and a drought that wilted the hopes of almost everybody, including me. My scoring grew worse with every round, and I finished in fifth place. Coming back from years of disappointment, Ken Venturi walked slowly home, dazed by the hundred-degree heat, and heroically claimed his well-deserved U.S. Open title.

When I shot 76-76 and missed the Open cut at Bellerive in St. Louis in June of 1965, the talk that my game was foundering reached a near-fever pitch in the press. I heard it nearly everywhere I went and I saw it in people's faces: I wasn't striking the ball with the same old zest and derring-do; I wasn't fearless over putts anymore; I didn't attack golf courses the way I always had. . . . *What on earth is wrong with Arnie?*

The Big Slump had struck. That's what was wrong with Arnie. My desire to win golf tournaments was as strong as it had ever been, but I suddenly couldn't seem to get the ball in the hole when it counted.

This is as good a point as any to talk about something I've been thinking about, in this respect, for many years. Namely, why did I begin in late 1964 to lose that magical ability to charge and capture major golf tournaments? As my record indicates, I played extremely well in most of the major championships for the next decade, but it's undeniably true that, as the press detected, something *was* different about my game.

Most golfers win tournaments, and certainly U.S. Opens, by avoiding mistakes. But I typically won my most important tournaments by overcoming mine. Charlie Sifford once noted that I was the most aggressive player in the history of the game. It's entirely possible that's true.

If the downside of that signature trait is that I was capable of risking—and losing—everything on a low-percentage shot that could take me from hero to goat in one swing, the reverse was also equally true. Faced with a situation like the one that I found at Cherry Hills, it never entered my mind that I *couldn't* pull off a so-called miracle finish. The doubt never entered my mind.

When Sam Snead commented that every time I drove the ball, it looked as if I was trying to hole my tee shot, he wasn't far off the mark. The way I looked at any shot was that if you played it as boldly as you could, you were guaranteed to have the results you desired at least some of the time. In my mind, that far outweighed the benefit of playing conservatively. It was precisely this quality, I'm convinced, whatever that elusive mental "it" may be, that enabled me to win the tournaments I won—certainly the majors.

Magnified by the unprecedented media coverage my life and my career received, the historic charge that made Cherry Hills such a memorable Open for my fans and transformed my life also made my inevitable collapses (like losing the Masters to Gary Player the very next spring, as well as the National Opens I all but had in my grasp) all the more vivid and painful for people to watch. In time, those major disappointments and losses even took a toll on me. Permit me to explain.

Before I had the hopes of an entire *Army* resting on my shoulders with every shot, the consequences of failing to pull off a successful charge were pretty much mine alone to bear. Prior to 1964, it hurt like hell to blow a big tournament the way I did at Brookline or three-putt my way out of the championship the way I did at Oakmont in '62. But the disappointment never lasted long and certainly didn't affect the way I attacked a golf course. By nature, I simply wasn't prone to dwell for long on failure or moan about my fate. That was the Deke Palmer in me, I guess.

But after Cherry Hills, the British Open titles, and three more Masters championships came my way, I can see now, from the vantage point of many years, there was a subtle but perceptible shift in my playing consciousness. Yes, the distractions of fame and demands of a burgeoning business life were many, and I'm certain they had some impact on my ability to focus during a golf tournament, though how much I still can't say. But the truth is, as Mark McCormack once pointed out, it was nice to have those distractions on which to blame my slump, like the one that struck me hard in 1965.

But here is the critical point. Somewhere about the time I won my last major championship in 1964—and I'm still not certain when this phenomenon began to occur—even I became slowly aware that I wasn't playing tournaments with the same indifference to consequences that had carried me to the summit seven times (eight if you count my National Amateur title, which I do).

Not to place too fine a point on it, somewhere along the way, the elusive "it" that defined my style of play and enabled me to go for broke after any prize I hungered for began to change, slip away, or simply evade my summons. For example, I would step up to a long putt, pause a moment, and think about the potential danger of running a bold effort too far past the hole—something that once would never have been part of my thought process. Furthermore, I would stand on a tee studying a difficult fairway and—without even realizing what was going on at first—feel deep inside that, above all else, at this critical juncture of the tournament, I didn't want to disappoint my fans by making a poor shot or a gamble that failed. In simplest language, I began to sometimes get careful when I shouldn't have. Without even realizing it, I was playing defensively— playing, at times, not to lose rather than to win. Frankly, once I started down that road, it was all but impossible to come back.

Maybe the thing I hated and feared most was the feeling that people might feel sorry for me. I still had the desire to show them what I could do, and I knew I still had the shots to do it. But as I admitted to several close confidants beginning in about 1965, every time I'd get close to a major prize, my hands would begin to shake, and for a moment or two, when it counted most, the demons of doubt would whisper in my ear and I honestly wondered if I could win again.

As a result, 1965 was a genuine torment from beginning to end. At age thirty-six, for the first time, I had major body pains to go with the mental anguish, particularly in my shoulder, where I was plagued by bursitis most of the year. I no longer smoked on the golf course, but I ate more to try to fill the nervous void. As a result, I put on extra weight that made me feel sluggish, out of sorts, slower, more cautious—not old, exactly, but no longer young, either. I know enough star NFL quarterbacks to know that this was how they felt when they realized it was almost time to hang up the spikes.

By year's end, I'd managed to win only one tournament in nineteen months, the Tournament of Champions, and for the first time after five consecutive years of ranking first or second on the Tour earnings list, I'd fallen to tenth place—almost $90,000 behind Jack Nicklaus.

I've often said, as others have before me, that the true test of a champion comes not when he's winning, but when the chips are down and he can't seem to find his way.

After my steep fall-off in 1965, Winnie and I did some serious soul-searching about where I was headed in my playing career. I know she felt one factor contributing to my decline was the growing length of the PGA season, which now stretched from Los Angeles the first week of the year to November and even early December. The Tour I had joined in 1955 was pretty much a six-month affair, but now, thanks to lucrative exhibition matches and a host of growing "unofficial" events and foreign tournaments anxious to capitalize on golf's booming popularity, it was possible to play golf without a significant break almost from Christmas to Christmas.

During my peak performance years, I'd always relished the chance to get away from the Tour and go home and do nothing but putter around the house and my workshop, play with the girls and go hunting with Pap, have dinner with friends, and be a nuisance underfoot to Winnie as she prepared the house for the holidays. One thing that was clearly missing now, as she pointed out, was that month of rest I once customarily took after Thanksgiving.

I was reluctant to admit she was right—but, as usual, she was right. We agreed after that disappointing "slump" year of 1965 finally came to an end that I needed to get back to the basics of family life, slowing down to enjoy it more.

I canceled a lot of engagements and took the rest of the year off to be with Winnie and the girls. It was almost like the old days, and the rest clearly did me good.

In the first tournament of the new year, 1966, the Los Angeles Open, I birdied seven holes in a row en route to a third-round 62, matching my career low and producing a three-shot victory over Miller Barber and Paul Harney.

I kept telling reporters and just about anybody else who would listen that my only focus for the year was winning golf tournaments, and in successive weeks, falling briefly off the cigarette wagon and puffing the odd coffin nail here or there on the sly, I placed second in the Crosby, third at the Lucky International, and lost in a playoff to Doug Sanders at the Bob Hope Desert Classic.

My Army was clearly pleased that "Arnie was back," and I wasn't at all disappointed myself.

After sixty-two holes at the Masters, I was tied for the lead, but I faltered and faded to fourth. Still, heading into the 66th U.S. Open at San Francisco's Olympic Club, our destination when Winnie and I had made our first big trip west more than a decade before as newlyweds, I was pleased that I'd made one of my best starts ever.

This time we stayed with our friends Ed and Rita Douglas, in their lovely home not far from the University of San Francisco. The Douglases had become close friends of ours over the years, and it was Ed, a regional manager for Pennzoil, who helped create a strong commercial affiliation that I enjoy to this day.

I'd made a few changes to my swing, learning to hit the ball with a slight fade that would fit Olympic's predominantly left-to-right features. It seemed to work pretty well, though I completed my first round in 71 despite some typically shaky putting on those billiard-table-fast greens. The first-round magic belonged to Al Mengert, a part-time tour professional from Washington State, who shot 67.

The next day I caught fire, and if I hadn't missed putts of less than four feet on each of the closing two holes, I would have matched the Open record of 64. As it was, my round of 66 and 137 total left me in a tie for first with Bill Casper.

Bill—as I preferred to call him instead of Billy— was a bit rejuvenated himself, having shed a lot of weight on a strange diet that reportedly involved buffalo and bear meats. The story goes—and I've never asked Bill about this, so who knows if it's true—that one morning before his round he ate swordfish and tomatoes, which would be enough to give me serious stomach distress. But the point is, Casper was leaner and meaner and had a more serious look in his eye than most of us had ever seen before. He was also one of the best short-game players who ever walked on an Open course, especially in the putting department.

For reasons both commercial and logistical in nature, the USGA's executive committee had decided to abandon "Open Saturday's" double rounds. Starting with Olympic, the tournament would conclude on a fourth day, a move most players applauded.

My third round wasn't particularly sensational, a steady 70, but it allowed me to open up a three-shot bulge over the slimmed-down Bill Casper, who completed his round with 73.

I felt the old adrenaline pumping, and I was once again attacking the golf course as I had in my younger days. Going into that final round, my feeling was that Olympic's front nine was more difficult than the back nine. If I could post a low score there on Sunday, I could play home with the confidence that it would take an extraordinary feat of shotmaking— or at least a spectacular collapse on my part—for somebody to catch me.

Everything just seemed to click. The shots were solid, the putts dropped. I'd posted a 32 by the turn and opened a commanding seven-stroke lead over Casper. To be perfectly honest, though, I wasn't thinking too much about Bill and what he might have to do in order to catch me. He was a steady player and sensational putter, but frankly not the sort who was known for last-minute heroics. The guy I had my eye on, and feared most, quite honestly, was a couple of strokes back of him: Jack Nicklaus.

How do you explain what happened over the next ninety minutes or so? I've spent nearly three decades attempting to do just that—explain to myself and to a lot of other sympathetic people the rhyme and reason of what transpired.

The simplest explanation is that, believing I had the Open already won, I quit playing Bill and Jack and started playing Ben Hogan's old 1948 Open record of 276. I'd done the same thing at Augusta when I almost gave away the Masters while chasing his mark there. I knew that if I could just finish the back nine in 36, a stroke above par, the new record of 275 would belong to Arnold Daniel Palmer.

In retrospect, it was the biggest mental error of my career.

In daring to think about breaking Hogan's record, I violated the very rule Pap had spent all those years drilling into my head—never quit, never look up, and, most of all, never lose focus until you've completely taken care of business. As we started together down the tenth fairway, Bill looked at me and made what sounded an awful lot like a concession speech. No doubt feeling Jack in hot pursuit, he reflected: "I'm going to have to go just to get second."

"Don't worry, Bill," I replied, uttering the words I was doomed to have to cat. "You'll finish second."

The nightmare began at that same hole, a bogey for Palmer at ten. Bill parred. Advantage Casper.

After that, like some ghostly newsreel playing in my head, I recall it going like this: I birdie at the 12th, but so does Bill. I remind myself that I'm still six ahead of him with six holes to play—no place to panic. At the par-3 13th, I miss the green with my tee shot and settle for bogey four. Maddening, but not fatal. We move to 14, where we both make pars; I'm still five up, but thanks to that bogey I now must par my way home to beat Hogan's old mark.

Fifteen is another par 3. The pin is tucked in the right-hand corner behind a bunker. Instead of playing safe, I decide this is the moment to put the tournament on ice. I attempt the perfect shot and go straight at the flag, watch my ball catch the edge of the green and tumble into the bunker. Another bogey. Then Casper, who has played safely to the middle of the green, thirty-five feet from the pin—I remember being annoyed by his strategy, wondering what he had to lose by *not* going for the pin— smoothly rolls home another birdie putt.

Thoughts of Ben Hogan and his record instantly vanish from my mind, replaced by the first rising vapors of genuine alarm. For the first time, it dawns on me that Bill Casper is the real threat here, not Ben Hogan. My lead has dwindled to three. We walk on to the 16th, the big par 5, 604 yards with a sweeping right-to-left curve that fits my natural ball flight. Most golfers would settle for two safe hits and a careful pitch to the putting surface, but all I can think at this point is how irritated I am that Casper has been "playing safe" and is catching up on me. I tell myself there is no way I can allow that to happen. There is *no way* I'm going to allow him to beat me by playing safe. I decide I will win or lose exactly the way I've won or lost every golf tournament I've ever played.

The long draw is my bread-and-butter shot, but either nerves or perhaps the fact that I've been hitting fades all week finally takes a toll. An untimely duck hook sends the ball off a tree into the deep left rough. I compound the situation by trying to slash a 3-iron out of the heavy rough. The ball squirts across the fairway, advancing less than a hundred yards. It stops once more in the heavy grass, leaving me no chance to reach the putting surface on my third. Now I still have over three hundred yards of fairway to negotiate and only three shots left for par. I chop the ball back to the fairway with my wedge and drill a 3-wood into the greenside bunker. You don't want to know what's going on in my mind here. It feels as if a volcano is about to erupt in my head. I blast out of the bunker and am fortunate to make no worse than six. Bill, playing impeccably safe golf again, scores his second consecutive birdie.

I have now lost four strokes on two holes, and my lead is one.

On 17, the hardest hole at Olympic, 435 yards uphill to a small green on the shoulder of the hill, I hook my drive into the long grass again, miss the green on my approach, but finally make a decent chip that leaves me ten feet for par. My putt just grazes the right edge of the hole. Bill, meanwhile, makes his par 4 and we are suddenly tied for the lead at the 66th U.S. Open.

At 18, Bill plays quickly, splitting the fairway with his drive. I tell myself there is still no reason to panic but certainly a need to get the ball into the short grass. I choose a 1-iron for accuracy but am so wound up I even pull that shot. I stare after the ball with a slumping heart as it scampers into the heavy left rough and disappears from my sight. What I wouldn't have given for an L&M cigarette about then.

Walking down the fairway, shaken to the core, I doubt if I have ever felt as alone or as devastated on a golf course. I know what a train wreck the world is witnessing, but I tell myself that I am *still* in the thick of it. I can glance at faces in the gallery and see their shock and grief, too. People call out reassuringly, and I don't even know if I acknowledge them. Perhaps I scan the crowd for Winnie, because her emotional thermometer is always set on seventy-two degrees and it never fails to calm me to see her. (Mark McCormack, on the other hand, was often such a visible nervous wreck, it made me feel nervous just to look at him—he often left the course at such moments to make business calls, for both our sakes.)

I try to relax and remember my father's lessons about keeping my head and body still, making a slow backswing and solid contact. All I need is one good shot. This one looks almost impossible, but I must somehow get it on the putting surface. I know Bill will get his shot on the green, and if I want any hope of making a playoff, I simply must have a par.

I decide on a wedge and set up over the ball, then hit it hard, slashing it out of the long grass. An instant later, still leaning over, I glance up to see where it is going. I watch the ball fly extremely high and appear to settle somewhere in back of the dangerously tiny green. The gallery there lets out a roar, and I know I've still got at least a chance to save par and halve the hole.

On the green, I face a difficult thirty-footer downhill to the cup across the lightning-fast putting surface. After a moment or two sizing up the situation, I stroke the putt and slightly misjudge the line a bit, leaving myself as tough a side-hill six-footer as I've ever faced to salvage par. Under the rule then in effect, I am forced to putt out first, which I do, then I step back to wait and see if Bill can beat my four. He misses his birdie attempt and we both finish with 278.

As Bill and I shake hands, all I really feel is a sense of deep relief and perhaps a bit of disbelief at what has just happened. My anger at myself will come later. In time, I realized I knew what Hogan must have felt like when Fleck caught him in exactly the same spot in 1955, forcing a playoff at the final hole of the Open—a tournament the greatest player in the game at that moment felt confident he'd won. My own confidence now shaken, I sign my card and walk slowly to the press tent, where a hundred unanswerable questions await. My friends in the press corps all look a little embarrassed to have to ask them. I can't wait to get to Ed and Rita's place for a drink.

There will be yet another U.S. Open playoff for me.

The playoff was an eerie reprise of the fourth round. Once again I played solid shots and went out in 33 against Bill's 35, and once again he started picking up strokes the way he had the previous day. He dropped a dramatic fifty-footer for a birdie two at 13, going ahead for the first time. In all the high drama of my collapse, it's sometimes forgotten that Bill Casper played almost flawless golf down the stretch. That point can't be driven home enough. I didn't just lose the 1966 U.S. Open—Bill Casper's brilliant play won it.

He finished with a 69 and I managed a 73, once again letting an Open championship slip through my fingers. Afterward in the pressroom, the shock of the previous day's free fall had begun to wear off, and I detected a swell of great sympathy about what those on hand had witnessed, the most historic collapse in Open history. As a postscript, or epitaph, to the event, some would write that the disaster only humanized Arnold Palmer even more—simply proved he was more like the people who admired him than any professional golfer in history.

I don't know whether that's true or not. All I know is that, curiously, afterward I was bitterly disappointed but I didn't feel the least bit sorry for myself. Why should I? It wasn't a disaster. A plane crash or an earthquake is a disaster. This was a golf tournament—admittedly a huge one and one I'd desperately wanted to win. But, as I consoled myself, I'd won it before and would probably have a chance to win it again. I was only the second man in history to break 280 and not win a U.S. Open. (Jimmy Demaret was the first, in 1948, losing by three to Hogan.) I'd played well enough to win the Open. But Bill Casper had played slightly better. That's all I can really say about it.

Fact is, I really felt worse for my fans and for those people with long faces waiting for me at Ed and Rita's house. I walked in following the play-off and discovered Winnie, both Douglases, and Mark and Nancy McCormack sitting silently around the kitchen table, as if they were at a wake. I didn't want anybody feeling sorry for me. That feeling extended to my own friends and family.

"What's wrong with you people?" I bellowed at them, forcing a halfhearted smile. "You look like you've been to a funeral."

I guess they thought they had.

Well, that's golf. My kind of golf, anyway.

Losing three Opens in playoffs was tough, but life is tough, and even though I felt emotionally drained and a little cheated by Old Man Par at Olympic Club, I wasn't through with the United States Open, nor it me.

The next summer, 1967, I chased Jack Nicklaus and his painted white Bullseye putter around Baltusrol's Lower Course and was tied for the lead with him for 54 holes. I shot a 69 to his 65 in the final round, becoming the second player in history to twice break 280 and fall short of victory, this time by four strokes.

At Champions Golf Club in 1969, I three-putted the 15th hole after making a great recovery from the woods. A birdie there would have put pressure on the leader (and eventual winner) Orville Moody; maybe that would have created an outcome more to my liking. Instead, I wound up three strokes back, in sixth place.

Playing the 14th hole at Pebble Beach in 1972, I had a putt of about eight feet for birdie that would have placed me in the Open lead with just four holes to play. Nicklaus was sizing up a similar-length putt on 12 for par. If I had made my putt and he had missed, the Open would probably have been mine. Instead, he converted and I failed—and the Open was his.

If only I could have had one of Doc Giffin's magic mulligans . . .

Then there was my return to Oakmont the very next summer. By then, of course, a host of new names were regularly pegged to the leader board: Lee Trevino, Raymond Floyd, Johnny Miller, even a bright young prodigy from Kansas City who looked as wholesome as a face off a cornflakes box. His name was Tom Watson.

At the par-4 11th hole during the final round, I was four under, facing a short, four-foot birdie opportunity that would have put me five under and in command of the tournament. I made what I thought was a good stroke, and watched in disbelief as the ball grazed the hole, staying out. Two more shocks to the system followed. First, thinking I was still in the lead at four under, I glanced over at a distant scoreboard and could make out that someone else had just posted a red five. I asked my playing partner, John Schlee, who that could have been. "Miller," he answered, meaning twenty-six-year-old Johnny Miller, who'd just finished with a sensational 63.

A few moments later, I struck what I was sure was a terrific drive at 12, only to discover a few minutes later that the ball lying in the fairway, which I thought was mine, really belonged to Schlee. Much to my surprise, my ball had caromed left instead of right and was in deep grass on the 603-yard hole. Now, instead of being tied for the lead and in good position in the fairway at a hole where I often made birdie, I was a stroke behind and facing a desperate situation. All I could do was thump a medium iron shot back to the fairway. With a four-wood, though, I attempted to reach the green but pulled the shot into the deep rough above a greenside bunker, pitched well past the hole, and made bogey six. I felt devastated and it quickly showed—two more bogeys at 13 and 14. I finally birdied 18, but it was meaningless. Once more I'd been unable to rally from my own mistakes, and someone else's good golf had cost me the Open.

Following a pair of top-ten finishes in '74 and '75 at Winged Foot and Medinah, respectively, my Open career began to fade. I played hard and never gave up; I gave my fans a few thrills here and there, but somehow I could never summon back any magic.

Then, in 1984, I came up two strokes shy at

sectional qualifying on the outskirts of Cleveland. That ended my streak of thirty-one consecutive U.S. Open appearances, a record I shared with Gene Sarazen. I'm still very proud of that.

In the summer of 1994, by special invitation from the USGA, I made one final journey to Oakmont, where I had played my first National Open, as an amateur (failing to make the cut), in 1953, for my last appearance at the U.S. Open. What an emotional roller-coaster ride that week was, with parties and dinners and private conversations with old friends who'd followed my Open escapades for several decades. I must have signed a thousand autographs. The letters and telegrams poured into the Latrobe office, and it was all I could do to keep myself together emotionally, if not on the golf course.

I shot 77-81 and as most people expected, I guess, missed the cut. In the pressroom afterward, as I mopped my brow with a small towel, I was asked to reflect on my long and illustrious Open career. The proper words were difficult to find. I wanted to express so much about the wonderful way I had been treated by fans and the USGA and what playing in the National Open had always meant to me. I began by talking about the tournament's great traditions and my own beginnings at Oakmont in 1953, moved on from there to say a few words about how grateful I was to have won at Cherry Hills and to have had a crack at winning probably seven or eight other times, then finally . . . I lost it.

I apologized and bowed my head, too choked up to go on.

As I got up to leave, the members of the press accorded me a great honor, something I had never seen or heard of them doing before. One by one, they stood and applauded—and kept applauding. It's traditional for writers to give the Open winner a standing ovation when he enters the pressroom after his victorious final round.

This time they gave me a standing ovation after my final Open round.

It was like having one of Doc's magic mulligans, after all.

CHAPTER TEN

The Claret Jug

Troon, Scotland
July, 1962

Dear Suze and Ken,

Having a nice time. Weather lovely but chilled a bit like late October. Much golf, little else. Course is not in particularly good shape and Arnie is putting awful. Nice to see our old friends but the magic is wearing off, I think. Glad to get back.

Love,
Winnie

Our Latrobe neighbor Susie Bowman brought this postcard Winnie sent her from Troon over to the house the other evening. We sat around the kitchen table and had a nice laugh about it. She'd found it while cleaning out some drawers and thought we might want to see it. I think maybe Winnie was the most amused of all, because of the fact that she *loved* going to the British Open, and the end of the note implies that the "magic" of the tournament was wearing a bit thin—or maybe it was *my* magic she meant.

"I definitely wrote that at the beginning of the week," she decided with a wry smile, "because the week ended pretty well, all things considered."

Indeed it did. In 1962 I won my second consecutive Claret Jug, the name of the venerable trophy presented by the Royal and Ancient Golf Club to the winner of the British Open. Champions keep the actual trophy for a year but are offered a smaller replica of the Claret Jug. Mine still sits in my Latrobe office.

Winnie had good reason to feel a little down and worried at the beginning of the week, though. The course, thanks to a lengthy drought, was in pretty poor shape. The wind was chilly and my putting was even colder, all factors that undoubtedly affected my mood and probably made me a little tough to live with. Remember, too, that just a few weeks before I'd lost to Jack Nicklaus in a playoff in front of the hometown folks at Oakmont. That was still gnawing at me.

What Winnie's note doesn't begin to reflect, though, is the great depth of affection and growing admiration she and I both felt for the British people and their beloved linksland golf courses, not to mention their reverence for the traditions of the game. It's no exaggeration to say we were having a love affair with British golf fans and their venerable Open.

But it's a love story that really began two years

prior to that, in 1960, just after I won the U.S. Open at Cherry Hills.

As it happened, we had almost no time to digest and savor the miracle that had taken place in Denver. Less than thirty-six hours later, Bob Drum, Winnie, and I met Pap and Harry Saxman (Pap's boss, Latrobe Country Club's president, and a close family friend) in New York for our TWA flight to Dublin, Ireland, and Portmarnock Golf Club, where Sam Snead and I were scheduled to represent America in the Canada Cup, the forerunner of the World Cup, against teams from thirty different nations. From there we would push on to St. Andrews, Scotland, where I would play in my first British Open.

To tell the truth, I knew little about Britain's linksland golf courses, aside from the fact that there the game began and the conditions were said to be considerably rougher than the courses we played in the States. I knew—or had been told—that fairways often resembled pastures and greens could be difficult to read. Also, the wind and weather were almost always dominant factors that greatly influenced play. Sam Snead had, at best, an ambivalent relationship with British golf. As his train was arriving in St. Andrews in 1946, and after sleeping on a bench in war-torn London en route to the tournament, he glanced at the Old Course and remarked that it looked like an abandoned golf course. His comment outraged a proper Scottish gent who overheard it. During the tournament, which he ultimately won, his first caddie had to be dismissed for being drunk as a skunk, while his replacement had a penchant for whistling through Sam's backswing. Needless to say, Sam, who wasn't shy about expressing an opinion, wasn't overly enamored of the place. Though he pocketed 150 pounds sterling for winning the Claret Jug, he bitterly complained to anybody who would listen that the trip cost him almost double that in expenses. Furthermore, he created quite a stir by announcing that he had no intention of coming back to defend his title. He later added insult to injury by saying that, perhaps thinking of his first night in Britain and the deepening rift between himself and golf's homeland fans, playing golf outside the United States "was like sleeping in the rough."

Other American players at the time shared Sam's attitude. Though they didn't feel as strongly about it as Sam, they were hesitant to make the pilgrimage to the British Open. It was expensive and time-consuming, and there was no guarantee you would make a penny for your efforts. Under the existing rules of the tournament, everyone, including the defending champion, had to go through two qualifying rounds. There were no automatic exemptions for top American players—even winners of our Open or the Masters. This fact alone kept most of the game's established and emerging stars home in America during the British Open week, and it had certainly been a major factor in the slow deterioration of the British Open's prestige.

But ever since I'd robbed Winnie of a Walker Cup honeymoon, I'd had it in my mind to go play the British Open championship, if for no other reason than that Bob Jones had felt such powerful kinship with the people of St. Andrews and the oldest major golf tournament in the world. Actually, come to think of it, my desire to go play the Open in Britain went back much further than that—to my days as a schoolboy golfer, when I followed newspaper accounts of the British Open and read exciting biographies of top American players like Jones and Walter Hagen, who not only played there but won there.

Somewhere on my first flight over there, during our extended cocktail hour, Bob Drum and I got to talking about Jones's great Grand Slam. Drum remarked to me that it was a shame that the growth of the professional game, among other things, effectively ended the Grand Slam concept as it had been known in Jones's day (the Grand Slam then comprised the U.S. and British Amateur Championships and both major Opens).

"Well," I said casually over my drink, "why don't we create a new Grand Slam?"

Drum gave me one of his famous contrarian glares that made him look like a cross between an annoyed college dean and a sleeping bear someone had foolishly kicked awake.

"What the hell are you talking about?" he muttered, though probably a little more colorfully than that.

I explained what I was thinking. "What would be wrong with a professional Grand Slam involving the Masters, both Open championships, and the PGA Championship?"

He chewed on that for a few seconds, then sipped

his drink and snorted. Usually, a Drum snort meant he thought your idea was so utterly ridiculous he sometimes wondered why he wasted his time sharing oxygen space with you. This time his snort meant he thought, *Well, kid, maybe you've got something there.*

Because his newspaper didn't want to foot the expenses, Drum was accompanying me to Britain on his vacation time, and for some mysterious reason a foolish editor at his paper even told him not to bother to file a story. The irony of that, of course, is that when it appeared that not only was I contending for the lead in the Open but also might *win* it, his bosses were begging him for a dispatch from the frontline. Drum was a wily old cuss, though. I believe he made them really grovel for a while, running up their phone bill to boot, before he gave in and agreed to go back on the clock and write something about my first trip to the British Open.

I'm not entirely certain he was the first to write about the idea of a modern Grand Slam, though. That's because when we stopped at Portmarnock en route, I'm certain he spread the idea of the new professional Grand Slam among his colleagues in the British press. So one of them was probably the first to actually write about the concept. Still, it was Bob who effectively first planted the seed that later grew.

I was immediately impressed by the rough links I discovered at Portmarnock and by the knowledgeable and interested crowds that roamed by the thousands up and down those windblown Irish dunes. Strange as it may sound, the style of golf was more like the kind of golf I'd played as a boy, when the courses were mostly ungroomed and fairly simple in design and nature, and I found that the reserved nature of the galleries—which annoyed some Americans and made them feel unwelcome—was actually a bonus for me. There was no shouting or carrying on, only polite sustained applause when you earned it by making a superior shot. They clearly loved the game for the game's sake and were a tough crowd to please, so pleasing them became a motivating factor for me.

Sam and I were the eventual winners, but a couple other things stick out in my memory of that week. To begin with, this was where I began my strong relationship with the wonderful British golf press, making a host of new acquaintances I would come to regard as good friends: men such as Pat Ward-Thomas of the *Manchester Guardian*, Leonard Crawley of the *Daily Telegraph*, Peter Ryde of the *Times*, and Henry Longhurst of the *Sunday Times*. The elegance of their reporting was exceeded perhaps only by their passion for the purity of the game. Their deep respect for the game's traditions set a wonderful stage for reporting on the tournaments, and they were a tremendous influence on both Winnie and me.

Pat Ward-Thomas became a particular favorite. Consider this well-turned snippet from his frontline dispatch in *Country Life* magazine, detailing our first interview one evening after I'd shot a miserable 75 and left Sam holding the bag at Portmarnock:

I was impressed by his manner, reserved, agreeable and polite, and yet forthright with the directness of a man who knows his own mind. On the evening of the third day at Portmarnock I had to talk with him on a radio programme, only a few minutes after he had finished his worst round. He was disappointed, and not a little angry with himself, because Snead that afternoon had played a magnificent round of 67 and Palmer's 75 meant that the American lead was far less than it should have been. Yet he said nothing more than he had played badly: there was no word of excuse or complaint, simply a contained impatience with his own imperfections. There was a quiet coldness about him that expressed determination and self-control more effectively than anything he might have said. Here I thought is a man capable of fashioning destiny and of being unafraid when it beckoned.

While I was busy "coldly" trying to fashion destiny and impress the Canada Cup crowds, Winnie was being squired all about Dublin by the elegant Chris Dunphy, an American blue blood who more or less ran Seminole Golf Club in those days and traveled in the higher echelons of British and American society. (It was Chris who eventually introduced us to the Duke of Windsor and his wife, Wallis. The Duke and I became pretty chummy, though his wife struck me as a bit flighty.) While I was trying my best to figure out the mysteries of linksland putting, Winnie was happily gallivanting through Dublin's famous linen shops and woolen mills with Dora Carr, Irish amateur star Joe Carr's wonderfully hospitable wife, and taking afternoon tea at Teddy O'Sullivan's Gresham Hotel with Chris Dunphy.

My first glimpse of St. Andrews one afternoon the following week wasn't exactly the religious experience I'd hoped for. To tell the truth, the sight of the Old Course links didn't exactly overwhelm me with fear. In fact, I thought it was probably as easy a golf course as I'd ever seen. Of course, this is exactly what most Americans think the first time they lay eyes on the place.

After my first practice round on the Old Course, I felt certain that my initial impression was correct—that the course wasn't all that difficult and could be mastered fairly easily if you avoided the gorse and stayed out of the fearsome pot bunkers. The wind off the Firth of Forth was usually frisky, but my tee shots were typically low-boring affairs that stayed below the currents that tortured higher ball-strikers and rolled a long way when they landed on the firm, wind-cured turf. This meant that, under certain circumstances, I could come close to if not actually drive several of the par-4 holes. I liked this quality about linksland golf quite a lot.

As I discovered, though, it's only after successive rounds at the Old Course that you begin to realize the subtle brilliance and high degree of difficulty the most famous golf course on earth throws at you. Bob

Jones wasn't particularly impressed by the course his first time around it, either, but he eventually became such a devoted student of the course that he compared it then to a "wise old lady, whimsically tolerant of my impatience, but ready to reveal the secrets of her complex being, if I would only take trouble to study and learn."

I couldn't put it any better than that. Study and learn. That's exactly what you have to do to try to prevent the Old Course from beating you.

Luckily, I had a good tutor to guide me through my lessons. Tony Wheeler, Wilson's representative in Britain, introduced me to a young, gangly, chain-smoking former St. Andrews junior champion named Tip Anderson, who knew his mind and the mysterious ways of the Old Course.

I suppose you could say Tip was your classic Scotsman—as stubborn as he was smart, not likely to suffer fools who didn't heed his advice. Despite our two strong personalities, we got along well from the start, though he wasn't the least bit hesitant to convey his disapproval if I overruled his opinion on a shot. Sometimes we must have sounded like an old married couple squabbling gently in the fairway or rough. At times, I confess, I'd get so annoyed with his hard-headedness I'd look at him in exasperation and remark, "Hey, Tip, I play this game myself. I *think* I know what I'm doing."

He would give me that deeply pitying look of his, perhaps shake his head, and look at the horizon as if to say, "Well, lad. There's no' much I can do to help you now, if you won't mind ol' Tip."

While I was busy qualifying for the Open on the adjacent New Course, firing 142 to easily make it into the tournament, trying my best to learn the eccentricities of the huge undulating greens and quirky bounces of links golf, Winnie was busy discovering the rustic charms of British hotel life just across Links Road on the second floor of Russacks Hotel. Figuring that midafternoon was an excellent time to slip down to the communal bathroom on our floor and have a nice hot, private soak in the tub, she was nearly flattened by a large semi-naked gent with a handlebar mustache who came barreling out of the bathroom. He apologized brusquely, but by then it was too late. Poor Winnie fled back to our room and shut the door in horror, refusing to risk another tub bath for the balance of the week.

I opened the 100th British Open with a round of 70 and followed that with a 71. This was something of a disappointment but not the end of the world. Kel Nagle was two behind leader Roberto de Vicenzo at that point, and Peter Thomson, who had won the tournament four times in the 1950s, was back with me at 141. The British Open traditionally started on Wednesday and finished with two rounds on Friday—so professionals could be back in their shops for the weekend. A few years later, the fourth round was moved to Saturday, and it wasn't until my business agent Mark McCormack convinced the Royal and Ancient in 1980 that American television would pay a lot more money to have the event spread over the weekend that the final rounds were moved to Saturday and Sunday.

After a third-round 70 enabled me to pick up five strokes on Roberto in the Friday morning round, I walked off the course to have a sandwich with Pap, Harry Saxman, and Winnie, feeling confident that the afternoon round might bode extremely well for me. Thanks to Tip, I'd managed to avoid the steepwalled bunkers and was playing better than my score indicated. I could feel myself getting into the right frame of mind to mount a charge the same way I'd done it at Denver a few weeks earlier.

Unfortunately, the golf gods had other things in mind. Just about the time we settled over our lunches, the skies above the links blackened and the rains blew in off the Firth of Forth. I mean it *rained*. It rained like I'd never seen it rain before, coming in wild gusts and torrents. Watching it pour, I remember assuring Winnie and Pap that a British Open had never been canceled because of inclement weather— nor had one ever finished on a Saturday, to that point. I was chomping at the bit to get back out there and catch the leaders. Aussie Kel Nagle had overtaken Roberto to lead with 207. I was at 211, four strokes back, but I felt the championship was well within my striking range.

I was deeply disappointed when I got to the first tee, dressed for the tumult and primed to play, and found that the afternoon round had been postponed, and furthermore was now scheduled to be completed—for the first time ever—on Saturday.

For what it's worth, I always thought, and still feel, that the postponement hurt my chances of winning that first British Open I'd played in. For the most part, because of my inexperience on linksland courses, I played conservatively—and that wasn't my style—which may also have cost me a bit. But in fairness it was really the infamous 17th or Road Hole that doused my hopes of completing the third leg of our newly created modern Grand Slam. The legendary 475-yard hole gave me fits all week. The first two days I reached it in regulation only to three-putt both times; and the same thing occurred in the Friday morning round before the historic washout.

By the time I reached the Road Hole's tee on Saturday afternoon, I'd cut Nagle's advantage to one shot and felt the tournament was mine to win. Perhaps because I was so pumped up, I overshot the 17th green on my 6-iron approach and wound up with my ball sitting on the pebble road behind the green. This time, however, I made perhaps my best recovery shot of the tournament, running the ball up the little bank and close enough to the pin to sink the par putt. I followed that with a massive drive and birdie at 18. Nagle, playing directly behind me, still one stroke ahead, needed par 4s on the last two holes to maintain his lead, and he got them. But it was really the Road Hole that wound up telling the tale. For the tournament, I had ten putts there to Nagle's four. Kel was such a gracious competitor, you have to give him all the credit in the world for hanging tough at the end.

Needless to say, I was disappointed that any hope of a Grand Slam was now gone, although I remember telling myself that an "American" Grand Slam was still possible, assuming I went home and captured the PGA Championship at Firestone in a couple of weeks. But frankly, our British Open experience had been everything I'd hoped it would be. The galleries had been so informed and so welcoming, the press so thoroughly engaging and entertaining (One of my fondest memories of the week was the hilarious pounding that defending champion Gary Player took from the tabloid press when he appeared on the first tee of the opening round wearing slacks that had one white leg and one black one. That fashion statement prompted an indignant scribe to pronounce that he looked more like a court jester than a dignified Open champion.), the entire atmosphere so strongly reflective of the good things I felt about the game, that when Pat Ward-Thomas and Henry Longthirst—oops, I mean to say Long*hurst*—urged us to go on to Paris for the French Open at St. Cloud, Winnie and I quickly consulted and decided to do just that.

We said so long to Pap, Bob Drum, and Harry Saxman and flew to Sculthorpe Air Base outside of London, where George Vogel, a U.S. Air Force major from my hometown, graciously offered to put us up in officers' housing for the week before the French tournament. We had a simply grand time of it. While I played golf and talked airplanes with the Air Force guys, Winnie shopped in London and saw the sights. Finally it was time to head over the Channel, and even that proved a memorable adventure. The Air Force insisted on flying us to Paris and arranged for us to go aboard a military C-47 cargo plane. While I sat up enjoying the ride with the

pilots, Winnie sat dutifully strapped in on a hard galvanized seat in the cargo area, her bottom cushioned
by a folded parachute, as we bounced through a fierce
thunderstorm. Many Tour wives, I can tell you,
would have filed for divorce after such a wild ride,
but as usual Winnie bore it all with good grace and
humor, her heart intent on a week in Gay Paree!

I remember getting to the hotel, which was somewhere near the famous Paris Opera, and immediately hustling out to the tournament site, the St.
Cloud Golf Club in the city's suburbs, where we had
supposedly been preregistered by our friends in the
British press corps. We walked into the club's dining
room to get a bite of lunch and ran smack-dab into
an unfriendly American socialite named Louise
Chapman, wife of Dick Chapman, the top amateur
player from Pinehurst, who smartly informed us that
there was no possibility I would be allowed to play
in the French Open. Her remarks didn't sit well with
me at all, but they didn't seem to faze Winnie. She
was already enjoying herself immensely, examining
the menu and trying out her café French, while I
stormed off to the tournament office to find out what
the hell Louise Chapman was talking about.

"I am sorry, Monsieur Palmer," the young woman
in charge of tournament registration said to me,
though she looked and sounded as if she was anything but sorry, "your entry has been . . . declined."

I explained that there must be some big mistake—
noting that our British writer friends, who urged us
to come, had promised to arrange my entry into the
tournament. I wasn't alone in this pickle barrel. Gary

Player was in the same situation though perhaps a bit less emotionally exercised about this ludicrous turn of events than I was at the moment. Were they really planning to turn away the current Masters and U.S. Open and former British Open winners? It would have been a laughable situation—if I hadn't been growing angrier and angrier with each passing second. The more I pleaded our case, the more indifferent the woman seemed to our plight.

In a cold fury, I stalked into the dining room and growled to a startled Winnie, "Get your jacket. We're *leaving*."

"Where are we going?" she wondered, visibly dismayed. I think her appetizer had just arrived.

"Home to *America*!"

Poor Winnie. She'd really had her heart set on being footloose for a week in Paris, enjoying the shops, the museums, and all those glorious restaurants and cafés. Ten minutes later, we were perched side by side in the back of a taxi racing to Orly Airport to make an afternoon flight to New York. Her heart was broken, and I was still so mad I swore to her I'd be dead before I came back to the French Open! A couple years later, I'm happy to report, we did come back to Paris, to play in the Lancôme Trophy tournament, and Winnie got to shop and explore the City of Lights to her heart's content. That's where, among other things, I really got to know the Duke of Windsor and we became pretty good friends. I never played in the French Open, though, and I promise you that for all the champagne and cheese in Paris I still never will!

*   *   *

On the heels of being selected both the Hickok Pro Athlete of the Year and *Sports Illustrated* Sportsman of the Year for 1960, two of my most cherished honors to this day, I suffered my first major collapse at Augusta that next spring of 1961, and posted a poor defense of my U.S. Open title at Oakland Hills in Birmingham, Michigan (I never broke 70 and wound up in twelfth place). In my mind, that made going to the 101st British Open at Royal Birkdale, on the Lancashire coast, all the more important. With the year suddenly slipping away, not only did I want to redeem myself for the poor showing in major events thus far, but the British Open and I had some unfinished business.

We arrived in Southport, a somewhat down-at-the-heels resort town even then, in possibly the worst spell of weather an Open had ever experienced. Certainly it was the worst *I'd* ever seen. Cold rain blew in gusty sheets off the Irish Sea, whipped by winds so fierce at times—reportedly seventy miles per hour in gusts—that not only did the tournament's concession tents blow off their moorings but someone later said cases of ale were flying through the air like box kites.

Fortunately for me, once again I had Tip Anderson as my caddie and steadying influence in the gale-force winds that whistled through Birkdale's high and ruggedly carved dunes. And my low, penetrating drives were of a tremendous advantage, because they kept my ball below the tops of dunes in many cases. Players who tended to hit high-flying shots saw their balls blown halfway to London. After once again being required to have to qualify because no automatic exemptions were given—a situation that was really beginning to get under my skin, I must admit—I opened up with 70, highly respectable under the circumstances. Scores were almost as horrendous as the weather, and when I heard Gary Player was withdrawing because of "illness," I passed along my condolences, telling him that I was sorry he was feeling so "under the weather."

I shot 73 in the second round despite a seven at the 16th hole, where the wind was blowing so hard that it moved my ball after I'd taken my stance in a bunker and I had to call a penalty stroke on myself. It was one of the lowest rounds of the day and moved me ahead of everybody except Welshman Dai Rees, who had come close many times but never won the Open.

The wind was still howling when we resumed play on Friday under a threat to cancel the tournament by the Royal and Ancient Championship Committee if there were further interruptions. I felt really on top of my game, took the lead for good with a birdie at the first hole, and went out in 32, six better than anybody else that morning. Dai Rees fought gallantly back with a 71 and might have caught me if I hadn't pulled off one of my best shots ever at the long 16th hole. My third shot to the par-5 hole nearly flew out of bounds to the right of the green, ending up in the thick and prickly gorse. I spotted a hole in the gorse, however, and somehow knocked the ball through the hole onto the putting surface, two feet shy of the cup. That salvaged par helped me to get home in 69, with a one-shot lead over Rees.

I didn't do anything spectacular on the front nine of the final round and was out in 36, good enough for a four-stroke lead. As it turned out, I needed every one of those shots, because I finished 4, 5, 3, 4 to Dai Rees's 3, 4, 3, 3 to win by a stroke. The moment that saved the tournament for me was the par-4 I salvaged at the 15th, following one of the best pressure shots of my career. I pushed my tee shot a foot or so into the rough near a bush—or, as I like to tell it, my ball was deeper in the rough than it was off the fairway. Either way, it was an extremely difficult shot, and I knew pretty quickly that Tip wanted me to play smart and just use a wedge to get safely back onto the fairway.

I remember the look of horror he gave me when I declined the wedge and reached for a six-iron, intending to go for the green. The thing was, I could see the ball very clearly and reasoned that if I could get the clubface on the ball cleanly, I could get myself out of trouble. I swung as hard as I could, waited a second, and looked up, watching my ball soar high and settle on the putting surface up the hill, fifteen feet shy of the hole. The spectators massed there let out thunderous applause. Unfortunately, I failed to ice the cake there by missing the fairly easy uphill putt, leaving it just short.

I parred home to finish with a 72 and a total of 284 to edge Dai Rees by a stroke, becoming the first

American to hoist the Claret Jug since Ben Hogan in 1953.

Winnie and I were both ecstatic, and I think our enthusiasm spread through the large galleries, who stayed to watch the presentation ceremony in the blustery winds. I was enormously pleased when I read how Henry Longhurst described the moment:

"It is doubtful that there was a man present at Birkdale who wanted Palmer to lose. It is impossible to overpraise the tact and charm with which this American has conducted himself on his two visits to Britain. He has no fancy airs or graces; he wears no fancy clothes; he makes no fancy speeches. He simply says and does exactly the right thing at the right time, and that is enough."

It's been said that my accomplishments at Birkdale helped spark new American interest in the British Open Championship, which admittedly was suffering some from the absence of most of the top American players. If that's so, I'm glad I could make a valuable contribution, because the British Open really is unlike any golf tournament in the world, and its place in the golf firmament, with its storied history and great traditions, was critical to the growth and development of the modern game.

After winning the Open, I took it upon myself, along with others, to quietly campaign with members of the sponsoring Royal and Ancient on the issue of the tournament's maddening qualifying policy. I argued that if they granted exemptions to the top players of major events and championships, they would not only generate more interest among

American players but probably attract even more of the world's top players as well. I'm happy to say it was a policy they eventually changed after the 1964 event, and I think *that* may have had a dramatic effect in reviving international interest in the championship.

I made 1,400 pounds sterling for my win at Birkdale—or roughly about what it cost us to make the trip, exactly the kind of financial wash that would make old Sam Snead go fleeing to his backyard to make sure the money he had buried in a coffee can behind the stump pile was still safe.

For our part, win or lose, it seemed that a tiny splurge of some sort was called for. We'd reserved a nice hotel room at London's Mayfair Hotel. After the presentation ceremony, with darkness falling, we hopped in a hired car with Wilson's Tony Wheeler to drive the four or five hours back to London. That's when the other memorable event of that week took place, one that Winnie and I still laugh about.

After driving a while, I suggested to Tony that we pull off the motorway for a bite to eat and a couple of beers. He spotted an American-style fast-food place (which was a new phenomenon on British highways then) and we pulled over. We went in, got a table, and ordered some snacks and beers. Just about that time, a group of obnoxious motorcyclists flooded the place, a gang of young, scruffy guys in leather jackets, who began harassing patrons and the waitress. Tony leaned forward and explained that the tabloids had dubbed these nuisance bikers "Teddy

Boys." They were modern-day rebels without a cause, with no shortage of rude behavior.

I watched them carefully, and Winnie could tell that their outrageous conduct really bothered me. In fact, the part of me that had grown up in the Youngstown Fire Hall was almost itching for those Teddy Boys to come over and give us a hard time. Like Pap, I would have tried to clean them up a bit. But they didn't come over, and we left a short time later to finish our drive to London.

Clearly, I still had those road punks on my mind, though, because when we checked into the hotel a few hours later and ordered a late-night supper of sandwiches, I confessed to Winnie that seeing those guys behave like that in public made me want to flatten their noses for good measure. She patted my hand and told me not to get myself too worked up— after all, I was the new British Open champion! So we brushed our teeth and climbed into bed.

I remember the dream quite well. We were still in that roadside pub when one of the Teddy Boys came over and began giving us a hard time. I was on him just like that . . .

"Arnie!" I heard a distant, alarmed voice calling. "Wake up, Arnie! You're *choking* me!"

I opened my eyes and found to my shock that both my hands were gripping my bride's lovely throat, her face wide-eyed in terror.

In the morning we laughed about it but agreed this was one story we should keep from the British press. "After all," Winnie observed, "they might have to write a story under the headline 'New Open Champion Strangles Wife in Hotel.' "

She had a point. We didn't tell anybody but close friends about the incident for years.

No British Open golf course is easy, but as championship tests go, Troon Golf Club has always enjoyed the reputation of being a giant killer. Playing at just over 7,000 yards in length, indecently narrow in places, with postage stamp–size greens that are as bumpy and unpredictable as a Manhattan cab ride, fairways surrounded by clutching eruptions of gorse, broom, and impossibly tough whin bushes dotted with ruthlessly sheer sod bunkers and deep burns, it's a tough and scary walk to par even on the calmest sunny day. It was at Troon in 1923 that Gene Sarazen, the cocky twenty-one-year-old U.S. Open champion, teed off as the wind began to howl. Four hours later, after a horrific 85, he packed up and headed for a long boat ride home to America.

In July 1962, as Winnie described in her note to Susie Bowman, the wind was blowing in classic Open style and the temperature was almost bone chilling those first few days after we arrived at Troon. She was correct in her assessment that I suddenly couldn't make a putt to save my life—I seemed to be leaving everything hanging on the lip. On the eve of the tournament I even complained to a handful of reporters that my back hurt, my drives were straying woefully to the right, and I'd forgotten how to putt. All of that was true—though I suspect I still suffered from an Open "hangover"—having lost the Open playoff to Jack Nicklaus at Oakmont only weeks before. In any case, I pronounced my game "terrible," but Sam Snead and the British book-makers would have none of my grumbling. The bookies established me as the favorite at 2-to-1 odds. Snead drawled that there wasn't "anything wrong with old Arnie that a two-stroke lead won't fix. He's just trying to sweet-talk that tough old course into lying down and playing dead."

Maybe it's true that I was. But motive didn't seem to matter, and the beginning of the week sure felt like a test for both Winnie and me. To begin with, the village of Troon, at least in those days, was a fairly isolated place with not much to do but either play golf or watch it being played. After greeting and dining with several of our British friends from the Royal and Ancient, there wasn't a whole lot for Winnie to see and do except trek after me around the spare links at Troon in the company of the ever-wise-cracking Bob Drum, watching me shiver and scowl at putts that maddeningly wouldn't drop.

If there was any consolation, it was that many of the field's top players were having similar difficul-ties. Dai Rees, who'd lost to me by a stroke the year before at Birkdale, played miserably and missed the thirty-six-hole cut. The same thing happened to Gene Littler, the 1961 U.S. Open champ, and Gary Player, the '61 Masters winner. The current U.S. Open champ, Jack Nicklaus, blew himself out of the tournament with a first-round 80. "An eighty!" he fumed in disbelief afterward. "It's impossible. I can't shoot an *eighty*."

But he did, and so did plenty of others. I played my first round wearing flannel long johns beneath my clothes, my aching back liberally swabbed with liniment. That prescription enabled me to fire a 71, good enough for third place after the opening round. I remember telling Winnie and Drum afterward, though, that my putter was even colder than the weather.

The following day, my putter suddenly began to warm up, and I got around that narrow torture chamber with a three-under 69 that placed me two strokes ahead of a pack that seemed to be losing ground fast. Perhaps the signature shot of that round, maybe the tournament itself, came at the daunting 485-yard 11th, which played dead into a stiff wind most of that week, where three players in the field had already scored sextuple bogeys and Jack made ten. I joked to somebody that the hole was "the worst hole I've ever seen," and I was only half kidding around. It was a monster, a real widow maker—especially in the wind.

After using a 1-iron to hit the narrow crescent of fairway, I pulled out a 2-iron and hit the ball just about as hard as I possibly could. The ball struck the front portion of the green and rolled up to within twenty feet of the hole. I stood over my ball for a moment and then struck the putt firmly, rattling it into the back of the cup for an eagle three.

That was the shot in the arm I needed. Because of

the severely dry and warm conditions preceding the tournament, I'd been anxious about the fairways and greens holding shots, but suddenly in the cold and wind that was no longer a concern. I hit booming drives (several over three hundred yards) to the heart of the fairway on almost every tee shot in the final thirty-six, and my approach shots were crisp, accurate, and confident. Only my putting needed a bit of tweaking, and I got that from a source near and dear as I strode off the par-3 17th, no doubt scowling because I'd just missed a makable birdie putt.

Winnie slipped to my side and quietly said, "Bob and I have decided that you are moving your head when you putt."

"Oh, *really?*" I replied, smiling broadly at my new traveling golf coach.

"That's right." She shrugged as if to say: *That's our opinion. Take it or leave it.*

I did consider what she told me, went straight to the practice green afterward, and worked on holding my head still as Pap had always taught me.

Something seemed to work. In the third round Friday morning, I had nine one-putt greens and cruised in with a 67, opening a five-shot lead over Kel Nagle. The irony, of course, is that a week that had begun so chilly and with so little promise ended in warm sunshine highlighting probably the finest finish of my career. My drives found every fairway, and the great galleries at Troon encouraged and rewarded me with enthusiastic applause for each good shot, feeding my confidence and pumping me up. I'll never forget how they swarmed around me as

I came up the 18th hole, held perfectly still as I made my approach shot to the final green, then swarmed ahead again to encircle the green. Winnie later commented to me that she thought they were going to charge right into the stately Troon clubhouse itself!

My goodness, what a feeling. I still get chills remembering that final walk through the crowds.

A few minutes later, I tapped in for a final-round 69, a six-stroke victory, and a 276 total that eclipsed the old Open mark by two strokes. Almost as important to me, I'd successfully defended the championship—the first American player to do that since Walter Hagen in the 1920s.

As I remarked to the British press afterward, I'd never—and I meant *never*—played better tournament golf. They responded by using up most of their stock of superlatives, heralding my final two circuits of Lady Troon as the finest finish in the history of the event. I remember that a correspondent for the *London Observer* wrote that I might well be the greatest player of all time. This was the first time anybody had written that, and that statement gave me tremendous satisfaction and a deep thrill.

I was thirty-two years old, standing proudly with my golf coach–wife in the weak sunshine at Troon, clutching the oldest trophy in the game, clearly at the top of my career. I had no way of knowing then that, despite lots of glowing predictions of Open championships to come, Winnie's postcard to Susie Bowman would prove a bit prophetic: I'd won not only my last British Open victory but also my next-to-last major golf title. My "magic" touch would never happen there again.

How can you know these things? The answer is, of course, you can't. If you're smart, you simply live and enjoy the moment. And at that moment all I knew and really cared about was that I'd accomplished something I'd set my heart on doing—winning the British Open and then winning it again. In every way conceivable, the moment marked one of the true highlights of my life.

In all, over three decades, I made twenty-three trips to the British Open. My best finish in the twenty Opens since Troon was seventh at Turnberry in 1977. My first weak performance came in 1963 at Royal Lytham and St. Anne's in England, where we won the Ryder Cup in 1961 and I played pretty well. In the Open, though, I got off to a bad start with 76 and went on to a twenty-sixth-place finish. The British fans weren't any more disappointed than I was.

Most everybody naturally assumed I would return to St. Andrews in 1964. But, for the reasons I've already talked about, I was physically and mentally exhausted and just didn't think my showing would be a good one. Considering that I won the Masters that April, if I'd managed to win the U.S. Open a few weeks before at Congressional, I suppose I might have indeed gone to the Old Grey Toon, with the Grand Slam still a possibility. But that didn't happen, so I stayed home and rested.

In a sense, though, I was there. Certainly in spirit. A few weeks before the British Open, Tony Lema called me to say he thought he might go over to see if he could qualify. He'd never made the trip, and I heartily encouraged him to do so, telling him I would arrange to have Tip Anderson serve as his caddie. I loved Lema's spirit and his natural flair for the dramatic—hence his nickname "Champagne Tony." I even gave him my favorite putter to use, and it must have worked some magic. With Tip as his guide, Tony went around the Old Course in 279, beating Jack Nicklaus to capture the greatest victory of his career. Just two years later, he and his wife died tragically in that plane crash near Chicago, and the golf world lost one of its most promising rising stars. I lost a cherished friend.

I was very disappointed with my performance when I went back to defend at Birkdale in 1965. The playing conditions were the opposite of what they had been when I won. The fairways were dry and hard, and I struggled to keep shots out of the rough all week, finishing a disappointing sixteenth. The next year I went on to Muirfield for the first time. I really liked the course, and Winnie especially liked the cozy hotel and other accommodations we found there in quaint Gullane, but for one reason or another the magic eluded me again and I finished eighth.

It was about then, as I said earlier, that I began to really have trouble with my putting. I putted not so much to win—as not to lose. That's a major difference, I see now, between the ability to contend, and to merely play, in a major golf championship. Over the next few years, I enjoyed other venues like Turnberry and Royal St. George's, in Sandwich, England, where I won the British PGA Championship in 1975, and the golf fans and press of Britain never failed to greet Winnie and me with anything less than the warmth they'd always shown us.

Which brings us to 1990. I was very enthusiastic about returning to St. Andrews, thinking that it would probably be my last shot at an Open championship. We flew directly from Latrobe to St. Andrews and checked in at Russacks Hotel by the 18th hole, just as we had done thirty years earlier. Tip was there to caddie for me once again, and I played and putted reasonably well during the first two rounds, reaching the halfway point at 144.

That score almost always makes the cut at the Open, and I felt good about my chances of playing through the weekend. So, apparently, did a number of other people, including Renton Laidlaw of BBC Television, who informed his audience that I would surely be around for the finish. Unfortunately, the winds abruptly died, the sun shone, and scores began to drop. I just missed making the cut.

Maybe that's why I went back again to St. Andrews five years later, in 1995. Quite honestly, I hadn't expected the Open to return to St. Andrews that soon, my game wasn't all that bad, and I still had hopes of making that cut. I'd also made up my mind to formally announce that this would be my farewell to the British Open, fittingly at the place where it all began for me thirty-five years earlier.

People were so extraordinarily nice to us that week. Everywhere we went it was easy to see that the appreciative British fans were as moved as we were by the fare-thee-well nature of the journey. Winnie and I greeted lots of old friends, had some big laughs, and shed more than a few tears.

On Friday afternoon of the second round, when it was obvious to everybody—including me—that I wouldn't make the cut, I walked toward the famous little stone bridge over the Swilcan Burn on the 18th hole. Photographers were calling out to me. They knew what the moment meant, and they wanted me to pause and give them a wave. So, at the top of the arched bridge, I turned, framed by the stern visage of the Royal and Ancient clubhouse, lifted off my visor, and gave the gallery a long farewell wave with it.

If you look closely at the photograph, which has become one of my favorites, you can see that I appear from my expression to be deeply pained and powerfully happy, as if I'm anxious to move off the stage and let others shine, but reluctant to finally go.

In fact, that's exactly how I felt. Memories were flooding my brain, and emotions were washing over me like you can't imagine. In the instant it took for the camera's shutter to flip open and close to capture that memorable photograph, I was also thinking how it all seemed to pass in the blink of an eye. True enough, my British Open magic was dimmed, but the magic of the British Open was as strong as it had ever been for me.

With that, I turned and walked up to the green and finished my Open career.

CHAPTER ELEVEN

Missing Link

At my age, any man can look back at his career and his life and have a few regrets. I suppose it's the extremely competitive world we live in that forces us to sometimes examine our lives in terms of what we don't have or haven't accomplished instead of looking at what we do have or have accomplished. I'll admit to being as competitive as anyone, so I guess it's natural that I share this inclination. Assessing my golf career this way is a prime example of looking at a glass as half empty or half full, the difference some say between being an optimist and being a pessimist. While I certainly consider myself an optimist, I have to admit to succumbing at times to the temptation to share the view held by many—that without the final jewel in my crown, the PGA Championship, my success on the golf course is somehow incomplete. In fact, for years I've held in reserve a spot for a PGA medal in a display case that holds awards from my major tournament victories.

I prefer to think that my career is neither half empty nor half full because of my repeated failure to win the PGA Championship. I'd certainly agree that it's less than full, and freely admit that I would have dearly loved to win the fourth major of the modern Grand Slam, a kind of golfer's Holy Grail that I pursued so hotly between 1960 and 1964. But whatever did or didn't come my way, I'm extremely proud of my effort and cherish many of the moments when I was in the hunt.

If it sounds like I have ambivalent feelings about my PGA experiences, that's because I do. My feelings about my performance in the PGA Championship—and the sponsoring organization itself—are complicated. At the risk of flogging a dead horse—the press has richly chronicled and analyzed these matters for decades now—I'd like to add some reflections on my "near misses" and upon the evolution of the organization itself. I hope they'll set the record straight.

To begin with, let me say that almost since the day I decided to become a professional tournament player in 1954, I quietly chafed under a host of what I considered to be unfair restrictions placed on players by the Professional Golfers' Association of America. The first of these restrictions was the six-month "apprenticeship" requirement that wouldn't permit a Tour rookie to accept any official tournament winnings. This was an unnecessary hardship imposed when he really needed a paycheck *most* in order to keep going. Another was the maddening five-year mandatory waiting period before a player was eligible to participate in the PGA Championship. I never agreed with the logic behind those rules. Could you imagine if those same restrictions were imposed on, let's say, baseball players? How would players and fans react if Ken Griffey, Jr., or any other player couldn't perform in the playoffs unless he'd been in the league for five years? Imagine the howls of protest over that. Yet the PGA got away with it.

At least as deeply frustrating to me was winning the 1958 Masters and nine other tournaments prior to that but being denied the opportunity to collect Ryder Cup points for my play. Those points undoubtedly would have placed me on the 1959 team that played at Eldorado Country Club in Palm Springs, where Winnie and I had a host of friends and would eventually have a winter home ourselves. This injustice stuck in my craw, I must admit, for *years*. Purely for a point of comparison, if such a restrictive clause existed today, players of such world-class caliber as Tiger Woods and Justin Leonard wouldn't have made the Ryder Cup squad that went to Valderrama in 1997.

As early as my first few weeks out on tour, in fact, I heard older and more established players grumbling about the "controlling" nature and undue restrictiveness of the governing PGA. They complained about how unfair it seemed to them that, just as tournament golf was beginning to experience a dramatic growth in popularity, an organization whose primary mandate was to look after the interests of thousands of teaching club professionals was dictating to touring professionals what they could or could not do with their careers, under guidelines and rules that seemed, to say the least, antiquated and inefficient.

Perhaps the seeds of my own discontent with the organization were sown farther back, deep in my own childhood, when my father, as devoted a club professional as ever taught a Vardon grip or fussed over the care of a golf course, was rudely denied membership in that organization under an outdated policy that prevented "cripples" from being granted PGA membership. That snub made Pap seethe with anger, as it should have, and when I started winning tournaments and gaining clout with PGA officials, that was among the first rules I went after with a vengeance. Eventually, I'm happy to say, my lobbying paid off and the offending clause (along with several outdated rules, such as the infamous "Caucasian only" clause) was excised from the organization's constitutional bylaws.

Many have said that without my suggestion and Bob Drum's publicizing it, there would have been no such thing as a modern Grand Slam. Including the PGA as part of the Grand Slam certainly increased its importance in the eyes of many, and it was further enhanced by my declared objective of winning the Grand Slam—or at least the American equivalent of it, all three major titles on our shores. While I can't offer absolute proof of that assertion, I am certain of this. In a move aimed at trying to increase gate receipts and capitalize on the potential windfall of television profits, in 1958, the first year I played in the event—at the Llanerch Country Club outside Philadelphia—the PGA decided to switch from its traditional match-play format to medal play. Following that move, the PGA Championship slipped a notch in terms of the prestige it enjoyed among some players and many in the media. To some, the once-great PGA Championship suddenly seemed like just another seventy-two-hole medal-play tournament, albeit an awfully important one, and with all due respect to my good friend Dow Finsterwald, who won that year, I did agree with those who thought it wasn't a good idea to change the format.

From the beginning, despite my growing differences with the sponsoring organization, I believed in my heart that the PGA Championship was a vitally important cog in the machinery of major-league golf. Once I became eligible to participate in the event and began accumulating points toward the Ryder Cup, I really did try my best to win that championship.

My first good chance came at Firestone Country Club in 1960. Just back from the disappointment of not winning the British Open at St. Andrews, I'd made up my mind to go all out for the *American* Grand Slam and was nicely in contention through the 15th hole of the Saturday round. At the famous and supposedly unreachable 625-yard par-5 16th, I pushed my second shot to the right and found myself blocked by trees. Spotting a gap through them, I decided to go for the green, nicked a branch, and my ball dropped into a hazard ditch. A penalty stroke and poor pitch followed, and I finished the hole with a triple-bogey 8—a score that effectively knocked me out of contention.

The next year, at Olympia Fields outside Chicago, Jerry Barber holed three monster putts in a row to catch Don January (he beat him in the subsequent playoff), while I scored better every round to finish in fifth place. Not quite where I wanted to be, but at least I was creeping closer to the top of the leader board.

In 1964, the championship was in Jack Nicklaus's backyard, Columbus Country Club, and Jack and I both responded to the occasion by playing ourselves into a tie for second place behind Bobby Nichols, who pulled off some of the most astonishing recovery shots I've ever witnessed. Come to think of it, I made a few impressive saves myself, including a birdie from the woods on 18 to tie Jack for second. My rounds of 68-68-69-69 made me the first player in PGA Championship history to shoot four rounds in the sixties and not win. Close but no cigar. Tough to swallow, that one.

Two years later, Jack and I won the second PGA Team Championship held at Palm Beach Gardens, Florida. That was the first of three such titles we would capture in the next five years (we won twice at Laurel Valley, in 1970 and 1971). Those victories, along with our four Canada/World Cup team wins in 1963, 1964, 1966, and 1967, prompted that memorable cry in the press of "Break up the Yankees," alluding to the reigning baseball dynasty of the time. Those team matches with Jack were really fun, I must say, in part because, for a change, I had the biggest threat in golf on my team. Perhaps we were golf's team match dynasty. All I know is that Jack and I are proud of the team record we assembled during those years.

I also know that I wasn't a factor again in the PGA Championship until 1968, at Pecan Valley in

San Antonio, Texas, a place so blessedly hot that players had to guard against heat exhaustion. As you would expect of southern Texas in July, the temperature made you feel like you were stepping into a Latrobe blast furnace, but surprisingly the greens were somewhat slow and therefore to my liking. Also, I liked playing in the heat. So, while the rest of the field wilted and had trouble breaking par, I got off to a respectable start with an opening-round 72 and got better by three strokes the next day. Standing on the tee at the 72nd hole, I was a mere stroke off the lead, held by Julius Boros, who was playing in the group just behind me.

I overcooked my swing and hooked the drive into some snarly grass near television transmission cables. Watching me pull the 3-wood to go for the green, Doc Giffin, who was on the scene, later said he felt the way Tip Anderson felt at Birkdale when I took out that 6-iron. In other words, he couldn't believe I was going to try as risky a low-percentage shot as that. A fairway wood from the deep rough is one of the toughest shots in the game, but the way I figured it, I might never get this close to the prize that had eluded me most, so I pulled out the wood and went for it.

I hit what was probably the finest wood shot of my career. The ball landed on the green and checked up eight feet above the cup. If I made that short putt, I would be tied with Boros, who was then standing on the tee. The ball went straight at the hole but curled off and rolled several inches past. I slumped over in despair. Boros made it an interesting finish, though, dramatic to the bittersweet end. Unable to reach the green in two, he made a superb pitch to get up and down in two, to win the championship. I finished in second place, tied with Bob Charles. A bridesmaid once again, I mentally kicked myself for having missed that putt.

Exactly two years later, at Southern Hills in Tulsa, another short-game master, Dave Stockton, worked his wedge magic on the closing holes to figuratively snatch another PGA Championship from my grasp. During the final round, at the dangerous 13th, a par 5 that had been converted into a par 4 for the tournament, Dave plunked his second shot into the pond, while I put mine on the green with an excellent chance at birdie. I was four down at that point, but it appeared there was going to be at least a two-, perhaps even a three-shot swing.

I watched as Dave dropped a ball by the hazard and made a sensational clutch recovery pitch, very nearly holing his wedge shot. He tapped in for a bogey, and I missed the birdie. The give-back was just a shot, but the disappointment I experienced at not taking fuller advantage of the opportunity was like a punch in the gut. Whatever momentum had been building suddenly vanished. Dave won by two over Bob Murphy and me. Another PGA *almost*.

In retrospect, for a variety of reasons, perhaps the one loss that hurt the most was the PGA Championship I hosted at Laurel Valley in 1965. In a sense, I suppose I'd rescued the PGA from the horns of a serious dilemma. Across the board in American sports, times were changing, but the PGA was

reluctant to change with them. In professional baseball and football, for example, racial barriers had
fallen, and blacks and other minority players were
finally being accorded the respect and paid the
money they deserved. Given certain antiquated policies of the PGA, though, it was inevitable that the
organization would run into trouble with politicians.
With the PGA set to take place the summer of 1965
at San Francisco Golf Club, the attorney general of
California used the golf organization's exclusionary
"Caucasian only" policy to bar the tournament from
his state.

I've been criticized by some who contend I didn't
use whatever clout I may have had at the time
(which I personally don't think was all that much—
at least with PGA members) to publicly oppose the
discriminatory policies and encourage minority participation in the game. I suppose by some yardstick
measurements, that's true—if by that my critics
mean I never called a press conference to confront
such issues or even challenge the organization's
policies in conversations with reporters.

On the other hand, given the way I was raised by
Pap, to respect any man regardless of his skin color
or nationality—to say nothing of my irritation over
the infamous "cripples" clause—it wasn't in my
nature to openly attack the organization or lead the
crusade for change, actions that probably would
have made me a lot of enemies in an organization
that had done so many good things for the game of
golf and was otherwise honorable and well inten-
tioned. I, and many others, wanted to see the PGA

change, to have its racial policies, and other policies, evolve with the times, but I didn't want to throw the baby out with the bathwater, so to speak.

Consequently, at the height of this first racial flare-up, I saw an opportunity to be of service to golf and the PGA of America by suggesting that the PGA move the championship to Laurel Valley, which was done. Unfortunately, as black golf stars like Charlie Sifford and Lee Elder can tell you, though, it really took many more years—decades, in fact—and a lot of quiet soul-searching and campaigning from within to finally get rid of the exclusionary language that I believe hurt the PGA's prestige. Inevitably, it took another nasty racial flare-up—this time after Hall Thompson made his controversial remarks at Shoal Creek in Alabama in 1990. The flood of negative publicity and public outrage that followed the incident prompted a thorough self-examination by the PGA of America and the PGA Tour and ultimately resulted in the establishment of new anti-discrimination policies that, I believe, have finally made professional golf a tent large enough to accommodate everybody.

As for staging the event at Laurel Valley in 1965, I wanted it to be picture perfect in every way, so, experiencing a kind of large-scale host anxiety, I worked and worried myself into a frantic state of mind, checking and rechecking on every detail in the days leading up to the championship. Perhaps I should have gone fishing in one of the nearby trout streams instead, because it was quickly clear from my play that I had invested far too many hopes and high expectations in the tournament. What a perfect setting Laurel Valley would have been to get the PGA monkey off my back once and for all.

The way I played the first hole of the championship nicely sums up my fate there that week. My 7-iron approach shot missed the green left and wound up just short of a small, temporary footbridge, which was directly in my line to the putting surface. Almost before anybody noticed what was happening, a gallery marshal with the wonderfully ironic name of Miles Span removed the bridge's railing. I pitched up and salvaged par, but I was informed a few holes later by an official that, by permitting improvement of my line of play, I'd violated a rule. I was assessed two penalty strokes. The wind went right out of my sails.

I finished with an even-par 72 but never summoned the focus to take my scoring any lower in the three succeeding rounds. I completed the tournament with 294, thirty-three places behind the winner, my good and gentle friend Dave Marr, who made it nerve-racking by *not* going for the green in regulation on the 72nd hole. He made a great long pitch to save par and win.

I gave Dave a good chewing-out for that strategy. Then I grinned and slapped him on the back and congratulated him on winning his first major championship. If I couldn't win it that year, I was very pleased Dave Marr had.

After the "near miss" at Southern Hills in 1970, I never really challenged in the tournament again, though in 1989 Jack Nicklaus and I did briefly give the boys in the press tent something to write home about. At Kemper Lakes outside Chicago, Jack and I both opened with 68s, and at one point near the finish of the opening round I actually held the lead and was cruising toward a 66. I was later informed that when word spread what Jack and I were up to on the golf course, something rare happened: the press tent virtually cleared out. Nearly all the scribes, including my crusty old friend Dan Jenkins (who rarely ventured onto a course unless a national emergency had been declared) came out to see for themselves what some hoped would be a reprise of the old Nicklaus-Palmer magic. Unfortunately, I treated them to a pair of untimely bogeys and finished with 68.

Despite ending the round that way, it felt great to briefly be atop the heap, and Jack agreed with me. And though I was one month shy of my sixtieth birthday, it was almost like the good old days. Jack and I had managed to turn back the calender a few years, and I couldn't recall the last time I'd made five consecutive birdies in competition. That really got the gallery buzzing, and it raised goose bumps on my own arms. Curiously, there was another champion lurking at the top of the leader board, quietly stalking the one major golf title that has forever eluded him, as well.

Tom Watson didn't take home the Wanamaker Trophy that year, and neither did I. With a 74 in the second round and a free fall to an awful 81 in the third, I finished in a disappointing tie for sixty-third place.

But at least I'd briefly felt that old current of

excitement that comes with being in the chase, and
perhaps that set the stage for my final appearance in
the championship, in 1994. There comes a point
when you have to say goodbye, and that point came
for me, fittingly enough, at Southern Hills in August
of that year. In an emotional setting that was similar
in scope to my farewell to the Open at Oakmont just
weeks before, I could barely get around the course in
one piece—and barely get the words out afterward
to express what the tournament and my long association with the PGA of America meant to me. I
played poorly and missed the cut, to nobody's surprise, but I thanked the organization from the bottom
of my heart for being such an important part of my
life. As you well know, you can't have a long-term
relationship with anyone or anything without some
conflict along the way.

And as I finished my final competitive round in the
PGA Championship, I was reminded of the long and
sometimes rocky road I'd traveled with the PGA of
America.

All families have honorable internal disputes, and
one of those conflicts helped to create the modern
PGA Tour. Jack Nicklaus and I lent strong hands to
the creation of the organization when a players'
revolt threatened to tear apart the PGA of America in
the late 1960s.

Here's my take on what happened:

As I've said, as early as the mid-fifties, top players
like Ben Hogan and Sam Snead openly complained

that it wasn't in the best interests of professional golf for the PGA of America, essentially an organization for the game's club and teaching professionals, to be running golf tournaments with an iron hand, making schedules, determining purses, and setting the rules by which players who made their incomes from playing in those tournaments simply had to abide.

The PGA's rationale for maintaining stewardship of the Tour, of course, was that it had not only created the road show of tournaments as a way to enable its members to pick up extra income playing in tournaments when their clubs were closed down for the winter. It had also supervised, maintained, and eventually (by the mid-sixties) made the Tour into an impressive and increasingly popular and profitable entity.

The increasingly sharp public debate was about control—who should be in charge of a tour that was growing by leaps and bounds as the popularity of golf exploded thanks to the exploits (among others) of Nicklaus, Player, and me? Should it be the club professionals or the tournament players themselves? Of course, the PGA of America had one answer, and an increasing number of tournament players had another.

As crass as it sounds, the issue was really money—more precisely, television money. For some players the last straw came when, in the summer of 1968, it was discovered that the PGA had entered into "secret" contract meetings for the television rights to *Shell's Wonderful World of Golf* and the *World Series of Golf* without consulting us. Gardner Dickinson,

one of the player representatives on the PGA's tournament commitee, led an angry contingent of tour
stars—including Doug Ford, Jack Nicklaus, and
Frank Beard—out the door to start their own golf
tour.

They formed a new entity called the Association
of Professional Golfers, or APG; hired the PGA's
own fine fieldman, Jack Tuthill, to act as interim
tournament director for the fledgling tour; then
began the complicated process of trying to bring
existing tournament sponsors on board. They were
damned effective, I might add. By the year's end, I
believe they had something like twenty-eight tournaments lined up for the approaching season and a
tour qualifying school established at Doral in Miami.
At one point, Jack Nicklaus wrote a thoughtful essay
for *Sports Illustrated* explaining the revolt and out-
lining why the move was in the end entirely necessary. My impression remains that the general public
was wholly in favor of the split.

I'll admit that at first I was a bit reluctant to join
the rebelling palace guards. For all its warts and
arrogance, the PGA of America *was* the goose that
laid the golden egg, and I am nothing if not loyal to
those who have helped me. Even if on more than one
occasion they stood in my way.

The irony, of course, is that Mark McCormack
had been battling the PGA for years on my behalf
over restrictive contracts and the issue of limiting
the participation of foreign players. Mark knew the
PGA's outdated rules were taking lots of money
from the pockets of players and, consequently, some

worthy charities as well. For example, in July 1964 we had scheduled an exhibition match in Princeton, New Jersey, with proceeds to go to the New Jersey Heart Association. At that time the PGA had something called the "Three Point Rule," which stated that a player could be off the Tour playing golf for prize money only three times a year while a PGA Tour tournament was in progress someplace else. That week the Tour stop happened to be the Insurance City Open in Hartford, Connecticut, a tournament I had not intended to play. So far, no problem there—I wasn't violating the Three Point Rule.

Unfortunately, the PGA had another restrictive clause that stated that no exhibition could take place within two hundred miles of a PGA tournament site, a sensible enough edict when you consider the kinds of crowds Jack, Gary, and I—and other stars of the Tour—were capable of drawing for an exhibition match. Since we were told that our exhibition was 202 miles from Hartford, we didn't anticipate any problem with the Princeton exhibition. The match had been set and advertised, and thousands of tickets were sold.

The day before the match, however, the PGA informed us that it would have to be canceled. They said that I could not play in Princeton because the site of the Hartford tournament had been switched to another country club in town that was only 196 miles from the site of the Princeton exhibition.

I thought they were joking, and I was baffled and later enraged to learn that they weren't. The PGA promised I would be fined and suspended if we went ahead with the charity exhibition. At the eleventh hour, Mark tried his best to persuade the PGA to yield, noting that the events were two states apart and that surely they could make a four-mile exception. But his mediation efforts failed. The sponsors of the heart exhibition were left holding an empty bag and had to cancel.

Who was the big loser? Not me. I lost a decent exhibition fee, but the Heart Association and the people of New Jersey, as Mark passionately argued, were the real losers in the absurd dispute. While I believe in strictly adhering to the letter of the law in following the rules of the game, this kind of hard-line, strict interpretation benefited no one.

Now consider the PGA's muddled thinking on the issue of participation in foreign events and the status of foreign players who wished to play on the American golf circuit. In March of 1961, Sam Snead and I were selected to represent the United States in the Canada Cup matches, scheduled that year to be held in Puerto Rico. But about two weeks before the event, the PGA notified us that I was ineligible to play because—under a PGA rule that involved my position on the money list—I had to either play in the PGA tournament in Memphis that week or not at all.

To make matters worse, the PGA powers that be decided that no foreign player to whom this rule applied could play in the Canada Cup either. Among others, that meant Gary Player couldn't represent his home country, South Africa, and Stan Leonard couldn't play for Canada. It was as outrageous as it was ridiculous, and believe it or not, the People-to-People Sports Committee even appealed to the PGA, pleading that their actions reflected "discredit on the United States and its sporting traditions."

Those pleas were met with unyielding silence. Jimmy Demaret played for me, Harold Henning played for Gary, and Al Johnston filled in for Stan Leonard.

The absurdity of this rule and other restrictive clauses like it—for example, the insane attempt in 1966 to restrict the number of tournaments foreign players could enter unless they went to a PGA school and became officially approved by the PGA—guaranteed that the revolt Jack and Gardner and the others led in the summer of 1968 would succeed.

As early as November 1963, at a time when the PGA was considering new regulations that would strengthen restrictions on U.S. players playing abroad, entering foreign tournaments, playing in exhibitions, and even appearing on television shows, I wrote a long letter to the PGA exhorting them to consider the consequences of their actions. I pleaded the case that golf was rapidly expanding in popularity beyond America's borders and that as worldwide interest in the game grew, it could only be good for the game itself and all of us individually to participate in the international growth and act as ambassadors of the game. Golf was much larger than any single organization, I said, arguing that it was not only unfair to restrict American players from playing overseas, but that limiting the exposure foreign players could have on our tour would ultimately damage professional golf in America. After a lengthy and frank airing of my concerns, I concluded with the following words:

> I sincerely hope that the action of the PGA tournament committee will reflect careful thought and consideration, not only for the good of the United States PGA but also for the good of the individual players who make up the tournament organization as well as for the game of golf in general throughout the world. If this is the case, then I am sure nothing will transpire now or in the future to seriously damage tournament golf as we now know it.
>
> Sincerely yours,
> Arnold Palmer

The PGA's lack of response effectively told the tale. The irony of my being hesitant to bolt with the others, of course, is that within a year, my unhappiness with the provincial attitudes and general arrogance of the PGA led me, at Mark McCormack's urging, to make some serious private explorations into the possibilities of starting a new tour. At that point Mark had convinced me that the restrictive clauses of the PGA bylaws would never hold up in a court of law, and at one point he counseled me to violate an exhibition rule, suffer a fine and suspension, then sue the PGA of America to draw public attention to the situation.

Eventually, a large and well-known corporation proposed a guarantee of $4 million in seed money to sponsor a tour of the game's top thirty players, the only stipulation being that three of them would be men named Jack, Gary, and Arnold. While some of the game's other top players might have turned down such a deal, it was believed that an overwhelming majority of the game's best players would enthusiastically sign on.

If you're thinking that in theory this sounds a little like Greg Norman's ill-fated attempt to start a world tour a few years back, you're right. There are distinct similarities in the concepts, and permit me to say here that in another twenty or thirty years, as golf continues its explosive growth worldwide and corporate interests increase, I fully believe that competing commercial golf tours will evolve. We may eventually see all kinds of new tours springing up. My greatest hope is that the various existing tours and governing bodies of the game will realize how imperative it is for them to work in concert now—as I believe they are doing—to handle the change properly, lest golf go the route so many other big-time sports have in the past twenty years. Lockouts and strikes and feuds only make players appear as nothing more than greedy bandits and harm everybody in the end.

At any rate, in 1964, like Greg Norman, I was attacked by some in the PGA establishment who circulated rumors that I was simply serving as a front man for Mark McCormack's secret plan to start a new world tour.

That simply wasn't the case. But unlike Greg, I mulled over the idea for six or seven weeks and decided the time wasn't right, and that this was not the proper way to go about gaining our freedom. Despite its arrogance and foolish attitudes, and its history of excluding the handicapped and minorities, I simply couldn't turn my back on the PGA of America. I knew the revolution had to come from *within* the palace walls.

In a nutshell, when Jack and Gardner's coup d'état happened four years later, at a time when I really did have some clout with PGA members, I saw an opportunity to serve as a bridge of sorts to a better world for everybody. But I chose a role that was far more in keeping with my values and personality.

Leo Fraser, a lifelong club professional who had many close friends, including me, on the Tour, had just taken office as the president of the PGA. Leo was far more open-minded to the idea of compromise and accommodation, and as much as anything else, his more flexible attitude stalled the alternative APG tour before it ever really got rolling. I remember going to see Leo at Atlantic City in late 1968 for a lengthy meeting, during which we discussed an idea that had been steadily growing in popularity. I was a leading proponent of a proposal to create a new players organization, a separate entity formally called the PGA Tour that would operate autonomously with a board composed of four players elected by the Tour, three businessmen, and the top three PGA of America officials.

Months of sometimes lively debate ensued, but Leo's essential fairness, good humor, patience, and determination to serve the best interests of the professional game eventually won the day. The rebels abandoned their cause, and the crowning touch came when Joe Dey, the longtime executive director of the United States Golf Association and a man of impeccable credentials, was named first commissioner of the new Tournament Players Division of the PGA— which would soon evolve into the PGA Tour.

Joe's presence gave the fledgling tour organization the instant credibility it needed. But more important, the birth of a new organization devoted expressly to fulfilling the needs and desires of professional tournament golf brought years of bitter feelings and acrimony to an end. We could finally get back to playing the game we all loved to play—instead of bickering about it. And, despite all the bickering, no one could ever do anything to completely diminish my sheer enjoyment at playing this marvelous game. I'd do it even if there was no money involved, and a lot of players share that view, as participation in the Ryder Cup, the Presidents Cup, and, to a lesser extent, the World Cup suggests.

Whatever hard feelings I privately nursed about being ineligible for the Ryder Cup of 1959, they vanished in 1961, the moment Winnie and I and the other members of the American squad and their wives walked onto the quiet, hushed grounds at Royal Lytham and St. Annes Golf Club for the opening ceremonies of seed merchant Sam Ryder's biennial match between the best players of America and Britain and Ireland. What I remember most was standing with my teammates near the first tee and feeling a lump rise in my throat and tears fill my eyes as the brass band played the "Star-Spangled Banner" followed by "God Save the Queen."

There is simply no experience in golf quite like being part of your first Ryder Cup opening ceremony, unless perhaps it's the closing ceremonies after your side has won.

In any case, my second-most-powerful memory from that weekend on the Lancashire coast, just up the road a bit from where I'd won my first British Open at Birkdale in July, involves Peter Alliss, who was my first match in the singles competition. Peter was an elegant man and an accomplished player. As most of the British players did, he shaped his shots for control purposes, from left to right in a controlled fade. I greatly admired the way Peter played the game, with such precision and accuracy, which was almost nothing like my style. And it says something nice about the man's quiet tenacity that I had to work my tail off simply to halve the match with him. Cordially shaking hands at the match's conclusion, I think both of us knew we'd been in a dogfight—and would probably be in a few more before things were over.

The highlight of my week came when Bill Casper and I teamed up in the foursomes to defeat Dai Rees and Ken Bousfield, 2 and 1. Counting my singles win over Tom Haliburton, a lovely gentleman, I departed Lytham with three victories, one tie, and 3½ points contributed to my team's winning total of 14 points.

For Winnie, the week proved almost as special. Even then, the unique social intimacy of the Ryder Cup—the lively and fancy dinners held in our behalf, the laughs and drinks we shared after the matches were through each evening—enabled her to get to know a number of the British players and their wives, as well as various members of the British press and various golf officials from their side of the pond. The sponsoring British PGA made certain the visiting wives had plenty to do, including arranging tours of great local homes and castles and scheduling shopping excursions to area woolen shops. As she said to me later, Winnie loved every minute of those side trips, mostly because of the many treasured friendships that were begun at Lytham.

Our departure from Lytham, however, was comical. I had arranged for a private motorcar to pick up our group of four at the hotel before dawn, the morning after the team victory celebration. Traveling with us were Martha and Bronson Ingram, old friends from Nashville, and the plan called for the four of us to drive from Lytham to London and from there slip away for a little end-of-season vacation in Rome, Italy.

So much for well-made plans! The first clue that the day was going to be a long one came when I discovered, to my profound displeasure, that the car I'd reserved had been commandeered by another American only minutes before. As it turned out, flamboyant Chicagoan Joe Jemsek (who owned several golf clubs in the Chicago area) was in a rush to make the morning train to London and had simply taken our car. Boy, was I boiling mad at his nerve!

Hurrying back inside to the hotel front desk, I arranged for a taxicab, which had to take its bloody time getting to the hotel because of a heavy fog. A short while later, we were informed that all flights to London would be delayed indefinitely because of the pea-soup fog, so we decided to sprint for the train station, hoping to catch the same train Joe Jemsek was taking. The fog was so thick we proceeded down the road at about the speed of an elderly caddie. I'll never forget the sight of our taxi driver with his bald head poked out the side window, squinting to see if we were still on the road.

We made it to the train with seconds to spare and discovered Dow and Linda Finsterwald settling into a compartment. We joined them and decided to have a little morning-after-the-victory-party victory party, buying up all of the train's grapefruit and orange juice and whatever they had in the way of muffins or snacks. We pulled out our Scotch and Irish whiskey bottles and made a few more toasts to Sam Ryder as the train slowly clanked out of the station, headed for London.

Ten or eleven hours later, we somehow found our

way through the even denser fog of London to the Savoy Hotel, where we settled in and had dinner. There we made the unanimous decision to still try to go on to Rome if and when the weather finally cleared.

Wouldn't you know it, the next morning the fog was even thicker! It was like the whole city was wrapped in a thick wool sweater. Winnie looked crushed as we learned that no planes were being allowed to take off from or land at London's major airports. Trying unsuccessfully to keep her grave disappointment from showing, my wife jokingly accused me of arranging the foggy weather simply to avoid the danger of having to go on a *real* vacation! Even so, we wandered around London for a couple more days, seeing the fog-covered sights, taking in a play in the West End, and buying gifts for the girls and other folks back home. As I recall, we had a pretty nice time, all things considered.

Ryder Cup participation came to mean an awful lot to me. At East Lake, in Atlanta, two years later, I narrowly defeated Dow Finsterwald in a close team vote for captain. I was honored to be chosen to head the American squad. Actually, I became the last playing captain in the matches. This time I lost a close singles match to that elegant swordsman Peter Alliss, who, for a man whose Rolls-Royce bears the license plate "3 PUTT," certainly made his share of fine strokes at East Lake. On the other side of the coin, though, I won four other matches against two defeats and contributed four points to our team's winning total in a lopsided romp, 23–9. Peter was one of their few bright spots—and don't believe a word of it when he claims he can't putt.

In 1965, returning to Royal Birkdale, old friend Dave Marr and I teamed to split foursome matches with Dave Thomas and George Will, followed by a similar split in the four-ball matches against my old nemesis Peter Alliss and Christy O'Connor. I captured both my singles matches, though, and left Birkdale with a 4–2 record. We retained the Cup, 19½ to 12½. Another rout by the Yanks.

A funny thing happened en route to another lop-sided American win at Houston's Champions Golf Club in 1967. Julius Boros and I were getting trounced early in the four-ball matches against Hugh Boyle and George Will when I glanced up and saw Jackie Burke looking on. Jackie was the host profes-sional at Champions and a longtime friend who loved to pull my chain whenever he could.

"Well, *Palmer*," he drawled slyly as we walked off the green where Julius and I had gone three down. "Looks like you two have gotten yourselves into a real mess."

I glanced at him as if I had no idea what he was talking about.

"What do you mean, Jackie?"

He grimaced. "I mean, I don't think even *you* will be able to get your team out of this one."

"Jackie, I'm sorry you don't have any faith in us."

"Sorry. Not this time."

"Well, if that's the case," I proposed thoughtfully,

"you wouldn't care to put a little something on it, would you?"

Now the old rascal smiled.

"I tell you what. If you somehow get out of this mess and win this match, I'll make you a clock."

"A clock?"

"Not just any clock. A beautiful handmade clock."

So a clock it was. On the very next hole, Julius and I started a rally and went on to secure a come-from-behind 1-up victory. That momentum propelled us through the rest of the weekend. I won five matches, gave the Brits a joyride in my airplane that brought the wrath of the FAA down on my head, and scored five points, contributing to one of the largest American margins of victory in the history of the Ryder Cup.

That handmade clock, incidentally, which has the twelve letters of my name where the numbers usually are, sits on a shelf in my office workshop. That's a place very special to me—the place I really love to go and work on clubs and be alone with my thoughts. So it's only fitting the clock is there, reminding me of a wonderful moment in my playing career and how much fun it was to take that clock off Jackie Burke's hands.

On a more serious note, permit me to set the record straight on a matter that has circulated erroneously for years—namely, that Ben Hogan, the American team captain that year, chewed me out at one point for assuming I would be playing every match. While I was hardly a favorite of Mr. Hogan, no such heated conversation ever took place. Ben conducted himself with his usual cool dignity, and I did my job, and the results of his captaincy and my team play pretty well speak for themselves.

In 1971, at Old Warson Country Club in St. Louis, Jack Nicklaus and I teamed in the first of several Ryder Cup collaborations, defeating Peter Townsend and Harry Bannerman in a closely con- tested 1-up four-ball match. Gardner Dickinson and I proved even more formidable as a team that year, however, winning three of our team matches to give me a record of four wins against one loss and one tie, in another romp by the hosts, 18½ to 13½.

Two years later, Muirfield, Scotland, happened to be the setting for my poorest performance in Ryder Cup competition. Jack and I beat Maurice Bem- bridge and Eddie Pollard, 6 and 5, in the first four- somes match, but turned right around and dropped the four-ball to Bembridge and Brian Huggett, 3 and 1. For the first time, I failed to win a singles match and my losses outnumbered my wins, 3 to 2. On the plus side of the ledger, Winnie was utterly charmed by the chef's lamb and the cozy elegance and staff charm of the small hotel where we stayed during the competition.

With my Ryder Cup career clearly waning, I pulled just about every string available with the sponsoring PGA of America to arrange for the Cup to come to Laurel Valley in 1975. Perhaps someone high up in the organization thought of it as a suitable reward for my decision a decade before not to bolt from the

organization when temptation was so strong. Whatever their reasons, I was very pleased that the Cup
was coming to my place at Laurel Valley for what
would clearly be my fare-thee-well to Ryder Cup
participation.

I'd hoped to play my way onto the team, but
it wasn't meant to be. Everyone knew that my
selection as team captain was a deeply symbolic and
sentimental choice. My record as a player in the
event spoke for itself in that regard. At that point in
time, no American had a better win-loss record
in Ryder Cup competition than me. But it was
obvious that my better days on tour were behind
me—as my mediocre tournament record from that
year indicates.

I was deeply honored to be selected captain, and
what a team I had that year. Golf's equivalent of the
Dream Team. Maybe the best Ryder Cup squad ever.

Nicklaus. Littler. Trevino. Miller. Weiskopf.
Floyd. Casper. Irwin. Geiberger. Dave Hill. J. C.
Snead. Lou Graham. Bob Murphy. If ever there
was a stronger and more talented American team, I
challenge you to name it.

I suppose the outcome was a foregone conclusion. In retrospect, the most interesting drama cen-
tered around the efforts of Jack Nicklaus, who had a
devil of a time with big Brian Barnes. It's kind of
funny now, but it was no laughing matter then. In
their first singles match, Brian shocked everybody—
and probably even himself—by upsetting Jack.
During the lunch break, everyone was buzzing that I

should engineer a rematch with Barnes so Jack could get his revenge. I could see that even Jack was itching for a rematch, so I pulled it off.

They met again a little while later on the first tee.

"Well, Brian," Jack said to Barnes. "You beat me this morning. You're not going to beat me again."

I don't think anybody there would have disagreed with that assessment. Certainly not a Ladbrokes bookie. That season Jack had already won six tournaments, including two majors, was the Tour's leading money winner, and was en route to PGA Player of the Year honors. He was the game's presiding master, at the top of his game.

But Barnes beat him again, 3 and 2.

All that proves in my book is what splendid unpredictability match-play golf provides. It's a reason I wish the PGA Championship would consider returning to its original match-play format.

I loved the Ryder Cup, because it simply wasn't about playing for money. It was about playing for something far grander and more personal than income and money lists. It was all about playing for your country, your people, and therefore yourself, and it was pure joy to try to beat the best of Britain and Ireland in an honorable game almost as old as the Magna Carta.

I'm proud of what the Ryder Cup did for me—and for what I contributed to my teams in six Ryder Cup competitions. I won 22 matches against 8 losses, with two ties and a total of 23 points.

That was a record that stood until Nick Faldo

entered the Ryder Cup at Valderrama Golf Club in Spain in 1997 with a record of 21–16–4 and 23 points. Nick won two matches and lost three, pushing his point total to 25. The Ryder Cup record is now his alone.

That's how it should be, for records are not meant to stand forever. Someday not too distant, I feel confident in predicting, considering the way the game is growing by leaps and bounds here and abroad, some former dashing young phenom like Tiger Woods or David Duval will nip Nick's record. The game brings out the best in us, and the best will always bring out their games at the Ryder Cup.

That same explosive international growth fittingly gave rise, in 1994, to the PGA Tour–sponsored Presidents Cup. From the moment I heard about the proposed Ryder Cup–style team competition I thought it was a great idea. It was a way to bring the finest players from the world's other major tours (Australia, Japan, and southern Africa) into the spotlight of international match-play competition.

For all the tremendous pride and pleasure I took in being part of seven Ryder Cup teams, I must say being selected to serve as captain of the second American Presidents Cup squad in their 1996 contest against the Internationals, as they're called, at the Robert Trent Jones Golf Club in suburban Washington was a thrill that almost stands by itself. Suffice it to say, it was one of the most enjoyable weeks of the past decade for me. And as the drama of the close finish indicated, the quality of the competition was extraordinary. If Freddie Couples hadn't run in that monster putt on 17 to win his match and cinch the Cup for the Americans, 16½ to 15½, I don't know if my old heart could have withstood any more drama.

As this past year's rout in Melbourne by the Internationals goes into the history books, I'm confident that the prestige and popularity of the Presidents Cup will only grow with each subsequent edition. Quite frankly, I'd like to see more match-play competitions develop within the individual tours, between the tours, and perhaps even between individual countries. Match-play golf is really where the soul of the game resides.

The Presidents Cup is a valuable contribution to the game.

If there is one other contribution I believe I have made to the growth and management of the professional game, I think that would have to be my role in the creation of the Senior PGA Tour, an entity that has rightfully been called the most successful sports story of the 1980s.

The truth is, however, before about 1980 I wasn't terribly excited about the idea of a separate tour made up of older players. In part that was because some of us disliked the idea of "abandoning" the regular PGA Tour, with the glamour and riches and drama we'd helped create. That reluctance invariably had something to do with our own egos and having to accept the verdict of time—namely, that we simply couldn't hit the ball quite as far and compete with the same gusto as the flatbellies of the modern Tour.

By the end of the seventies, I'd seen my putting touch go into the tank and was having fits with my vision, wrestling with eyeglasses and finally growing accustomed to wearing contact lenses. True enough, I was still capable of shooting 65 on any given day, but it was maddening that I couldn't seem to duplicate the effort when it counted most in majors or on the regular circuit. The truth is, despite an outward appearance of contentment with my *life*, I was pretty unhappy with the state of my *game* at the age of fifty—so, in effect, the Senior Tour came along at a perfect moment for me. I needed a new challenge and something big to play for.

The thing that really kicked off interest in forming a senior tour was the popular Liberty Mutual *Legends of Golf* telecasts, produced by Fred Raphael of *Shell's Wonderful World of Golf* fame, which first ran in 1978. That first televised best-ball match couldn't have had a more dramatic finish. Gardner Dickinson and Sam Snead trailed the Australian duo of Kel Nagle and five-time British Open champion Peter Thomson by two at the 16th hole until Snead rolled in a clutch birdie to keep his team alive. He then knocked in an eight-footer at the next hole to even the match. At 18, he hit his approach stiff to the flag and made the birdie to win. You couldn't have asked for a better scenario: Golf's all-time leader in tournament wins (81 by the PGA's official count) making three birdies in a row for a come-from-behind win.

The television ratings were high but soared even
higher the next year when the *Legends* had the most
dramatic finish in its history. Julius Boros and Roberto
de Vicenzo put together six *consecutive* birdies in a
playoff to nip Art Wall and Tommy Bolt, who made
five of their own! I recall the irresistible drama of this
particular match, because there was a men's closing-
day dinner going on at Latrobe Country Club that
evening, and nobody in the men's grill would go
upstairs to the dinner until the action was over! Both
teams kept making birdies, a mind-boggling display
proving the "old" guys really could still play.

Aiming to capitalize on the *Legends* momentum,
several former Tour greats gathered for an informal
meeting on January 16, 1980, in Commissioner
Deane Beman's office at the Tour headquarters in
Ponte Vedra, Florida. They didn't know precisely
what they wanted to do, but they had a hankering to
play tournament golf again and thought the ratings
success of the *Legends* proved there might be a good
market for a limited number of senior professional
events. Present were Sam Snead, Julius Boros, Dan
Sikes, Bob Goalby, Gardner Dickinson and Don
January—career money-list leaders and fierce competitors all. Not shy about individually airing their
views, I gather this group of balding eagles argued
about this potential benefit and that potential draw-
back but finally agreed that Deane Beman would put
his considerable organizational expertise behind the
idea of forming a senior tour.

As it was later explained to me, it was also generally agreed that the fledgling tour needed another marquee name or two to help "sell" the idea of an over-fifty tournament circuit to the public and, most critical, to attract potential sponsors who might consider the start-up tour a competitor of the regular PGA Tour. Since I was pretty well connected in the corporate world, and was still showing up to play on the regular Tour from time to time, that person turned out to be me.

As I said, at age fifty, I wasn't sitting around thinking what a great time I could have playing "senior" golf. Business was booming, and I felt that I still had some unfinished business left on the regular Tour circuit—namely, the PGA Championship. But a couple things happened to change my thinking in this regard.

First off, since my friends organizing the new tour asked me to lend the clout of my name and presence, and considering all the things the PGA and PGA Tour had done for me over the years, I felt morally obliged to help out. I began speaking to potential sponsors and people I knew in the business world who might benefit from an association with the new Senior PGA Tour. Then, as if scripted by the golf gods themselves, I managed to fend off an attack of the nerves and win the 1980 PGA Seniors' Championship, held that year at the Turnberry Isle Resort in Florida. The excitement and sudden interest in the new tour that win created across the business world, I suppose, proved incalculable.

By the way, it also felt wonderful to win.

*   *   *

That summer, the United States Golf Association held its first USGA Senior Open Championship at Winged Foot, an event won by Roberto de Vicenzo. Based on gate receipts and other factors, the tournament was a major commercial disappointment. The problem, someone quickly deduced, was the age restriction. You had to be fifty-five or older to enter—as was the case for the established Senior Amateur—which meant a number of the best-known players from golf's so-called golden years weren't eligible to play, myself included. In a move that completely turned around public interest in the event, the USGA wisely lowered the age requirement to fifty for the next rendition, and the result was an enormously successful Senior Open Championship staged at Oakland Hills, which I just happened to win in an exciting playoff against my old Open competitor Bill Casper and the lesser known Bob Stone. To some folks (and even to us) it almost looked like old times.

I'm told my victory was just the shot in the arm the Senior PGA Tour needed to really get rolling, a boost of vital support once again delivered by our good friends at the United States Golf Association. After that, the sponsors started coming forward and senior tournaments started forming at an impressive clip.

As a footnote, in terms of the rules and procedures the new tour would follow, I was personally opposed to the suggestion to permit the use of riding carts in tournaments and, initially, strongly felt the tournaments should be 72-hole events in length, the same as on the regular PGA Tour. Ultimately, I changed my thinking on the length of the tournaments but still feel allowing riding carts in competition was a big mistake. I got outvoted on this issue but warned others that it just might open Pandora's Box somewhere down the line—as it did, indeed, in 1998, when physically handicapped player Casey Martin won his landmark court case, demanding to be permitted to use a riding cart in competition, citing, among other things, the Senior Tour's use of them. I'm totally opposed to exclusionary practices, but equally opposed to providing an unfair competitive advantage.

In terms of popularity, it didn't hurt the seniors' cause that a stream of some of the biggest names in the history of the game was coming along the feeder pipe, guys like Gary Player, Chi Chi Rodriguez, Ray Floyd, Lee Trevino, and, of course, Jack Nicklaus. Maybe the thing I liked best about those early days of the senior circuit was the relaxed atmosphere that pervaded the galleries and competition. Players routinely attended sponsor cocktail parties and mingled with corporate sponsors and fans. Many of the players were grateful for the opportunity to be the center of attention once more and felt as if they'd been given a new lease on life. In effect, we had.

The competition was dead serious, but friendships were rekindled and revealed themselves in the midst of play when Chi Chi and I needled each other or Ray or Lee and I traded affectionate jabs. Those

exchanges, I think, went a long way toward drawing fans into the galleries and sponsors to tournaments, ultimately making the Senior PGA Tour the
$50-million, forty-two-event prime-time road show
it has become. The bottom line is, we had fun in
those early days, and the world saw some pretty
good golf—including aces on two consecutive days
in the pro-amateur event at TPC at Avenel, during
the first Chrysler Cup Match in 1986 (a team competition between America and twelve top international
players) by a guy named Palmer. That really sent an
electric charge through the gallery, I can faithfully
report, and created a buzz in the national media that
lasted for several days. Within hours, a plaque was
installed at the tee. I was pretty excited about it, too.

Year in and year out, the Senior Tour has been a
model of sporting consistency, earning its distinction
as the most successful sporting enterprise of the
1980s. True, as it's grown, the tour has lost a bit of
the intimacy and free-spiritedness that always made
it so much fun to be part of, but the overall impact
and benefit to individual players' lives and associated charities have far exceeded anything, I think,
the founding graybeards could have envisioned.

I'm proud of the ten senior titles I won between
1980 and 1988. I'm also proud of the fact that a tournament I helped start in 1980—now called the Home
Depot Invitational in Charlotte, North Carolina—
was one of the founding events of the Senior PGA
Tour. My involvement with the tournament began
the same year as the Senior Tour began, when friends

from Charlotte approached me about the idea of getting personally involved with a proposed Senior Tour event for that city. I liked Charlotte a lot. The region has deep golf roots, my longtime friend Johnny Harris and his family lived there, and I had numerous other friends and business interests in the area, including a large Arnold Palmer Cadillac dealership. I also knew the golf fans of the Carolinas were still smarting from—and sore at— Commissioner Deane Beman's controversial decision to pull the regular PGA Tour's Kemper Open out of the Queen City and move it to Washington.

People in Charlotte wanted a golf tournament badly, and I decided to be the guy who helped them create it. That same summer, with enthusiastic community support and IMG's invaluable assistance, we started a tournament we called the World Seniors' Invitational at Quail Hollow Country Club. Though I've never managed to win my own senior tournament, which has grown tremendously in purse money and is now named for and sponsored by the Home Depot—and is played at Palmer-designed TPC at Piper Glen Golf Club to boot—it still gives me deep pleasure to personally host the event each year.

That's because, as my own senior playing days continue to dwindle, acting as host gives me an opportunity to remain in touch with old friends and greet the younger bucks of the Senior circuit. I understand, for instance, that as I write this some frisky upstart from St. Louis has won so many

Senior Tour events in the past year alone, he's taken to lobbying to have the Senior Tour officially renamed the "Irwin Tour."

Well, as much as I admire his style (not to mention his long-iron game), Hale Irwin had better watch his flank carefully, because some younger guys named Watson, Wadkins, and Strange are all about to become senior citizens of professional golf and will probably have something to say about that in the very near future.

Should be fun to watch for years to come.

The agony and the ecstasy. I experienced both during my forty-two-year tenure at the U.S. Open.

Agonizing over another near miss at Olympic Club in 1966.

Staring down a missed putt at Oakmont in 1962.

Bidding farewell to the U.S. Open at Oakmont in 1994.

Celebrating my first U.S. Open victory in 1960 in Denver.

John Clock, USGA president, presents me with the trophy emblematic of my 1960 National Open championship at Cherry Hills.

The British Open was always one of my favorite tournaments for many reasons, and I still love to cross the pond to play the old links and courses.

Playing in 1960 at St. Andrews, my first British Open.

. . . and at Troon in 1962.

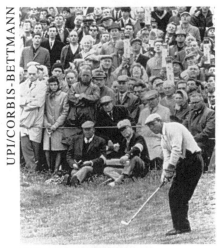

The British version of Arnie's Army watching me at Royal Birkdale in 1965 . . .

Holding the Claret Jug for the first time in 1961.

'I guess it's over,' said Palmer, who finished his British Open career amid cheers from both spectators and admiring pros.

This framed photo of my last appearance at the British Open in 1995 at St. Andrews hangs in my offices in Latrobe.

*I suffered more than my share of ups and downs at
the PGA over the years (as did that bridge railing in
'65 at Laurel Valley. Fortunately, I was able to capture
the Senior version of the event twice.*

AP/WIDE WORLD PHOTOS

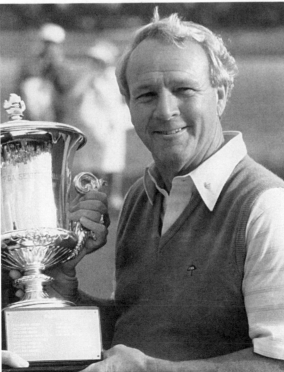

*Playing golf in international events like the
Presidents Cup (which my good friend George
Bush helped initiate) and the Ryder Cup, as well
as playing in various exhibitions, has helped me
see a good bit of the world.*

**With Gary Player
during a 1961 visit
to Japan.**

**Hitting a golf ball off the
Eiffel Tower during a
promotion in Paris.**

The 1963 Ryder Cup team.

**Receiving the Presidents Cup in 1996
from George Bush.**

**The Bob Hope Desert Classic, one of my
favorite stops on the Tour. In this photo
I'm joined by Bob Hope, Lawrence Welk,
broadcaster Lindsey Nelson, and Joe
DiMaggio.**

The Big Three enjoying a refreshment break at the 1966 Florida Citrus Open, a tournament that eventually became the Bay Hill Invitational. That's Jack Nicklaus in the center and Gary Player to my far left.

Sometimes, when you least expect it, and you most need it, somebody does something that makes your day. Here in 1991 Peter Jacobsen and other touring pros present me with a cake at the Bay Hill Invitational.

Golf is a humbling game, and nowhere is that more true than at Pebble Beach—a place of astounding beauty. Here I contemplate my fate in the 1962 Bing Crosby National Pro Am.

I'm still amazed at the number of people I've managed to meet because of my involvement in the game of golf. None of them is any more special than Dwight David Eisenhower, but it's hard to forget the day that I got a summons from President Nixon to the Western White House.

With Winnie's help, President Eisenhower surprised me with a visit on my thirty-seventh birthday.

Winnie and President Eisenhower watching the action in Palm Springs.

In San Clemente with President Nixon, Vice President Ford, Henry Kissinger, and Bob Hope among the attendees.

The Big Three plus one.

**A gathering of distinguished Americans for
the tenth Anniversary cover of
Private Clubs magazine.**

A few of my favorite things. I always told people that if I hadn't been a golf pro, I'd have been a movie cowboy. Instead I had to settle for being a pilot, but I'm most proud of the good I've been able to do on behalf of children because of my involvement with the March of Dimes and Arnold Palmer Hospital for Children and Women in Orlando.

OFFICIAL PHOTOGRAPH U.S. NAVY

**Posing with my brother
Jerry in front of a wood
sculpture of Pap that Jerry
commissioned in 1998 and
now stands on the
18th hole at Latrobe.**

Jack, Gary, and me in a recent photo. As members of the Big Three, we've shared a lot of history.

Winnie and me in 1997.

No matter what ups and downs I've experienced on and off the course, I've always enjoyed the game of golf. This photo taken in the locker room at Oakmont following my final appearance in a U.S. Open says it all. I've tried to enjoy every moment of this golfer's life.

CHAPTER TWELVE

The Handshake

Someone once said that ten men out of one hundred can handle failure. But only one man out of those ten can really handle success.

I don't remember where I heard this, but over the years I've come to believe it's really true. A little bit of success can be a dangerous thing to some men, and a lot of success, improperly handled, can be a prescription for disaster.

I was fortunate to experience success fairly early in my professional playing career, and though I always thought I had a pretty good head for numbers and handling my own business affairs, in retrospect I can see that one of the most fortunate things that ever happened to me was finding Mark McCormack or his finding me.

The truth is, I'm not entirely sure which way it happened.

According to Mark, the first time he saw me I was warming up on the practice range in the spring of 1950 on a golf course in Raleigh, North Carolina, where Wake Forest was preparing to play a collegiate golf match against the College of William and Mary. I was scheduled to play in the number-two slot behind Bud Worsham, and Mark was supposed to play that position for William and Mary. For some unknown reason he got bumped to the fifth match for that particular tournament. He claims that was a lucky break because the way I was striking low irons on the practice tee put terror in his heart.

I don't believe we even spoke to each other that week, or for that matter actually talked to each other for another half-dozen years. The amusing thing is, I've seen stories written that tell how Mark and I became fast friends playing against each other in college or forged our friendship when he was a young attorney starting out in Cleveland and I was stationed there completing my Coast Guard commitment. Nice tales, but untrue.

I'm not even certain I remember our second encounter. According to Mark, that took place at the Masters in the spring of 1956 when his friend Bob Toski failed to make it into the Masters field but asked Mark to pass along a special putter to me. Mark was in the U.S. Army at the time, stationed conveniently enough at Camp Gordon right there in Augusta. As Mark tells it, he strolled over to the putting green where I was practicing after the first round and introduced himself, then conveyed Toski's best wishes and handed me the putter. We had a friendly chat about our college days and a few other things we had in common. He says I introduced him to Winnie, and she remembers that introduction. So it must have happened just like that.

Three years later, after he had graduated from Yale Law School and was working for the prestigious Cleveland law firm of Arter, Hadden, Wycoff, and Van Duzer and I had won my first Masters golf tournament, we met again.

This time the setting was the Tour stop for the Carling Open at Seneca Golf Club in Cleveland. I was playing, and Mark had come out with his bride, Nancy, to watch the action and say hello again. We had a pleasant conversation, and Mark let it slip that he and Carling's PR man, Dick Taylor, were knocking around the idea of starting up a small company to represent the business interests of a few top professional golfers, mostly in the form of booking exhibitions. Legendary Boston sports promoter Fred Corcoran had done a lot for the career of Sam Snead and others—not to mention the fledgling PGA Tour itself—but nobody I knew had a personal business manager or "agent" to handle their affairs to the extent Mark was talking about. I remember thinking the idea potentially had real merit. He asked me to think about it, and I promised him I would. That was about as far as things went then.

We didn't meet again until that November. This time the setting was a motel room in Atlanta, where Dow Finsterwald and I went to speak to Mark and Dick Taylor about the possibility of their formally representing us with their new enterprise called National Sports Management, Inc. We listened to what Mark had to say, and learned they were already booking exhibitions for guys like Gene Littler, Doug Ford, and Toski. Dow and I agreed to see what they could do for us. A few decent exhibition fees came out of that agreement, mostly in the $300-to-$500 range, and that was extra income we were both really glad to get.

By then it was becoming ever clearer to me that, due to my sudden success playing professional golf, I was going to be presented greater opportunities in the golf world (and possibly outside it) than extra Monday golf exhibitions. I wasn't entirely sure how to capitalize on such potential or even how to proceed from an organizational standpoint. Winnie was soldiering along bravely as our team accountant, travel planner, and general business manager, but with people suddenly approaching us asking for pieces of my time for everything from exhibitions to commercial endorsements, I knew we were rapidly entering a new league and needed professional business help.

I told Mark bluntly that I wanted him to manage these opportunities. Moreover I wanted his help *exclusively*. As surprising as it may sound, this wasn't the easiest decision for Mark to make. NSM was a new but prospering concern by then, and he and Taylor had recently snared Bill Casper and Art Wall as clients as well. He explained to me that his specialty was negotiating contracts and that there were many areas in which he was totally ignorant, a better reason, he argued, to have the full services of an organization like National Sports Management rather than one man handling his affairs.

It was a logical argument (Mark is nothing if not persuasive), but I was adamant that I needed *one* man to handle my business affairs and one man alone. Sometimes you have a gut instinct and intellect about these things, and my gut told me Mark McCormack was the man for me. Mark's sophistication impressed me. He is a man of letters and a voracious reader who also is tough, is possessed of fierce integrity, intuitively knows the value of things, and knows how to say no—something I'm still learning how to do.

In many ways I was still a bashful, backward kid, and I suppose because I'd grown up in the Great Depression I got easily excited when people mentioned things they wanted me to do, or talked about business opportunities and so forth. Central to my constitution was a determination never to disappoint anybody, but I had no way of appreciating the kind of personal commitment involved—or its potential toll on my practice time and my game.

For example, as early as 1956, Munsingwear and Haggar offered Dow and me and a few others on tour money to wear and promote their golf apparel. The deals were hashed out independently—handled more like friendly clubhouse conversations after a golf round than business negotiations—so I had no grasp of the complexities of my real worth and whether or not I was selling myself short or asking too much. About that same time, I also did my first book, *Hit It Hard,* with Bob Drum, a modestly successful how-to book that opened a host of new opportunities in publishing and instruction. Almost overnight there was talk of Arnold Palmer golf schools, driving ranges, regular golf "tips" in periodicals, as well my writing a syndicated column.

Basically I needed somebody like Mark who

could sort all of this out, separate the good opportunities from the bad, and help protect, buffer, and ensure the quality of life I was building back home in Latrobe with Winnie and, soon thereafter, our children. I needed somebody who knew when to say yes but wouldn't hesitate to say no.

That's a tall order. Especially at a time when nobody was doing that sort of business advocacy work for professional golfers. I did see a relationship that I thought might work, to some extent, as a model—the manner in which Clifford Roberts worked on behalf of Augusta National and President Eisenhower. I knew—or at least had heard such was true—that Mr. Roberts handled most of President Eisenhower's business and investment affairs and was the man President Eisenhower turned to whenever he had a question about anything from a stock tip to a matter of national security. Clifford Roberts was the ultimate inner-circle man, adviser and protector, friend and counselor, through good times and bad, thick and thin, and President Eisenhower trusted him implicitly. In a nutshell, I told Mark I wanted him to become my Clifford Roberts.

Mark took a few days to think it over and we met again.

"All right," he said. "I'll be your Clifford Roberts."

With that, we shook hands. The deal was consumated that simply. Mark agreed to give up National Sports Management with the understanding that I would be the sole focus of his attention and expertise—my Eisenhower to his Roberts, so to speak—though at some point down the line he could consider taking on a few special additional clients. I agreed to listen to and heed his advice—especially when he said no to something. There was no written contract between us, because Mark knew my word was my bond and there would be no turning back on my part. The same was true of him, I knew, and those stories that you've heard about us never formalizing our business relationship in printed legalese are true. As life went along, eventually a host of formal legal documents linking us and our business interests would be hammered out and signed—for that's the way, alas, of the modern world. A world that, at times, seems to be run by lawyers.

But that handshake was the beginning of our relationship and pretty much all the contract either of us required in order to get down to business.

Beginning in late 1959, one of the first things Mark closely examined was my business relationship with the Wilson Sporting Goods Company. My first professional endorsement deal was with Wilson, begun the moment I signed a contract giving up my amateur status several weeks after winning the National Amateur in 1954, a standard $5,000-per-year agreement with a few incentive clauses written into it that was pretty much identical to the contracts of every other player on the Wilson staff. It called for me to play Wilson clubs and use Wilson balls, and though I wasn't particularly fond of their equipment—and less fond of the quality of their golf balls—I was nevertheless proud to represent the same company Sam Snead, Cary Middlecoff, and Lloyd Mangrum spoke so highly of. I also immensely liked and trusted the folks at Wilson, especially player rep Joe Wolfe, Plug Osborne, the company's regional sales manager for the Southeast, and Fred Bowman, the company's president. They treated me very well and had every reason to expect, as I did, that the marriage would be a long and prosperous one.

Mark eventually had another opinion, however. In going over my original contract with the company, he learned I was prohibited from doing virtually anything to commercially capitalize on my success that didn't have Wilson's approval and/or name on it. If I endorsed cornflakes, for example, I would have to say I started my day each morning with a bowl of cornflakes . . . and be sure to mention something about Wilson golf equipment. The agreement I'd signed, in fact, though I'd failed to realize it at the time, contractually locked me up as a commercial entity until 1963. To be perfectly frank about it, I didn't feel it was either smart or appropriate, as Mark counseled, to try to alter the agreement via new negotiations.

Mark pointed out that I was being severely restricted from marketing my name and services, and he worked on me at every turn to change my mind on this subject, but I held fast. As I repeatedly pointed out to him, loyalty was a big deal with me, and I trusted the people at Wilson to do the right thing. Looking back, it's fitting that the absence of loyalty on Wilson's part was ultimately what changed my thinking and drove me from that great sporting house.

After my second Masters win in 1960 the business environment around me changed at a pace that almost took my breath away. Mark was fielding commercial offers and endorsement deals from all directions, some of them truly eye-opening, everything from television specials to hair tonic ads, trying his best to accommodate my wishes and abide by the rules set down by the folks at Wilson, but working his tail off trying to figure out a way to achieve more financial autonomy and control of my own fate.

In my view, the real beginning of the end of my association with Wilson—and thus the beginning of Arnold Palmer Enterprises—came just after that post-Masters frenzy when I was approached by a man named Jack Harkins.

I knew about Jack Harkins, and a lot of other people around the Tour did, too—not all of it particularly flattering. Harkins was a loud, profane, cigar-chewing club maker and big-talking high roller who was known to drop an occasional bundle at the craps tables in Vegas. But he also owned the First Flight Golf Equipment Company out of Chattanooga, Tennessee, which made some pretty decent professional-quality golf clubs, in my estimation, and was the first man, as far as I know, to innovate the concept of swing-weighting individual golf clubs. He was also highly personable and, as I quickly found out, a man of surprising integrity and vision despite his bluster.

Jack wanted me to leave Wilson, come on board at First Flight, and design a set of the highest-professional-quality golf clubs under the Arnold Palmer signature. I was flattered by his suggestion, and I was also deeply intrigued. Since I was the son of a club professional, building and rebuilding golf clubs was not only a hobby and avocation of mine, it was also one of my genuine passions. For years, I'd lobbied Plug Osborne and the others at Wilson to improve the quality of the irons they put out under my name, but that had never come to pass.

On the other hand, I was reluctant to do anything to upset the apple cart at Wilson. Stuck between a rock and a hard place, I held Harkins off while I put Mark on the case to see if he could figure out a way for us to fulfill our agreements with Wilson and possibly start our own lines of high-quality golf clubs. At the time this was all developing, however, I was operating under the impression that my contract with Wilson was at an end and up for renegotiation in 1960. In fact, as I've said, Mark quickly put me straight on the fact that we wouldn't legally be free of my obligations to Wilson until 1963.

So something had to give. We asked for and were granted a big meeting to discuss our concerns with the management at Wilson Sporting Goods.

Right after the Tournament of Champions, Mark, Winnie, and I flew to Chicago for a conference with Wilson executives at their factory in nearby River

Grove. We were taken straight to the offices of the company's new president, Bill Holmes. Joe Wolfe was there, but gone were my friends Plug Osborne and Fred Bowman. The conversations dragged on through lunch and the afternoon, and all that was really accomplished was that all sides agreed to see what could be worked out by the lawyers to liberate us a bit from the restrictions imposed by my existing contract—and, to Wilson's way of thinking, end once and for all any danger of my abandoning ship to go over to Harkins at First Flight.

A few weeks later, I won the U.S. Open at Cherry Hills, and as Mark engagingly put it in his own account of the moment, "Instead of a mere hot commodity, you became an immortal in alligator shoes."

Mark was constantly agitating through the end of summer and autumn to have a "serious" discussion with me about my future, but I delayed him, pending final word from Wilson on the new contract, until a snowy night in December, when he finally cornered me at the Oak Bar at the Plaza Hotel in Manhattan and gave it to me straight. He said that I had to make some major decisions about the direction my business and personal life were going to take. I hated it when Mark got that serious glint in his eye—it always meant I was going to probably have to disappoint somebody, which of course was alien to my nature.

I remember sipping my whiskey and listening to him advance the idea that we were at a major crossroads, that I had an opportunity to become a very wealthy man, and one way or another I probably wouldn't do badly if I decided to stay put with the offer we assumed Wilson was preparing in good faith at the time. On the other hand, as he laid it out, if I freed myself from the Wilson contract and together we explored the many opportunities suddenly flying my way, well, who knew what the limits could be?

I heard what he was telling me, and I thought hard about it. The snow was falling outside and I was anxious to get home to Winnie and my family. Nothing had ever prepared me to make such momentous business decisions, but I loathed conflict of any kind and knew in my heart that my conservative nature demanded that I give Wilson the full benefit of the doubt. We had to take things to the bitter end. I told Mark that we owed Wilson that much, to see what kind of deal they came up with, and Mark did his best imitation of a lawyer who's been given the opposite verdict than the one he'd expected or sought. Despite his efforts at hiding it, I could tell he was surprised, angry, and disappointed. But I also knew he'd do his best for me.

Mark worked hard over the next few weeks to hammer out guarantees of more freedom over our own commercial endorsements and a new deferred-income provision, as well as a split-dollar insurance program that would ease my worries about my family's future if something should happen to me. I was encouraged when the new Wilson execs all agreed to the changes and said that a mere formality remained before we put ink to paper on the matter. The final draft of the new ten-year agreement had to go to Wilson's legendary chairman, Judge James Cooney, for his approval. No one anticipated any problem.

I didn't know much about Judge Cooney, but I understood he was a tough old bird who once fired hundreds of striking meatpackers at the height of a bitter labor strike (Wilson and Company was a giant in the meatpacking business long before they began using gut to make tennis strings and hides to make footballs). I remember how everyone trooped into his office all smiles and took a seat around the judge's desk, ready to sign the revised contract after months of hard work on both sides.

The judge held my future in his hands, and I watched him as he read over the agreement. I knew we were in big trouble when his face contorted and he looked as if he had personally been insulted. He tossed aside the contract and made a harsh little speech to a stunned Mark and me about how he couldn't possibly grant such "liberal" terms to me when nobody else in his employment had the same kind of deal. Furthermore, he wondered, or words to this effect, who the hell was Arnold Palmer to be dictating terms when he already had Sam Snead and Patty Berg under contract.

I was devastated, and mad as hell. So mad I could scarcely speak. Mark kept his usual poker face, though I figured he was mentally turning cartwheels of joy at the unexpected development—already planning the brave new future for us. This embarrassing tantrum on the judge's part meant, as Mark, with no small portion of irony, told someone, that I "was going to have to become a millionaire whether he [I] liked it or not."

In the busy months that followed, we reached an agreement with Harkins and a number of Chattanooga business interests establishing what was to be known as the Arnold Palmer Golf Company, makers and distributors of top-quality professional-grade golf clubs. We even hired away a few of Wilson's top management people and tried to buy out the remaining portion of my contract with Wilson, offering exceedingly generous terms. The judge would have none of it. In fact, he basically ignored our every approach and forced us to wait out to the last second the expiration of my contract in 1963.

I'm happy to say we made up lost ground pretty rapidly. Within a year, the Arnold Palmer Golf Company was selling about a hundred thousand sets of clubs a year, and Mark's vision of an ever-expanding empire of Arnold Palmer business interests was dramatically coming into focus.

The other part of Mark's overall business strategy that emerged from that wintry powwow in Manhattan was to establish, in 1961, Arnold Palmer Enterprises, a corporate signature for a host of business ventures gathered beneath one umbrella.

The tale of how the multicolored umbrella became our corporate logo is a rather interesting one. One day not long after APE was formed, a group of us were sitting around a conference table at the Holiday Inn in Ligonier attempting to brainstorm

some kind of signature logo we could use on clothing, business stationery, golf clubs, and so forth. In
the preceding days we'd come up with a number of
promising ideas ranging from crossed golf clubs to
laurel leaves, but upon deeper investigation found
these symbols were either too commonplace to have
any real meaning to anybody or else were already
copyrighted by someone else.

The frustration level was rising pretty quickly
when an idea popped into my head.

"What about an umbrella?" I said.

Nobody seemed particularly wowed by the
suggestion.

"What kind of umbrella?" somebody asked.

"I dunno. What about a multicolored golf
umbrella?"

A few heads bobbed slightly, but nobody thought
it was as close to as good an idea as I did. Someone commented that I shouldn't get my hopes
too high because it would be a miracle if Travelers
Insurance hadn't already trademarked an umbrella
as a corporate logo. Even so, it was decided that
the lawyers would investigate the symbol and get
back to us. A couple weeks later, we were surprised
and pleased to learn that nobody worldwide had
copyrighted the umbrella symbol. We suddenly had
our new company logo, an open golf umbrella done
in four colors—red, green, yellow, and white—
to signify the varied components of our new
enterprises.

*   *   *

Contrary to what some people think, Arnold Palmer and Mark McCormack didn't invent the concept of sports marketing in golf. During the early days of the century, Harry Vardon pitched any number of products, including cigarettes and liquor, as did Walter Hagen and even Bob Jones. Gene Sarazen may have been the king of golf's early pitchmen, however, promoting everything from lawn sprinklers to shotgun shells at the height of his public appeal.

The selling of products based on the appeal of famous athletes was a well-established practice in American advertising. But as I made clear to Mark from the beginning, I didn't feel comfortable pitching a product or service I wouldn't use or didn't think was very good. That just seemed dishonest to me, and I was pretty sure the public would see right through it. Mark agreed with me and even suggested that such criteria should be the basis for picking and choosing what we would endorse. If at all possible, they had to be products Arnold Palmer would personally use. As an operating credo that sounds pretty simple, right?

Well, down the line, as I'll explain in a moment, we ran into a few situations that had almost comic consequences. We'll call these mistakes our marketing "duds."

Two of my early deals were with makers of products I had no problem whatsoever endorsing—Coca-Cola and L&M cigarettes. I've already spoken about my addiction to cigarettes. If you've ever seen any of a number of print and television ads for L&M cigarettes from the early sixties, some of which won top advertising-industry awards, you know there's no ambiguity whatsoever about my affection for the product in hand. Likewise, if you happened to be following me during the Open at Cherry Hills or any number of other Masters tournaments where my nerve endings were being frayed by the tension of the chase, you undoubtedly saw me gulping down Cokes at an alarming rate. I suppose I thought that sugar in the blood might help to keep me calm. The simple fact is, I also happened to love the taste of Coca-Cola and found it comforting. Another early product endorsement was Heinz catsup. I appeared in Heinz ads in *Sports Illustrated* and *Life* magazine about that time.

A brilliant part of Mark's marketing strategy was never to tie my endorsement of a product to how I was faring on the golf course. No congratulations or acknowledgment of a tournament won ever appeared in an ad or commercial I was part of. Mark's reasoning was simple but effective: "win ads," as they were popularly called in the industry, were about winning or losing, and his aim was not to position me as a "winner" because there always comes a day when a winner no longer wins—and his appeal, accordingly, dramatically dims.

The purchasing public's attention span, as any Madison Avenue marketer can tell you, is remarkably fickle. This year's big sports winner can easily become next year's forgotten gridiron hero. Mark's creative solution to this problem was to market my image in a far more "timeless" way—that is to say, in terms of values closer to my own heart, to the qualities I admired both in the products I used and what other people supposedly admired most in me: character and endurance, reliability and integrity.

That was the philosophical base of his thinking, and in advertising circles it quickly proved to be a pioneering strategy, as offers to represent everything from toothpaste to underwear, snow tires to farm machinery, made their way to the offices of Arnold Palmer Enterprises. Some companies we felt comfortable making deals with; many we didn't. In addition to an array of golf-related products and services ranging from indoor putting greens to franchised driving ranges and instruction academies, we soon entered into broader clothing and apparel contracts, a deal with Lincoln Mercury, various kinds of household and hardware products, and other merchandise we deemed fit nicely beneath the APE umbrella.

At one point we even entertained visions of ourselves becoming dry-cleaning moguls. I must confess I didn't originally see the point in creating a chain of Arnold Palmer Dry Cleaning Centers. I mean, I relied heavily on superior dry-cleaning services myself, but I suppose part of me secretly feared that I might be accosted at tournaments by unhappy customers whose pants had been improperly ironed or whose best shirt had been inadvertently ruined.

Within a few years, though, we had a franchise chain of something like 110 Arnold Palmer Dry

Cleaning Centers (with countermen dressed in grass-colored green jackets, no less) scattered around the United States, prompting my old buddy Dave Marr to quip, "If I'm going to take my laundry to a golf pro, it's going to be Chen Ching-po."

There was also talk of Arnold Palmer soap and Arnold Palmer Christmas trees being sold exclusively through JCPenney. Consider this somewhat embarrassing paragraph from a little *Golf Digest* bio of the time, published in 1967: "Arnie can supply you with a complete golf outfit from clubs to socks, dry clean your clothes, put an ice skating rink in your backyard, steer you to the right place to get stock certificates printed, and, if you are bothered by a hook or slice, his 'Palmer' method of golf instruction will attempt to straighten you out in one of his indoor schools he is franchising around the country. If you want some insurance, one of his companies can oblige. And someday soon you might be able to stay in an Arnold Palmer motel . . ."

Well, the motel thing never really worked out. In fact, some of the duds were at least as interesting as our successes in the sports marketing realm. For example, we once foolishly allowed my name to be associated with a "revolutionary" backyard driving net and showed up on the practice tee at Doral with several press photographers on hand to capture my first ceremonial shot into the new net. Unfortunately, I hit the ball so hard it flew through the net and nearly crowned Bill Casper, who was practicing at the opposite end of the range. The Arnold Palmer "foot detergent" was also something less than a roaring success, and near endorsements for shaving cream, suntan oil, talcum powder, and a deodorant in plastic containers molded into my likeness fortunately never really got off the ground.

I was once asked to try to drive a golf ball through a television screen to prove it wouldn't break—I did; happily it didn't. Among other offers I politely declined were a line of houseboats, a revolutionary manure dispenser, a golfer's vacation club, countless children's toys, a brand of walking sticks, an endless procession of personal exercise gizmos, several brands of liquor, French cologne, more offshore golf resorts than I care to remember, fallout shelters, orange groves, an African safari, apartment houses, and a one-act play that hoped to make it to Broadway called *What Is the Verdict?*

The real verdict, as I often and loudly complained to Mark, was that it sometimes felt like we were in danger of killing the goose that laid the golden egg—namely me, stretching me so thin to accommodate so many product endorsement deals. Not only would that diminish my value as an endorser, it would take even more of a toll on my golf game.

I've described how I complained to the press that my expanding business interests took an increasingly larger bite out of my days and perhaps were a contributing factor to the decline of my play. That much is true—though to what extent it was true still somewhat eludes me. In fairness to Mark, he didn't arrange any business deal I didn't ultimately have veto power over, and as Mark and anybody else around me from the beginning knew, I was fanatical about fulfilling commitments and given to saying yes to things before I had taken the proper time to think about the potential impact on my life and schedule.

More often than not, he faithfully protected what precious time I did have for family and practice by saying no up front in situations where I never could or would have. In essence, he played a very necessary "bad cop" to my "good cop," and I once confided to close friends that it was good to have all my business interests to publicly complain about, as Pap did after my majorless 1963 season, because at least it offered some kind of explanation for the decline in my performances.

In that regard I suppose I contributed to a widespread belief with the press and to some extent in the public that the evil, hard-driving Mark McCormack was "wearing out the greatest player of his generation" (to quote one prominent columnist from that time). By allowing that notion to take hold, I was sowing the seeds, in effect, of a phenomenon that developed when Mark, with my reluctant agreement, moved on to establish International Management Group and represent selected other golf stars and eventually a broad range of top sports and celebrity figures.

Years later, whenever I heard a prominent player complaining that he was being "IMG-ed to death"— in other words, run by Mark and his associates around the world in order to exploit the player's marketability—I was sorely tempted to, and on selected occasions did, offer my own seasoned opinion on this subject. As far as I knew, Mark never put a gun to a player's head to do something he didn't want to do, and ironically, at least in my view, most of the real complaints stemmed from the fact that the star player in question—and I include myself in this category, which I'll talk about shortly—either felt he wasn't being given the attention from the boss that his stardom merited or else nursed some belief that his "fame" wasn't being marketed properly and failed to yield the big paydays he'd expected.

We humans are funny critters, even the famous ones—and maybe especially the famous ones. Over the decades I've watched some great professional golfers come and go through the portals of IMG, an "A" list that includes Jack Nicklaus, Raymond Floyd, and Greg Norman. For one reason or another, some very legitimate ones and, in my view, some that had far less to do with profits than personalities, these men and a number of lesser luminaries decided Mark and company weren't their cup of tea. As Mark would tell you flatly, that was fine, a reasonable and honorable enough reason to strike out on one's own.

But, for all of my own considerable differences with Mr. McCormack, the truth is I never heard a player who was loyal to him complain that Mark wasn't loyal in return many times over. I know of many private acts of generosity and personal charity he will simply never speak of—things he did for this player or that one at a critical or difficult moment of their lives that helped to ease their burden. At the end of the day—and most telling, in my estimation—the list of players who have remained with Mark and loyal to IMG through the ups and downs of their careers dwarfs the list of those who grew disgruntled and left.

Me included. But more on that touchy subject in a bit. First, a few more thoughts on the life of Arnold Palmer the pitchman.

To me, perhaps the most enjoyable of those early business relationships were the clothing deals we had with Munsingwear, Sunstate Slacks, and, a little further on and more enduringly, Robert Bruce Clothing. The licensing of these companies was handled for us brilliantly by Jules Rosenthal, a New York clothing-industry man Mark hired specifically to oversee the manufacturing and distribution of Arnold Palmer logo clothing and sports attire.

Additionally, thanks to Harold Neuman at Robert Bruce—as gracious and astute a businessman as I ever met—I was given a strong hand in the design of the Robert Bruce golf attire line. I remain proud of the style, high quality, and functionality that came out of the Arnold Palmer clothing of that era. Every now and then someone will pull me aside and show me their treasured Robert Bruce golf sweater, and I always feel a kick of pleasure at that, because I still own half a closet full of Arnold Palmer alpaca cardigan sweaters myself! Wouldn't sell them for anything, either.

The first such sweater we brought out cost $18.95, and when we stopped making them fifteen years later, the going price was more than $150, owing to the steeply rising cost of top-grade alpaca wool. What a shame. I still feel these were the best golf sweaters ever made, and a number of other people apparently think so, too, because I still get letters from people wondering where they can purchase them.

I loved those clothes, but, in retrospect, making the print and television ads for them, which happened over something like a twenty-year period, was sometimes more pain than pleasure. Posing with fashion models for hours at a time was a hell of a lot harder than I imagined it would be. The good news was that many of the models were gorgeous young women or celebrities in their own right and we did have more than a few laughs before and after the productions were over . . . with Mrs. Palmer's complete and amused consent, of course.

As I remember, the television spots we filmed at Latrobe and sent to Japan were particularly effective. So much so that after Laura Baugh of the LPGA and I were depicted cutting up as we rode together down a fairway in a golf cart—this was sometime in the early 1970s—millions in Japan speculated that I'd ditched Winnie and that Laura was my new (and very young) wife!

Not too many years ago, I was checking into a Hong Kong hotel and signed my name. The clerk looked at it and beamed widely at me and said,

"Ah, you bring more Arno Par-mare shirts!" For a moment I was confused, and then it came to me. He had no clue that I was the real Arnold Palmer—no idea, it quickly became clear, in fact, who or what Arnold Palmer did to have his name on the shirts. But thanks to Renown of Japan, our hugely successful clothing licensee in the Far East since the early days of the clothing enterprise, he knew Arnold Palmer clothing very well indeed. For many years running, our signature line was the top-selling brand of all clothing lines in Japan, and the hotel clerk merely thought I was a salesman bringing the latest Palmer shirts to Hong Kong—proof that the brand name had developed a life of its own that exceeded that of the man himself.

One of the more amusing print ads from that faraway time is one for Ajay Golf in which, of all things, Jack Nicklaus and I are depicted walking together on a fairway, chatting pleasantly and towing our bags on pull carts. There's a bit of history behind how that ad came to be.

Sometime in late 1960, Jack approached me in the locker room at a tournament site and told me he was thinking of turning professional. He wondered if I could help him out by introducing him to Mark McCormack. I told him I would be happy to do that, and pleased to help him out in any way that I could.

As I've said, I liked Jack from the very beginning. The extraordinary quality of his game spoke for itself, but he was also extremely courteous and mindful, thanks to his father's strong influence, of the greater traditions of the game. I really was happy to help him figure out the best way to turn professional. And as much as I didn't like the idea of "sharing" McCormack with anybody, I'd already hooked Gary Player up with Mark, to great effect. It seemed only fair that a kid of Nicklaus's obvious ability and unlimited potential should speak with somebody who could give him an idea of what to do with himself. As I suspected would happen, Jack soon became a McCormack client.

A few years along, some of the first great things to come out of this unique alliance were the television programs our company, Trans World International, produced, which would eventually involve Jack, Gary, and me. The first series was called *Challenge Golf* and ran for thirteen weeks spanning 1963 and 1964. That series was produced by Jay Michaels (father of Al Michaels of *Monday Night Football* fame), who originally wanted to call the show "Arnold Palmer Against the World," until I pointed out to him that if somebody beat me in a golf match we would have to change the show's name—that could get costly and confuse viewers.

In settling on *Challenge Golf*, it was decided that Gary Player and I would compete against top twosomes in a best-ball format, at famous venues like Riviera Country Club in Los Angeles, Pauma Valley, and Pebble Beach. I can think of few other players I'd rather have had on my side in any match than Gary.

Gary's surname suits him perfectly, for I don't know if there has ever been a more dedicated player than he. The diminutive son of a South African mine worker, Gary came to the game with a strong grip, a flat swing, and a confident bearing that many early on mistook for simple arrogance. After his first trip to try to make it on the British tour resulted in disappointment in the 1950s, he was advised by some to go home to South Africa and find a good club job. Instead, he worked on refining his game as few ever have and transformed himself into a golfing dynamo. Not only did he capture three British Opens (1959, 1968, and 1974), but while playing a limited schedule in the United States between 1958 and 1979, he won twenty-one events, including three Masters (1961, 1974, and 1978), two PGA Championships (1962 and 1972), and one U.S. Open (1965). In the process, he became one of only four men in history (Sarazen, Hogan, and Nicklaus were the others) to win all four major championships. With a practice work ethic that was unmatched except perhaps by Hogan's, and an ever-sunny, always-upbeat attitude that was very genuine and receptive to the press—which masked, I think, a deep worry about not being accepted—Gary went on to collect something like 120 tournament wins worldwide in his regular playing career and became the greatest foreign player ever on the American tour.

No player I can think of made more of his gifts than Gary, and I think there was something to Billy Maxwell's remark that among the Big Three Gary was perhaps the greatest competitor—simply because if he hadn't been, he wouldn't have been among the Big Three. Relatively short off the tee, he made himself one of the premier sand players and clutch putters of all time. Beneath the trademark black clothes and movie-matinee-idol good looks, the fad diets and ridiculously intense exercise regimens, is a man who loves his family and his native South Africa to pieces. He is also one helluva nice guy.

Gary and I had tremendous social chemistry. Our games fit hand-and-glove and we were always able at a critical moment to make each other smile or laugh to relieve the tension—especially, as I said earlier, when we were forced to sit in a studio booth and record voice-overs for those *Challenge Golf* matches. Being a far poorer sand player and script reader than Gary, I'd goof up something in the script and he would make a wisecrack and all hell would break loose between us. The studio engineers would shake their heads in dismay as we clowned around and they rewound the tape for yet another take. Those were some of the best laughs I ever had.

I'm proud of what we did together on the golf course, too. We took those matches very seriously and always tried our best to win. In the two years and twenty-six matches that *Challenge Golf* aired on ABC, I'm happy to say, Gary and I lost only eight times, including twice to Julius Boros and George Bayer, twice to Sam Snead and Ted Kroll, twice to Tommy Jacobs and Mason Rudolph, once to Joe Campbell and Dave Ragan, and once to Ken Venturi and Byron Nelson. The ratings were always high, and most of all we truly enjoyed making the shows.

It was about the same time that Bob Hope asked me to make a cameo appearance in his movie *Call Me Bwana*. As I recall, Mark and I had recently come back from our first trip to see Gary at home in Africa, a trip that amazed us in so many ways. The beauty and sweeping grandeur of South Africa and neighboring Rhodesia (now Zimbabwe) were breathtaking, and it was easy enough to see why little Gary was so keen on his big native land. People were unfailingly kind to us everywhere we went. During a stop for a match in Johannesburg, Gary's hometown, his father took Mark and me six thousand feet down into a gold mine, a thrilling experience that darkened later when we learned that a tragic cave-in not far away that same day killed more than a hundred workers. The scale of such human tragedy was almost unimaginable, but it reminded me of some of the coal-mining tragedies I'd heard about while growing up in Pennsylvania.

On a brighter note, as Mark recounts in his tale of the visit, there was an old South African legend that if a man could lift two of the gold ingots poured in the mine and walk away with them, he could keep them. I decided to give the tale a test and managed to get my large hands around two gold bars. I hoisted them and started for the door—visibly surprising the mining people, I guess, by either my physical strength or my nerve. They politely asked me to put the gold bars back, and I was happy to oblige them. They laughed with great relief—like men who'd just gotten many thousands of dollars back.

On that same memorable road trip, we hopped to

Zambia aboard Central African Airways, and I was invited up to the cockpit of the airplane to visit with the pilots, as often happened whenever I flew on commercial aircraft (United Airlines, which I once represented, even gave me my very own cockpit "pass"), leaving Mark to sit in white-knuckle terror and Gary to drolly remark that if I didn't find a different hobby he would have to find a different airline.

A few days later, we flew to Zululand, where Gary's brother, Ian, was a top game preserve ranger, actually having to buzz the landing strip in a single-engine plane to chase off a herd of rhinoceroses. What a thrilling sight that was! We toured the preserve by jeep en route to the golf course, where the tees were built on hills built by giant ants once reputed to be maneaters. We saw prides of lions and heard Ian's terrifying tale of nearly dying from the bite of a black mamba snake. I remember his pointing out a deadly gaboon viper in the bush, and all I could think about as we played the course a little while later was that if I hit my usual number of balls into the rough, Africa could simply keep them.

That night in the little town of Edinburgh, in a modern hotel with all of the expected Western-style amenities, yet surrounded by the vast dark African continent, I guess our nerves were still keyed up from our close encounters with lions and snakes. Mark and I were sharing a room and talking, just before turning out the lights, about how strange and truly far away we felt from home. All of a sudden Mark let out a terrified yell. I turned and saw a frightening face pressed against our room's window! Mark wheeled for the door and I hit the floor, fearing I don't know what. An attack by unfriendly natives? One of those sudden violent revolutions that seemed to be always in the evening news?

It turned out to be our little host Gary Player making scary faces at us. He'd climbed out his bedroom window and inched along the hotel ledge just to see how badly he could frighten us. He later told us that he laughed so hard at the way he worked us up he nearly fell backward off the ledge, and at that moment neither of us would have cared if he had.

I'd like to say that the South African trip was beneficial research for my big-screen debut, but that would be less than truthful. As a result of my "work" in *Call Me Bwana*, nobody from Hollywood phoned to suggest I give up my day job. I must confess that Jay Michaels and I once seriously discussed the possibility of producing a feature film in which You Know Who would get to fulfill his childhood ambition to play the good guy in the white hat who rides up to save the day and vanquish the bad guys with his six-guns blazing.

I don't recall how Mark felt about that possibility, whether he was fer it or agin it, but Jay and I at least were pretty serious at one point about exploring the project's possibility. Unfortunately, it always seemed to get shoved aside for something else, and then, in the early 1980s, Jay Michaels unexpectedly passed away, a real jolt to us all. Jay was a fine man and an exceptionally gifted producer who left us all far too soon.

If I did entertain movie hopes, that's perhaps because making my little part of *Call Me Bwana* was so easy and such fun. We shot my segment over a couple of hours in a studio west of London, a scene in which I suddenly walk through a tent flap looking for my stray ball, which Bob Hope's character, having breakfast, mistakes for an egg. Bob offers his usual droll banter, and I mostly had to be myself.

Much harder, in some ways, given my wariness of prepared scripts, were my appearances on Bob's television shows over the years. Bob knew I was a far better ad-libber than reader, but the timing of our comedy routines was such that I had to memorize my lines and hope like the dickens I saw the proper cue cards when the moment arrived. The gag was almost always the same: Bob would fish for compliments about his game and I would put him down with crisp one-liners.

> BOB: How come you never invited me to
> appear on *Challenge Golf*?
> ME: We don't do comedy, Bob.
> BOB: I mean to play golf, Arnie.
> ME: We don't do comedy, Bob.

Or this tidbit:

> BOB: Arnie, they tell me I have a picture
> swing.
> ME: True. I saw your last picture. Fun-nee.
> BOB: My short game is good.

ME: That's right. Unfortunately, your short game is off the tee, Bob.

Making several appearances over the years on Perry Como's show was a little more serious in nature but also great fun. Maybe the major highlight of my dubious television career was being asked to serve as guest host on *The Tonight Show with Johnny Carson.* We had Vic Damone and Buddy Hackett on as guests for that particular show, and even today, more than thirty years later, I get a bit nervous remembering how anxious I was on that hot seat. As a result, most of the show remains a mental blur to me and I'm hesitant to even go back and view the old tapes of the show. Let's face it, when it came to acting or being a stand-up comedian, I was really the one who was a bit short off the tee.

Nevertheless, it was thanks to those shows—all arranged by Mark and his people—that a boy from a small western Pennsylvania steel town got to rub elbows with some of the biggest stars in the entertainment field. Only in America could such a thing happen. Through these encounters, Winnie and I made some deep and lasting friendships with people like Bob and Dolores Hope, Bing Crosby, Jack Lemmon, James Garner, and dear sweet Dinah Shore.

Gary Player would agree with me, I think, that the most fun we had filming golf shows was when Jack joined us for *Big Three Golf,* another production I had a large financial stake in thanks to Mark. It ran on NBC for eight episodes in 1964. The format brought the three of us together in a series of golf matches staged at spectacular locales ranging from Los Angeles Country Club to Firestone Country Club to Carnoustie and the Old Course at St. Andrews. At stake was $50,000 for the winner. A problem arose when it became obvious that by the sixth match, Jack had the series clinched. We decided to extend the series two more matches, hoping the drama of Gary and me competing for second place would sustain the earlier ratings—which reportedly rivaled the average daily viewing audience of *Captain Kangaroo*—but it didn't quite work out that way.

The playing highlight for me, I suppose, came when I had an opportunity late in the series to beat Gary and Jack at St. Andrews but missed a short putt, leaving the match in a tie that would be settled when we moved on to Dorado Beach in Puerto Rico, where I finally beat Jack in a playoff.

The competition was fierce, I must say, but so was the horsing around after the cameras finished shooting. I forget who started the friendly fracas the night after we finished shooting in Montreal, but you have it on good authority from me that Gary and Jack were always ganging up to try to beat me— even in a food fight! Someone spilled a little ginger ale or champagne on somebody else, and soon corks were popping and bottles were fizzing and food of one kind or another was flying through the air. Poor Mark McCormack, who tried to hold the leash on all three of us, was none too pleased to receive the substantial cleaning bill from the hotel's management.

Filming *Big Three Golf* was really when I got to know Jack Nicklaus on a more personal basis, and I liked him even more than before. Given his relentless German stare and his seemingly unshakable emotional composure, it might have surprised golf fans at the time to learn that off the course Jack was just one big fun-loving kid who not only had an instinct for keeping his fame in proper perspective but was even known to let his hair down (what little he had in those days, thanks to his famous buzz-cut hairstyle) when the cameras were off.

My relationship with Jack has been the source of endless speculation and reporting, scholarly analysis, and even the stuff of mythmaking for almost forty years. Some of what you've read is true; some of it is pure bunk.

Let's start with a tale that is true—though a bit foggy for me—from the early moments of Jack's stardom. The scene was Oakmont Country Club, the event the U.S. Open of 1962. Prior to our Sunday playoff Jack and I were talking in the locker room, and according to him and others who overheard the conversation, I casually offered to split the purse with him and he politely declined, apparently noting that he didn't think that would be fair to either of us.

Unfortunately, I don't remember having made this suggestion, though I certainly may well have done so. In any event, neither of us would have considered anything particularly wrong with such a suggestion. Purse splitting—wherein two players make an agreement before the tournament to combine their winnings and equally divide the pot afterward—was a common practice on the PGA Tour in those days. Though I hadn't done it much it was a staple of life for some marginal players, desperate to make ends meet to keep their income levels up.

If I made such an offer to Jack—and I have no reason to think I didn't—I honestly believe I made it out of simple consideration for him, a Tour rookie who had yet to win on the circuit. The fact that he remembers it so clearly and I don't means that the offer simply didn't matter that much to me. It has bothered me, however, that over the years some accounts of the event have given the incident a shadowy overlay, as if some major code of conduct or sportsmanship were being breached. Jack, I feel safe in saying, didn't regard it as such, and neither did I. Later that year, in fact, we did split a purse at a tournament, and for the record we agreed to split the gate proceeds of the playoff with the USGA of that same Open at Oakmont. That practice was common, too.

At any rate, the ethics of purse splitting got a thorough public airing when *Sports Illustrated* stated in a special report on the issue that purse splitting went on in 50 percent of all playoffs and a vast majority of Tour players saw nothing improper with the practice. That same week, I think, a rumor circulated around the World Series of Golf in Akron that that season's major champions (whose names happened to be Palmer, Nicklaus, and Player—all clients of the same business manager, Mark McCormack) agreed beforehand to pool their winnings and divide them equally. There is no truth to that whatsoever.

The *Sports Illustrated* piece quoted prominent Tour players as saying that a tournament's title was far more important than the money, but the public's reaction was swift and unambiguous on the subject: They felt cheated. After a bit of soul-searching, since the annual money title was decided by a player's winnings, the PGA decided to place a ban on the practice. In retrospect, I'm glad they did—it kept everything out in the open where it belongs.

Much has been made of The Rivalry. Arnie versus Jack. Volumes have been written, verdicts given. My own personal take on the subject is a fairly simple and I think true reading. Jack Nicklaus was and is my greatest competition in golf, both on the course during my peak years and off it years later as our separate interests evolved in the business world.

Honest competition is a wonderful thing, as central to the American way of thinking as anything. The Arnie-Jack connection may have started at Oakmont in '62, but I believe it reached fever pitch in November of 1964 when we both flew to Lafayette, Louisiana, to compete in the season-ending Cajun Classic. It was an event so low on the scale of importance to either of us, I must say, with all due respect to the fans and sponsors there, that neither of us would have been in the tournament's field unless something big was at stake. In this instance, it was the Tour's yearly money title hanging in the balance.

Entering this last tournament of the year, I was

leading Jack in the money race by a mere $318.87. I was also still mentally kicking myself because I'd had a chance just a few weeks before to sew up the title at the Sahara Invitational at Las Vegas, leading by two going into the final round, before my game fell apart and I wound up nineteenth to Jack's third place—throwing the money title into a real horse race. To compound matters, Mark had scheduled ambitious separate exhibition tours for both of us to Australia and New Zealand, which meant we had to make up our minds to play in Lafayette weeks in advance. I told Jack that I doubted I would be able to fit the Cajun event into my crazy schedule, and he nodded and pretty much agreed he probably couldn't either. I planned to go on to Japan, and it was almost hunting season back home in Pennsylvania. As I said to Jack, I needed and wanted the time off to be with the girls and to look after a few business matters. He told me he had plenty of things he needed to do and wanted to get home to Barbara and the kids.

As someone later said, it was pretty much an Academy Award–winning performance on both parts.

"I knew if I entered," Jack slyly admitted to a reporter later, "Arnie would, too. We were just trying to outpsych each other."

Thus our rather unenthusiastic trips to Louisiana. Suffice it to say, neither of us wanted to be there, but neither could abide the possibility of skipping the tournament and effectively presenting the money title to the other on a silver platter. I had been the Tour's leading money winner in 1958, 1960, 1962, and 1963, and I really wanted that fifth title very badly to salvage an otherwise disappointing year. Despite my runaway Masters victory in April, I'd managed to win only one other tournament, the Oklahoma City Open, and I was beginning to feel great frustration with my game, particularly my putting.

To make matters worse, I caught a nasty cold en route to Louisiana and opened the first round with a dreary two-over 74. Jack was four under after eight holes. Fortunately for me, that's when the Gulf squalls came up and washed the round off the boards. The next two days were dry but the temperature plunged steadily, forcing players into knitted ski caps and padded rain jackets to try to keep warm. I posted a 68 in the new first round and had to rally on Saturday from five straight bogeys to finish with 74. Jack's rounds of 68-71 left me three strokes behind him as we faced what promised to be a painful final thirty-six-hole finish on Sunday.

We were forced to start at dawn's early light, and the weather, as someone remarked, would have been great for an Army–Navy football game but was hardly the setting for great golf. With temperatures just at or slightly above freezing, Jack looked more like a polar bear than the Golden Bear, dressed as he was in a couple sweaters, a knitted dickey, and a rain suit. I wore my own layers and managed to complete the third round of the Frostbite Open with a 71, leaving me tied for fourth, two behind Jack. He stretched that lead to four in the final round before I mounted a respectable little charge only to fall short with a poor effort on a short par putt that stopped inches shy at 15, pretty much sinking my hopes.

By that point, Miller Barber had effectively won the tournament by five strokes over the field, but the drama wasn't quite over for me. Gay Brewer had a lengthy putt on 18 that could give him second place—and me the money title. If he made it, Jack would finish third and I would be the season's leading money winner. If he missed, Jack would tie for second and take the money title. It came down to that.

I watched intently but Jack didn't, later telling someone that it was the first putt he'd turned away from since the Oakmont Open in '62, when I missed a six-footer that would have beaten him.

Brewer missed the putt and Jack got the money title. Even as we shook hands and I congratulated him, the disappointment I felt was immense. "This is the eighth time I have finished second this year," Jack told reporters, "but the first time in my life I have felt happy about it."

I'm glad *he* was happy.

That pretty well summarizes the intensely competitive relationship that has always existed between Jack and me. On the course, there was—and still is—nobody I ever wanted to beat more, and as I've said, if I was at the top or anywhere near the leader board on Sunday, his was the name I watched for and feared most, especially if he had the lead. This was just as true at Oakmont in '62 as it was at our first Skins Game in 1983. And I'm certain Jack feels exactly the same way.

On a more philosophical note, I must say I think Jack and I were very good for each other and very good for the game of golf in general. Our rivalry—especially when you add Gary Player to the mix—happened at a time when golf was just beginning to take deep root in the broader American sports psyche, and the intensity of our competition, as well as the distinct differences in our personalities, created tremendous natural drama and a fan interest in the professional game that had never been seen before. I needed Jack to remind me what my Pap had warned me from the beginning—there was always going to be some talented young guy out there who could beat you ten ways to Sunday, so you'd better never let your guard down. I think Jack needed me to serve as the high standard he was aiming for. If he could beat me, which he ultimately did, he could beat anybody and become the greatest player in the game.

The fans and sponsors, I'm happy to say, were the beneficiaries of our fierce but gentlemanly thirty-five-year competition on the links. Tournament gates doubled, even tripled, I'm told, when it was announced that Jack and I would be playing in the same field. Both of us were keenly aware of our unique positions and responsibilities in this respect. We knew we were good theater—and we enjoyed it at least as much as the fans and reporters did. Believe me when I say, despite the pain of losing major tournaments to each other and the wild swings in fortune that defined our relationship, we had a lot of fun being the center of all that attention. But most of all, we wanted to beat each other to a pulp. That's the nature of healthy sportsmanship and the spirit of tournament golf. That's just the way it should be, too.

Behind the scenes of those celebrated Arnie-versus-Jack years we traveled together quite a lot, dined together, privately discussed at great depth issues of the Tour and family life, agreed philosophically on far more things than we disagreed on, and ruthlessly pounced on any opportunity to needle each other in private about beating the other at his own game. Our wives became good friends early on and remain even closer today. It reveals something nice about the nature of our complex friendship, I think, that, given the right project, Jack and I could still work together, as our four Canada/World Cups and three national team championships demonstrate. We were natural adversaries, to be sure, but also clearly a good fit.

Unlike our wives, though, Jack and I never became what you might call pals off the golf course. Perhaps our rivalry was indeed too intense and too deep to permit that. Perhaps our personalities just didn't mesh that way. Whatever it was, he followed his destiny and I faithfully followed mine. But we never failed to enjoy each other's company in a social setting, like the time I plopped a lady's wig on his head (or maybe it's the other way around; the story has been repeated so many times and so many ways, I'm beginning to forget which way it really happened) and we briefly danced together like a couple of drunken teddy bears at a tournament function, delighting everyone except the poor lady who lost her hairpiece.

The simple truth is, I like Jack and I admire him in more ways than I can probably express. But that doesn't stop me from feeling a surge of the old competitiveness—or even a stab of jealousy—when one of his companies or course design crew wins a job contract I thought we deserved or whenever our mutual business interests collide and the Umbrella and the Golden Bear find themselves in direct competition for a project, as we occasionally do. That's just simple human nature, and I know he feels the same kind of competitive fire about me and my organization.

We're different men with different views, and our differing view of Mark McCormack explains a lot about us.

In July 1970, not long after his father's death, Jack assembled his own business team and decided it was time to go his own way, amicably terminating his business relationship with Mark and International Management Group. He wanted to determine his own destiny, and in retrospect I think he really needed the new mental stimulation of making his own way in the business world. Jack is, at heart, analytical, a detail man, always taking things apart to see how they run. He's also a bit of a lone wolf who prefers to do everything himself. You can see it in the way he focuses in on a golf shot, the way he appears to be scrutinizing every blade of grass for a clue when he putts. You can see it in the way he builds a golf course or runs a golf tournament, where

he is master of the smallest detail. From what I've
heard and even from what Jack has admitted to me,
that's exactly how he runs his businesses. I, on the
other hand, have always enjoyed having a number of
trusted people around me and rely on them to do
their jobs without too much interference from the
boss. I suppose that, too, is the Pap in me. Once I
trust somebody socially or in business, they have my
respect and support until they prove otherwise. Jack
navigates more by brain. I go more by heart. Intellect versus instinct. Jack versus Arnie.

I must confess, though, at the time it happened I
was pretty ambivalent about Jack's decision to leave
Mark, and I told him so. Part of me thought it was a
foolish mistake on his part, proof of his hardheaded
German determination to always do things his own
way. But as I like to say, "Jack is Jack," and part of
me was also glad to see him go, because I hated not
having Mark's full and complete attention.

In retrospect, I see that it was clearly the right
decision for him to make, and I think we've finally
come full circle on that issue and others. We're
closer now, in some respects, than we have ever
been. We share a golden history and a thousand
memories of laughter and tears. I'd feel remiss if I
didn't say that. On the larger issues facing the game,
for example, questions like the dominant role the
equipment revolution is playing in altering the face
of the game or the development of new competing
tours and the formation of players' unions, it should
surprise nobody that we come down in complete
agreement on the side of protecting the integrity

of the game, preserving the traditional values and qualities that have always made golf the most splendid and democratic pastime on earth.

Competitive golf has been the center of both our lives, and yet the differences between us—the factors that made us such intense and faithful competitors, I believe—are still as apparent as ever to anyone who wishes to take the time to look. Jack likes golf, but I don't think he actually loves and needs the game the way I still do. I try to play every day, and when I don't play—if you'll pardon the expression—I feel like a bear with a sore tail because of it.

Jack plays because he must play, and, not surprising to me, he is still capable of summoning that legendary ability to concentrate and perform that will have historians talking about his game two hundred years from now. His family and his business command more of Jack's attention than anything—and that's just the way he wants it.

My family and my business mean everything to me, too, but the third component of the mix is my need to still be out there chasing after Old Man Par, trying to make cuts and please the galleries.

Bottom line: Jack is still Jack.

And Arnie is still Arnie.

In the mid 1970s, my own relationship with McCormack and International Management Group underwent what I think of as a major shift, if not a sea change, with the arrival of Alastair Johnston on the scene at IMG. A tall, angular son of Glasgow with a dry wit and reserved manner befitting his training as an Arthur Anderson accountant, Alastair was handpicked by Mark to do a special job—namely, look after me on virtually an exclusive basis and become, if you will, my "new" Clifford Roberts while Mark continued building IMG into the giant of entertainment representation it has become.

Once again, I had great ambivalence about the change. I was frustrated that Mark seemed to have less and less time to personally handle the affairs of his number-one client. The last thing I wanted was to have to get used to a new man. However, I did want someone who really was solely focused on my concerns and needs—as Mark had long ago promised he would be but never quite accomplished, in my book.

A personal trait of mine is that I take my time sizing up people whom circumstance has placed close to me. I think I'm a pretty good judge of character, and I always notice small things about how someone handles himself—the way he dresses, treats people, pays attention to small details, and so forth. It goes back to that need I described earlier to be able to trust those closest to me—so I can give them the freedom to do what they do best and not have to peer over their shoulders, wasting their time and mine in the process. From the beginning, Alastair Johnston earned high marks in these respects, but I was naturally resistant to having the head man of an organization I essentially helped found hand me off to a protégé, even one as debonairly polished as Alastair Johnston.

The turning point for us both, I think, came at a business meeting at Los Angeles Country Club in 1978 when Alastair helped engineer and essentially designed, in concert with my longtime friend Ed Douglas, my commercial affiliation with Pennzoil, an enduring business relationship that has brought me untold pleasures over the past two decades and, as I write this—amid a twentieth-anniversary celebration—has just been extended to the year 2005.

That was the beginning of a fruitful and fun period of my business life, new commercial representations for me that included my longtime affiliations with Cadillac and Rolex Watches and slightly shorter but no less fulfilling relationships with GTE, Lanier Business Machines, Rayovac Batteries, PaineWebber, and Hertz Car Rentals. In the past few years, Alastair has been the point man and main driving force behind the scenes of my proud associations with Lexington Furniture (a Palmer Home Collection array of furnishings that Winnie has enjoyed having a strong hand in designing), Cooper Tires, and Office Depot.

To say I've come to trust and rely on Alastair's judgment and instinct for arranging and monitoring my business affairs would be a tremendous understatement. I'm sure I've also driven him crazy on more occasions than he'd prefer to think about. Especially since I still pick up the phone from time to time and shout at him that he's running me ragged and probably ruining my golf game with all the deals and commitments he makes for us.

In other words, the more things change, the more things stay the same. That's just the way I like it.

Alastair listens with his irritatingly calm, calculating Scottish patience and then reminds me, as his predecessor used to do, that we never do anything I don't really want to do, which at the end of the day is really true. The difference between Mark and Alastair is that Mark usually states his opinion and leaves it at that. Alastair can seemingly talk nonstop for hours on the subject at hand, sketching out pros and cons, weighing this or that—a tactic, I sometimes think, he uses simply to wear down my resistance. When I hang up the phone, I usually feel better for having gotten something off my chest, but little else has usually changed.

Though he drives me crazy at times, I'm extremely fond of Alastair and trust his judgment in most matters. Several times over the past twenty-odd years I've suggested to Alastair that he leave IMG and come work for me exclusively, but every time I make the proposition he logically counters that he can be far more effective serving the interests of Arnold Palmer Enterprises and its affiliated companies by remaining on the inside of the largest sports marketing firm in the world. That's a tough argument to top.

If that implies that Mark McCormack and I have grown somewhat apart over those same twenty years, I suppose that's accurate. Mark would tell you exactly the same thing. He has his busy life and I have mine, and it's probably fortunate that Alastair is there to serve as the link between us.

I could show you something I call the "X file," a file folder full of angry letters I wrote Mark over the years but for one reason or another never mailed to him. There is no sugarcoating what those letters really are: they're resignation letters, terminating my relationship with IMG. A few I might have even actually sent, fired off at a moment when I felt he was failing to live up to his end of the bargain sealed by that long-ago handshake.

In truth, I've never left IMG and I've never left Mark. There are a number of powerful reasons for that, my abiding sense of personal loyalty and trust being chief among them. For his part, for all our differences of opinion on a range of subjects and the increasing physical distance that separates us, Mark's business savvy has made us both materially successful beyond our wildest dreams.

At least as important to me, he has never failed to be there in the good times nor flinched from his duty in standing shoulder to shoulder with me through the hard times. Like a marriage that endures the challenge of decades, takes the good with the bad, survives the gravest threats and somehow grows stronger because of them, our union may seem a bit perplexing to some on the outside looking in.

But to us, it's as real and lasting and simple as the famous handshake that created it.

I cite, for example, the extremely trying times that befell my businesses, and therefore me, beginning in 1987 and lasting into the early nineties. Two protracted and expensive controversies—actually three if you care to count an aborted sale of Bay Hill to a Japanese holding group and the public relations disaster that grew out of that affair, which I'll discuss in another chapter—happening almost simultaneously, threatened to destroy a lot of what Mark and Alastair and I had spent many years creating. That's not even taking into consideration the number it did on my psyche owing to the hits my personal reputation took in the press. Some of the criticism was warranted—we made honest mistakes in judgment, and we paid dearly for those errors in terms of lawsuit settlements and the collapse of a personal dream of mine called Isleworth. But some of it was also mean-spirited and just plain inaccurate reporting, intensely personal attacks on Mark and IMG and ultimately me that reflect, I fear, the nature of the times we live in.

In 1987, a group of residents living adjacent to a pristine lake bordering a new upscale Orlando golf community called Isleworth filed suit over environmental concerns stemming from runoff water from the golf course I built there. Our engineering people on the project repeatedly assured us there was no basis for concern about contamination of the lake as described by the lawsuit. A mountain of legal, engineering, and environmental studies grew over the next three years, until an Orlando court awarded the residents a $6.6 million judgment against the development. Thanks to Mark and Alastair, my own financial exposure was fairly limited. I designed the golf course and the clubhouse, and Winnie and I owned a couple of lots in the development and were planning to build a home there.

Isleworth was a dream of mine, a golf club and residential community I hoped would be the crowning touch of my career as a course designer. It was a dream that quickly turned into a nightmare.

The upshot is that when the unexpected judgment came down hard against the development's major partners, the banks withdrew their support and the project slipped into receivership, prompting a flurry of additional lawsuits and a bunch of headlines that made IMG and me appear to be dangerously uninformed, if not outright heavies. There's a grain of truth in the accusation that we didn't pay close enough attention to the details. Owing to a complex financial arrangement involving foreign capital and separate partners developing the real-estate end of the project, our fate wasn't entirely in our own hands. In retrospect, our mistake—and it was a doozie—was failing to gain proper control of the project from the beginning, thus being able to monitor what was really happening on several different fronts and perhaps sparing ourselves a lot of anguish and no small expense in legal fees and fines. The settlement was ultimately reduced and all parties came to an agreement to end the dispute. I'm happy to say that the project eventually got back on track. A new owner was found and today Tiger Woods, Mark O'Meara, Mark McCormack, and quite a few other prominent people own homes at Isleworth. The development has become all of what some, including I, originally envisioned. Yet the memory of that failure still bothers me.

Frankly, the episode that hurt much more, financially and otherwise, came out of a troubled episode involving my automotive dealerships and the demise of a trusted friendship with a man named Jim O'Neal. Over a four- or five-year period of time during the late '80s and early '90s, as widely reported in the *Wall Street Journal* and other places, O'Neal, whom I met at Bay Hill in about 1976, directed the creation of my chain of six automobile dealerships that ultimately got into trouble and cost McCormack and me $14 million apiece to get squared away.

In some ways, it was simply another of those unfortunate business tales that came out of the late '80s—one man's over-reaching ambition with not enough monitoring and skepticism on our parts. Suffice it to say, we took control of things ourselves and saved the dealerships. They are once again thriving, but I learned the hard way that there are times when you really shouldn't mix business and friendships, although, in most other similar instances, I think I've fared pretty well. In spite of the problems with Isleworth, O'Neal, and my own health, I've come out of it all in pretty good shape, and I continue to believe that friendship is still far more valuable in life than money.

As for Mark, say what you will about the man, but the plain fact is that working together we both found success beyond our wildest dreams. Through good times and bad, he's never broken the faith of that long-ago handshake. At the end of the day, if you really know me, that's what has meant so much to me.

CHAPTER THIRTEEN

The Left Seat

There's no doubt in my mind that if professional golf hadn't become my way of life, something to do with aviation would have.

I suppose I've had this thought a thousand times while standing on a golf course somewhere awaiting my turn to hit, watching as a private jet or commercial airliner passed overhead, landing or taking off.

Fact is, since I was a boy making elaborate balsawood airplanes and flying them on my father's course at Latrobe, and especially after Tony Arch took me on that harrowing joyride at age twelve when the plane's tail bumped the golf course, I dreamed of what it would be like to fly my own plane. I could not have even remotely imagined how vital aviation would eventually become to my golf and business careers.

In this respect, the fates have been extremely generous. I've been fortunate enough to have owned eight airplanes, beginning with my twin-prop Aero Commander, bought secondhand for $27,000 in 1962, and ending with my latest joy, the Citation X, a $15 million wonder ship that is the fastest private jet of its class in the world.

In between those compass points of my life there have been a lot of grand adventures in the air, usually with me in the left seat (command position) beside a group of the finest men in private aviation—the chief pilots I've employed over the years. Business deals have been made that wouldn't have happened, I've fulfilled playing and charity commitments that I simply couldn't have otherwise met, and I've even experienced a few close calls that probably shouldn't have happened—but invariably do to any pilot who's been in the air as long as I have, nearly 20,000 hours of cumulative flying experience, according to my flying logs. All because I love to fly.

The story of how flying and golf became so interwoven in my life really dates from the first golf tournament I flew to as an amateur in 1949 at age twenty. It was a trip to Chattanooga, Tennessee, in a commercial DC-3 that encountered a tenacious thunderstorm that sent a ball of static electricity (known as St. Elmo's fire) hurtling down the aisle among the terrified passengers, one Arnold Daniel Palmer among them.

Back safely on the ground, I got to thinking about what had happened and realized that flying, like golf in some ways, was a mystery that I simply had to know more about, a technical puzzle to be solved, a science to be mastered, with a history and even an aura of mythology attached to it, as thrilling as it was challenging. Even then it came to me that flying from one tournament site to another might be a great way to play even more golf, but I did not have a clue how many other benefits would eventually come my way as a result of such woolgathering.

My first flying lesson was under the unflustered

gaze of Babe Krinock at tiny Latrobe Airport. I went out to the field one day when I was in my late twenties, just after I had begun playing professional golf and could afford Babe's fee, and asked him to give me flying lessons. We went out and climbed into a single-engine Cessna 172. He took us up and started explaining the proper procedures of flight.

It was almost that simple. But in other ways it was anything but simple for me to finally master the principles of flight. I'm sure I scared the hell out of a number of people at the airport, and probably Winnie as well, as I struggled to learn to fly. Fortunately, I had a gifted instructor at my elbow who not only saw the wisdom in allowing me to make mistakes he knew were survivable, but also had a lot of confidence in my soon-to-be-discovered ability to fly an airplane. That made all the difference, I can tell you.

For example, early on in the training process, we were flying in a Cessna 182, a larger and more powerful plane than the 172, and Babe was in the copilot seat allowing me to land the plane at Latrobe. My approach suddenly got out of hand, and I actually straddled a large hole workmen were digging at the end of the runway. Most instructors would have gone crazy and issued the student a stern lecture for being so reckless. But Babe looked at me calmly and didn't say a word. He knew I knew I'd made a miscalculation—a potentially deadly one—and he also knew I wouldn't ever make that mistake again. "That's all right, Arnie," he'd say calmly but firmly whenever I screwed up. "Stick with it. You'll get it."

He made me learn to relax and feel comfortable in the air, but also never to take a single thing for granted. He was a stickler for proper procedures, the most thorough teacher I've ever had, but also patient beyond belief at times. I owe him a big debt of gratitude for that.

After I got down the basics, I had the thrill of my first solo flight—a spin over the Allegheny Mountains during which I felt the power of having the controls of the airplane entirely to myself. That solo flight earned me my single-engine pilot's license, permitting me to fly under what the Federal Aviation Administration calls "Visual Flight Regulations." I could fly only with clear visibility, circumnavigating "weather" by either flying below the clouds or in some cases above them. In those early days of my flying career, Babe accompanied me to several tournaments, but it quickly became clear to us both that he had other students to teach.

In late 1958, the year I won my first Masters, I leased a Cessna 175, hired my first copilot, and began flying to tournaments and exhibitions. Occasionally, if the trip could be accomplished in daylight hours, I even flew myself there alone and back, without the benefit of the serious navigational cockpit tools we have today. It was really hands-on flying—and I loved it. I remember once, early on, flying over to Indiana for a scheduled exhibition match, missing the designated airfield (which was little more than a mowed-down cow pasture), nearly flying to Indianapolis before I realized my mistake. Doubling back, I finally found the right airstrip and did the exhibition, but then had trouble finding Latrobe again on the return leg. It made for a long but oddly enjoyable day in the air.

For the most part, though, a couple of able local pilots, Harold Overly and Frank Shepherd, accompanied me to tournament sites and on longer business trips. It wasn't until after my 1960 U.S. Open win at Cherry Hills, though, that Mark McCormack and I both began to seriously discuss the potentially huge impact owning my own airplane could have on our blossoming business opportunities. Corporate executives owned airplanes in those days, but an athlete owning and operating his own aircraft was virtually unheard of.

Shortly after I took possession of my first airplane in early 1961, a twin-engine Aero Commander 500 that had been owned by Commercial Credit Corporation out of Baltimore, I showed up at the FAA inspector's station at Allegheny County Airport in Pittsburgh, ready to take what's called a "check ride" and shoot for my multi-engine private pilot's license.

It's an engaging memory.

The inspector was a dour-faced sort who clearly didn't suffer any fools in the air, and after I completed the oral part of the examination without any hitches, he looked at me and suggested that we go for a ride in my new plane. The actual flying was the really critical part of the test, of course, but unknown to him I was anxious as hell about just getting the engines properly started. We walked out to the plane with me saying a silent prayer that the fickle left engine would start. The problem was a fuel valve that stuck when the engine was cooling off, and— sure enough—I'd no sooner switched on the right engine and gotten it running than the left refused to crank. I was suddenly sweating golf balls.

"I can get this going," I promised the stone-faced instructor. "Let me do something and I'll be right back."

He watched me climb out of the plane and re- move the engine cowling on the left wing, where- upon I took a hammer and gave the fuel pump a good sharp whack. I replaced the cowling, hopped back in, and cranked up the engine, revving it good.

"Well, Arnie," he said with perfect deadpan timing, then smiled at me. "You've passed your mechanics exam. Let's see if you can actually fly this thing."

Beginning in 1961, I was in the air a lot. The man who played the critical role in helping me be there was Russ Meyer. A Harvard-educated attorney and former U.S. Air Force and Marine reserve pilot who initially worked with Mark McCormack's Cleveland law firm, Arter, Hadden, Wycoff, and Van Dusen, booking my various exhibitions beginning in late 1960 and early '61, Russ was the man who engi- neered that purchase of the Aero Commander from Commercial Credit. Over the years, through a thou- sand deals and business transactions, he also became a cherished friend and the man I have turned to for anything having to do with aviation.

Russ was an early partner in the formation of IMG, and I fondly recall that one of his first jobs on my behalf was the ghostwriting he did, first penning a brochure of golf tips for *Newsweek* and then, more ambitiously, producing 260 fifty-second "Arnold Palmer Golf Tips" for radio syndication. My memory of trying to read Russ's beautifully written scripts and screwing them up is probably at least as amusing as it is painful, a prelude to the screwups Gary Player and I committed in the studio booth while doing voice-overs for the *Challenge Golf* series a few years later. The good news from Russ's standpoint, I guess, was that he used his part of the $10,000 fee to pay off his Harvard Law School loans.

A few years after Russ negotiated the purchase of my first plane, with an ever-growing interest in private aviation, he took a leave of absence from the Cleveland law firm to run a small aviation company called American Aviation Corp. I was flattered when he asked me to come on board as vice president of public affairs—though my role really didn't involve a lot more than consulting on a new single-engine airplane the company planned to produce called the American Yankee, and meeting with salespeople and members of the company's board of directors. I loved talking airplanes, and these were my kind of fellows.

American thrived under Russ's leadership, developing a second popular four-seater plane called the Traveler. Eventually American acquired the assets of Gulfstream Aviation, in a reverse merger deal, becoming Grumman-American Aviation in 1972. It was a good move and paid off for all parties concerned.

The jet age was dawning fast for private and corporate aviation, and Russ's talents didn't go unnoticed by industry leader Cessna Aviation, in Wichita, Kansas. Cessna convinced Russ to become executive vice president of operations in 1974 at a critical moment in the growth of the private-jet industry. Cessna was a fifty-year-old company that had had only two chairmen in its illustrious history and was the world leader in the manufacture of single-engine airplanes, producing more small aircraft than every other company combined, more than six thousand planes a year.

The problem was, lawyers and insurance companies had driven the product-liability costs of producing and selling single-engine airplanes so high that the market was rapidly dwindling—just as the jet age was coming on. Part of Russ's mandate was to take Cessna into the next phase of its business life, which he did in spectacular fashion after being named the company's third chairman and CEO in 1975.

That same year, he made available the company's first private jet, the Citation I. I'm proud to say I was one of the new craft's first owners. At that time, his planes were the new kid on the block, but within five years the company had abandoned single-engine airplanes entirely and was rapidly becoming the major design and engineering force in private jet aviation. Today, almost twenty-five years later, Cessna is the dominant player in the thriving private-jet industry, with something like 60 percent of the market share. Better yet, Russ and I are closer friends than ever. He's still my number-one man in aviation, the guy I consult about anything that has to do with flying, and I guess I must be considered one of his best-paying customers, since I've owned six different Cessna Citation jets.

More on them in a bit, though.

In 1963, I purchased my second airplane, a Rockwell Aero Commander 560F. It was brand new, more powerful, and roomier, than the 500. It had a cruising range that would enable us to make it to Palm Springs from Latrobe with just one stop, cruising at 240 nautical miles per hour. One of the simple joys of owning that plane, I realize when I think back, was taking Winnie and the girls up in it for Sunday-afternoon spins, or "training" flights, as we called them. Winnie loved flying, but the girls, I'm afraid, weren't terribly impressed. They were far more interested in the dolls they were playing with in the rear seats.

I, on the other hand, found that piloting an airplane did something very special for me, especially after I acquired my instrument and multi-engine ratings, which enabled me to fly through all kinds of weather, in and out of small airports—really anywhere I wanted. Above all, the speed and convenience of air travel was infinitely preferable to the old way touring pros got around the circuit; as I said to a reporter about that time, "I loathe driving a couple hundred miles every Monday." I literally and figuratively had put that old trailer home as far behind me as possible, and I liked it that way.

Moreover, though, after climbing into the left seat of my plane following a tournament, whether I had won or not, I found it impossible to dwell too long on what had happened, good or bad, on the golf course. Flying the plane demanded my full attention, clear thinking, and an unerring performance under pressure I found almost soothing. Flying a plane was good therapy, perhaps even like a form of meditation for me—I could disappear into the clouds and not have to worry about what I had or hadn't done on the golf course, what opportunities I had grabbed or chances I'd blown, whom I'd pleased or let down. The phone couldn't ring. I didn't have to try to answer impossible questions about whether my putting would ever regain its brilliance or how it felt to be considered the hottest commercial pitchman in the world.

I was just another pilot in the air, heading home somewhere over America. I found the experience both stimulating and comforting. Ironically, nothing I've found except perhaps hitting a golf shot provides me with such instantaneous feedback on the decisions and the moves I execute.

Over the next two years, I put over a thousand hours on that plane, which was the first to wear the special registration number granted to me by the Federal Aviation Administration: 701AP. Just over a year later, in February 1966, I upgraded to my latest capitalist tool—a new Rockwell Jet Commander, which we leased for two years with an option to buy.

There's no question that private jet travel significantly enhanced my earning potential, though in retrospect I'm sure it also cost me a few tournaments I might otherwise have won, including a couple of majors. Indulging two obsessions sometimes resulted in fatigue, robbed me of needed practice time on the golf course, and generally found me overstretching my physical and mental limits. Relieved of a reliance on commercial air carrier schedules for longer hauls, I literally could be five or six places in a single day. From a business standpoint, this was ideal. By this time, the late sixties, I had Palmer businesses cropping up in at least ten major cities in addition to playing in, on average, about twenty-five tournaments a year and no fewer than twenty exhibition matches. Combined with a growing number of commercial endorsements and the scores of speaking engagements I was asked to do, I probably visited from thirty-five to fifty other cities in a single year.

In my old flying logs I see I was sometimes in the air twenty-six days out of any given month, but the convenience of having a jet also permitted me to sleep in my own bed most of those nights. A typical non-tournament business day from those years might have gone something like this: I would have breakfast at home with Winnie and the girls, fly down to New Orleans or Jacksonville for an afternoon golf exhibition, maybe stop somewhere en route for a business meeting, then fly home to

Latrobe. On lucky days, I actually made it home for dinner with the girls or at least in time to kiss them goodnight before they went to bed.

This leap into the corporate jet age—with an aircraft whose range was two thousand nautical miles and that cruised at speeds of five hundred miles per hour—came with a factory test pilot named Darrell Brown, who taught me the ins and outs of flying a jet and eventually became a trusted friend and valued pilot for many years. When Darrell went briefly back to Rockwell in Oklahoma City, as planned, a new copilot named Dick Turner took his place, but he and I had a few rocky moments adjusting to both the new jet technology and to each other. I learned that good chemistry and communication are as essential between pilots as they are between a golfer and his caddie.

I remember vividly one incident early on in our brief association, when the plane was still new to both of us. Dick and I realized that our fuel supply was seriously out of balance—a real no-no in a jet, a formula for disaster—but neither of us had the technical expertise to correct the problem. Fortunately, we got the plane down and went scurrying for the right information, and the problem never reared its ugly head again. Even so, I felt much more confident when, at the time of the Buick tournament in Flint, Michigan, and shortly before my most celebrated collapse at Olympic Club, I phoned Oklahoma City and convinced Darrell to join me on a full-time basis. Darrell, I was pleased to learn, was as happy as I was about this development. We made a good cockpit team.

I suppose in some ways the confidence I felt on the golf course extended to the way I flew an airplane, with both good and not-so-good consequences. You really can't do anything halfway in the air. In those early years of flying—with memories of Tony Arch's foolish stunts emblazoned in my head—I was for the most part a stickler for following the proper procedures for safety's sake. But I'll also admit to the occasional bit of youthful hotdogging.

The FAA, it must be said, was a bit more lenient in those days, and far fewer private pilots were in the air then. I'm proud of the fact that I have no blemishes on my flying record, and that I always tried to stay within the rules. But early in my flying career, I confess, I did sometimes give in to the temptation to buzz airfields or golf courses where friends were playing, careful to stay above the 800-foot minimum. The most infamous buzzing incident came in September of 1967 when I took several members of the British Ryder Cup contingent up for a pleasure ride in my Jet Commander during the matches at the Champions Golf Club in Houston. Tony Jacklin, Hugh Boyle, Malcolm Gregson, and George Will all wanted to go for a ride. With them aboard, I circled over the golf course and then took them straight up to 8,000 feet before peeling off and rolling the plane.

A couple of them lost their cookies, and I later had to do some serious explaining to the FAA after a local dairy farmer complained that I was flying below the legal minimum elevation, and, worse, was disturbing his livestock. Lucky for me, an FAA inspector happened to be at the Ryder Cup and confirmed, after a brief investigation, that I had done nothing illegal—just pushed the envelope a bit, as they say.

A year or so later, Darrell and I were approaching Latrobe Airport in my newly leased Lear 24, which I got in early 1968, when the tower informed us that the Powder Puff Derby planes had stopped by. The lady pilots had assembled at the airfield and were anxious to watch us land our latest aircraft.

The Lear, with its sleek aerodynamics and so-called fixed wing, was fast, hot, and extremely nimble, and I felt as if I could do almost anything in it, which may be one reason I would fly it quite contentedly for many years. At the time, there was a great deal of concern about the plane's safety record, because of a series of unfortunate crashes. My personal view of the situation was that the technology was too new and the aircraft was simply too fast for most private pilots to handle. Jets of its speed capabilities were not commonplace, so there weren't many experienced pilots available to fly them. A potentially dangerous supply-and-demand problem. Darrell resigned his position as my pilot when I first leased the Lear, citing the plane's spotty safety record. It was only after I convinced him to fly with me and he saw what the plane could do, how easy to fly and safe it really was, that he agreed to stay with me for a while longer.

Anyway, as we approached the 4,000-foot landing strip at Latrobe, I turned to Darrell and suggested we give the famous lady aviators on the ground a little show. He grinned and nodded. We first made a low drag pass with the flaps down, then climbed rapidly and came around again—rolling the plane and flying past the ladies upside down. I'm told the gallery—I mean to say *audience*—went crazy with pleasure.

I could read you a long list of famous folks who've flown with me and signed my plane's guest book—ranging from my old Palm Springs flying pal Dinah Shore to President and Mrs. George Bush—but maybe the most fun I had flying friends around was with the annual trip I took to the Tournament of Champions in Las Vegas with my doctors from Latrobe Hospital as my guests. For them, it was some needed R and R, a mini–golf vacation, while for me it was a bit like having an extended family along. With all my aerial guests, I'm careful to make sure every comfort they might desire is at hand, including snacks and cocktails (though if they feel the urge to smoke, I'm always quick to point out management's official policy, posted on a small sign in the cabin: "If you must smoke, please step outside").

I'll never forget one such trip with my doctor friends. My personal physician, Dr. Bob Mazero, an old friend and classmate from Latrobe High, was standing in the aisle just behind the pilot seats holding a martini as we began making our initial approach to Las Vegas over Hoover Dam. Just for fun, I rolled the plane 360 degrees. I executed the maneuver so quickly, Bob didn't appear to realize what had happened. He blinked with confusion.

"Arnie, what the hell was *that*?" he asked finally, realizing he'd felt something funny. On the other hand, his martini hadn't lost a drop.

"I don't know, Bob. What did it feel like?" Seated at the controls, I was the picture of sweet innocence.

"I'm not sure," he admitted, his brow knitted in puzzlement.

A few seconds later, I rolled the plane the other way and he let out a yelp. "Good heavens. What are you *doing*, Arnie!" He'd figured out that I'd turned him upside down for an instant in the air.

"Nothing, Bob," I remarked calmly. "Don't get so excited. I wound you up one way, so I thought I'd just better unwind you."

The plane erupted with laughter.

Not quite so amusing, but happily far rarer, are those tense little moments when something unexpected happens in the air and you must react with as much coolness and levelheaded thinking as you can muster. Fortunately for me and my passengers, flying has been such a major passion of mine that I regularly go through recurrent intensive training every year at Cessna's Wichita headquarters. It doesn't hurt that I've had a succession of gifted, experienced pilots flying with me over the years who were great in the clutch. They include, in addition to the ones I've mentioned, Lee Lauderback,

Charlie Johnson, Ken Gero, Roy Martin, Don Dungey, Woody Woodard, Dan Keating, Cliff Crews, and my current fellow pilot, Pete Luster.

One of the first tense moments I ever had, besides straddling the runway hole with Babe Krinock sitting impassively at my elbow, came when I was practicing touch-and-go landings (briefly touching down and then taking off again) at the Latrobe Airport in my Aero Commander 560F and brought the plane down a few yards shy of the asphalt, dropping the wheels in the soft ground but luckily bouncing over the lip of the runway. That's the kind of beginner mistake you make only once, one way or another. If you're lucky enough to survive it, you never make it again.

Another time, a few weeks after the end of the regular Tour season, I flew down to Albany, Georgia, in my Aero Commander to do some hunting and to generally unwind and get away from it all. I was met by a friend and his pilot, who flew us in his older Beechcraft to his 650-acre preserve, putting down on a grass airstrip surrounded by pine forests.

After the hunt (during which I never killed anything—for me the real pleasure was just being in the autumn woods) the pilot asked me if I wanted to fly the plane back to Albany, and I didn't wait for him to offer a second time. We loaded up, cranked up, and rumbled down to the end of the field for takeoff. About halfway down the field, I noticed that I didn't feel the plane's rudder functioning.

"I don't feel any rudder," I said loudly to the pilot.

"Aw, it's fine, Arn," he replied nonchalantly. "Just give it some power." And with that, he shoved my hand on the throttle all the way forward. We bounced toward the pine forest and I finally got the plane airborne, either just clipping the tops of the pines or missing them by the hairs on our terrified heads. Once we were in the air I *knew* the plane had no rudder—the cable had snapped, as it turned out—but, despite a shaky ride that probably terrified the other passengers, I was able to get the craft safely down at the airfield at Albany. When I had switched off the engine, I was sorely tempted to flatten that pilot's embarrassed red nose. But before I could say a word to him, he was off behind the hangar throwing up!

A few years later, Winnie and I were returning from out west in the Lear very early on a winter morning. It was just after dawn, too early for the tower at Latrobe to be open, as it turned out, so we made a pass over the airfield to make sure it was clear enough to land. During our absence, there had been a large snowfall, but the runway was neatly plowed and looked fine in the morning sunshine. We went around and came in expecting a normal landing—only to touch down on a solid sheet of ice. I felt the Lear begin to skid wildly beneath us. I used the engine's thrust to regain control of the plane and brought her to a halt in the face of a snowbank at the end of the runway. The plane sustained negligible physical damage. I wish I could say the same thing for the pilot's ego. I got out to inspect the situation, and I nearly cracked my skull when I slipped on the ice.

Now flash ahead twenty years. Lee Lauderback and I are returning to the mainland from Hawaii, where Lee has met Ed Seay and me on the return leg of a trip to the Far East. Our destination is San Francisco, but halfway across the Pacific from Honolulu to the California coast, we suddenly calculate that, because of the unexpectedly severe head winds, we don't have enough fuel to make it to San Francisco—we may be extremely fortunate just to get to the California coast. It's too late to turn back to Hawaii, so we do some swift course alterations and replot for the closest landing site—Monterey, California.

We had six people on board, including two of Ed's employees, and, I must say, they were pretty cool under the circumstances. Up front, meanwhile, I was reviewing emergency ditching techniques in my head and could tell from Lee's tense expression that he was doing the same thing. No one said a word, but there were audible sighs of relief when land came into view and we saw the airstrip at Monterey. The tower suggested that we go around once for our approach, but I told them that wasn't possible—we needed to come straight in immediately. It was a good thing we did, too. The fuel gauge was registering dead empty, so we took her straight in for a landing. After we were on the ground, I asked the maintenance crew to check the actual supply of fuel left in the tank and they reported there wasn't enough fuel to have made a second approach. Talk about a close shave.

Another time, while flying into Los Angeles International Airport in a leased twin-engine plane from Palm Springs, Ed Seay and I nearly got turned topsy-turvy by the jet blast of a commercial airliner landing on an adjacent runway. Luckily, I got the plane level before its wing could touch the runway, and we landed without further incident—just a little paleness around the gills.

I've also had a few harrowing moments in heli-copters, which I am licensed to fly and enjoy doing from time to time. One of the most frightening expe-riences I've ever had in the air occurred in Korea in 1989, when Ed Seay and I took Dave Marr and a film crew making a documentary about our course-design work into the mountains more than a hundred kilometers from Seoul.

As we were preparing to board the client's new twin engine state-of-the-art chopper for the brief flight back to Seoul, I noticed that the weather was closing down fast, which greatly alarmed me. I questioned the pilot, one of Korea's most decorated military fliers, as it turned out, and was assured that he was fully qualified to fly IFR, which means Instrument Flight Rules.

So up we went. We weren't a hundred meters up in the air when we disappeared into fog. I became even more concerned. I was watching the pilot and his instruments like a hawk and realized that either he was becoming disoriented or, far less likely, the craft's instruments had gone haywire. The electronic horizons were all over the place and the helicopter was on the verge of getting into serious trouble.

My worst fears were confirmed seconds later when we broke free of the clouds and there was a huge rock—the side of a mountain, actually—mere yards away! Everyone in the chopper gasped and the pilot immediately responded and pulled away from the mountain. What felt like an eternity later, we got safely below the clouds again, popped out over a highway, and proceeded at low altitude to Seoul. If you ask Ed Seay about the incident, he'll just close his eyes and shake his head, maybe mutter, "Holy cow."

That expresses my sentiments exactly.

Every pilot with any significant time in the air has a tale or two like this to tell—and the fact that he is still around to tell them means he probably knew just what to do when the difficult moment arrived. Maybe the most amusing ticklish moment came early in my flying career, in the old Aero Commander, when Winnie and I were flying down to Birmingham, Alabama, for a tournament. Because I was flying under Visual Flight Rules, I knew I might need her to jot down critical information from the tower if and when the weather changed. Sure enough, visibility got worse as we neared Birmingham, and the controller began to pass along important information. I was working hard in the left seat but happened to look over at Winnie, assuming that she was dutifully writing down all the instructions. Instead, I discovered she was brushing her hair and putting on fresh lipstick!

Thanks in large part to Russ Meyer, I've been fortunate enough to get to know many of the movers and shakers in the American aviation industry, which is really a smaller community than you might imagine. I was once invited by the chairman of Boeing to fly with the test pilots of one of the first 747s to come off the production line in Seattle. Brother, did I jump at that opportunity, and I wasn't in the plane five minutes when the head test pilot said to me, "Arnie, you want to fly her? Go ahead. Get in the left seat."

Man oh man, was I in heaven taking that big baby up. We put her through some impressive maneuvers and brought her back down to earth—but I stayed up in the clouds for days just thinking about the experience.

Lucky for me, somebody at competing aviation giant McDonnell Douglas heard about my Boeing test flight and offered me a chance to fly *their* new production jumbo airliner, the DC-10. I didn't hesitate to accept that invitation either. I took fellow Tour player Ken Still up with me on that test ride. For many years afterward, we would both talk about the day like giddy schoolboys.

I was also privileged to fly not once but on several occasions with the world-famous Blue Angels, the U.S. Navy's high-performance jet squadron whose precision flight maneuvers have thrilled millions worldwide. The first time was when I was invited down to Pensacola, where the Blue Angels are based, by a friend in the insurance business named Jack Colter. Jack insured many U.S. Navy pilots and, since this was at the height of the Vietnam War, it just so happened that the navy was interested in drumming up some publicity for its recruiting efforts. I was more than happy to become their civilian poster boy.

The plan called for me to take up the wives and girlfriends of the Blue Angels in my Aero Commander—a prop plane, mind you—climb to 10,000 feet, then begin a slow descent, at which point the Blue Angels in their much faster F-9 fighter jets would descend upon us and hold their position for a few minutes while a photographer on board captured the moment for posterity, or at least for an interesting training poster. We also had on board Gordon Jones, a former U.S. Marine pilot and Tour player; he was supposed to communicate via hand signals with the Blue Angels, since we had no direct radio communication available.

Anyway, all goes precisely as planned and we make a slow descent and the Blue Angels appear off our wings and the girls are waving to their men to beat the band and the photographer is snapping pictures madly . . . when suddenly I realize our onboard communications man is throwing up like a son of a gun on the floor of the plane. To make matters worse, the next day we learn that the camera malfunctioned! The base commander was deeply apologetic and all, but begged us to go up and do it all again; I consented to a shorter run, minus our interpreter. The resulting photos still hang with pride in my Latrobe office.

I later had a similar opportunity to fly in an F-16 with the U.S. Air Force's famed Thunderbird performance team, and I was even allowed to help land a military jet on the aircraft carrier *Eisenhower*. Talk about precision flying. There's simply no room for error in such a situation. Trying to hit that famous island green at TPC Sawgrass on a Sunday was a piece of cake compared to the challenge of trying to safely set a multimillion-dollar aircraft on a floating runway. No mulligans there.

But the biggest thrill, hands down, came in the summer of 1976 when the people at Gates Aviation, the Learjet manufacturer, asked me to participate in an effort to establish a new speed record for circumnavigation of the globe.

On May 17, 1976, during America's bicentennial-year celebration, two other pilots, Jim Bir and Bill Purkey, veteran journalist Bob Serling, and I left Denver's Stapleton International Airport at 10:24 A.M. and flew to Boston in a specially outfitted Lear 36. After a quick refueling stop in Beantown, the next scheduled stop was Paris, but severe head winds ate up our fuel supply, so we had to land in Wales instead. From there it was on to Paris, Teheran, Sri Lanka, then Jakarta. At each stop, the drill was pretty much the same. We would hop out waving flags and distributing bronzed replicas of the Declaration of Independence, socialize a bit with local folks and dignitaries, then maybe trot off briefly for a bit of refreshment while the plane was being serviced. In Iran I was taken to have high tea with the crown prince, while in Sri Lanka I was put on top of an elephant and paraded about the local town. As amazing as these little ceremonies were, we managed to hold each of our visits to less than an hour's time.

I flew the plane most of the way, and there were moments I'll simply never forget, like heading toward Sri Lanka over the Indian Ocean late at night, with everybody onboard asleep but me. We were cruising at 45,000 feet when I suddenly noticed that, because of ice formation, our global navigation computer had kicked off. I remember being briefly frightened, but as I sat there flying the plane, fooling with the radar and radio signals, I began to calm down, and I told myself I'd be damned if I'd wake the others. I knew my proper coordinates and I aimed the radar down, picking up an image of the coastline of India. I flew the coast all the way to Sri Lanka, and as we descended the plane's state-of-the-art electronic guidance system came on and we glided in as though we were on the wings of an angel.

A tenser moment came far out over the Pacific, on the dangerous leg from Manila in the Philippines to Wake Island, which is approximately halfway across the Pacific Ocean from Hawaii—the same stretch where Amelia Earhart vanished without a trace.

We left Manila in the first serious blows of a fast-approaching Pacific typhoon and soon had a big decision to make. Halfway between Manila and Wake Island, the only refueling stop thereabout, you must decide to either proceed or go back, or at least divert to Guam. Problem was, Manila was being pounded by the typhoon, and amid all the radio static it wasn't clear whether Wake Island was faring well, either. We did, however, hear that Guam was being evacuated in the face of the storm, and we made a decision to keep going, placing our hopes on tiny Wake Island, little more than a speck, a bleak chunk of coral rock in the world's largest ocean.

Well, obviously, we made it. After refueling at Wake, we flew to Honolulu, arriving in the dead of night, then straight into Denver's Stapleton International Airport, where we buzzed the tower to signal the end of our great aerial adventure at 7:49 P.M. on May 19, before angling off to nearby Arapaho Airport, where Winnie and our eldest daughter, Peggy, were waiting to greet us. I remember Winnie's great bear hug, followed by her comment that I really needed a shave. I think I slept maybe three hours the whole trip.

Our circumnavigation of the globe had set a new aviation record for that class of business jet of 57 hours 25 minutes 42 seconds, eclipsing the old mark, set a decade before, by almost thirty hours. In writing about our little adventure, *Time* magazine cheekily concluded: "Considering the water hazards and long pars, the 46-year-old Palmer didn't do a bad job. He was 77½ days ahead of Phineas Fogg."

Later the same year, Russ Meyer brought out his first production jet at Cessna Aviation, the Citation 500, which I leased until an improved version of the plane came along two years later. After flying a Citation II for three years with great satisfaction, I upgraded to a Citation III, and that became the first of my planes to bear my new FAA-designated registration number: N1AP.

From there we moved into a slightly larger version of the model III and then jumped, a couple years later, to the beautiful, roomier, more powerful Citation VII model.

Every airplane Russ delivered seemed to be slightly more wondrous than the last, with innovations that would make Cessna the eventual dominant player and world leader in the private-jet aviation field. Every year when I would go back to Wichita for my annual check ride and three-day brushup in the simulator, I would learn what was coming down the Cessna production pipeline. To say I was anxious to get my hands on the controls of the new Citation X would be understating the matter by a mile.

Russ kept a designated delivery date close to his vest, the old rascal. Then one afternoon in August of 1996, while I was standing in the sixth fairway waiting to hit an approach shot in our annual gala that benefits the Latrobe Area Hospital, I heard a familiar jet roar and looked up to see just about the most beautiful thing I'd ever seen—the new Citation X gliding right over us as it approached Latrobe Airport.

The feeling that the sight of the new plane gave me was comparable to the thrill of winning a golf tournament, I can honestly say, and I took a few of my guests to the airport to see the new ship up close and for brief "test rides." Everyone was ga-ga over the beauty and technical wizardry of the plane, but

I'd already had a nice preview of Cessna's latest creation.

A few weeks before the gala, Winnie and I got up early for breakfast in Latrobe, then drove to the airport, where a prototype of the new plane we were scheduled to soon receive, with Russ and his wife, Helen, aboard, was waiting. We took off and flew for 5 hours and 58 minutes, straight to St. Andrews. We drove into the Old Grey Toon and had a drink with Tip Anderson at the Bogey Ben Pub. The next morning, we played the Old Course and later attended the majestic opening ceremonies of the Royal and Ancient's annual autumn meetings, during which the out-going club captain is thanked and the incoming one installed, along with any new members.

I happened to be one of the new members that year. What an enormous thrill, given my lengthy association with the British Open and the the golf fans of Britain and Scotland. I performed the ageless ritual of "kissing the captain's balls," and we had a dandy time catching up with old friends, reminiscing about several Open championships that are near and dear to my heart. The following morning, we got up and flew home, arriving in Latrobe in time for lunch at the club.

It had been some trip. Among the nicest two days of my life.

Afterward, I got to thinking about what Old Tom Morris would make of the age we inhabit, how thanks to flying Winnie and I have been fortunate enough to have seen virtually every corner of the globe, met thousands of people we never could have met, seen astounding natural wonders, met queens and kings and hotel doormen armed with sparkling wit. I've even managed to play a fair bit of golf amid all that air travel, and I somehow don't think Old Tom, patron spirit of the game that he is, would begrudge me the pleasure of saying that flying an airplane all these years has given me a joy that's the equal of golf.

Well, almost.

CHAPTER FOURTEEN

Bay Hill

In the fall of 1963, as my most frustrating year on tour, to that point, was drawing to a close, Pap began building the new nine at Latrobe Country Club. He'd waited a long time for this project to begin, and not surprisingly, being the original hands-on boss, he did much of the manual labor and almost all of the design work himself. Nobody knew the character of that rolling Allegheny farmland any better than my father did, and he seemed to know exactly what he wanted to do with it from the very beginning. For my part, I suppose I was anxious to lend a helping hand, shaping some of the fairways and greens with a bulldozer, if for no other reason than it gave me time to ponder the mystery of my performance in 1963.

Although I had seven tournament victories in twenty starts that year, I failed to win any of the majors. A few people were saying that I was "washed up," perhaps ailing, undoubtedly an elder statesman of the Tour at the grand old age of thirty-four. Some said that I no longer had the incentive to play like the Palmer of yesterday, and it didn't help my mood a bit that Bob Jones, when asked by a reporter to comment on my "major" drought, said that the so-called Palmer Era could be over—if it ever existed anyway. Jones wasn't trying to be unkind; he was merely describing what he thought he saw. So was Pap when he sharply observed to a reporter who had asked more or less the same question as the one posed to Mr. Jones, "There's nothing wrong with Arnie's game—he just has too many irons in the fire. He's got to decide whether he wants to play golf or make television films with Bob Hope. With this boy Nicklaus coming along the way he is, Arnie can't do both."

The truth is, of course, at first I thought I could do all those things—but I was slowly beginning to realize that maybe I couldn't. My back ached a bit, but my playing skills from tee to green were essentially fine, as strong as they'd ever been. For whatever reasons anybody cared to name, though (and everyone had a theory), my powers of concentration on the golf course had obviously suffered a fall-off, and so had my putting touch. Frankly, it was nice just to climb up on that bulldozer and shove dirt around on those new holes at Latrobe without having to figure out whether my golf career was coming or going. In retrospect, seven victories in twenty starts isn't such a bad year, but major championship victories are the standard by which careers have always been judged. And rightly so, I might add.

Designing and owning my own golf course had been part of my game plan as far back as I could remember, and by 1964, if you counted the golf courses Buddy Worsham and my other teammates and I built at Wake Forest plus the between-the-runways course I hacked out of a field for the U.S. Coast Guard, I'd acquired a fair bit of experience in building one. As early as November of 1957, George Love, a former chairman of Chrysler, had invited me to take over the creation of Laurel Valley Golf Club, build it, run it, do whatever I needed to do to make it a world-class golf club. But I'd tactfully declined such full involvement, citing my desire to instead play the Tour full time. (A wise decision, since my first Masters win came the next spring.) Instead I opted to become the club's touring professional. Architect Dick Wilson ably built a fine golf course for the Laurel Valley members, with some minor input from me, and many years later, after my own course design firm was in full operation, I updated the course.

My first substantial experience designing a golf course from start to finish, though, came at Somerset, Pennsylvania, at a resort area in the mountains about forty miles east of Latrobe, a place called Indian Lake, which I did virtually on my own with only a crew of day laborers supplied to me by the project's owner, developer Jim McIntire. I cleared the land and drew up the course plans in my head. The original concept was a somewhat novel scheme: building houses people would use principally as vacation and second homes connected to an airstrip. So theoretically you could fly your plane to Indian Lake, pull up to your front door, go inside, put on your golf spikes, then head out the back door to the course, or something like that.

The reality was that McIntire had only enough capital to build the first nine holes, which I proceeded to do, creating a layout with tight fairways and small push-up greens that, thirty years later, some say is still one of the best tests of golf in western Pennsylvania. On one hole, players have to go under the runway to get to the next tee. Ironically, I never got paid for my work there, though I was given two house lots, which I still own.

After the Indian Lake and Latrobe projects, word began to get around that Arnold Palmer was interested in taking on course designing jobs and the offers began to come my way—slowly at first, but with increasing frequency. When the Cleveland gang got into this, Mark suggested the best thing to do was to associate ourselves with a professional architect. That man turned out to be Frank Duane, a former president of the American Society of Golf Course Architects and a highly respected course designer. Mark arranged a meeting, and we quickly came to terms.

As a result of an unfortunate infection, Frank's mobility was severely limited. An insect bite in the tropics had led to an illness that left him paralyzed and confined to a wheelchair. But that proved to be not a serious obstacle to our success. As the collaboration evolved, I became the field work supervisor and on-site consultant for the team. I was often up in the bulldozer, doing the work hands-on, just as Pap had shown me. I loved moving earth to shape the golf course. Frank was a superb architect who, like me, drew inspiration from the classic courses of America's golden era of course design—the works of Tillinghast and Ross, Raynor, Thomas, and Dr. Mackenzie. The Winged Foots, Merions, Oakmonts, and Brooklines—these were the Holy Grails of our design thinking. They were the kind of beautiful, honest, classically shaped layouts golfers of every skill level could appreciate and enjoy playing.

And, I must say, Frank and I were a pretty effective team. One of our first collaborations was Myrtle Beach National, followed shortly thereafter by the Bay Course at Kapalua, in Hawaii. The high visibility of those courses created even more demand for our services, and that, combined with my burgeoning business interests and commitment to the Tour, created some tense "educational" moments in our evolving professional relationship.

For instance, the phone rang once with Jim Deane on the other end of the line. Jim owned the new Half Moon Bay club south of San Francisco, where Frank and I had just completed work on a championship golf course. Because of my extremely busy schedule that summer, Frank had done the lion's share of the work. The final grading had been done and the course was almost ready for grassing, but Jim was spitting mad, issuing not a few choice expletives. To mercifully summarize, he was upset that I'd been too busy to oversee the final contouring of the greens, and he advised me in no uncertain terms that if I intended to become a major-league course designer, using my name to sell a signature golf course concept, I'd better make absolutely certain I was on hand to properly oversee every phase of the construction. Especially the greens.

He had a point. He knew it and he knew I knew it.

Embarrassed, I got straight on my plane and went to see Jim. I got on the bulldozer and personally reshaped all eighteen greens at Half Moon Bay, which today, I'm proud to say, is one of the premier clubs in the Bay Area. I learned a painful but valuable lesson from the experience—that I couldn't send someone else to complete a job my name was on. That's been a guiding tenet of our design work ever since.

My collaboration with Frank Duane lasted about five years, during which time we built ten or twelve excellent courses, all of which I remain very proud of. But as our workload continued to increase, Frank's health took a sudden decline, and it became obvious to both of us that the demands for our services were exceeding our capacity to provide the kind of attention Jim Deane had rightfully demanded.

About 1970, I began looking around for another full-time course design partner, and one day while playing an exhibition match at the new Bermuda Run Country Club in Winston-Salem, North Carolina, with three younger Tour players who'd all been Worsham scholarship players at Wake Forest (a golf scholarship I established in Bud Worsham's memory), I happened to glance over and see this freckle-faced, bald-headed, ugly son of a gun inspecting the greens.

"Who's that guy?" I asked one of my playing partners.

"Oh," he said. "That's Ed Seay. He and Ellis Maples designed the course."

I asked him to invite Ed over, and he did. Ed and I shook hands, and I told him I liked what I saw at Bermuda Run. He thanked me. Then I gave it to him straight: would he be interested in working with me on a few golf course projects? Ed is a big excitable sort, a bullnecked U.S. Marine Corps veteran who probably took a few too many shots to the head (as I like to kid him) when he played for the corps football team in the middle sixties. Anyway, Ed grinned and said he would love that opportunity, and I told him I would be in touch after we checked out his credentials.

A few weeks later, I knew I had found someone special in Ed Seay. After getting out of the U.S. Marines in 1965, he'd gone to work as a junior design partner for Ellis Maples, the dean of southern architects, who many feel is as fine a course designer as the Carolinas ever produced. As the handsome layout at Bermuda Run proved, Ed had obviously learned his lessons well at Ellis's elbow. Timing is everything in life and in golf. Shortly before Ed and I met, Ellis informed Ed that he was anxious to slow down a bit and suggested to Ed, in the nicest possible way, that he venture out on his own.

Six days after that first meeting in the fairway we

had worked out an agreement. Being a big old country boy with a heart of gold but a mouth as big as a Florida gator, Ed flatly told Mark McCormack he wasn't interested in signing a lengthy legal contract. A handshake, he said, was as good as his word, and his word ought to be good enough for anybody.

That was a sentiment I could fully appreciate, since it was pretty much my own arrangement with Mark. So we all shook hands and got down to work.

Our first job was in Tokyo.

"You mean Tokyo, Georgia?" Ed drawled.

"No, Ed. I mean the real Tokyo. Tokyo, Japan. Do you have a passport?"

"No, sir."

"Then I recommend you get one, Ed. *Fast.*"

The trip, to consult with developers and plan three different golf course projects, had more than a few amusing moments with my new partner in tow. Apparently, Ed had never strayed too far from his native Florida, including his time in the military, so the customs, rituals, and finer points of Japanese business protocol left him, shall we say, a little confused. At one point, I remember, after a seemingly endless series of meetings with the clients and their lawyers and corporate subordinates, during which vast quantities of tea were served and consumed, poor Ed gave a look of grave dismay and blurted out to one of our very proper hosts, "Well, we're gonna actually need to see some damn ground before we can talk any more about this thing."

The comment threw the Japanese contingent into a major panic. They exchanged worried glances as the interpreter conveyed Ed's blunt assessment to them. At that point they began profusely apologizing and explaining that the course site was at least 150 miles from Toyko and it would be simply impossible to see the actual proposed site for at least a day or two.

All Ed meant, of course, was that he needed to see the site before he could make any more suggestions about the design. His eyeballs seemed to be floating from all that green tea, and I knew, even if they didn't, that he was dying to get outside, see some land, get his hands dirty, and get down to work. Ed Seay is nothing if not a worker.

I smiled and explained to the interpreter that my partner hadn't meant he wanted to see the land that very minute but that further discussions would be helpful after he'd finally been able to view the property.

Whew. You could feel the tension leaking out of the room. There were relieved smiles all around the table.

This was the first time Ed's brand of blunt southern charm had startled a prospective client—but it certainly wouldn't be the last. In fact, Ed's nickname for himself is the "Tactful Sledgehammer," and I suspect others have less flattering names for him. But I have to say, in his defense, that his plainspoken good-ole-boy way of cutting through the baloney, combined with an agile intelligence and frat-brother humor, has defused many ticklish situations when the negotiations were stalled and seemed at the point of going off the rails or at least getting bogged down in legalese.

Shortly after that, we started work together on the third course at the Broadmoor in Colorado and the new Ironwood course at Palm Desert. A few years later, after a host of successful collaborations, I invited Ed to work with me exclusively and we officially formed the Palmer Course Design Company, with offices at Sawgrass in Ponte Vedra Beach, Florida.

Since then, we've gone on to handle more than 250 projects around the world, ranging from simple low-cost municipal courses to high-end private clubs, each one different and special in its own way.

You'll have to forgive me if I don't call any of our designs personal favorites. As Ed would say, that's the ultimate designer no-no. Like your own children, every project has its own special quality. When you add to that a set of construction challenges, cost factors, geographic eccentricities, and endless other variables, trying to compare your creations is really like comparing apples to oranges. What I will say is that whether you are constructing something as no-frills as Birkdale, the fine municipal course we built in 1997 for Johnny Harris and his partners for less than $4 million in Charlotte, North Carolina, or something as exclusive as the Old Tabby Links at Spring Island in South Carolina, with its subtropical grandeur and four-hundred-foot-wide playing corridors where almost all the holes are isolated from one another, the objective is always the same: to give as much value to the client for his dollars as is humanly and creatively possible, to make the course beautiful and challenging to golfers of all skill levels, and most of all, to make the experience of playing a Palmer Design course one that will make the first-time player walk off and say, regardless of his or her score, "Wow. I want to go back and play that sucker again." (Pardon me for sounding a bit like Ed there, but that is what I get from hanging around him for the past thirty years.)

Having said that, I should offer another observation. I'm often asked by prospective clients, fans, even other Tour players what qualities or factors, in my opinion, make a golf course great. My response is always the same: because it is a golf course.

I'm not being flip. I'm dead serious. That is to say, every golf course is going to be great to somebody for some reason or another, and what you think is important in a golf course may not be what I think is important or a particularly notable feature—and vice versa. Who's right, who's wrong? No one. That's why, to be honest, I hate lists and rankings of the "world's best golf courses." They make me very uncomfortable. Golf courses are just about the most purely subjective things on earth—subject to a thousand variables in the mind of the person beholding them. Some people like links; some prefer gentle parkland courses. You like big greens with minimal breaks; I prefer small greens with plenty of elevations. What Ed and I work hard to do is always keep in mind our vision of a "natural" design whose hallmarks are playability and versatility. And I think, given our record of achievement, the proof is in the pudding.

If I may crow a bit, I'll say that you'd be hard-pressed to find a busier bunch than the twenty-five designers, draftsmen, secretaries, and the big bald-headed guy who heads up the crew employed at 572 Ponte Vedra Boulevard. I'm proud of Palmer Course Design and the work they do, Not long ago, I was notified by the American Society of Golf Course Architects that I'd been selected to receive the Donald Ross Award for 1999, a coveted prize given to architects who have made a strong contribution to golf course design. As honored as I am to personally accept the award, it's really a tribute to Ed Seay and all of the talented folks he has gathered around him.

The first time I laid eyes on the Bay Hill Club and Lodge, during a winter exhibition in early 1965, not long after we opened the new nine at Latrobe, the place was little more than a still-raw golf course with a tiny pro shop, a small guest lodge, and a few modest bungalows carved out of the orange groves and desolate razor brush of central Florida. It was a true wilderness area, home to a few pristine freshwater lakes filled with waterfowl, snakes, and gators.

In other words, it was nearly perfect. A golfer's paradise, in my book.

For years, Winnie and I had discussed how great it would be to have a quiet little out-of-the-way place in Florida we could go to every winter where I could retreat to work on my game and the girls could relax in the warmth. We'd looked around a lot, but it wasn't until I played Bay Hill, another fine design of Dick Wilson, that I went back to the house we were renting that winter in Coral Gables and said to Winnie, "Babe, I've just played the best golf course in Florida, and I want to own it."

By then she was accustomed to my sudden bursts of inspiration, but after viewing the property herself she agreed with me that Bay Hill was something special. With its splendid isolation and Eden-like abundance of wildlife, it really was a little bit of paradise on earth. We envisioned ourselves being happy there for a very long time, building a second home where we could go to relax before beginning the madness of another Tour season, where I could practice to my heart's content, with only a few club members and their guests around to interrupt my concentration. Best of all, we could adopt a slower pace of life—something that we greatly needed at this point in our hectic lives.

At my request, Mark McCormack and Russ Meyer went to work trying to put together a deal that would allow Arnold Palmer Enterprises to purchase the club and all of its assets—a job easier said than done, as it turned out. Bay Hill had been built as a getaway club by several prominent businessmen from Nashville and Detroit, and negotiations with those owners, a collection of almost a dozen men, became a lengthy ordeal that took almost the next five years to put together.

At last, in 1969, we finalized and signed a five-year lease with an option to buy the club. We immediately set about making improvements to the course and to the lodge, figuring we would own the whole shooting match outright by the end of the lease.

However, almost a year to the day after we signed the agreement, disaster struck—at least to my mind.

I happened to read one morning in the *Orlando Sentinel* that the Disney Corporation had just announced its purchase of twenty-seven thousand acres near us at Bay Hill. The entertainment behemoth was planning to begin immediate construction of its grandest family theme park ever, a vision called Walt Disney World.

Friends immediately called to congratulate me on my incredible business savvy. With Disney in the neighborhood and the land rush of commercial development that was bound to follow, property values were expected to soar out of sight. Contrary to their belief, I was really depressed as blazes by the news, heartsick that I would soon have Disney as a neighbor. Gone forever would be my quiet little corner of Florida, my private practice Eden of birds and birdies.

Eventually, though, I calmed down. I even was among the first to go out and take a ride on our new neighbor's impressive monorail system when it became fully operational. I met Disney officials and looked over the ambitious blueprints for the immense theme park. The people at Disney couldn't have been more gracious, and the experience brought home to me what an unprecedented impact the park's presence was going to have on Orlando and the surrounding environment. I suppose I still privately despaired a bit for little Bay Hill. On the other hand, nature herself had given us an ace of sorts. Thanks to those freshwater lakes to the west and north, access to our little sanctuary would remain fairly limited. With no through traffic and only small residential streets connecting something like six hundred residential lots, I figured that with luck we would become an oasis of calm in the midst of it all.

I'm happy to say that's exactly the picture that evolved; however, Bay Hill almost slipped through our fingers because of circumstances beyond our control. By 1974, owing to some business setbacks of our own, Arnold Palmer Enterprises was just about to ask Bay Hill's owners for an extension of our lease-option agreement when we were thunderstruck to learn that they'd made their own deal to sell Bay Hill to somebody else—in fact, it was pretty much a done deal. The new owner was George Powell, president and CEO of Yellow Freight transport lines out of Kansas City, a man who turned out to be a real gentleman. When I approached George, he graciously agreed to renegotiate our deal, and we eventually purchased the golf club and course from him. The final price we paid was a bit higher than we had hoped it would be, but at least Bay Hill was finally ours.

Pap loved Bay Hill dearly. He could come there and do the things he loved most: play golf with friends, see his grandchildren, and enjoy a few adult beverages in the locker room after a round of golf. For a while, until I talked him out of it, he was even dead set on purchasing one of the club's original cottages, which, as I recall, was up for sale for $17,000. After a life of hard work and taking care of everybody else's needs, Pap was about to officially "retire" (although he never really retired), and I for one was pleased that he would finally be able to enjoy some of life's finer things, which Bay Hill offered in spades. On the other hand, my mother, already beginning to show the effects of the crippling rheumatoid arthritis that she dealt with bravely until her death, wasn't terribly fond of Florida. She always found her time there a little boring, to say the least. I suspect she needed the unfolding drama of the northern seasons, the comfort of her Latrobe friends, and the social traditions of western Pennsylvania to keep her happy. At any rate, they didn't purchase the bungalow—which, incidentally, recently sold for about a quarter of a million dollars. So much for my real-estate business savvy.

It is a bit ironic that Pap was so keen about Bay Hill—on our owning and operating the club and lodge, I mean to say.

A few years before, he had nearly lost his mind when I informed him that I was thinking about purchasing Latrobe Country Club. I'll never forget the look he gave me.

"Are you crazy? Why on *earth* do you want to do that, Arn?" he growled.

"Well, Pap," I reasoned, "you've been here your whole life. That's a good enough reason for me."

I waited a second or two before adding, "Besides, it means you'd have to work for me."

He didn't find that particularly amusing. But the deal was all but signed and sealed at that point. The fact is, owing to cheap imports and the steep decline in the high-grade specialty steel market, Latrobe's economy was suffering, the effects of which were visible even at the club. The watering system was antiquated, greens and fairways sorely needed rebuilding, and the clubhouse and pool area could have done with a serious face-lift.

This was exactly Pap's logic for *not* buying the country club. He knew what it took to run the place, what a drain on capital resources owning the club outright would be. The figures simply didn't add up in his mind.

As I presented it to Pap, though, it not only seemed an opportune moment for me to step in and spruce up the place—but also, given our family's long identification with the place, it was the right thing to do. Harry Saxman had first raised the intriguing possibility with me. With Harry's help, over a series of months, we tracked down and purchased all of the outstanding shares of stock in Latrobe Country Club. That proved to be a bit of a paper chase in and of itself that I do not wish to repeat anytime soon, because, since the club was founded in the 1920s, much of the stock was scattered far and wide, squirreled away in people's strong boxes and attics. Some of the certificates ultimately had to be revised before they could be sold.

But, eventually, Latrobe was ours. Winnie and I became the sole stockholders in September of 1971. The club became, in effect, a true mom-and-pop operation. Over the years, we rebuilt the course and upgraded the club's amenities, adding a new cart barn, halfway house, and tennis courts. We refurbished the locker rooms and the pool area and expanded the clubhouse to include a new grill and dining facility, which opened in the nick of time for the wedding of a close friend's daughter. A few years later, we built a special covered patio off the club ballroom facing the 18th green, and we named it "Peggy's Porch," inaugurating it at my eldest daughter's wedding to Doug Reintgen in June 1978.

For the record, I tried to convince Peggy that she and Doug were far too young to get married, but Peg is a strong-willed lass who takes after her mother and completely shrugged off my concerns in this regard. I liked Doug quite a lot. He was a local boy from a good family and he used to caddie at the club. At that time Doug was still in medical school but clearly had a promising future. Peg was undecided about her career and unsure of what she really wanted to do with her life, save marry Doug. My principal fear, however, was that their lives were just too unsettled to jump into a lifetime commitment. In this respect, I guess, my concerns did prove a bit prophetic, because a few years later they separated and eventually divorced. All families have their ups and downs, but I am pleased to say we all remain good friends with Doug and his family, and true to form Doug has gone on to become one of the country's top cancer surgeons, based in nearby Tampa, Florida.

Back to the country club. Following his stint in the U.S. Air Force, my younger brother, Jerry, returned to Latrobe and tried his hand at inside jobs for a few years, until he decided it was more fun to be outside working on the grounds as Pap's assistant. He completed agronomy studies at Penn State and was a logical successor to the club's superintendent job, which I gave him when Pap passed away in 1976. A decade after that we named him general manager of the club, the title he holds today. It pleases me no end that his son Deken attended Wake Forest University and has gone on to work for the USGA in Colorado Springs, and that his daughter Amanda is studying agronomy at Penn State and is seriously considering either following her old man into the golf course business or maybe even joining her uncle Arnie in the course design field.

Whatever happens in the future, and with all due respect to Pap, I feel confident in saying that buying the club from the members twenty years ago is one of the smartest moves I ever made. It enabled me to preserve a facility I care deeply about and to give something back to the people of Latrobe. It pleases me in ways you can't imagine when members stop me to say how fine the golf course looks or how terrific the food in the dining room has been these past few years. It seems like almost every Saturday afternoon when I'm at the club during the summer months, a big wedding reception or anniversary party is going on in the ballroom or out on Peggy's Porch—a sight that never fails to make me a bit reflective. While much has changed around here, the spirit of the place, the most important part, remains the same.

In a word, I couldn't be happier with the way things have turned out in Latrobe. And I'll wager, wherever he is looking on from (though you can sure bet he won't admit it), so is Pap.

Someone asked me a surprising question the other day.

Was I afraid of dying?

I suppose my answer might have surprised him a bit. No, I replied. I'm not particularly afraid of dying—as long as I go the way my father did.

In February of 1976, Winnie and I flew back to the West Coast from Hawaii and said goodbye to each other and headed our separate ways. She went on home to Bay Hill, where Pap and Doc Giffin had just arrived for their winter golf getaway, and I flew on with great anticipation to the Bob Hope Desert Classic in Palm Springs. The Hope, simply put, was one of my favorite tournaments, and the week it was held was one of the finest of the year. That's due in part, I'm sure, to my long and close friendship with the host, Bwana Bob, but also because I always seemed to find my game there and won the tournament a record five times. The expanded five-day format, the colorful mingling of entertainment-industry folk and golf pros, the large and responsive galleries, the relaxed atmosphere, and the opportunity to catch up with old friends and fans—all of it combined to make the Hope tournament a very special event in my heart, despite what I would have to inevitably think of every time the calendar turned to February.

I'd just walked off the course in 1976, buoyant after shooting 64 in the opening round, when my old friend Ernie Dunlevie, the tournament's president, pulled me aside and said he needed to speak with me privately on a matter of grave urgency.

I didn't like the way his face looked one bit.

We went into a room and he told me my father had suffered a massive heart attack and died. I was devastated. I sat down in a chair, feeling completely drained. That I was numb is the best way I can describe it. I thanked Ernie and immediately called home. Pap had played nine holes that morning on the Charger Course at Bay Hill, grabbed a quick bowl of soup, and headed out for another full eighteen on the big course with Doc Giffin. Afterward, they'd had a drink and Pap had said he felt tired and decided to go take a nap before he and Doc had dinner and played a hand or two of gin rummy. He went to his room in the lodge and stretched out on the bed. A short while later, Doc returned to his adjoining room and found the door between their bedrooms ajar. He stepped into Pap's room to investigate and discovered him lying on the floor. Pap apparently got up when the massive coronary struck—and died before he reached the floor.

To say the least, I was stunned beyond belief.

This was the news I'd feared hearing, in some way or another, all my life. It simply didn't seem possible that my father could be gone. He was the man I most admired in the world. He was the man whose hard rules and painful lessons had made me everything I'd become, everything I stood for, everything I was. And now he was gone.

That's when I lost it.

I won't even attempt to describe to you what those next few hours and days were like for me. I sleepwalked through them, living in a blur of sorrow and anger and sadness. Pap was such a dominant presence in our lives, and he'd worked so hard for so long with so little material reward. It just seemed cruelly unfair that just as he was able to finally relax and enjoy the fruits of his labors, he would simply stretch out on a bed and pass away. That's enough to test any man's faith—in himself, in the fates.

It was Pap's wish that his body be cremated.

A week or so later, we held a small memorial service at the Lutheran church in Youngstown, where Pap never felt comfortable darkening the doorway. Afterward, the family went to a spot that would have pleased him far more, the place where I think he performed the Lord's work in his own quiet, dignified, bullheaded way: a small knoll just above the 18th green at Latrobe Country Club.

There, keeping it short and sweet and simple as he would have liked it, with only a handful of friends and family members gathered around, we scattered his ashes near a small red bush above the putting surface, where he could easily keep a wary eye out for anyone who failed to properly repair their ball marks.

A few years later, we scattered my mother's ashes near the same spot. After that, the little red bush seemed to grow like crazy. My mother, always the life giver and nurturer. I'm convinced that the two of them are happy there, and I know that I can feel their presence every time I'm on that course—or anywhere else, for that matter. They say that to those who have been given much there is much that is expected. That little truism goes a long way toward explaining why I've lived my life the way I have. I don't care how old you are, you still want to earn your parents' approval and live up to the example they've set. That's a tall order in my case, but a worthwhile goal.

The ebb and flow of life, like a golf match, never ceases to amaze me.

A short time after my father's death, I got a phone call from Orlando businessman Frank Hubbard. Frank was concerned that the Citrus Open was dying on the vine at Rio Pinar, and he wondered if moving the tournament to Bay Hill and attaching my name to the event might somehow revive what had once been a very popular and prosperous stop on the PGA Tour.

When I thought about it, I realized that this indeed was a way I could give something valuable back to the PGA Tour, which has been so very good to me and my family. A year later, in the spring of

1979, with me playing the host role, the new Bay Hill golf tournament debuted with a strong field of PGA players on hand, including Jack Nicklaus. I don't remember much about the 70 I shot in the opening round; what I do recall is being incredibly nervous about having the entire golf world, my old friends, and several million network television viewers come to Bay Hill. Needless to say, I hoped to get their stamp of approval on the premises and the new tournament. No Broadway producer ever sweated bullets any larger on opening night of his theatrical baby.

As it turned out, I needn't have worried quite so much. Among other things, we got rave reviews from the golf press, and appropriately enough, that first Bay Hill event was won in a thrilling playoff by a Wake Forest lad, Bob Byman.

Over the next twenty-odd years, I'm happy to say, even as the names of the tournament's title sponsors shifted from Hertz to Nestlé to Office Depot to Cooper Tires, the list of Bay Hill champions included the best and brightest of the PGA Tour: Andy Bean, Tom Kite, Gary Koch, Fuzzy Zoeller, Payne Stewart, Paul Azinger, Robert Gamez, Dan Forsman, Andrew Magee, Fred Couples, Ben Crenshaw, Loren Roberts, Phil Mickelson, and Ernie Els. Not a bad collection of trophy winners.

Best of all, the players themselves made it abundantly clear to me how much they looked forward to coming to Bay Hill each spring, sometimes bringing their families along and making "working vacations" out of the festive week. Orlando is a great place for family fun. Amid all the drama of golf, there were some great parties and a lot of laughs and deepening friendships with younger guys like Curtis Strange, Peter Jacobsen, and Mark O'Meara, to name just a few. I'm especially pleased that all this has taken place at a spot my family, Pap included, has always been so fond of.

Since I'm being a little sentimental about it, I should point out that it was the same Frank Hubbard who asked me to get involved in the tournament who, a few years later, approached me with another proposition. This time he wanted me to lend my name and financial support to something he and many others believed was greatly needed in the Orlando area—a first-rate children's hospital. In the beginning, all Frank wanted was to use my name and maybe get a financial donation from me toward the announced fund-raising goal of $10 million.

I was more than happy to do that. Children are my soft spot, and the idea that I might be able to do something to help a lot of sick children, well, that was essentially a "no-brainer," as my own grand-children would say today. Winnie and I enthusiastically signed on.

Then, after we toured the cramped, outdated children's wing of Orlando Regional Medical Center, meeting brave little kids battling cancer and other illnesses, seeing all those shockingly frail and tiny premature babies on life support, by golly, the floodgates in me opened. I used whatever clout I had to get that new hospital project up and flying. Pretty quickly, the campaign target had swelled from

$10 million to $30 million, and a bit further along the line, I was pleased that other prominent tour stars like Greg Norman and Scott Hoch gave their time and financial support to the institution. Upon winning the Las Vegas Invitational in 1989, Hoch presented the entire first-place winner's check to the hospital, a gesture that touched thousands of lives and a guy named Arnold Palmer very deeply.

It was Winnie's idea to make the children's hospital the principal beneficiary of the charity monies created by the Bay Hill tournament, a tie-in that has been a perpetual source of income to a project near and dear to our hearts. Eventually, I signed over all of my stock in the tournament to my two daughters, Peggy and Amy, and their families, and today my primary function with respect to the tournament is to serve as host, make sure things get done right and everybody has a good time, and do whatever I can to lobby on behalf of the charitable beneficiaries.

August 23, 1989, is a day I'll never forget. Thousands were on hand for the opening and dedication of the Arnold Palmer Hospital for Children and Women. There was a host of young entertainers and singing characters from Disney World, a marching band, various area dignitaries and friends, and the press.

It was just days before my sixtieth birthday, and I guess I was in a pretty reflective mood. The hospital project had grown to mean so much to both Winnie and me and our family—the ultimate pet project in some ways. As speeches were made and thousands of balloons were released, I was feeling fine and in control. That is, until six-year-old Billy Gillespie, a new patient at the facility, held the microphone and spoke to the gathering—and to me personally. Billy thanked me for making a "dream come true."

I remember glancing at my daughter Amy, with her husband, Roy, and her four healthy children gathered around her, and feeling a knot of gratitude tighten my throat and chest. Though we couldn't possibly have known it then, Amy would soon go through her own ordeal with cancer—and come out on the other side, wiser and healed, thanks to a world-class treatment center like the hospital we had just helped create. When I saw the tears of pride and thanks forming in Amy's eyes, that's when I lost it.

Once again, I was crying in public.

My own children, as you might expect, mean so incredibly much to me. Sometimes I indulge in wishing I'd also had a son, but upon further reflection, given what I've learned about my own obsession to please my father and ultimately outdo him, I realize that a son might have had a difficult time growing up in my shadow. I look at Jack Nicklaus and his four boys—Jackie, Steve, Gary, and Michael—and realize not only what a challenge it must have been for them at times to be Jack's sons but also what a terrific job Jack and Barbara have done in shielding and raising them. Jack and Barbara also have a spirited daughter, Nan, so Jack knows a bit about what it's like to live in my house. Even if destiny had given me a son, I realize that even a son who chose to follow me into the greatest game on earth couldn't possibly have pleased me any more than have my two wonderful daughters, Peggy and Amy. As I've said, with all due respect and affection, I think Peg and Amy get their love of books, the arts, all things beautiful and creative, not to mention their maddening streaks of hardheadedness, *entirely* from their mother. The apple doesn't fall far from that tree, I suppose, and though we've had our share of lively dinner-table debates and father–daughter battles over everything from boyfriends to women's rights, the joy and pride I've taken in both my daughters has never wavered, and has simply increased over time.

As I look back, though we've never really discussed the subject, I realize how difficult it was for them to grow up being Arnold and Winnie Palmer's children. In the early days of their school lives, for example, we were dead set in our conviction that Peg and Amy should attend local public schools. They were no different from any other kids, so why should they be treated as such? When you have significant money, as we did about the time they were old enough to notice the differences between people's circumstances, it's easy to spoil a child but difficult to instill discipline and values.

Our aim, Winnie's and mine, was to make sure our daughters didn't feel more privileged or more fortunate than any other child. Maybe we erred a bit in that thinking, because the truth was that, like it or not, through no fault of their own, they were privileged. And even if they didn't quite feel and act that way, lots of other kids in the public schools simply

assumed the girls came from a privileged background and felt it was therefore their duty to make
things rough on them both at times.

Regrettably, we eventually had to place the girls
in a private school where presumably their father's
name wouldn't mean so much, or if it did the schools
simply wouldn't tolerate the kind of harassment Peg
and Amy had faced. Even then, Winnie and I were
determined that our girls should essentially make
their own ways through life. We are, by nature,
frugal people—always saving for next year's crisis.
Through their high school and college years, Peg and
Amy both worked jobs like any other teenagers. In
college neither one had the benefit of a personal
automobile. I suppose this was a source of embar-
rassment for them because of the attitudes and values
of some in their intimate social circles.

In any case, under the circumstances I don't think
we did so badly as parents. After her marriage to
Doug Reintgen amicably dissolved, Peg entered the
financial world and came down to Orlando to join
our organization as an executive with Arnold Palmer
Enterprises.

Fortunately, as all sides can confirm, it was a mercifully brief business association. Peg had her own
bold and creative ideas about how a business venture
should be run, and I think the year she ran some of the
Bay Hill operations cost me, conservatively speaking,
at least a million dollars.

I'm sure Peg would have her own take on our
challenging year in business together. In fact, I'm
sure that she would point out that I drove her nuts,

and that if that complicated relationship revealed anything at all it was that going into business with her old man was a really bad idea. By nature and temperament, Peg is a strong woman who likes to do things her own way, a quality I greatly admire. As I think of it, maybe she's more like her old man than I'd first imagined.

Anyway, she eventually went back out on her own and found a far better niche, in the investment business. She married Peter Wears, a fine man and successful stockbroker, and they've built a family life with their two children and his daughter in Durham, North Carolina. That makes me very pleased and proud.

Peg's big adventure in management came at a difficult moment in the life of Bay Hill. Sometime in the mid-1980s, we were approached by a large Japanese concern that was anxious to purchase the whole two-hundred-acre complex, and the money they were offering was, to say the least, eye-opening—roughly $50 million.

From just about every standpoint, it was a public-relations nightmare. To begin with, when it was widely reported that we were planning to sell Bay Hill to Japanese investors, we received an avalanche of criticism from the public and local newspaper columnists and even some of our neighbors that was, in my mind, only partially justified. Winnie herself was considerably displeased with the prospect of giving up the club and lodge, which she had spent more than a decade fussing over and improving with her crack decorator's eye. She also accurately reminded me that the community was home to a number of World War II–era veterans who considered the idea of Japanese owning Bay Hill a slap in the face.

The truth is, the decision wasn't mine alone to make. I had numerous partners in my businesses who believed we couldn't rebuff the Japanese simply because of hostilities that took place half a century ago. Besides, from a purely business standpoint the proposed deal was almost too good to be true (and, in fact, turned out to be just that). Under the deal's proposed terms, I would continue to run the day-to-day operations at the club and keep our longtime association at Bay Hill fully intact. In theory, nothing would visibly change. It might even be better— thanks to the windfall of cash I would be able to plow back into various operations in and around the premises.

That was the theory, at least.

Perhaps because of the intense controversy and the panic of the club's members, or perhaps because their own financial situation wasn't nearly as solid as we had at first thought, the Japanese concern balked and the deal ultimately collapsed under its own weight. The would-be buyers used a loophole vaguely related to environmental issues (asbestos insulation was discovered in some of the lodge's oldest rooms) to back out of the proposed agreement— costing each side at least a couple million dollars in lawyers' fees and other expenses.

Given half a chance, I've decided, things usually work out the way they should.

Later on, Roy Saunders, Amy's husband, came to work for me, and soon Amy herself was growing more and more involved in the day-to-day operation of the club. I'm happy to say that since that rather difficult time (which also included the Isleworth fiasco and O'Neal episode, I might add), Amy and Roy have worked hard and had a wonderful impact on the quality of life at Bay Hill, for both members and lodge guests. We've recently undergone a $7 million face-lift of the golf course and grounds, refurbished the lodge's forty-eight guest rooms and six suites from top to bottom with Lexington's Arnold Palmer Collection furniture, and taken the wraps off a splendid new pool and spa facility.

For all the dramatic changes that have altered the landscape around us in central Florida (Disney isn't our only neighbor; we also have Universal Studios now on the opposite side, and the largest convention center in the Southeast not much more than a few good pokes with a fairway wood away), Bay Hill remains, by and large, a tranquil residential oasis that most of us are very happy to call home.

Like the comfortable lobby furniture or the famous green clock on the putting green, I guess I really am something of a fixture around the place. It pleases me to be able to go into the club grillroom every morning before seven, greet some of the same staff members I've said hello to for ten or fifteen years, have my breakfast of fruit and toast, and greet any early-rising lodge guests who happen to be about.

It also pleases me to be able to finish up a

morning's work in my office just up the stairs from Jim Deaton's handsome pro shop, then mosey out to the range and hit warm-up balls from my little corner of the range. I don't mind it a bit when strangers come up and politely speak to me. On the contrary, unless I'm preparing to play in a tournament or have some other pressing obligation, I relish the opportunity to say hello to a visitor, pick their brains about the lodge and the course, and maybe sign an autograph or two.

It seems to me that autograph seekers have gotten out of hand in American sports, even around the PGA Tour, where entrepreneurs, I'm told, now pay kids to collect famous signatures on photographs and hats and other collectibles. That practice distresses me, and I must confess that there have been times when I simply refused to sign my name. Not long ago, for instance, someone sent a pile of glossy photographs of me waving farewell to the gallery from the bridge at St. Andrews with the instructions to "just sign your name." There must have been two hundred photographs, and no "please" or "thank you" attached. We sent the package back with the photographs unsigned. Whoever sent that package, I suppose, will think Arnold Palmer is a jerk for not signing his pictures. Well I think that he's the kind of "fan" I don't really care to have—someone who was clearly aiming to make money off my signature.

At my offices in Latrobe and Bay Hill, we get literally many thousands of requests from people each year. In Pennsylvania, Doc Giffin, Gina Varrone, and Debbie Rushnock have become pretty good at spotting true fan requests, as have my secretary, Pat Boeckenstedt, and receptionist, Janet Hulcher, at Bay Hill. They know chapter and verse my policy on signing autographs: I'll happily sign anybody's personal photo or hat or scorecard, whatever they choose, as long as it's a personal request. I won't sign golf balls, though. That's an unwritten policy designed to combat forgeries on the market. I try to do as much signing for genuine charity events as the strength in my right hand will allow.

I feel it's important for an athlete to sign autographs, and I get riled up when I see some younger Tour player blowing past a group of kids who merely want him to pause and acknowledge their presence. Where, I wonder, does that fortunate young man think the next generation of golfers will come from, to say nothing of the game's fans? In my mind, it's all about giving back whatever you can whenever you can.

In any case, signing autographs at Bay Hill keeps me connected with what's taking place around there and, well, it's pretty widely known that I will talk to just about anybody who happens to be breathing. Especially fans and paying customers.

You may have heard tales about my dentist, Dr. Howdy Giles, described by some accounts as the Ultimate Arnold Palmer Fan. I'm certain Howdy wouldn't take the slightest exception to that designation, and the way we met and became close friends, I think, says a great deal about us both.

Once upon a time, Howdy Giles was a golf-crazy dental school student in Philadelphia, who used to get ribbed by his classmates for always wearing Arnold Palmer logo sportswear he purchased at Wanamaker's department store in Philly. To mark their engagement in 1966, Howdy's fiancée, Carolyn, presented him with a new set of Arnold Palmer irons. Howdy and Carolyn attended their first Masters in 1968, but we weren't introduced until an exhibition in Wilmington, Delaware, in 1970. After that, the Gileses began coming to Bay Hill on vacations and soon purchased a condominium there. Through the club, we became good friends socially, and I didn't mind a bit that Howdy was always snapping photographs of me in action. In addition to being an excellent dentist, he's a crack photographer. Undoubtedly, you've seen his photographs of me, because scores of them have wound up in books and magazines. By Howdy's count, he's taken a staggering half a million photographs of me, displaying every mood and emotion I'm capable of.

What you may not know about Howdy is that he's also become a top junior golf and rules official for the United States Golf Association, having served field duty at both Senior and U.S. Opens, and has two lovely daughters, Robin and Julie, who attended Wake Forest University.

Now I call that a *fan*. But more important, I also call that a friend. Howdy and Carolyn are two of the nicest, most down-to-earth people, a pleasure to know in every respect. Only in America, as Howdy likes to say to anyone who will listen, can a kid grow up to meet his hero—but also become his hero's friend. Even though I sometimes have tell Howdy to *quit* taking pictures, I remind him whenever I can that the gift of that friendship goes two ways.

In a nutshell, it seems fitting that our friendship really took root in the friendly atmosphere at Bay Hill. The whole idea behind Bay Hill was to create a special low-key place where both the members and guests would be made to feel comfortable and welcome. It says something good when so many of the club and lodge staff, including caddies and housekeeping and kitchen personnel, are holdovers from the time when we arrived. We are surrounded by the entertainment business, and the competition for workers of all skill levels is, to say the least, fierce. That our turnover rate is so low is just one indication that we're doing something right—and not just for our guests.

One of my great pleasures is playing in the daily Bay Hill Shootout. When I'm home from the road, that's usually where you'll find me after a morning's work in the office and a quick lunch: preparing to tee it up with a bunch of golfing cutthroats, friendly rogues, old friends, and generally all-around good guys. The Shootout is an event that precedes me and dates back to the club's founding members, a bunch of golf nuts who couldn't wait to try to take each other's pocket change every afternoon.

You've probably heard tales about the Shootout, how everybody who is anybody on the PGA Tour has played in it at some point. That's true. Many of them have. The Shootout is not only famous—it's great fun. Here's how it works: On a typical day, eight to ten foursomes, and occasionally a fivesome, are selected as "teams." Each team has a range of golfers—an "A" player, "B" player, "C" player, and so forth, with each player's rating based on his handicap. We manage to attract a range of handicaps, and the best thing about it is that anyone who wants to play and can play reasonably well can get in the Shootout.

Originally, it cost twenty bucks per man to enter, and if your team was good enough to win you could pocket a couple hundred dollars for buying drinks afterward in the men's locker room. Now the entry fee is up to $30, and on special occasions it's $50 per man. That doesn't count all the side bets and private nassaus and walk-in wagers flying around on an average day. On New Year's Eve we play what's called the Grand Shootout, which attracts more than two hundred players and has a pretty impressive pot.

In a typical Shootout, I'll sometimes have four or five bets going in different directions, and there are certain members (who know who they are) whose folding money I simply *adore* collecting. On the other hand, more times than you might think, I'm the one who walks home to my condo with the lighter pockets.

Everyone has stories about the rough-and-tumble competition, but here's one of my personal favorites. Many years ago, my foursome came to the difficult par-3 17th. The hole plays across a large pond and bunker to a green many find extremely challenging to hit, especially from the championship or "Palmer" tees, where I play from. That day the distance was about 210 yards to the flag, and I asked

Tomcat, one of my longtime caddies at Bay Hill, to hand me my 2-iron.

He shook his head solemnly.

"What do you think, Tomcat?" I asked him.

"Mr. Palmer, it's a three-iron."

"No," I said. "I don't think I can reach it with a three-iron."

The truth is, a lot was riding on the shot. I was tied in several different matches and needed to at least make par, preferably birdie.

"Yes, sir. You just take the three and go ahead and hit it." Tomcat had no doubt about it whatsoever.

So I set up and hit the 3-iron. I hit it pretty well, too.

Straight into the water.

As the jackals in my group broke up laughing, I growled, "Tomcat, that was the wrong damn club. Give me the two-iron, please."

He handed me my 2-iron and I glanced over at the others and said, "Okay, guys. Laugh all you want. I'll still make par the hard way."

With that, I busted the ball. It flew across the pond, landed on the green, skipped once, and popped into the hole.

Par the hard way.

That nearly killed the guys. I turned to Tomcat and barked with mock gruffness, "See there, Tomcat? I *told* you it was a two-iron!"

He wasn't the slightest bit fazed.

"No, sir," he said with perfect timing, wiping the club and putting it back in the bag. "It was a *three* iron. You hit it fat."

I guess some people at Bay Hill really know me better than I know myself.

Another private moment speaks volumes about my attachment to the place, the people, the tournament, the hospital that bears my name and benefits from the tournament's proceeds, and everything else Bay Hill has come to symbolize in our lives over the past thirty years.

It happened in 1991, the start of a new decade, but hardly the most rewarding year of my life on and off the golf course. It came at the moment when we were in litigation over the Isleworth fiasco and my friendship with O'Neal had been severed, with painful financial repercussions to come. Every time I turned around, I seemed to be reading something bad about Arnold Palmer in the newspapers.

As the saying goes, when it rains, it pours. I guess it is also true that it's at moments like these when you discover who your friends really are. At any rate, fittingly, it had been pouring all week at the Bay Hill Invitational, causing smaller crowds and a general atmosphere of gloom, especially after the bad weather forced us to shorten the event to fifty-four holes.

Needless to say, I was in an awful state of mind, feeling sorry for myself and wondering what I could do to try and get the tournament, if not life in general, back on track. That's when I was summoned to an urgent meeting in the locker room.

There I found most of the tournament's players

assembled, waiting for me. I must have looked really baffled and not a little bit worried. What on earth, I wondered, were they gathered for? It looked like a tribunal of some sort, an impromptu trial. That was exactly what I needed to put me over the edge.

Then Peter Jacobsen came forward and presented me with a specially inscribed cake congratulating me for making the thirty-six-hole cut the day before and, as someone later said, for being such a good ambassador for the game of golf.

Applause followed, and then some whooping and hollering.

I can't really tell you how much that meant to me, coming at that moment in my life when so many other things seemed to be on the verge of crumbling, my own ability to make a tournament cut included. It was the perfect tonic for what was ailing me, and lifted me right out of my blues! When the boys finally quieted down, I was called on to make a few comments but was struck speechless. When I finally found the words, I once again barely had the physical capability to speak. I hated for the guys to see me choked up like that, but there was no holding back my emotions, I'm afraid. They knew that and I knew that. But they were telling me in the most poignant way possible—like giving a birthday cake to a kid—what Bay Hill and I *both* meant to them.

I'll always cherish that moment.

Perhaps it goes without saying at this point, but I'll always cherish Bay Hill, too.

CHAPTER FIFTEEN

Hat's Off

Let me tell you about a very special evening I recently experienced in New York. As memorable nights go, this one was almost as painful as it was wonderful.

The occasion was the world debut of a Golf Channel documentary on my life called *Arnold Palmer: Golf's Heart and Soul.* If the title of the film alone wasn't enough to make me an emotional basket case, the news we received on the eve of our departure for the screening and big reception certainly was. The day before the festivities honoring my life got under way, we learned Winnie was suffering from peritoneal carcinoma.

To a person, we were all thunderstruck and terrified by the implications. My initial reaction was to cancel our trip to the debut party and get Winnie to the cancer specialists in Orlando as quickly as possible, but Winnie's cooler head prevailed (as it almost always seems to) in the crisis. She insisted that I go on to New York and do my duty to be with our good friends, many of whom had come a great distance to be there, and to say thank you to Joe Gibbs and his talented people at The Golf Channel who'd spent more than two years putting together the documentary.

I've had many memorable evenings as a public figure, but this one was right up at the top in terms of its emotional impact on me. I'm sure most of the folks I spoke to and shook hands with afterward at the reception were under the impression that my visibly subdued mood was due to the powerful tribute of the documentary, a beautifully wrought piece of filmmaking that did indeed leave me short of words and brought tears to my eyes on several occasions. Of course, they couldn't know that, try as I might, I couldn't keep my mind from drifting elsewhere, to thoughts of Winnie and the life we'd made for ourselves. It was an evening made for reflection, and seeing so many of those images from years past was bittersweet at best. But I knew that other people were counting on me, and that Winnie would be unhappy if I didn't put the best possible face on. So I tried to focus on the good and let the rest go—for a time.

That the premiere should come only days after Joe and his staff announced that The Golf Channel was about to reach the milestone of its 24 millionth subscriber was icing on the cake—and made the occasion even more meaningful for me. It amazed me to think that it had been less than a decade since the afternoon Joe and I met at the Birmingham Airport in Alabama to discuss his personal dream of a television cable channel devoted exclusively to the coverage of golf and its many aspects.

Joe had convinced me then that the concept had real potential and had asked for my help. A short time later, I enthusiastically signed on as chairman of the new enterprise and promised to lend my name and use my influence wherever it was proper with folks inside and outside the golf world. I also hoped I could attract prospective sponsors to help get that dream off the ground. Start-ups of any kind are tough. In those first years, I must admit, convincing people to share our vision of The Golf Channel wasn't the easiest selling job. Quite a few people in the television industry and even the golf world itself ridiculed the idea and flatly predicted we would go broke in no time flat, stating that programming devoted to golf twenty-four hours a day just wouldn't fly. No matter who the pilots were.

Obviously they didn't know Job Gibbs. The man has a southern preacher's charms and a mongoose's tenacity. Or maybe all those doubters simply underestimated the allure and drawing power of the history-rich game of golf. In any event, someday perhaps Joe will put his own pen to paper and tell the inside story of how The Golf Channel survived against the odds and finally thrived. Until then, you'll have to take it from me that no human being ever worked harder or overcame more obstacles in his path than Joe Gibbs did to bring his dream to life.

That *my* life should be the focus of the channel's first major documentary effort will always mean something very special to me and my family. For a number of reasons I had resisted previewing the film beforehand. Afterward I was so choked up by what I watched, I slipped into a quiet reflective daze that lasted the hour or so I lingered to shake hands at the reception.

Obviously, only a tiny handful of people really knew what was weighing so heavily on my mind that night. The fear of the unknown had never rattled me a bit on a golf course or in the business arena. For that matter even my own struggles against prostate cancer eventually settled into a personal challenge I was eager to confront and go for broke against. But when it comes to a member of my own family having to face an uncertain ordeal like cancer and its treatment, as we experienced with my daughter Amy and her frightening odyssey through the medical world a few years back, I realized all too clearly my own mortal limitations and the frustrations that come in facing them.

The very word "cancer" used in the same sentence as Winnie's name struck cold terror in my heart. For if Arnold Palmer was supposed to be the Heart and Soul of Golf, as Joe and company's lovely documentary described me, Winnie Palmer is surely the Heart and Soul of Arnold Palmer.

A couple of weeks later, we returned to Latrobe from Bay Hill.

As is our daily habit, Winnie and I got up well before dawn and had breakfast together in the kitchen. I began my day as I always do, by exercising and then downing a quart of water as my grandmother used to do in order to get the plumbing properly functioning. Winnie seemed like her old self. Her treatment program was well under way and already showing promising results, and she was briskly arranging this clipping or that to dispatch to a friend (the woman reads at least half of everything published each week in the English language—books, magazines, speeches, and I'm only exaggerating a little bit), talking about our plans for the arrival of our grandchildren at the holidays just ahead, and shamelessly dropping hints that she wouldn't mind having an early Christmas gift from me in the form of a new garden rototiller. It was nice to have some semblance of our ordinary life back.

As millions of you who have been down this road ahead of us know, though, you're never quite the same after you've received news of cancer in your life. If nothing else, it deeply sharpens your powers of observation and makes you aware of and grateful for the small blessings you have all around you every minute and every day.

After breakfast, I put on my favorite old red alpaca sweater, and Prince, our golden retriever, and I strolled up the hill to my office, passing beneath towering evergreens that once upon a time my little girls and I planted. Those trees now are nearly fifty feet high, standing vigil like giants in some child's book of fairy tales. And now my little girls have little girls—who themselves are almost no longer little girls—of their very own.

Amazing how it has all gone so swiftly.

I let myself into the office, and while Prince went off to find one of the stuffed animals he's forever carrying around, I went straight into my workshop to finish making a new set of irons I was anxious to take to the golf course later that morning. I love being in the office before Gina, Debbie, and Doc arrive to start the day. It gives me time to be alone with my thoughts, work on clubs, think about the day ahead—or not think about it, as the case may be. This particular morning, however, Cori Britt was there already doing something. Cori is our staff "jack-of-all-trades," who does everything from keeping the copy machine filled to wrestling with Prince. He's the kind of young man I like, a bright, optimistic local kid who went to work for us years ago around the grounds and the house, graduated from St. Vincent College in Latrobe, then returned to work for us, literally learning the business from the ground up. Our office accountant, Bob Demangone, followed the same route. They're fine young men, hometown boys in the best sense of the word, and I'm pleased they work for me.

If it sounds a little like I was taking inventory of the things I love, I suppose I was—and am. It would be a shame, it seems to me, not to pause and acknowledge the things and the people that have made my life so genuinely rewarding, my days so full. My father used to say that this life would pass so quickly it would make your head spin, and, you know what? He was right about that. This life, my life, has done just that.

A few days before the Golf Channel documentary party, I'd had the good fortune to shoot a round of 63 at Latrobe. That wasn't quite as sensational as the 60 I fired in a casual round back in 1969, but it got the office phones ringing with wire service reporters on the other end, wondering if Arnold Palmer had maybe found the fountain of youth.

The answer was, no, I hadn't. But it was nice to post that kind of number again, and my effort reminded me that I *still* feel in my heart that, given the right combination of rest, equipment, and mental preparation, I could compete with the flatbellies of the PGA Tour.

I'll admit that I sometimes fantasize about how great it would be to win a tournament, any tournament, one more time. In that sense, I'm not much different from the young man who spent most of his youth on the fairways of this place, his heart and his head filled with visions of heroic comebacks. If I were to win again, that would *really* make the office phones ring off the hook. At my age, wouldn't that set the golf world on its collective ear? Frankly, I'd love nothing better than to have to face the tournament press corps after a most unexpected victory and field their questions. Knowing me—the almost seventy-year-old me, that is—I might even use the occasion to get a few things off my chest that have been chewing away at me for some time.

Please indulge me for a moment.

There are just a few observations I need to make, and they might seem incredibly trivial and unimportant to some people. But they certainly aren't to me. They arise from lessons I learned as far back as my father's own dinner table. They have to do with proper manners. And just because I choose to share them with you now instead of waiting till the next time I'm standing victorious in the press tent doesn't mean I'm giving up believing that will happen. I'll be hitting it hard, and then I'll be off to find it to hit it hard again, believe you me.

A few days before our return to Latrobe, I hosted a luncheon gathering at Bay Hill, part of a charity golf outing to benefit the Arnold Palmer Hospital for Children and Women. The event drew a couple hundred enthusiastic participants, including a couple of well-known PGA Tour stars, and raised close to three quarters of a million dollars for the hospital, for which I was deeply grateful.

But as I prepared to sit down at the luncheon, I was dismayed to gaze across the function room at the club and see several men still wearing their golf caps as they sat down to eat.

To many, I'm sure this seems to be an incredible nitpick, a totally inconsequential matter in the overall scheme of things, but as I sat there it made me alternately sad and angry to think we now reside in an age in which intelligent and supposedly well bred men enter a building, encounter a woman, or come to someone's dinner table still wearing their hats! To make matters worse, a well-known professional was preparing to take his seat just yards away from me, still wearing his cap with clearly no intention of removing it. It was apparent that the thought had not entered his head.

Luckily, or maybe not, one of the tournament's directors sensed my acute discomfort and made an announcement that Bay Hill had a club policy of asking men to please remove their hats when indoors. One by one the hats came off, save for a stubborn few—including that of the famous Tour player, who apparently was so offended by the idea that somebody would consider it a sign of natural courtesy for him to remove his lid, he promptly got up and walked out of the luncheon in a sulk.

I thought about what had just happened for a few moments. I briefly felt bad about the situation, wondering if maybe I'm just a social dinosaur in this world to insist on such an old-fashioned courtesy. I promptly asked someone to go catch the Tour player and inform him that he was invited to come back and continue wearing his cap, if he chose to. The sponsors wanted him there and I did, too. He did come back and took his seat for lunch, still wearing his cap. We chatted pleasantly as if nothing had happened, though deep inside I was irritated and amazed that a man of his stature in the game could have grown up in and around golf and, approaching age forty, be either so blithely ignorant of or unconcerned about the fundamentals of basic politeness.

Call me old-fashioned for saying this, but I happen to believe manners do count—knowing when to speak and what to say, knowing when to remove your hat as a sign of basic courtesy to the host of a home, knowing how to win by following the rules, knowing the importance of when and how to say thank you.

I know I've said this before, but it bears repeating: golf resembles life in so many ways. I also happen to believe that golf, more than any game on earth, depends on simple timeless principles of courtesy and respect. I don't think it's by accident that golf is the most polite and well-mannered game on earth, a sport where every man or woman rises on the merits of his or her own skills and personal integrity, following rules that have remained essentially the same for the past five hundred years. What some players don't seem to quite grasp is that golf's enormous success can be attributed almost entirely to the fact that it hasn't changed much in a world where values are constantly shifting or, as some believe, eroding.

Not removing your hat, even after being asked to do so, is symptomatic of larger ills that could threaten the game. That's why I bother to tell this story.

The truth is, when I see modern stars of the game ignoring the basic fundamentals of personal courtesy or—worse—treating fans and even sponsors with indifference or disrespect, suggesting they simply feel entitled to the enormous amounts of money, opportunity, and social prestige the game brings their way, I worry about the future of golf, because it means something vital is no longer being given back to the game and those who support it. It saddens me to no end when I realize many younger players don't know the history of the game that gives them such rich and splendid lives, possess little appreciation of how and why the professional game has grown the way it has in the past fifty years, and have no apparent interest in understanding the important traditions of the game and perpetuating them. Ours is a game—and for that matter, ours is a nation—of such simple abundance I sometimes feel it's downright criminal to take the many ordinary blessings we enjoy for granted. It's my belief that we do so at our own peril.

As I finished writing this memoir, for example, we were at an interesting moment in history that says something disturbing, I think, about our troubled national identity, a willingness to ignore rules of basic conduct and courtesy in the interest of self. For only the second time in our nation's history, a president of the United States had been impeached by the House of Representatives for alleged high crimes and misdemeanors. Almost simultaneously, the National Basketball Association was hours away from canceling its entire playing season for the first time ever due to stubborn players and unyielding owners, both of whom, polls showed, the overwhelming majority of fans believed were simply spoiled multi-millionares who had made Mr. Naismith's game a hostage of their own greed.

Believe me, as someone who had a hand in creating the concept of sports marketing, I'm all for athletes getting handsomely paid for what they are worth, but as these two events, juxtaposed against each other in the evening news, indicated, nobody is above the rules of game. Not NBA All-Stars. Not sitting presidents. And certainly not Arnold Palmer.

I'll let you in on a little secret, something I've admitted to a handful of folks. I never cared for the nickname "The King." At times, it makes me uncomfortable and even a bit irritated to be referred to that way. There is no king of golf. Never has been, never will be. Golf is the most democratic game on earth, a pastime of the people that grants no special privileges and pays no mind to whether a man is a hotel doorman or a corporate CEO. It punishes and exalts us all with splendid equal opportunity. And when and if we begin to think the game belongs to one group of people or class of individuals the way certain NBA, NHL, or major-league baseball stars of a few years back seemed to believe of their respective games, our traditional and honorable game will decline so fast it will, as my father used to say, make our heads spin.

I'm the son of a hard-nosed caretaker who had large hands and an even larger heart, but a man who drilled into me the importance of always leaving the golf course better than I found it. Today, in a time when there is talk of multiple global tours, and sums of money that would have once been unimaginable are flowing into and around golf, I feel we have to be more vigilant than ever to make certain the things that make golf such a great game remain the same, are protected and nurtured and preserved for the next people coming along. We don't need to tear down in order to build up.

Now that I've grumped a bit, as my grandchildren like to say, permit me to say a few positive things about the state of the game—as well as say a lot of thank-yous.

I do like being seen and called an ambassador of the game. It is a role I take very seriously in my work with the USGA and whenever I am in the public eye. But I suppose at the end of the day what

I really am, inescapably—and how I prefer to be thought of in terms of my legacy—is a caretaker of the game just the way my father was before me.

My early playing days were driven by a passionate desire to see what I could accomplish and do for people, initially my father and mother, then Winnie and the girls, finally friends and my fans. Now I see my primary role as someone who feels a moral obligation to take care of the game that enriched his own life so profoundly, to fuss a little bit when I feel it's necessary, to do whatever it takes to make sure I pass along a game that is in even better shape than I found it.

As I've gotten older, I've realized that we need to be constantly challenged to examine ourselves and see what we can give back to this life. Several years ago, for instance, my friend and neighbor Dr. Tom Moran, former chief of surgery at Latrobe Hospital, challenged me to come up with a way to assist the hospital where I was born. The hospital was in the midst of a critical expansion of much-needed services and facilities. What I proposed and carried out, with the help of a few insiders, especially my sister Cheech, and the support of many generous people in western Pennsylvania and elsewhere, was an event we dubbed our "golf gala."

We created a one-day affair with a four-man skins game along with a lavish dinner and amateur scramble. All I had to do, it seemed, was ask my Tour buddies, several of the top players, and they said they would be happy to help out. We did this for six years running, alternating between Latrobe and Laurel Valley, and cleared more than $3.5 million for the hospital, putting it in the hands of a newly formed foundation headed by Dr. Bob Mazero.

To give you an idea of why we had no trouble drawing a crowd for the skins game, here's who we had each year: 1992—Curtis Strange, Chi Chi Rodriguez, and Dow Finsterwald; 1993—Greg Norman, Dave Marr, and Rocco Mediate (who, by the way, grew up and played his golf at nearby Greensburg Country Club); 1994—Jack Nicklaus, Jay Hass, and Peter Jacobsen, my regular playing pal in the Fred Meyer Challenge and the Shark Shootout; 1995—Lee Trevino, Gary Player, and Fuzzy Zoeller; 1996—Nick Price, Raymond Floyd, and Fred Couples; and 1997—Tiger Woods, Tom Lehman, and Davis Love III. They not only came as a favor to me, but, under the most gentle of prodding, turned their winnings over to the hospital as well.

That's how professional golf gives back to the lives of people, and I'm very proud to be a caretaker or an ambassador in that process.

While I'm on the subject of charities, let me mention something about Greg Norman. Several years ago he inspired an important fund-raiser for my hospital in Orlando when he was living at Bay Hill. He and I played with a couple of other pros in an annual exhibition he called the Shark Shootout. It has since evolved into the aforementioned pro-amateur event at Bay Hill that we renamed Champions for

Children. Through the efforts of a number of people, but most particularly Tommy Scarbrough, a hard-working Bay Hill member and past chairman of the Bay Hill Invitational, most of the many Tour pros who live in the Orlando area participate in the annual fall event.

I have been associated with and worked for quite a few other charitable organizations and causes over the years, the most extensive connection being with another charity that focuses on children in need. That was my twenty-year tenure as Honorary National Chairman of the March of Dimes Birth Defects Foundation. I still get emotional when I look at campaign promotional photos taken with bright, brave youngsters each year back in the 1970s and 1980s who, I know from letters I receive, have gone on to have successful and productive lives. I'm pleased to have made whatever contribution I made, and it was great to work with such devoted March of Dimes people as Arthur Gallway, Ed Fike, Jean Wilson, and a marvelous photographer, John Blecha.

Now to a few of those thank-yous.

I sometimes think you can best judge a man by the people he most closely associates himself with. In that respect, I've been exceedingly fortunate to have a special group of people close to me. For years, I've had the benefit of an informal advisory group of friends and top businessmen off whom I could bounce the many ideas and proposals that come my way. I can also seek counsel from them to address the problems and dilemmas that cross my desk from time to time. This inner circle of trusted friends includes Russ Meyer, Johnny Harris, and Dick Ferris, the former chairman of United Airlines, who, among other things, heads the policy board of the PGA Tour. Lately, I've also been fortunate to be able to tap the outstanding business acumen of Charlie Mechem, the Ohio broadcasting executive who served the Ladies Professional Golf Association as its commissioner with great distinction in the mid-1990s, before semiretiring. Admiring so much what Charlie had done with the LPGA, I asked him if he would be willing to act as consultant on some of my business activities. He readily accepted, to my delight. Charlie has provided wise counsel on a number of occasions and has been particularly helpful with the Arnold Palmer Golf Company, helping guide it through the turbulent days the golf equipment industry has been experiencing of late. Among other contributions, he played an important role in bringing LPGA Hall of Famer Nancy Lopez aboard with the creation of a new line of women's clubs bearing her name now on the market. Charlie and his lovely wife, Marilyn, have a winter home at Bay Hill, so we get to see a lot of each other.

I can just see and—worse—hear Pap, at this point, if he were reading this memoir.

"For Pete's sake, Arnie," he'd growl. "Just say thank you and get *on* with it so we can play golf!"

He's probably right. I'll get on with it. But there

are so many other people who deserve heartfelt thank-yous from me, I suppose I really could go on for many more pages.

The list begins of course with my own parents and extends through the many casual and close friends I've had over the decades, to the group of hearty fans who recently turned up unexpectedly on the tee in the chilly desert dawn at the Hope tournament to watch me tee off. As I joked with them, I was so far out of contention I was having to tee off in the dark, but there they were, a faithful knot of Palmer loyalists true to the bitter end, dressed hilariously in their pajamas and bathrobes and holding little signs proclaiming their enduring membership in Arnie's Army.

I can't tell you what that little gesture meant to me.

Yet again unable to speak, all I could do was take off my hat to them and mutter thank you.

It's been a great life. Rich with unexpected rewards and people—just like those loyal fans—at every turn in the road. I want everyone who reads this to know that. Allow me to take my hat off to you all. Thank you for letting Arnold Palmer be Arnold Palmer.

You'll never know how deeply grateful I really am.

Thoughts like these and others crowded my head that recent autumn morning, when I finally got out of the office and over to the course to try out my newly made set of clubs.

By the turn at the tenth hole, I realized the clubs

weren't quite as magical as I'd hoped they might be. I wasn't playing particularly well. But, on the other hand, it felt good to play along at a leisurely pace, looking closely at the golf course and thinking about the changes I planned to make over the winter. Like my father before me, I'm forever fussing with the golf course, changing this or adding that to try to make it an even more special golfing experience for those who play it.

At one point I briefly left the golf course and walked over to admire the big red barn we recently finished restoring just off the 14th hole. It looked like something from a Currier and Ives postcard and is Winnie's pride and joy, fitting beautifully into the landscape with the three red covered bridges Pap added to the golf course when he built the new nine in 1963.

As I stated at the outset of this reflection, autumn's arrival in western Pennsylvania always fills me with a bittersweet pleasure; it means we'll soon be headed to the warmth of Bay Hill, but it also announces that another golf season back home has come and gone.

Lacking the gift of prophecy, I can't tell you how many more times I'll get to go around that old golf course before I join my parents on the hilltop near the 18th green. But I can promise you that going around it never fails to delight and surprise me, and on this particular Indian summer day, our first day back since the start of Winnie's medical treatment, I was walking up the 18th fairway when I saw him.

He was standing just off the fairway about three

hundred yards out from the tee, where only a few weeks before a tall and regal pine tree had stood. That tree was very special to me. I can remember as if it was yesterday the day my father and I planted it. I was about six years old and was allowed to ride on the root ball of the young tree as we hauled it to the freshly dug hole beside the 18th fairway in back of our old Ford truck.

The tree, which was roughly the same age as me, had grown nearly seventy-five feet tall and lived a good life. But now it had died a natural death of old age, and I hated to say goodbye to it. In fact, I commented to my brother, Jerry, that I wished we could find some fitting way to memorialize it—maybe carve a statue out of its stump or something. A few days later, Jerry found a talented wood carver who worked with chainsaws, and the result of his artistry was now standing ten feet high on the side of the fairway with his hands on his hips, staring up the hill at the 18th green.

It was unmistakably Pap, keeping a sharp eye out for anybody who was foolish enough not to fix his divot or properly repair his ballmark on the green.

I stood there looking up at him for the longest time, deeply moved to have him back, pleasantly lost in my own thoughts, vaguely aware of the high-school band practicing for the big homecoming game that weekend just across the valley from the golf course, wondering what my Pap would make of this golfer's life.

Some things never change. I still hope he'd be pleased.

HIGHLIGHTS OF AMATEUR CAREER

1946:   Winner, WPIAL and PIAA Championships
          Runnerup, Hearst Junior

1947:   Winner, WPIAL and PIAA Championships
          Winner, West Penn Junior (df C. A. Brown, 5 and 4, at Highland Country Club)
          Winner, West Penn Amateur (df Knox Young, 3 and 2, at Shannopin Country Club)
          Semi-finalist, Pennsylvania Amateur

1948:   Winner, Southern Conference Championship
          Winner, Sunnehanna Amateur
          Semi-finalist, North and South Amateur
          Lost, first round, U.S. Amateur

1949:   Winner, Southern Conference Championship
          Winner, West Penn Amateur (df Jack Benson at Oakmont)
          Semi-finalist, North and South Amateur
          Medalist, National Intercollegiate (NCAA)
          Lost, third round, U.S. Amateur

1950:   Winner, Southern Intercollegiate
          Winner, West Penn Amateur (df Steve Savor at Longue Vue)
          Winner, Greensburg Invitational
          Medalist, National Intercollegiate (NCAA)
          Lost, first round, U.S. Amateur

1951:   Winner, West Penn Amateur (df Jack Mahaffey at Alcoma)
          Winner, Worsham Memorial

1952:   Winner, West Penn Amateur (df Frank Souchak at Fox Chapel)

Winner, Greensburg Invitational
Runnerup, Pennsylvania Amateur (play-off)

1953:   Winner, Ohio Amateur
Winner, Cleveland Amateur
Winner, Greensburg Invitational
Winner, Mayfield Heights Open
Semi-finalist, West Penn Amateur
Lost, fourth round, U.S. Amateur
Missed cut, U.S. Open

1954:   Winner, U.S. Amateur (df Bob Sweeny, 1 up, at
Country Club of Detroit)
Winner, Ohio Amateur
Winner, All-American Amateur
Winner, Atlantic Coast Conference Championship
Winner, Bill Waite Memorial Tournament
Runnerup, World Amateur
Missed cut, U.S. Open

NOTE: Palmer also won the West Penn Open at Fox Chapel Golf
Club in 1957; then a professional.

ARNOLD PALMER'S RECORD IN
U.S. AMATEUR CHAMPIONSHIP

1948   Memphis Country Club, Memphis, Tennessee
        Lost in first round to William K. Barrett Jr., Colonial
        CC, Memphis, Tennessee, 6 and 5.

1949   Oak Hill Country Club, Rochester, New York
        Lost in third round to Crawford Rainwater,
        Pensacola, Florida, 4 and 3, after defeating Frederick
        Mayer, Westchester, New York, 3 and 2, and Charles
        Robinson, Belle Meade, Tennessee, 4 and 3.

1950   Mineapolis Country Club, Minneapolis, Minnesota
        Lost in first round to Frank Stranahan, Toledo, Ohio,
        4 and 3.

1951   Did not compete, serving in U.S. Coast Guard.

1952   Did not compete, serving in U.S. Coast Guard.

1953   Oklahoma City Golf and Country Club, Oklahoma
        City, Oklahoma
        Lost in fourth round to Don Albert, Alliance, Ohio,
        1 up, after defeating John Frazier, Finlay, North
        Carolina, 7 and 5, Jack Westland, Everett, Washington,
        1 up, and Ken Venturi, San Francisco, California, 2 and
        1. (Shot 78 in losing match to Albert.)

1954   Country Club of Detroit, Grosse Pointe Farms,
        Michigan
        Won championship with following sequence of
        victories:
        Defeated Frank Strafaci, Garden City, New York, 1 up
        Defeated John Veghte, Pine Brook, New York, 1 up
        Defeated Richard Whiting, Red Run, Michigan, 2 and 1
        Defeated Walter Andzel, South Shore, New York, 5
        and 3

Defeated Frank Stranahan, Toledo, Ohio, 3 and 1
Defeated Don Cherry, Wichita Falls, Texas, 1 up
Defeated Ed Meister, Kirtland, Ohio, 1 up, 39 holes
Defeated Bob Sweeny, Sands Point, New York, 1 up

PROFESSIONAL VICTORIES

1955
- Canadian Open

1956
Panama Open
Colombia Open
- Insurance City Open
- Eastern Open

1957
- Houston Open
- Azalea Open
- Rubber City Open
- San Diego Open

1958
- St. Petersburg Open
- Masters Tournament
- Pepsi Open

1959
- Thunderbird Invitational
- Oklahoma City Open
- West Palm Beach Open

1960
- Bob Hope Desert Classic
- Texas Open
- Baton Rouge Open
- Pensacola Open
- Masters Tournament
- U.S. Open Championship
- Insurance City Open
- Mobile Open
Canada Cup (Partner: Sam Snead)

1961
- San Diego Open
- Phoenix Open
- Baton Rouge Open
- Texas Open
British Open Championship
- Western Open

1962
- Bob Hope Desert Classic
- Phoenix Open
- Masters Tournament
- Texas Open
- Tournament of Champions
- Colonial National Invitational
British Open Championship
- American Golf Classic
Canada Cup (Partner: Sam Snead)

1963
- Los Angeles Open
- Phoenix Open
- Pensacola Open
- Thunderbird Classic
- Cleveland Open
- Western Open
- Whitemarsh Open
Australian Wills Masters
Canada Cup (Partner: Jack Nicklaus)

1964
- Masters Tournament
- Oklahoma City Open
Piccadilly World Match Play Championship
Canada Cup (Partner: Jack Nicklaus)

1965
- Tournament of Champions

1966
- Los Angeles Open
- Tournament of Champions
Australian Open
- Houston Champions
  International
- PGA Team Championship
  (Partner: Jack Nicklaus)
Canada Cup (Partner: Jack
  Nicklaus)

1967
- Los Angeles Open
- Tucson Open
- American Golf Classic
- Thunderbird Classic
Piccadilly World Match Play
  Championship
World Cup (Partner: Jack
  Nicklaus)
World Cup International
  Trophy (Individual Title)

1968
- Bob Hope Desert Classic
- Kemper Open

1969
- Heritage Classic
- Danny Thomas Diplomat
  Classic

1970
- PGA Team Championship
  (Partner: Jack Nicklaus)

1971
- Bob Hope Desert Classic
- Citrus Open
- Westchester Classic
- PGA Team Championship
  (Partner: Jack Nicklaus)
Lancôme Trophy

1973
- Bob Hope Desert Classic

1975
Spanish Open
British PGA Championship

1980
Canadian PGA Championship
◆ PGA Seniors
  Championship

1981
◆ USGA Senior Open
  Championship

1982
◆ Marlboro Senior Classic
◆ Denver Post Champions of
  Golf
1983
◆ Boca Grove Senior Classic

<u>1984</u>
- ◆ PGA Seniors Championship
- ◆ Doug Sanders Celebrity Pro-Am
- ◆ Senior TPC
- ◆ Quadel (Boca Grove) Classic

<u>1985</u>
- ◆ Senior TPC

<u>1986</u>
- ◆ Unionmutual Classic

<u>1988</u>
- ◆ Crostar Classic

TOTAL VICTORIES: 92

Key

- • PGA Tour (61)
- ◆ Senior events (12)

ARNOLD PALMER'S PROFESSIONAL CAREER SUMMARY
1955 THROUGH 1998

U.S. EARNINGS—REGULAR PGA TOUR	$2,100,239
SENIOR PGA TOUR	$2,134,076
FOREIGN/INTERNATIONAL/ NON-TOUR U.S. EARNINGS	$1,257,930
TOTAL COMPETITIVE EARNINGS	$5,492,245

(Excludes pro-ams, skins games)

VICTORIES: 92
(U.S. Tour—61; Foreign/International—19; Seniors—12)

INDIVIDUAL RECORDS

BEST 18-HOLE ROUND:	62, 1959 Thunderbird Invitational, fourth round; 1966 Los Angeles Open, third round
BEST OPENING ROUND:	64, 1955 Canadian Open; 1962 Phoenix Open; 1970 Citrus Open; 1970 Greensboro Open; 1971 Westchester Classic
BEST SECOND ROUND:	63, 1961 Texas Open
BEST THIRD ROUND:	62, 1966 Los Angeles Open
BEST FOURTH ROUND:	62, 1959 Thunderbird Invitational
LOWEST SCORE, FIRST 36 HOLES:	130, (67–63), 1961 Texas Open

LOWEST SCORE,
FIRST 54 HOLES: 195, (64–67–64), 1955
                                                Canadian Open

LOWEST 72-HOLE SCORE: 265, (64–67–64–70), 1955
                                                Canadian Open

BIGGEST VICTORY MARGIN: 12, 1962 Phoenix Open

MOST CONSECUTIVE BIRDIES: 7, 1966 Los Angeles
                                                Open, third round

HOLES-IN-ONE: 17, three in PGA Tour
                                                events, four on Senior
                                                PGA Tour, one in Japan

ALL-TIME LOW
18-HOLE SCORE: 60, Latrobe Country Club,
                                                September 1969

SPECIAL GOLF ACHIEVEMENTS

PGA Player of Year—1960 and 1962
PGA Tour Leading Money-Winner—1958, 1960, 1962, 1963
Vardon Trophy—1961, 1962, 1964, 1967
Ryder Cup Team—1961, 1963, 1965, 1967, 1971, 1973;
    Captain—1963, 1975
Chrysler Cup Team and Captain (Senior Golf)—1986–90
Presidents Cup Captain—1996

ACADEMIC HONORS

Honorary Doctor of Laws, Wake Forest University, Winston-Salem, North Carolina

Honorary Doctor of Humanities, Thiel College, Greenville, Pennsylvania

Honorary Doctor of Laws, National College of Education, Evanston, Illinois

Honorary Doctor of Humane Letters, Florida Southern College, Lakeland, Florida

Honorary Doctor of Humane Letters, St. Vincent College, Latrobe, Pennsylvania

AWARDS

GOLF:

Charter member, World Golf Hall of Fame, Pinehurst, North Carolina, 1974

American Golf Hall of Fame, Foxburg, Pennsylvania

PGA Hall of Fame, Palm Beach Gardens, Florida, 1980

All-American Collegiate Golf Hall of Fame, Man of Year, 1984

Ohio Golf Hall of Fame, 1992

Phoenix Open Hall of Fame

Bob Jones Award, U.S. Golf Association, 1971

Walter Hagen Award, International panel of selectors

William D. Richardson Award, Golf Writers Association of America, 1969

Charles Bartlett Award, Golf Writers Association of America, 1976

Herb Graffis Award, National Golf Foundation, 1978

Gold Tee Award, Metropolitan (NY) Golf Writers Association, 1965

Golf Digest "Man of Silver Era," 1975

Old Tom Morris Award, Golf Course Superintendents Association, 1983

Golfer of Century, New York Athletic Club, 1985

Commemorative Honoree, 1987 Golf Digest Commemorative Seniors Tournament

Golfer of Decade (1958–67), Centennial of Golf, *Golf* Magazine, 1989

American Senior Golf Association National Award, 1989

Chicago District Golf Association Distinguished Service Award, 1989

Ambassador of Golf Award, World Series of Golf, 1991

Bing Crosby Award, Metropolitan Golf Writers Association, 1992

Memorial Honoree, Memorial Tournament, 1993

PGA of America Distinguished Service Award, 1994

Distinguished Service Award, Tri-State Section, PGA of America, 1996

Centennial Award, Golf Associations of Philadelphia, 1996

Francis Ouimet Award, Francis Ouimet Caddie Scholarship Fund, Boston, 1997

Lifetime Achievement Award, PGA Tour, 1998

Golfer of Century, Western PA Golf Association, 1998

Donald Ross Award, American Society of Golf Course Architects, 1999

GENERAL:

Associated Press Athlete of Decade, 1960–69

Hickok Athlete of Year, 1960

Sports Illustrated Sportsman of Year, 1960

Western Pennsylvania, Pennsylvania, Westmoreland County, Cambria County, North Carolina, Florida Sports Halls of Fame

Wake Forest Hall of Fame

Arthur J. Rooney Award, Catholic Youth Association, Pittsburgh, Pennsylvania

Dapper Dan Man of Year, Pittsburgh, Pennsylvania, 1960

Lowman Humanitarian Award, Los Angeles, California

Distinguished Pennsylvanian, 1980

Partner in Science Award, March of Dimes Birth Defects Foundation

Theodore Roosevelt Award, National Collegiate Athletic Association

Business Leaders Award, Northwood Institute

National High School Sports Hall of Fame

Gold Medal, Pennsylvania Association of Broadcasters, 1988

Order of Eagle Exemplar, U.S. Sports Academy, 1989

Sports Appreciation Trophy, Atlanta AC Country Club, Atlanta, Georgia, 1990

Van Patrick Career Achievement Award, Dearborn, Michigan, 1990

Eagle on World Award, Japanese Chamber of Commerce and Industry of New York, 1990

Pathfinder Award, Youthlinks Indiana, 1992

Outstanding American Award, Los Angeles Philanthropic Foundation, 1992

National Sports Award, Washington, D.C., 1993

Sports Legends Award, Jr. Diabetes Foundation, Pittsburgh, Pennsylvania, 1993

Humanitarian Award, Variety Club International, 1993

"Good Guy" Award, American Legion National Commanders, 1993

Man of Year, Palm Springs Chamber of Commerce, 1994

Ford Achievement Award, Dearborn, MI, 1994

Golden Plate Award, American Academy of Achievement, 1995

History Makers Award, Historical Society of Western Pennsylvania, 1995

Community Service Award, Latrobe Chamber of Commerce, 1995

Reagan Distinguished American Award, Jonathan Club, Los Angeles, California, 1996

Lifetime Achievement Award, March of Dimes Athletic Awards, 1998

Caritas Award, Richstone Family Center, Los Angeles, California, 1998
Spirit of Hope Award, University of Pittsburgh Cancer Institute, 1998

GOLF BOOKS AND VIDEOS

Arnold Palmer's Golf Book, 1961
Portrait of Professional Golfer, 1964
My Game and Yours, 1965, revised 1983
Situation Golf, 1970
Go for Broke, 1973
Arnold Palmer's Best 54 Holes of Golf, 1977
Arnold Palmer's Complete Book of Putting, 1986
Play Great Golf, 1987–9 (book, videos)
The Arnold Palmer Story, 1991 (video)
Arnold Palmer, A Personal Journey (by Thomas Hauser with Arnold Palmer), 1994
A Golfer's Life (with James Dodson), 1999

ARNOLD PALMER'S CAREER HOLES-IN-ONE

1—LATROBE COUNTRY CLUB—#2—134 yards—wedge
2—LATROBE COUNTRY CLUB—#2—134 yards—wedge
3—GREENSBURG COUNTRY CLUB—#16—9-iron—1945
4—DESERT INN COUNTRY CLUB, Tournament of
   Champions, Las Vegas, Nevada—#16—6-iron—1959
5—PENSACOLA COUNTRY CLUB, Pensacola Open,
   Pensacola, Florida, #11—7-iron—March 3, 1965
6—JOHNSON CITY COUNTRY CLUB, Johnson City,
   Tennessee—Exhibition—#2—1965
7—SPRING VALLEY COUNTRY CLUB, Sharon,
   Massachusetts—Exhibition—#7—243 yards—1965
8—WILMINGTON COUNTRY CLUB, Wilmington,
   Delaware—Exhibition—1966
9—BAY HILL CLUB, Orlando, Florida—#2, Charger
   course—151 yards—7-iron—September 27, 1979
10—INDIAN WELLS COUNTRY CLUB, Palm Desert,
   California, Bob Hope Desert Classic—#6—144 yards—
   8-iron—January 10, 1980
11—LATROBE COUNTRY CLUB—#2—134 yards—Deacon
   pitching wedge—September 7, 1982
12—TPC AT AVENEL, Potomac, Maryland, Chrysler Cup Pro-
   Amateur—#3—182 yards—5-iron—Tuesday, September 2, 1986
13—TPC AT AVENEL, Potomac, Maryland, Chrysler Cup
   Pro-Amateur—#3—182 yards—5-iron—Wednesday,
   September 3, 1986
14—OAK HILLS COUNTRY CLUB, Narita, Japan, Fuji
   Electric Grand Slam—#14—185 yards—4-iron—
   March 25, 1988
15—TPC AT PIPER GLEN, Charlotte, NC, PaineWebber
   Invitational—#12—183 yards—4-iron—August 5, 1990
16—INGLEWOOD COUNTRY CLUB, Kenmore, Washington,

GTE Northwest Classic—#8—193 yards—3-iron—
August 21, 1992
17—LATROBE COUNTRY CLUB—#2—122 yards—pitching
wedge—September 6, 1997

INDEX